CALIFORNIA LOCAL FINANCE

CLAREMONT SOCIAL RESEARCH CENTER
OF THE ASSOCIATED COLLEGES
CLAREMONT GRADUATE SCHOOL · CLAREMONT MEN'S COLLEGE · HARVEY
MUDD COLLEGE · POMONA COLLEGE · SCRIPPS COLLEGE

CALIFORNIA
LOCAL FINANCE

JOHN A. VIEG   HUBERT C. ARMSTRONG
FRANK FARNER   GERHARD N. ROSTVOLD
JOHN P. SHELTON   PROCTER THOMSON

STANFORD UNIVERSITY PRESS, STANFORD, CALIFORNIA
1960

STANFORD UNIVERSITY PRESS
STANFORD, CALIFORNIA

LONDON: OXFORD UNIVERSITY PRESS

© 1960 BY THE BOARD OF TRUSTEES OF THE
LELAND STANFORD JUNIOR UNIVERSITY

LIBRARY OF CONGRESS CATALOG CARD NUMBER: 60-8565
PRINTED IN THE UNITED STATES OF AMERICA

FOREWORD

One of the major fields of interest of the Haynes Foundation has been that of local governmental agencies in California. In furtherance of such interest the Haynes Foundation has supported several projects in the general field of local government, but none of these projects related specifically and exclusively to the financial aspects of local government. Because of the substantial increase in the expenses of administering local governmental entities in California, with the attendant requirements of greater revenues, the public has become acutely conscious of the tax burden which local governmental agencies have imposed upon their inhabitants. These conditions suggested to the Trustees of the Haynes Foundation the desirability of a descriptive and analytical study of local government finances in California.

Inasmuch as the Claremont Social Research Center is composed of a group of highly competent scholars, who are specialists in the several fields of the social sciences, its plan to undertake a study of California local finance found enthusiastic acceptance by the Trustees of the Haynes Foundation. The Trustees are hopeful that this publication will not only be successful in promoting a better understanding of this complex subject, but also that the recommendations contained in the study will result in some improvement of the fiscal affairs of local government in California.

In conformity with its traditional policy in its relation to recipients of its grants for research projects, the Haynes Foundation accorded complete freedom and independence to the Claremont Social Research Center in its investigation and study of this problem and its formulation of the findings, recommendations and conclusions set forth in this publication. Accordingly, such findings, recommendations and conclusions do not necessarily reflect the views of the Trustees or staff members of the Haynes Foundation.

FRANCIS H. LINDLEY
President
The John Randolph Haynes and Dora Haynes Foundation

Permission to quote from or summarize
the report is granted provided appropriate
reference is made to the Haynes Foundation
and Claremont Social Research Center.

This publication was prepared and published under a grant of
The John Randolph Haynes and Dora Haynes Foundation, a
charitable and educational trust organized "for the purpose
of promoting the well-being of mankind."

PREFACE

Justice Oliver Wendell Holmes said, "When I pay taxes I buy civilization," but Mr. and Mrs. Citizen sometimes fail to appreciate the truth of his remark when, along with October's bills for payments on home, automobile, furniture, television and patio set, they receive their annual notice of the cost of local government. Public finance is necessarily a matter of dollars taxed, spent and borrowed but it is also a question of people and how they are affected by the quality and cost of government services. This study cannot claim to be everyman's guide to state and local finance. It does, however, try to examine California's local revenue problems with an appreciation for the human values involved.

As our title indicates we concentrate in this book on problems of local finance. Yet state aid and shared revenues have come within the last generation to assume such vast proportions that we have found ourselves obliged to give consideration to state finance as well. It is not by accident that the jurisdiction of the Legislature's major committees in this field covers both state and local taxation. What California ought to strive for is not two separate systems, one for state and one for local finance, but a single comprehensive plan designed to assure adequate revenue at both levels. How much comfort taxpayers will be able to derive from this study will doubtless vary considerably from person to person. A seer once said, "To know the worst is peace; it is uncertainty that kills." In any event those who read the book should gain an understanding of the predicament local public officials face as the result of creeping inflation, explosive growth and the citizen's insistent demands for more and better service.

We count it a pleasure to acknowledge all the debts of gratitude we have incurred along the way:

To Alan Cranston, State Controller, and Robert C. Kirkwood, his predecessor; Ronald B. Welch and John B. Marshall of the staff of the State Board of Equalization; Assemblyman Ernest R. Geddes of Claremont; Allen D. Manvel, Chief of Governments Division of the U.S. Bureau of Census; Henry W. Magnuson, Peter Tashnovian, Drayton B. Nuttall, Ray H. Johnson and Dorothy Kirshman of the staff of the State Department of Education; John R. Quinn, Assessor of Los Angeles County; Frank Passarella of the staff of the Los Angeles County Auditor-Controller's Office; Garfield Gordon of the California Teacher's Association, and T. Stanley Warburton of Fullerton Union High School District.

To those long-time observers of the problems of California local government and school finance who were kind enough to advise with us, especially Professors Marvel M. Stockwell of the Department of Economics of the University of California, Los Angeles, Malcolm M. Davisson of the Department of Economics, Victor Jones of the Department of Political Science and Edgar L. Morphet of the Department of Education of the University of California, Berkeley, and Elmer D. Fagan of the Department of Economics, Stanford University; Paul Salmon, Superintendent of Schools at Covina; Frederick W. Sharp, City Administrator of Pomona; and Bradford Trenham, former General Manager of the California Taxpayers Association; to Richard H. Hill and Kendall Wright of the staff of the Western Data Processing Center at UCLA; to the authors of that extensive series of California legislative reports on state and local finance whose work made our own labors so much lighter and to finance officers in other states who generously sent us copies of their reports;

To our Research Assistants, Bruce F. Davie, James T. Doyle, Paul R. Kaufman, William N. Littlefield and George McMillan; to our secretarial assistants, Robin Chen and Marion Moxley; to the typists of the preliminary edition, Dorothy Overaker and Sydney Scrivener, and to our own colleague Gerhard N. Rostvold, who, as Deputy Director of the project, handled arrangements for that edition; to Laurel Fujishige, typist of the final edition; to the Executive Committee of the Claremont Social Research Center and especially its chairman, Dean Luther J. Lee of the Claremont Graduate School;

To Leon E. Seltzer and the staff of Stanford University Press; and finally, to the John Randolph Haynes and Dora Haynes Foundation and its Committee on Research and Grants chaired by Arthur G. Coons, President of Occidental College, for making the study possible.

We thank them all for their aid and counsel. We alone, however, are responsible for any shortcomings in the finished product.

CONTENTS

TABLES

FIGURES

PART I

THE IMPENDING CRISIS: MYTH OR REALITY?

PROCTER THOMSON

Assisted by George H. McMillan

"It is a known fact in human nature, that its affections are commonly weak in proportion to the distance or diffusiveness of the object. Upon the same principle that a man is more attached to his family than to his neighborhood, to his neighborhood than to the community at large, the people of each state would be apt to feel a stronger bias towards their local government, than towards the government of the union, unless the force of that principle should be destroyed by a much better administration of the latter." — Hamilton, The Federalist, Number 17.

By any reasonable standard, local government in California serves the people of the state honestly, efficiently, and equitably. Yet like local government everywhere, it suffers from a number of chronic maladies that impair its efficiency, hinder the adjustment of structure and function to changing economic and social conditions, and, ultimately, threaten local freedom and initiative. Efficiency, flexibility, and initiative in local government are a vital part of that "balance of capacities" within a federal system through which individual liberties are safeguarded and public decisions are made by a highly complex society with some reasonable degree of equity and order.

The local functions that are the chief subject of this study — many of them have, of course, inevitable ramifications at the state level — fall into four main classes: (1) the basic housekeeping services, such as street and park maintenance, policing, fire-fighting, sewage disposal, health inspection, sanitary regulation, and the impounding of stray cats and dogs; (2) the expanding field of welfare services, such as old-age assistance, aid to needy children, hospital maintenance, and general relief; (3) the social function of education, indispensable to both individual growth and social freedom; (4) the operation of public enterprises, a catch-all designation covering a bewildering variety, such as gas, water, and electric utilities, docks and warehouses, airports and swimming pools, which, in most — though not all — cases, are financed by fees and charges levied on the consumers of their services. San Francisco and Los Angeles have even undertaken to finance ball parks for two migratory teams from the East.

INTRODUCTION: THE CITIZEN AND HIS GOVERNMENT

These functions, commonplace and ordinary as they are, represent the cutting edge of government, the place where the ordinary citizen comes in most intimate and continuous contact with the public process. As such, they ought to elicit the active concern and sustained interest of every citizen of the community. The jealous regard that people entertain for things closest to home, or at least for their comfort and

pocketbook, combined with the opportunity to make their influence felt
in the local arena, ought to generate lively concern over municipal
housekeeping. As De Tocqueville commented:

> It is difficult to draw a man out of his own circle to interest him
> in the destiny of the state, because he does not clearly understand
> what influence the destiny of the state can have upon his own lot.
> But if it is proposed to make a road cross the end of his estate, he
> will see at a glance that there is a connection between this small
> public affair and his greatest private affairs; and he will discover,
> without its being shown to him, the close tie that unites private to
> general interest. Thus far more may be done by entrusting to the
> citizens the administration of minor affairs than by surrendering
> ... the control of important ones, towards interesting them in the
> public welfare and convincing them that they constantly stand in
> need of one another in order to provide for it. A brilliant achieve-
> ment may win for you the favor of a people at one stroke; but to
> earn the love and respect of the population that surrounds you, a
> long succession of little services rendered and of obscure good
> deeds, a constant habit of kindness, and an established reputation
> for disinterestedness will be required. Local freedom, then, which
> leads a great number of citizens to value the affection of their
> neighbors and of their kindred, perpetually brings men together
> and forces them to help one another in spite of the propensities
> that sever them.[1]*

But this sanguine expectation is doomed to disappointment if we
examine the workings of local government. Perhaps because of the wide
range and vast importance of the issues decided by the national government or because of the increasing size and complexity of "local" politics
in a metropolitan civilization, the citizen no longer is energetically concerned with the machinery of local government. All the great themes
and many of the minor variations of social policy are sounded, so he believes, in Sacramento or Washington; and when his interest in public
affairs is aroused, his ears are attuned to these distant centers.

This broad tendency, however, is subject to some significant exceptions. The tumult and the shouting have not quite died away on the
local scene. For example, two of the most interesting political contro-
versies of recent years, one in Southern California and another in
Northern California, erupted during the past biennium. In Los Angeles
County the taxpayers' revolt of 1957-58 indicated that citizens could be
as vigorous in defending their rights as they were mistaken in identifying the forces that threatened them. The following account testifies to
the state of public feeling at the time:

> A San Gabriel Valley Taxpayers League meeting last night ended
> in shouting confusion after a speech by Tax Assessor John R.
> Quinn. The meeting was interrupted by shouts and boos, several

* Numbered references will be found at the end of each chapter.

people were ejected, and at one point a West Covina City Councilman Jay Brown was ordered out of the room. The session finally
ended with at least three factions shouting for attention and the
rest of the audience drifting away.[2]

The tragic, or comic, feature of this episode, of course, lay in the fact
that the County Assessor was only then getting around to making in the
San Gabriel Valley the same type of comprehensive revaluation which,
on his approximately five-year circuit, he had already made in other
sections of the county. Many assessments had been raised rather markedly but the prime cause of high taxes lies in high expenditures and for
these the assessor bears not the slightest responsibility. The entire affair is a classic example of the illusions that can entrap those who become aroused without being informed.

A somewhat different controversy has been unraveling in Northern
California where Sacramento County is wrestling with a king-size version of an old and familiar problem: 150 thousand residents of an urban
area of roughly 165 square miles lying to the northeast of the City of
Sacramento want to secure the benefits of municipal services. But to
incorporate or to annex: that is the question. The City of Sacramento
itself (27 square miles, 165 thousand people) is divided upon this question. On the one hand, it looks with disfavor upon the incorporation of
a new municipality that would compete for industry and prestige. On the
other hand, annexing the entire area at one fell swoop involves a number of accommodations and rearrangements that not all the interested
parties are presently prepared to make.[3]

Both history and common sense suggest that political liberty and
governmental efficiency are won or lost bit by bit and piece by piece.
The battle to maintain and, if possible, to extend these objectives is
made up of a prolonged and exasperating series of minor skirmishes
against public apathy, bureaucratic inefficiency, and fiscal incompeten-
cy. In these arenas, quite as much as in those of interstate competition
or of international rivalry, basic liberties are "meanly lost or nobly
won."

THE DEFICIENCIES OF GOVERNMENT

A "crisis" in local government has been with us, in one form or
another, for well over half a century. While "crisis" is a call to action,
it is also a trap for the unwary. The maladies from which California
suffers are chronic rather than epidemic, debilitating but not fatal. They
result from a long process of historical development.

A few jurisdictions have gone bankrupt, but in most cases "maladjustments and deficiencies" represent a more appropriate label for the ills that afflict these governments.[4] Taking the widest and most general view of the subject, we can distinguish three major types of "maladjustments and deficiencies" that are endemic for local government.

Inefficiency

The indictment for "inefficiency," a standard item in most of the writings on local government, not only covers a multitude of sins but has a variety of meanings. Inefficiencies are of two distinctly different kinds, technical and economic. Technical inefficiency is failing to secure as much output as possible from the inputs of resources available. Economic inefficiency means failing to employ an optimum combination of inputs or failing to secure an optimum combination of outputs.

Unrepresentativeness

A government is unrepresentative when the system for translating private preferences into social decisions consistently fails to implement the consensus of the body politic. But in the view of the slippery and elusive character of the "consensus," most people would settle for a slightly less heroic test of the representativeness of government, a test phrased, say, in terms of the fairness or unreasonableness of the processes of choosing candidates, presenting issues, and electing representatives. If the machinery itself is fair and reasonable, most people are perfectly willing to bear its occasional failures and mistakes.

Two examples of that test may be appropriate at this point. California, in company with a number of other states, has established fiscally independent school boards, that is, boards which are elected by direct vote and which do not submit their budget to the city council. Most school people favor an independent board on the grounds that since educational issues would be merged with other issues in the selection of the city council, the latter body, given veto power over the budget or appointive power over the board, would not reflect the consensus of the community on educational policy.[5]

While the voters and officials of the state appear to have found this argument persuasive, it has by no means won universal acceptance from political scientists and other students of the governmental process.[6] With school and city budgets being drawn up and adopted separately, a unified decision on fiscal policy for the entire community goes by default. Moreover, the separation of these two important branches of government means that economies of large-scale operation in the purchasing of supplies, the hiring of personnel, the handling of cash balances, and the issuance of bonds cannot be secured save by ad hoc cooperative arrangements.*

A curious and interesting example of the tests that can be applied to the system of electing representatives is provided by the County Charter Study Committee's recent proposal to increase from five to eleven the number of supervisors in Los Angeles County.[7] For five elected officials in a county of five million to determine the wishes of the electorate is a difficult matter indeed. While (approximately) doubling the ratio of supervisors to constituents would improve the situation considerably, an even more dramatic improvement would be registered if fifty or a hundred were elected. Representativeness, however, does not depend on ratios but is governed by a number of complex political and social relationships. Even more importantly, the larger the size of the representative body, the greater the difficulty of transacting business efficiently. Thus, a large number of supervisors is required to insure the representativeness of the body but a small number is needed to perform business with dispatch. However, both these worthy objectives cannot be achieved simultaneously; each must be reconciled with the other upon some higher ground of principles.

Inequity

Local government may violate the rights of its citizens or treat individuals and groups unfairly. Violations may follow some consistent pattern and exhibit a congenital bias against a particular set of interests, or they may create large numbers of random instances of individual injustice. Consistent bias usually arises from defects in representation, and random injustice from defects in organization and administration.

While in practice inequity is often difficult to identify and all but impossible to prove because the "rights" in question cannot be opera-

---

* Fiscal dependence and appointed school boards are quite common among large cities in the East and Midwest. Chicago's board is appointed by the mayor and its budget is subject to veto by the aldermen, though this power has not been effectively exercised since the depression of the 1930's. New York has an appointive board and the school budget is drawn up, along with that of all other departments of city government, by the mayor and his budget director for submission to the Board of Estimate and the City Council. See Robert M. Haig, Carl S. Shoup, and Lyle C. Fitch, The Financial Problems of the City of New York: A Report to the Mayor's Committee on Management Survey; General Summary Volume of the Finance Project (New York, 1952), Chap. xiii, esp. appendix pp. 508-22.

tionally defined, the elemental and widely accepted principle that equals should be treated equally provides a point of departure for investigating some simple but important cases. If, for instance, two persons in the same jurisdiction with the same wealth and the same income pay different amounts of taxes for identical services, equals are unequally treated and inequity obviously arises.

(This example must be very carefully specified, for in economics the obvious is often incorrect. In the long run, different rates of property taxation — assuming this is the community's method of taxation — do not mean differences in economic burdens, since properties with higher rates will sell at lower prices and those with lower rates will sell at higher prices until returns on capital are everywhere brought to equality. In the short run, however, owners sitting on the property when high rates are imposed suffer losses while those presented with low rates reap gains. The following discussion assumes short-run conditions.)

A familiar complaint of municipalities in metropolitan areas is that county services for unincorporated territory are occasionally subsidized by county taxes levied on city residents. Since cities provide and pay for municipal services within their boundaries and counties sometimes supply similar services in unincorporated urban territory, some portion of the taxes that counties levy on cities may go to pay for services someone else enjoys. The sheriff's office, which patrols heavily populated but unincorporated urban territory, is one example. Another is health service and sanitary inspection, which are available to all the cities of the county but are not provided for cities such as Los Angeles, Pasadena, Alameda, and Berkeley which operate their own departments.

While these inequities should be corrected, the sums involved are apparently much smaller than is ordinarily supposed. Many county services, such as charities and corrections (which account for two-thirds of the budget in Los Angeles County and correspondingly large fractions in other counties), are provided for cities as well as for unincorporated territories. In sum, according to the research staff of the Senate Interim Committee on State and Local Taxation, a survey of five metropolitan counties revealed that the percentages of their budget involving "the subsidization of one group of taxpayers by another" ran from a low of 2% in Napa County to a high of 6.5% in Kern County with Sacramento (2.4), Los Angeles (2.6), and Alameda (3.0) counties lying in between.[8]

Summary

To summarize, then, the major economic and political virtues to be sought in local government (or any government) are efficiency, representativeness, and equity. Government must allocate resources wisely; it must represent the will of the people; and it must implement the common standards of decency and justice. To the extent that it fails to reach these high objectives, it fails in its essential purpose and must be reformed, revised, or supplemented by other arrangements.

In the remainder of the chapter, we shall investigate some of the more obvious and notorious shortcomings of California's local governments, shortcomings that are both cause and symptom of the inefficiencies and inequities of public bodies. The first deficiency refers to the climate of opinion in which government operates, and suggests that some of its ills can be traced to a defect of understanding on the part of the citizens it attempts to serve. Next we examine rather superficially the interplay between the institutions of government and the social and economic factors of the California scene; a major disability of local government, we suggest, is its failure to adjust to socio-economic change. We next turn our attention to some of the outstanding deficiencies in the collection of local revenue, a topic more fully treated in chapters 5 and 6. Finally, we look at governmental organization.

Each member of this quartet touches upon a different aspect of the central problem, and some of them are causes of the others: inflexibility, for example, is a contributory factor to improper organization, and it, in turn, complicates the problem of securing an equitable and efficient fiscal base. In assessing the defects of local government per se , as is done in the discussions on taxation and organization, we employ criteria of efficiency, representativeness, and equity; the defects we discover have already been described in general terms.

SOCIAL CHOICE AND INCONSISTENT EXPECTATIONS

Follies and absurdities that would immediately be apparent in the management of an ordinary household are tolerated and even encouraged in the conduct of public affairs. The occasion for this churlish observation is the universal tendency of local communities to demand more services than they are willing and able to pay for. Within recent years in California, this particular variety of fiscal schizophrenia has become more virulent than usual since complaints about inadequate public services have increased in equal measure.

To move to the same conclusion from another direction, complaints about the burdens of taxation can emanate from many sources. The four principal points of the compass are: (1) people whose preference for government services is lower than the community's in general, (2) people who disapprove of certain kinds of public expenditure, (3) people who believe that the tax system is unjust and that they bear too large a share of the burden, and (4) people who want government services but object to paying taxes. The first three of these groups have logical and reasonable grounds for complaint; the fourth group suffers from an optical illusion, but this illusion is by no means uncommon. For obviously the link between costs and returns is far less direct for public goods, where individual taxes bear little relation to individual benefits, than it is for private goods where payment is proportional to benefits.

The members of a free society are, and must be, able to choose the government under which they live. As a result they may, and often do, prefer to live in a charming community that is too small to operate efficiently. They may be unwilling to consolidate their schools with someone else's schools in order to achieve a balanced and integrated program. They are reluctant to relinquish the autonomy of their local police force in order to achieve the economies of centralized record-keeping, fingerprinting, and reporting. They may prefer to deal with a host of elected officials, rather than with a small number of impersonal administrative agencies.

Students of local government can raise no legitimate objection to the consequences of these choices. They are entitled to enquire, however, whether all available alternatives were taken into account. Do people know the price they pay for the governments they have elected to establish? When a jealous regard for local autonomy animates some crossroads community to oppose school district reorganization, do parents know the fiscal and educational costs of operating these isolated districts? When some small municipality is hastily gerrymandered from a few scraps of unincorporated territory for a temporary advantage in lower taxes, do property owners realize how illusory these benefits will become with the passage of time? Or when the residents of some urban fringe area decide to form their own city in order to forestall annexation, do they realize how costly this privilege will become when they are forced to bear the expense of full-scale municipal operation?

The moral that lies behind these events is that in government as in other aspects of life one worthy objective frequently conflicts with another so that rational policy requires choices to be made between them.

A citizen who prefers a small autonomous community, for example, must be willing to relinquish the prospect of securing governmental efficiency through large-scale municipal operation. And a harassed city dweller who moves to a no-down-payment suburban paradise, populated by small homes and large families, must be prepared to bear the burden of heavy school taxes with a certain degree of equanimity.[9] To complain about the terms of these choices is only natural; but to fail to recognize the pattern of conflict among objectives, to expect the irreconcilable to be reconciled, and to refuse to accommodate to the necessity of making choices — these inconsistent and erroneous attitudes are a formidable barrier to wise policy in local government.

SOCIAL CHANGE VERSUS INFLEXIBLE GOVERNMENT

In this state as elsewhere, government is the prisoner of history, and the compromises that seemed fair and reasonable in 1879 (when the present constitution was adopted), or 1907 (the date of the last change in boundary lines, when a piece of San Diego County was established as Imperial County), or 1926 (when the present system of senatorial representation by counties was established), or 1933 (when the Riley-Stewart Amendment authorizing state sales taxes was adopted*) no longer seem so today.

The Metropolis

The growth of population and industry has created in California as in other states a number of huge metropolitan centers comprising hundreds of thousands of people, thousands of different industrial plants, and hundreds of different governmental units. Each of these huge agglomerations consists of a central city and a galaxy of satellite communities rotating in eccentric orbit amidst densely populated fringe areas

---

* Government documents are notoriously dull. But, in connection with the Riley-Stewart Law, a recent report of the Assembly Interim Committee offers an interesting exception to this tendency: "The seizure of the initiative by the State Board of Equalization (of which Riley and Stewart were members) was more than just mere coincidence. In 1933 the importance of the board was at a very low ebb. The equalization of public utility property valuations had been stripped from it by the 1910 constitutional amendment, and much of its remaining prestige was lost in 1929 when the assorted corporation fees and taxes were incorporated into the Bank and Corporation Franchise Tax and placed under a newly created administrative unit, the Franchise Tax Commissioner. Prohibition was still in force so that liquor control did not then exist as a function of the board. Because of these factors it might be presumed that the board was eager to find something to justify its existence and thwart such criticisms as were rendered by the 1929 Tax Commission, e.g., that it be abolished."

Table 1.1. Population & Governmental Units
in California's Nine Standard Metropolitan Areas: 1957

Name of Area	No. of Square Miles	Population (In Thousands)		Number of Governmental Units				
		Met. Total	In Cities	Total	Counties	Cities	School Districts	Other Districts
Fresno	5,985	336.7	170.0	191	1	15	101	74
Los Angeles-Long Beach	4,853	6,109.7	4,693.3	319	2	68	157	92
Sacramento	985	427.1	177.5	135	1	5	42	87
San Bernardino-Riverside	27,310	677.0	393.7	200	2	24	105	69
San Diego	4,258	900.4	686.5	117	1	10	52	54
San Francisco-Oakland	3,314	2,630.7	2,215.0	414	5	53	156	200
San Jose	1,305	527.5	347.4	92	1	15	47	29
Santa Barbara	2,745	116.0	80.1	69	1	4	32	32
Stockton	1,410	238.4	121.7	138	1	5	71	61
TOTAL	52,165	11,963.6	8,885.2	1,675	15	199	763	698
% of State Total	32.6%	81.1%	60.3%	43.2%	26.3%	60.1%	41.5%	42.3%

Source: U.S. Bureau of Census, Census of Governments: Local Governments in Standard Metropolitan Areas.
1957, pp. 8-10.

Source for City Population: Estimates listed by city clerks in State Controller's Report of Financial
Transactions Concerning Cities of California, 1957.

which themselves are on the point of fusing into incorporated communities. The forces that bind these masses together are (1) the economic and social advantages of having complementary resources and processes gathered in a single geographical center, (2) the advantages of minute specialization and division of labor, which such a collection assists, and (3) the advantages of living in a metropolitan center where an infinite variety of amusements and services are at one's beck and call. (A small city, for example, cannot support an opera.) The tangible evidence of these ties is the transport and communications network connecting the different nuclei of the metropolis with one another. The intangible evidence is the system of commercial arrangements coordinating the various parts of this vast apparatus.

As enumerated by the Bureau of the Census, California has nine of these centers: Los Angeles-Long Beach, comprising Los Angeles and Orange counties; San Francisco-Oakland, comprising Alameda, Contra Costa, Marin, San Francisco, San Mateo, and Solano counties; San Diego, comprising San Diego County and (though not for census purposes) Tijuana below the border; San Bernardino-Riverside-Ontario, including San Bernardino and Riverside counties; San Jose, including Santa Clara County; Sacramento, city and county; Fresno, city and county; Stockton, including San Joaquin County; and Santa Barbara city and county. All these areas include counties or groups of counties containing at least one central city of 50,000 or more population plus adjacent metropolitan territory economically integrated with the central area. At present the United States contains 174 such areas.

Unfortunately, the Census definition, including as it does the entire county or counties within which the central city and related metropolitan aggregates are located, is a bit too inclusive for several areas in California, since neither the desert villages of eastern San Bernardino County nor the agricultural settlements in Antelope Valley of Los Angeles County qualify as "metropolitan" communities. The total population of these metropolitan areas provides, therefore, an upper limit of the true metropolitan population. The population of incorporated cities in each region provides the lower limit — lower because it excludes people in densely populated fringe areas.

Table 1.1 summarizes the data for California's metropolitan areas. The 11.9 million people living in these areas make up the bulk of the state's population: 81% of the people in California are concentrated in the 16 metropolitan counties and 60% of them live in incorporated cities of metropolitan regions, a somewhat higher degree of concentration than exists for the United States as a whole where, roughly, three-fifths of the total population live in standard metropolitan areas.

Units of Government

How has government adapted and changed to meet the changing demands of metropolitan civilization? A glance at the last five columns of Table 1.1 suggests part of the answer. Each area is served by a veritable hodgepodge of local authorities: Los Angeles has over 300, San Francisco-Oakland over 400, and even Santa Barbara, the smallest of the lot, boasts 69 separate units.

The number of governing agencies is actually a great deal larger than the magnitudes shown in the table. Under the strict definition employed by the Census Bureau, a "unit" of government must have fiscal autonomy, an independent governing body, and a certain degree of administrative freedom, a test that many special districts — regarded as governments by other students of the subject — often fail to meet. By taking a loose and flexible view of the character of the unit, the numbers reach astronomical proportions. For instance, the Los Angeles Metropolitan Area, according to one pair of authorities, contains "at least 1000" governments, and San Diego at least 150.[10] An enumeration made in 1953 by the Senate Interim Committee on State and Local Taxation listed 544 governmental units in Los Angeles County, of which 380 were special districts,[11] a decided contrast to the strict Census constructionists who tabulated only 50 such districts in 1957.[12]

Adaptability

While social institutions are mutually interdependent, some of them change much more rapidly than others. Under modern conditions the economic arrangements of society undergo continuous and rapid transformation while government, many of whose features are rooted in law and custom, alters much more slowly. The result is that public institutions are frequently out of adjustment with the remaining forces of society.

The differences in flexibility created by the impact of law and custom are reinforced by the mechanisms of adaptation in the public and private sectors. For an economic organization, survival depends on efficiency, and inflexibility spells bankruptcy; while for a political organization survival and efficiency are not linked so intimately. The mechanism for creating efficiency in both government units and busi-

ness firms depends upon an appropriate combination of direct and indirect sanctions. The direct checks and balances are obvious: a firm
that is doing badly will be taken in hand by its managers upon the ad-
vice and counsel of its stockholders. Similarly, the governing authorities of a city or county will endeavor to correct the abuses that they or
the citizens discover.

For business enterprises, however, the indirect checks and balances are the ultimate guardians of efficiency. For if the firm is not up
to snuff its customers will trade elsewhere; since the marginal customers spell the difference between prosperity and famine, only a few such
desertions are needed to usher the inefficient firm into oblivion. But
these indirect checks and balances, so devastatingly effective for business, are impotent and harmless for local government, since the citizen who moves away because he is dissatisfied with the services he receives cannot possibly threaten the survival of the city. The dissenters
leave, the satisfied or immobile remain, and the municipality continues
its wasteful ways on a slightly more modest scale than before.

THE FISCAL BASE

The property tax, the main source of local revenue, illustrates
the ancient maxim "uneasy lies the head that wears a crown." The
property tax is both defective in principle and deficient in practice.
"Its sole virtue," one writer states, "is its age."[13] But according to
some authorities, in addition to the virtue (if any) that age confers upon
it, taxation of real property is the only source of revenue local units
are competent to administer. If this contention is true, if other forms
of taxation are too complex for cities and schools to handle or if the
attempt to employ them would erode their economic base, then discussing the disabilities of property taxes is an invitation to despair. For
nothing is either good or bad, to paraphrase the Bard slightly, save
alternatives make it so. And if the property tax has no feasible alternatives — save loss of local initiative or wholesale reduction in local services — we must accept it as it is and pass on to more fruitful areas
of inquiry.

But alternatives do exist. The principal sources of public revenue
are wealth, income, and consumption. Of these three the taxation of
wealth secures the minimum amount of revenue with the maximum
amount of fiscal inequity, economic inefficiency, and administrative
difficulty.

Inequity

Fundamentally, the property tax is unjust because it fails to treat equals equally. Income from property is only a fraction of income in general, somewhere between 1/4 and 1/3, in fact, for the U.S. economy as a whole, and different families have widely different ratios of wealth to income. To the extent, therefore, that taxes on property are ultimately borne by owners of property and to the extent that personal income represents the most equitable measure of that illusive magnitude, "ability to pay," the property tax violates one of the basic criteria of taxation in a democratic society.

Inefficiency: The Flow of Capital

The property tax distorts the pattern of investment between different communities. Communities with high tax rates have a lower volume of commercial and residential investment and those with low tax rates have a higher volume of investment. Differences in tax rates lead to improper allocation of resources.

Some of these effects, admittedly, take a very long time to work themselves out and all of them are mixed and interspersed with a number of other forces. A growing community with a high tax rate, for example, will not expand quite as rapidly as it otherwise would. But regardless of disturbing factors, the long-run return on capital in one area must be roughly equal to the return in any other area. As a result, buildings are relatively scarcer and their rents before taxes are relatively higher in high tax communities while the reverse is true in low tax communities so that net yields in both are approximately equal after taxes are paid.

How does this adjustment affect economic efficiency? It is bound to affect it adversely because the location of business, residential, and commercial activities no longer reflects the natural advantages of different communities. Differences in tax rates create artificial scarcity and artificial abundance. If X would have been a good place for a shopping center or an apartment house and Y a relatively poor site, the differences in taxes ought not to repeal the comparative advantage which nature establishes. [14]

Inflexibility

As most California communities have discovered, the property tax is inflexible. It is inflexible in principle because the market values of assets, which are the capitalized net worth of income streams running into the distant future, do not always keep pace with year-to-year

changes in community income. It is inflexible in practice because assessed values tend to lag behind market values.

These twin disabilities create, in California as elsewhere, the
sorry spectacle of wealthy communities and impoverished governments
during periods of economic growth and cumulative inflation. And state
legislatures have enthusiastically compounded the natural disabilities
of the tax by imposing legal barriers on both the operating margin and
the borrowing margin of cities, schools, and other local agencies. Altogether, no more perfect formula for fiscal mismanagement could be
devised than to place the governments of expanding metropolitan areas
upon a narrow fiscal base and then deny them the power to use that
base when they need it. Legal limits on local tax rates are, in one
sense, however, a kind of left-handed recognition of the inherent inequities and diseconomies of the property tax per se. The remedy, we
trust, is sufficiently obvious that he who runs may read: Retire the
property tax from active duty as rapidly as possible.

Administration

A favorite indoor sport of writers on public finance is to complain about the assessment practices and administrative standards of
the local property tax. The bill of particulars varies little from one
community to another. In the first place, property is never assessed
at its full value; for California as a whole the assessed values are about
a quarter of the market values and the ratio has been falling intermit-
tently throughout most of the postwar period.* Second, different tax
areas have widely differing ratios of assessed to market value; as far
as can be determined, California counties in 1957 varied from 20 to
27%, i.e., the highest level is 35% greater than the lowest. Third, different kinds of property within the same tax jurisdiction are assessed
at different ratios of market value. Fourth, in all jurisdictions some
property escapes assessment altogether; this is particularly true of the
personal property tax, which falls mainly "upon those unfortunate individuals who are burdened either with a vigorous conscience or a ground-
less fear of legal consequences."[15]

The causes of these variations are not hard to isolate. Apart from
the inherent difficulties of identifying and measuring millions of parcels
of residential property according to a fair and equitable formula, the

---

* The State Board of Equalization reckons the 1958 ratio at 23.7%,
and the highest state-wide ratio achieved in recent times was 50% in 1935-
37. For details and documentation see Chapter 6, Table 6.6.

virtual impossibility of conducting search and seizure operations to
catch hundreds of millions of pieces of personal property, and the un-
believable complexity of the recording and reporting arrangements required by this bootless enterprise, there are six causes susceptible of
remedy this side of Utopia:

1. The elected, often technically untrained, assessor who is
    subject to political pressure both to reduce individual as-
    sessments and to lower the general level of assessments in
    the area under his jurisdiction,

2. State aid programs which, however desirable on other
    grounds, provide an incentive for competitive underassess-
    ment because state money is paid to schools in inverse pro-
    portion to the amount of assessed value per child,

3. The ancient tradition of underassessment and differential
    assessment in local units which perpetuates itself by its
    own inertia,

4. The preoccupation of professional assessors with a meta-
    physical magnitude called "true value" which renders them
    incapable of recognizing the impact of inflation on asset
    prices,

5. The political climate which converts a technical issue, the
    value of property, into a power struggle between the tax-
    payer, or taxpayers as a group, and the assessor,

6. Failure to coordinate and centralize the assessment of
    property in the hands of a unified agency with effective power
    to achieve equalization between different tax jurisdictions.

THE ORGANIZATION OF LOCAL GOVERNMENT

The fascinating and interesting complexities of local organization
in California defy analysis and frustrate generalization. The present
(1958) structure, the joint product of historical development and ad hoc
improvisation, consist of 351 cities, 57 counties, 1 city-county, 1,790
school districts,* and around 3,000 special districts. Except for the
counties, whose boundaries have remained stable for nearly half a century, these numbers are constantly changing. New cities are incorpo-
rating; new special districts are spawning in the suburban hinterlands
of metropolitan regions. But, as a welcome exception to this pattern of
governmental fertility, the number of school districts has steadily decreased during the last few decades.

While the pattern of local government in California is a patchwork quilt of many hues and colors, its infinite variety bespeaks both
confusion and experimentation. In broadest outline the problem of
"government" — the making of group decisions, the allocating of poli-

* These numbered 1,818 on July 1, 1957.

tical power, expressing group loyalty — is inherently quite simple. But this problem admits of a multiplicity of solutions, solutions that must recognize the historical conditions of the locality, the geographical advantages and disadvantages of the region, the social composition of the area's population, the economic trends and prospects of the community, the personal ambitions of community leaders, the diverse expectations of interest groups, and so forth. Even in the absence of these sources of diversity, no one "correct" solution to the problem of government exists; there are many roads to the summit.

Consequently, the governments we observe in the municipalities and counties and districts of this state can be regarded as a series of viable experiments, a set of rough approximations to an ideal dimly visible beneath the mass of confusion and detail that confronts the observer on every hand. As one pair of authorities on metropolitan government recently remarked:

> We reject the pessimistic view that metropolis is all dissatisfaction, the overly optimistic view that metropolis will automatically grow bigger and better, and the manipulative view that the expert alone, with his laudably growing competence, should control most of the behavior choices which shape metropolis. Rather, what we have in mind is that just as the citizens of this country have repeatedly succeeded together in spite of many a stupidity or peculation along the way, so they will see their own interest in meeting the challenge of Metropolis in Ferment, too, and will devise a hundred ways of meeting it for every form it takes. We are not sure that Metropolis, like Paradise, is lost; but if it is, then, like Paradise, it can be regained. [16]

Social Decisions and Individual Choices

Policy. The infinite variety and vast complexity of public organization in a metropolitan community frustrate the efforts of the ordinary citizen to make rational decisions on public policy. Wholly apart from its other demerits, the multiplicity of governmental units taxes the voter's understanding of public issues, increases the number of agencies and authorities he must keep track of, diffuses his interest in any one public agency, multiplies the number of candidates he must examine and vote upon, and, finally, subverts the democratic process by encouraging neglect and disinterest. In addition, the uninstructed citizen who wishes to petition his government for some simple and ordinary service is shunted about the labyrinth like a character in a Kafka novel.

The ordinary citizen in California may deal with ten to a dozen different governments and encounter a roster of names at election time that would tax the memory of an insurance salesman. In addition to state and national governments, the list includes the city, the county, the school district, and half a dozen special districts. If he follows the prevailing California pattern, living in one locality and working in another, he will encounter another parcel of local agencies at his place of business. Inhabitants of unincorporated urban areas with their burgeoning quota of special districts have an even larger list to keep track of. To compound his difficulties the California custom of legislation by constitutional amendment — an inevitable outgrowth of an unrepresentative legislature — confronts him with an elongated ballot of state propositions.

Now representative democracy is itself a device for economizing on the labor of decision-making. The selection of representatives to decide complex issues of taxing, budgeting, administering, and staffing for local governments is designed to spare the ordinary citizen from the uncongenial and time-consuming task of examining those issues with the care their importance deserves. The citizen determines only the broadest and most general outlines of policy and trusts his elected representative to translate this policy into specific legislation. But the multitude of candidates and agencies and issues exceeds the citizen's span of attention and defeats one of the essential purposes of representative democracy.

Money. The vast number of different governments erected on the same fiscal base and given autonomous power to draw up budgets and levy taxes means that no single agency reviews and compares the relative value of money spent for different purposes — no single agency, that is, except the voter himself in a very roundabout and indirect fashion. Each agency, of course, can reallocate funds between the various functions it controls but no agency can transfer money from the city to the school budget, or from the county to the independent district's budget to equalize returns at the margin between each field of use. This limitation is serious. It is as if one person in a household were empowered to decide how much should be spent for food, another to decide for clothing, another for recreation, etc., but no one could decide to transfer funds from clothes to food if the last dollar spent for the former brought less satisfaction than the last dollar spent for the latter.

Even in principle, with a unified decision on the allocation of resources between functions, maximum satisfaction from the expenditure of a given total is difficult to achieve and impossible to verify because the satisfactions accrue to different people. (See Chapter 3.) Nevertheless, a kind of rough intuition about community values and relative satis-

faction is available to guide this decision. But even this imperfect moni-
tor cannot be mobilized when different bodies make independent decisions for different purposes.

Of equal if not of greater importance, the multiplicity of units
means that no single agency decides whether the sum total of public
money is either greater or smaller than the community desires. For
the alternative to public expenditures is private consumption and investment (as any taxpayer well knows) and the ultimate cost of public
goods is the clothing and cars and houses and books that do not get made
and sold because resources are used for highways, clerks, prisons,
teachers, and schools. The rationality of this decision also goes by default when a number of independent local bodies make autonomous expenditures and tax levies.

In practice, and as a result of precedent and experience, things
are not quite so bad as we have indicated. Members of one taxing authority do communicate occasionally and informally with their opposite
members in other governments; an underlying community consensus
on both the pattern and the total emerges after much painful experience
with unsatisfactory alternatives; and voters do pick and choose on the
basis of their fiscal preferences among various functions. But adjustment is painful and prolonged and, moreover, in a new or rapidly growing community — as what town in metropolitan California isn't? — the
consensus is difficult to sample at best and impossible to ascertain when
decisions are diffused.

Big Problems and Small Governments

Students of metropolitan civilization are united in the belief that
local governments must be large enough to deal with the problems confronting them. Many of these problems are the responsibilities of the
metropolitan area as a whole and cannot be resolved by the uncoordi-
nated efforts of individual agencies.

As Luther Gulick, one of the grand old men of public administration, pointed out in a recent paper, an essential element of local structure is, "the need to achieve geographic, social, and economic com-
prehensiveness so that the metropolitan government may not be confronted by the impossible task of building half a bridge, regulating
traffic on one part of a through highway, controlling land use for one
side of a street, or fighting to hold down crime in half of a slum."[17]

Three distinctly different meanings are, however, hidden in the
principle that local government must be big enough to handle the problems that confront it.

Return to Scale. Given the state of the arts and the potentialities
of administrative organization, many functions can be performed more
efficiently and at lower cost per unit of output by a large-scale organization.

Police protection, utilizing a fingerprinting and identification
system plus a crime laboratory and a broadcasting station, provides
an excellent example of the economies of large-scale operation. Though
most communities jealously guard the autonomy of their police department because they do not wish to place themselves under the protection
of an outside authority, many of them are too small to employ the technical facilities required to cope with the modern criminal. Traffic regulation can be handled quite adequately by the police force of a small
town; a missing persons bureau, on the other hand, would need to cover
the entire country. Optimum sizes of other functions fall at various
points between these limits.

A library provides another illustration. Since its utility is directly proportional to the number of different volumes and periodicals it
contains, two small communities can virtually double their effectiveness at no increase in cost by combining resources and interchanging
books. Keeping a larger card catalogue at each of two branches, carrying books back and forth, and administering the larger system represent
potential sources of increased cost. But an 80 or 90% rise in the variety
of offerings could be achieved with exactly the same total expenditure
by combining budgets, reducing the total spent on books, and applying
the difference to the extra cataloguing, transportation, and administrative expense.

The financial management of local government, a technical area
that most citizens find as mysterious as it is boring, offers another
example of the savings that size can secure. These economies are especially significant in the handling of cash balances, since most governmental units, confronted by the need to finance a continuous stream
of payments from a discontinuous flow of receipts, hold large reser-
voirs of cash or resort to short-term borrowing in order to tide them
over the dry season when no taxes are coming in. Consolidating the
balances of two or more units reduces the amount of stagnant cash and
borrowed funds which all of them hold in reserve.

> In this context Sacramento County merits commendation for
> aiding in ending the expensive practice by school districts of
> borrowing money to tide them over before revenue is collected.

Thanks to action by the state to make its aid money available to the districts at an earlier date and to County Executive **M. D.** Tarshes for initiating the pooling of county and school reserve funds, the districts are not having to go to the banks for interim money.

These new policies mean Sacramento City and County taxpayers will save this year about $40,000 in interest charges and a great deal of bookkeeping. While this amount is not large, it represents a cost which has been eliminated by good planning.[18]

Even larger financial economies could be achieved if cities, counties, and school districts abandoned the issuance of local bonds and persuaded the state to place its full faith and credit behind the long-term debts of local units. No matter how good its credit rating, a medium-sized city or school district is simply not an optimum unit for borrowing money from the bond market and invariably pays a higher risk premium, i.e., a higher rate of interest, than the state as a whole. If — and admittedly this is a very large "if" — the transfer could be effected without loss of any significant degree of local control, the saving of many millions in interest would be worth the trouble and red tape such an arrangement would invariably create.

One of the central problems of federalism is that the optimum-sized taxing unit is larger than the optimum-sized spending unit. A small city, a medium-sized school district, and even a medium-sized county are not equipped to tax wealth, income, or consumption as effectively as some larger unit. In the first place, an effective system of taxation demands an elaborate establishment for record-keeping and enforcement which governmental units of moderate dimension cannot easily afford. In the second place, the elasticity of evasion, the opportunity for avoidance by migrating to another district, is particularly large for taxation of income and consumption by small units of government. Many of these local units, indeed, are far better equipped to perform the functions of government than they are to raise the money to support this performance. The agencies of metropolis, consequently, must pool some of their tax resources in order to prevent their fiscal limitations from compromising their administrative advantages.

Hundreds of other advantages of large-scale operation could be cited. In view of the prevailing delusion that a big enterprise is always more effective and efficient than a small one, however, we ought to state emphatically that the costs of coordinating massive aggregations of men, money, and material eventually counterbalance the benefits of large-scale operation. Moreover — though governmental consolidation

is not responsible for these cancerous offshoots — increases in size
confer certain peculiar handicaps upon cities: crime, congestion, and
poverty apparently increase in geometric proportion to the size of the
population.

A few urban organizations, therefore, are too large rather than
too small. If operating economies are a paramount consideration,
they should be cut up into smaller pieces rather than allowed or encouraged to proliferate further. An illustrative example is probably
the school system of the City of Los Angeles.

Indivisible Problem and Coordination Costs. A second, and
somewhat different, reason that governments must be big enough to
handle the problems confronting them is that some "problems" are indivisible and extend over wide areas with the result that piecemeal
solution by separate agencies involves either waste and duplication or
excessive costs of intergovernmental coordination. Crime prevention
and freeway construction offer excellent examples of indivisible problems.

The necessity for a unified attack on syndicated crime and the
problems that arise when a number of independent agencies attempt
to pool their forces for such an effort are illustrated in the following
account:

> Within twenty miles of Chicago there are some 75 independent
> jurisdictions, all wedged one against another. When a crime
> is committed in Chicago and the malefactors are making for
> the country, the Chicago police department may notify five or
> often ten police departments to be on the watch. Radio has
> helped to minimize the time spent, but even now only a small
> minority of the surrounding towns are in communication. The
> perpetration of one bank robbery necessitated twenty minutes
> of telephoning to advise the proper towns along the route taken
> by the bandits. Later it was found that they had broken through
> the cordon before the calls could be taken and acted upon, and
> by the time half a dozen police departments were on the lookout,
> the bandits' car was speeding along, a dozen miles away from
> the searchers.[19]

Designing and providing for the major highways of the metropolitan region has long been recognized as an area-wide problem requiring
solution by an authority with appropriate scope and jurisdiction. Many
metropolitan regions have had to rely on the state government to perform this role, as in the recent case of the second span of the Bay
Bridge where the Legislature was finally called upon to adjudicate the
dispute. With or without benefit of a metropolitan highway authority,
a veritable hornets' nest of vested local interests is stirred up when-

ever a new link is contemplated in the trunk system leading through or around the region. Consideration of these interests, rights, and loyalties is both ethically justifiable and politically inescapable. The presence of a regional authority, therefore, does not eliminate the necessity of adjudicating opposed claims; it merely establishes a more or less neutral arena within which such disputes can be aired.

Social Costs and Benefits in Local Operations. A third reason that local governments must be big enough to handle the problems confronting them is that the activities of some governmental units impose costs upon (or create benefits for) other units. The following striking example, drawn from a situation prevailing several decades ago but not without relevance today, will convey the essence of the argument:

> The municipalities on the east shore of the San Francisco Bay deposit between 250,000 and 500,000 tons of wet sludge annually on the shallow mud flats of the bay. The odor is nauseous, the sight from the Bay Shore Highway at low tide is repellent, and the sludge is a source of infection to those who seek recreation on the bay.[20]

While metropolitan civilization would be impossible without modern sanitation and sewage disposal, present arrangements are admittedly unsatisfactory and some communities manage to create serious health and aesthetic problems for other communities. In southern California, the Los Angeles County Sanitation District, with its Hyperion and White Point outfalls that empty wastes into the ocean about a mile or more from shore, runs into perennial conflict with the beach cities.[21]

Smog, of course, represents another instance in which the activities of one group or of one bunch of communities create costs for other groups. And crime and vice allowed to flourish in one area invariably tend to spill over into other parts of the metropolis. If nothing else, the civic reputation of the entire area tends to suffer as a result of these local centers of corruption. As an example, some, though by no means all, of the interesting activities of Chicago gangsters in the great days of the twenties and thirties were actually headquartered in the "open city" of Cicero. Or, if one takes newspaper accounts seriously, the Sunset Strip, an unincorporated island of county territory populated by high-priced bistros and unemployed actors, offers a number of entertaining and slightly illegal pastimes not generally available in the neighboring communities of Los Angeles and Beverly Hills.

This relationship is a street that runs both ways, of course. A city that cleans up its local smog factory confers benefits upon the surrounding territory. A school district with an above-average program trains future citizens for other communities. And alert law enforcement officials in one town are a boon for other towns as well.

In general, however, when the community or one agency does not bear the full cost or reap the full benefit of the activities in which it engages, it will tend to push too far on things that impose costs on other areas and not far enough on things that create benefits. It will, that is, in the absence of any arrangements for consolidating or coordinating some of the activities of these independent local units.

Size and Efficiency: A Summary. We have indicated three important reasons that governments must be large enough to tackle the problems that confront them. First, for many governmental functions large-scale operation is more effective and efficient than small-scale operation. Second, many governmental problems are indivisible, and cannot be solved by an agency that covers only a small portion of the metropolitan area. Third, activities of some independent communities or agencies impose costs upon (or create benefits for) other communities and agencies. While these factors are logically quite distinct, a specific problem area may, and usually does, involve all three of them. Crime prevention, for example, is characterized by returns to scale (in administrative organization), indivisibility (with respect to area), and social costs (between communities).

Administration

The art of public administration in local governments, most students of the subject agree, is primitive and unsatisfactory, marked as it is by wholesale violations of the most elementary principles of sound organization. Apart from the fact that history and political feasibility have forced local governments to operate on much too small a scale — we paid our respects to this situation in the section immediately above — they fail to make effective use even of the limited resources at their disposal.

Some of the obvious administrative disabilities of California's local governments are covered in the following list:

1. Too many elective officials, especially officials whose functions are primarily technical.

2. Failure to achieve a unified administrative structure.

3. Mixing legislative functions with administrative functions.

4. Budgeting, auditing, and accounting procedures that are confusing, antiquated, and time-consuming.

Counties. With a few outstanding exceptions the counties of California are the weakest link in the chain. Given the emerging pattern of urban development, counties ought to serve as the nucleus of metropolitan government. But they cannot rise to these responsibilities so long as they are tethered to the traditional pattern of country government, including a host of elected officials — a board of supervisors, a school superintendent, an assessor, a coroner, a road commissioner, a clerk, an auditor, a treasurer, a sheriff, a district attorney, and so on — operating independently of one another, and a county board of supervisors that tries its valiant best to handle both legislative and administrative responsibilities. Policy-making officials such as the supervisors, the district attorney, and possibly the sheriff should be directly responsible to the voters, but officials with technical responsibilities — the assessor, the coroner, the treasurer, the road commissioner, the clerk — ought to be appointed by the county manager on the basis of competitive examinations. The administrative business of the county should be handled by a county manager or chief administrative officer responsible to the Board and empowered to appoint officials, draw up a proposed budget, and determine salary schedules.

Special Problems of Special Districts. Special districts are created for a number of reasons. First, and most important, is "the desire to obtain municipal-type services without having to create or annex to a city government.[22] In turn, reasons for preferring to remain aloof from city government include the belief that tax rates will be lower if services are provided by special districts, the desire to retain a separate identity, and the suspicion that city politics are dark and devious. Second, however, special districts may be created by both cities and unincorporated territories because the optimum-sized unit for water supply, sanitation, smog control, and other services exceeds the scope of existing governmental jurisdictions. Third, special districts may be created in rural areas to facilitate the production of crops by providing irrigation, soil conservation, and reclamation.

Most of the acute problems of special districts in California arise in unincorporated areas where large numbers of such units, each with its own separate function and taxing power, are stacked on top of one another. As an agency of government, this "stack" of districts lacks administrative unity, creates confusion, and dissipates responsibility. As a taxing body, the districts must rely on property levies and cannot utilize sales taxes or be eligible for state subsidies, both

of which are available to cities. As an agency for sampling the community census, elections to the governing boards of special districts are
noteworthy for the extreme apathy they generate among citizens.[23]
Finally, as a producer of public services, this batch of special districts may cost more than an incorporated city covering the same territory. The following story from Sacramento County illustrates this
point to a T:

> In tax code area 99-70* the people are paying a walloping
> $11.69 for each $100 of valuation. What runs the tax bill up so
> fantastically? Mostly the many special assessment districts and
> the borrowings for school operations. In the code area just men-
> tioned the people are paying $1.73 for North Sacramento elemen-
> tary schools operation. There is another $ .32 for carrying bonds
> for this school operation. These same people also pay $1.94 for
> the operation and bonds of the Grant Union High School. They pay
> $ .66 for the Hagginwood Sanitary District, $ .36 for the Ameri-
> can River Junior College operation and $ .17 on bonds for the
> college.

> But this is still not all. These voters pay a tax levied by the
> American River Flood Control Zone No. 11 amounting to $2.49.
> This one item is greater than the county basic tax (of 2.33 per
> $100).

> Thus it is clear that the county tax tells only a minor part
> of the story about the expense of government in unincorporated
> areas. In the main these various assessments have gone steadi-
> ly upward. What is more, the taxpayers rarely break down their
> governmental costs to discover just what the components of their
> tax bills are.

> Here is illustrated the high cost of buying city type services
> one at a time. A city, however, furnishes a package of all essen-
> tial services for one tax rate.

> It is therefore easier for citizens of the city to understand
> their costs and control them. The people in the unincorporated
> areas are confronted by so many boards, trustees, districts and
> bond issues that most of them cannot follow what is happening
> and stay away from the many elections in droves.

> Sooner or later these conditions drive people who want city
> type services to get themselves into a city.[24]

Not only are special districts "pyramided geographically, one on
top of the other, resulting in endless confusion to the taxpayer and officials alike ...[and creating] innumerable tax code areas,"[25] but the
vast number of state enabling acts for these agencies are vague, contra-
dictory, and "even barren, as to basic powers and procedures." Further, new districts are often created when existing agencies could serve
quite handily; dissolution of superfluous districts and consolidation of
inefficient special units is often quite difficult, and coordination or plan-

---

* For an explanation of "tax code areas," see Chapter 2, pp. 31-34.

ing for these agencies is altogether lacking in many instances. Finally
and not surprisingly, even their number is not known with any degree
of certainty — the Assembly Committee on Municipal and County Government reckoned that there were "between 5,000 and 6,000 districts
of all types" in 1957 — because there is no central office to which all
of them are obliged to report.[26]

As matters now stand, the layer-cake system of special district
government in metropolitan fringe areas is an exasperating anomaly
rather than an organic defect. But given present and prospective growth
trends in the nine metropolitan areas of the state, with the bulk of the
population destined to bypass the central city and flock to the suburban
hinterland, proliferation of special agencies could well prove a fatal
handicap to efficient and effective local government in the decades ahead.

NOTES TO CHAPTER 1

[1] Alexis De Tocqueville, Democracy in America (rev. ed.; New
York: Alfred A. Knopf, 1948), II, p. 104.

[2] The Progress Bulletin (Pomona), January 18, 1958.

[3] Issued by the Executive Committee of the Sacramento City-
County Chamber of Commerce, a lengthy pronouncement opposing the
creation of a new municipality which would "compete" with the present
city of Sacramento was reported in The Sacramento Bee, August 8,
1958. The same issue of the Bee contained a news story under the title
"City Offers Realism on Issue of Annexation" which suggested that the
City Council was unwilling to annex the entire area but would welcome
piecemeal acquisitions as conditions warranted.

[4] Alvin H. Hansen and Harvey S. Perloff, State and Local Finance in the National Economy (New York: W. W. Norton & Co., 1944)
pp. 11-13.

[5] Paul R. Mort and Walter C. Reusser, Public School Finance:
Its Background Structure, and Operation (2d ed.; New York: McGraw-
Hill Book Co., 1951) pp. 56-65.

[6] Robert L. Morlan, "Toward City-School District Rapproche-
ment," Public Administration Review (Spring, 1958), 113-18; and
Nelson B. Henry and Jerome Kerwin, Schools and City Government
(Chicago: University of Chicago Press, 1938).

[7] Los Angeles County Charter Study Committee, Recommendations of the Charter Study Committee Presented to the Board of Supervisors (Los Angeles, July 22, 1958), pp. 1-4 (Mimeographed).

[8] Report of the Senate Interim Committee on State and Local
Taxation; Part Seven, Fiscal Problems of Urban Growth in California;
California Legislature 1953, Regular Session (Sacramento: California
State Printing Office, 1953), p. xv.

[9] Lyle C. Fitch, "Metropolitan Financial Problems," The Annals of the American Academy of Political and Social Science, CCCXIV (November 1957), 73.

[10] Richard Bigger and Stanley Scott, "Problems of Metropolitan Government" (Mimeographed draft), Los Angeles and Berkeley, Calif.; Sept. 1, 1957. Messrs. Bigger and Scott, it is only fair to note, include 5 counties instead of 2 within the Los Angeles Metropolitan area.

[11] Senate Interim Committee, Fiscal Problems of Urban Growth, p. 125.

[12] Same source as Table 1.2, p. 10.

[13] Philip E. Taylor, The Economics of Public Finance (rev. ed.; New York: The Macmillan Co., 1953), p. 313.

[14] For an excellent discussion of this and related points see: Herbert A. Simon, Fiscal Aspects of Metropolitan Consolidation (Berkeley: Bureau of Public Administration, University of California, 1943), pp. 3, 20.

[15] Taylor, Public Finance, p. 297.

[16] Martin Meyerson and Barbara Terrett, "Metropolis Lost, Metropolis Regained," The Annals of the American Academy of Political and Social Science, CCCXIV (November 1957), 9.

[17] Luther Gulick, "Metropolitan Organization," Annals (November 1957), p. 60.

[18] The Sacramento Bee, August 9, 1957.

[19] Merriam, Parratt, and Lepawsky, The Government of the Metropolitan Region of Chicago, quoted in Victor Jones, Metropolitan Government (Chicago: The University of Chicago Press, 1942), p. 66. The source having been published in 1933, the incident presumably occurred sometime in the Roaring Twenties. Nowadays the Windy City has grown old and respectable and such adventures are no longer typical.

[20] Jones, Metropolitan Government, p. 59.

[21] See a story in the Progress Bulletin (Pomona) of August 12, 1957, entitled "L.A. Sewage Fight Older Than Smog."

[22] Winston W. Crouch, Dean E. McHenry, John C. Bollens, and Stanley Scott, California Government and Politics (Englewood Cliffs, N.J.: Prentice-Hall Inc., 1956), p. 266.

[23] See ibid., 267-68.

[24] The Sacramento Bee, May 19, 1958.

[25] Assembly Interim Committee on Municipal and County Government, Special Districts; Assembly Interim Committee Reports 1955-57, Vol. 6, No. 4 (Sacramento: Assembly of the State of California, 1937), p. 6.

[26] Ibid., pp. 6-8.

With 159,000 square miles,[1] California, the third largest state in the Union — ranking immediately behind Alaska and Texas, and just ahead of Montana — is a good deal bigger than many of the important nations of the world. It exceeds Japan (143,000 square miles), Italy (116), and the United Kingdom (94), and is several times as large as Greece (51) or Czechoslovakia (49). Indeed, of the countries of Europe outside of Russia, only France (213), Spain (194), and Sweden (174) have a larger area than California.

POPULATION

Throughout its eventful history the population of the state has grown at a prodigious rate — from 93 thousand at its admission to the Union in 1850[2] to 14.7 million in 1958. Following the decade 1850-60, when an increase of 309% was tabulated, the population of the state rose by 40 to 60% every ten years except when migration was retarded by depression during 1890-1900 and 1930-40. (See Table 2.1 for details.)

The migrations that created this century of growth had widely different origins and characteristics.[3] Following the gold rush, which put the state in business — about 80,000 people reached California in 1849 — the fertile lands of the Sacramento and San Joaquin valleys attracted a large number of farm families. Completion of the transcontinental railroad in 1869, combined with the dislocations created elsewhere in the country by the Civil War and its aftermath, also accelerated the rate of migration to the Golden State.

After the turn of the century, the state received a substantial number of migrants from Missouri and nearby areas; while in 1910-20, Iowa discovered California. During the prosperous twenties, a host of retired oldsters attracted by its benign climate, youngsters beguiled by the glamor of Hollywood, and businessmen in search of expanding economic opportunity added over two million people, or 60%, to the population of the state.

While the displacements of the Great Depression brought the "Okies" and other victims of natural and man-made calamities — Steinbeck's Grapes of Wrath or Carey McWilliams' Factories in the Field are required reading in this connection — California in the 1930's acquired only 1.3 million people, a smaller absolute rise than that of the 1920's and the smallest percentage increase (22%) in the state's history.

But, aided by military operations, defense industries, and postwar relocation, particularly by servicemen who returned to the scene of the crime as it were, 3.7 million people, or 53%, were added to the population of the state in the decade of the 1940's, and an additional 4.1 million have been tabulated since 1950.

At the present rate of growth — 562,000 between July 1, 1957 and July 1958 [4] — the excess of births over deaths provides around 227 thousand people every year, and migration about 335 thousand. [5]

To give point and emphasis to these astronomical magnitudes, present growth rates indicate that California is acquiring about 1,540 people each and every day, or a population roughly equivalent to that of Santa Clara County every year. About 920 new residents cross the state borders every day, or enough to match the 1957 population of Fresno County every year.

Both the children who are born and the migrants who enter the state bring with them a host of new demands for local government services, and strain the existing capacity of fixed equipment — highways, hospitals, fire stations, public offices, and, unfortunately, prisons — to the utmost. These new demands, moreover, fall in different proportion upon different areas. No one who has watched the citrus groves of Orange County, which experienced a 14.6% rise in population this past year, being bulldozed into suburbs can fail to appreciate the devastating impact of migration upon the social and political arrangements of local areas.

With an estimated 14.7 million people in July 1958, California ranks second only to New York (16 million) and exceeds a number of European countries such as Czechoslovakia (13.2), Hungary (9.8), or Sweden (7.3). [6]

Population data, including some crystal ball work for years up to 1970, are presented in Table 2.1.

CALIFORNIA'S GOVERNMENTS

California has over 5,000 local units that are empowered to levy property taxes. As of February 1, 1958, these included 57 counties, 1 city-county, 351 cities, 1,790 school districts (down from 1818 since July 1, 1957) and 2,901 special districts for a grand total of 5,100. The numerical status of special districts is, as usual, vague and doubtful. The State Board of Equalization tabulated 68 different categories of such districts for which it assessed utility property and for which county officers assessed common property, but irrigation districts — there were 110 of these in 1957 — assessed their own proper-

Table 2.1. California Population Estimates and Projections
for Selected Fiscal and Calendar Years, 1900-1970
(Population Figures in Thousands)

Year	Total Population including armed forces stationed in the state		Civilian Population excluding armed forces stationed in the state		Civilian Population as a % of Total Population
	1 January	1 July	1 January	1 July	1 July
	a	b	c	d	e
1900	1,460	1,490			
1910	2,344	2,406	Not		....
1920	3,427	3,554			....
1930	5,621	5,711	Available		....
1937	6,434	6,528			....
1940	6,868	6,950	6,813	6,899	99.2
1947	9,696	9,832	9,485	9,672	98.3
1948	9,948	10,064	9,783	9,895	98.3
1949	10,200	10,337	10,028	10,161	98.2
1950	10,473	10,609	10,299	10,438	98.3
1951	10,834	11,058	10,599	10,681	96.5
1952	11,400	11,743	10,990	11,299	96.2
1953	11,956	12,168	11,523	11,748	96.5
1954	12,382	12,595	12,001	12,254	97.2
1955	12,815	13,035	12,476	12,699	97.4
1956	13,318	13,600	12,979	13,260	97.5
1957	13,880	14,160	13,545	13,830	97.6
1958	14,445	14,730	14,115	14,400	97.7
1959	15,012	15,295	14,682	14,965	97.8
1960	15,578	15,860	15,247	15,530	97.9
1965	Not Available		18,150	18,454	....
1970			21,432	21,790	....

Sources: California State Department of Finance, Budget
Division, Financial Research Section, Carl M. Frisen, senior research
technician. Titles of publications, tables, and page numbers are shown
below:

Cols. a & b, all years; col. d prior to 1958: California's Population in 1957. Sacramento: The Department, July 1957. Col. a, tables not shown in this table but are available in the source material.

Col. d, 1958-1970: "Projections of California's Civilian Population by Single Year of Age, 0-20 Years, and for Selected Age Groups." Sacramento: The Department, September 1957, Table A.

CLF Computations:
Col. c: Straight-line interpolation of col. d. Col. c for 1940 based on col. e multiplied by col. a because adjacent year for interpolation (1939) not available.

Col. e: Col. d divided by col. b.

ty and collected their own taxes; the same was true of 10 sanitation and sanitary districts. In addition, at least 150 districts possessed property-tax-levying powers but did not exercise them. Adding the go-it-alones and the sleepers (1957 estimate) to the above yields 3,171 special districts and raises the grand total to 5,370.[7]

Since some of these units are superimposed on others, with boundaries overlapping but not coinciding, and since each unit has its own particular tax rate, the state as a whole is divided into a patchwork quilt of 13,602 "tax code areas."

Geographic, Demographic, and Political Characteristics of California Cities and Counties

In at least one respect, the city and county governments of this state are relatively uncomplicated. There are only two main categories of city and county governmental authority, namely, charter or general law, and two main types of administrative organization for cities, namely, mayor-council or council-manager.

Table 2.2 sums up the picture as of the first quarter of 1958.

Table 2.2 City and County Government in California

Unit	Type	Number	Per Cent of Total Active Units
(a)	(b)	(c)	(d)
Cities:	Active	351	100.0
	Inactive	3	
	Charter	60	17.1
	General Law	290	82.6
	Special	1	.3
	Council-Manager	170	48.4
	Mayor-Council	181	51.6
Counties:	Active	57	100.0
	Charter	10	17.0
	General Law	247	83.0
City-Counties:	Charter	1	100.0

Source: Table 2.a (Appendix)

Table 2.a in the Appendix brings together a variety of basic facts about California counties and cities. In addition to governmental type and date of incorporation, we have included information on recent population trends, land area, and the urban rural distribution of population for the various counties.

As one would expect in a state as diverse as California, the geography and demography of its cities and counties varies greatly. Though city boundaries give very little insight into the underlying realities of metropolitan development, the three cities with the largest land area are Los Angeles (454.8 square miles), San Diego (131) and Oakland (53.3), while Wheatland with 0.2 square miles possesses the smallest area in the state.

The prodigious rate of population growth in certain areas of California is highlighted by such figures as a 4,098% rate of increase for West Covina (1,072 to 45,006 in absolute numbers) and 305% for Del Norte County during the 17 years from 1940 to 1957. Other cities with large percentage increases are Concord with 1,978% and El Cajon with 1,789%. Orange County with 291% and Contra Costa County with 255% also registered sizeable rates of increase.

During this eventful period only eight California cities and three counties registered a decrease in population. The cities were Amador (down 61%), Angels (-1%), Avalon (-9%), Colma (-19%), Davis (loss of 1 person), Grass Valley (-3%), Jackson (-8%), and Plymouth (-20%). Sierra County lost 26% of its population, Mariposa 24%, and Nevada 6%. Two other counties, Amador with +0.3% and Lassen with +2% registered very small rates of increase.

In light of the power structure of the State Legislature, the percentage of county population residing in urban areas (cities or unincorporated territory with 2,500 or more population) is a statistic of some importance. Varying from a high of 100, 97, and 91 for San Francisco, Los Angeles, and Alameda Counties, respectively down to zero for ten counties in the state (Amador, Alpine, Calaveras, Lake, Mariposa, Mono, Plumas, Sierra, Trinity, and Tuolumne), the urban population is more than half the total for only 23 of California's 58 counties (including the city-county of San Francisco). While no hard and fast predictions can be made on the basis of this arbitrary division, the "rural" counties (counties with more than half their population outside of urban areas) outnumber the "urban" by about 1.5 to 1 and continue to hold the balance of political power in the upper chamber of the Legislature. Recollecting that some 81% of total population resides in the 16 metropolitan counties, with 60% in incorporated cities in those counties, California is a metropolitan commonwealth with a quasi-rural Senate, a not uncommon situation in many other states in the Union.

Eight of California's cities were incorporated in 1850, the year the state was admitted to the union. While a number of thriving communities existed at that date, many of them situated near the missions

that Father Serra so thoughtfully located a day's journey from one
another, the list of 1,850 incorporations includes only Benecia, Los
Angeles, Sacramento, San Diego, San Francisco, San Jose, Santa
Barbara, and Stockton. Each subsequent decade witnessed lively activity in the founding of municipalities, 112 additional cities (including
3 now on the retired list) having been incorporated by the turn of the
century, 130 in the decades 1901-20, another 36 between 1921-40, and
21 in 1941-50. The seven and a half years from 1951 to the middle of
1958 ushered in a bonanza crop of 48 new towns.

Springing full-blown from the forehead of the tract home builder,
many of these recent additions were incorporated as large-scale cities.
Lakewood in Los Angeles County, founded 1954, is a noteworthy member of this group of lusty infants, with a population in 1957 of 75,000,
assessed valuation of $57 million and an area of 7.4 square miles.
Other such additions to the Los Angeles family include Downey (1956)
with 89,000 people, $91 million in valuation, and 11.8 miles of terri-
tory in 1957; Bellflower (53,000, $40 million, and 6.1 square miles);
Norwalk (83,000, $64 million, and 9.1 square miles); and Paramount
(20,000, $25 million, and 4.3 square miles). Quite a different aspect
of the problem is illustrated by the incorporation of Rolling Hills and
Rolling Hills Estates, a pair of residential communities with two and
three thousand people, respectively. To preserve the amenity values
of their estates and to keep the common herd at bay through judicious
use of municipal zoning regulations appear to have been the primary
motives for incorporation.[8] The City of Industry (588 people, $8 mil-
lion valuation, and 5.4 square miles), a spaghetti-shaped community
that includes a number of factories strung along a railroad track but
excludes the residential areas on either side, was incorporated to provide municipal services at a minimum cost.[9]

Quite a few of these recent incorporations, fostered by permissive state regulations and encouraged by the availability of shared
sales tax revenues under the Bradley-Burns Act of 1955, are geographical monstrosities and sociological isolates. They are not organic entities; they are gerrymandered into all sort of odd shapes and
sizes, and when the transitory circumstances which gave them birth
pass away, they promise to create a host of problems for future metropolitan development.

Types of City Government

Council-Manager Government. An increasing number of California communities have adopted the council-manager form of government, a device that combines an elected legislature, whose members usually serve on a part-time basis, with an appointed professional administrator. In such municipalities the council, elected on a nonpartisan ballot, usually chooses a mayor from among its own members to chair its meetings, deliver the annual Fourth of July oration in the city park, and officiate at laying cornerstones or spading up the first shovelful of earth for the numerous public projects inaugurated by California's growing communities. In theory and sometimes in practice, the division of labor between council and manager follows the pattern both tradition and efficiency prescribe as appropriate spheres of influence for the legislative and executive arms of government. That is to say, the manager draws up the city budget for council modification and approval. The manager also administers the legislation that the council enacts and has primary responsibility for hiring or firing employees, purchasing supplies, and arranging for building contracts.

But in these latter spheres, the city council — as is customary with local governments everywhere — takes a bit more responsibility than is usually exercised by state or national legislative bodies. This relation holds true even when the city executive is an elected official. The council often reviews the employment of city personnel, examines the purchases of supplies and equipment, and ratifies the granting of construction contracts. In California school district government, the superintendent, as administrator-in-chief, is even more narrowly restricted because the legislative arm, the elective board, has to ratify every teacher's contract and every purchase of supplies down to the last paper clip before such acts are legally valid. In any event, many city councils find difficulty in restraining themselves from second guessing the manager in these crucial areas of administration and instances of hidden or open conflict have been rather numerous.

Mayor-Council Government. California has two major variations on the mayor-council theme, the centralized and the decentralized. In the former, found in some charter cities, a strong mayor elected as a full-time chief executive has substantial control over most aspects of city government though some of his authority may be shared with other independently elected officials. In the latter, found in all general-law and some charter cities employing the mayor-council device, executive authority is exercised by the city council, the mayor being a ceremonial appointee from the membership of the council, and no single

official is responsible for conducting the administrative business of
the city. Needless to say, only a very small community — in which
a group of presumably alert and dedicated amateurs can easily handle
the uncomplicated details of municipal affairs by formal meetings and
informal consultation for a few hours every week — can afford the lux-
ury of decentralized administration.

Los Angeles and San Francisco, in common with most large
cities in the United States, where the mayor is an important political
symbol and the cynosure of civic loyalties, have established the strong
mayor form of government. Distrust of executive centralization, a
trademark of California government, is responsible, however, for a
number of interesting oddities in the governmental structure of both
cities. Though elected for a four-year term and vested with power to
draw up the budget, recommend legislation, and veto acts of the council, San Francisco's mayor may appoint, but cannot remove, the chief
administrative officer who has assured jurisdiction over ten technical
or business departments. The authority of the mayor of Los Angeles,
who is elected for four years and also possesses budgetary, appointive,
veto, and supervisory powers, must be filtered through the opaque
medium of some 17 appointed boards that supervise operations and
select personnel for the various departments of the city. While the
charter is tilted more heavily in favor of the council in Los Angeles
than it is in San Francisco, additional elements of decentralization for
the government of California's largest metropolis deprive both legislative and executive arms of a significant fraction of their proper authority: seven city departments are run as independent empires, with
their own budgetary, employment, and salary powers. Our modest
recommendation for remedy of these anomalies is that the city scrap
its charter and start anew. Residents of the metropolis, however, appear reconciled to these administrative curiosities despite the fact
that, as observed in a recent Haynes Foundation report, "for more
than sixty years forward-looking Angelenos have been searching for
solution to the problems" of governmental organization in a rapidly
expanding economy. [10]

The Effect of City Size on Type of Government

In general, one would assume that the costs of decentralized
government and diffused authority are greater for large cities than
for small ones. When the span of control is small, the volume of municipal business moderate, the number of key personnel in the commu-

nity fairly small, and the relevant facts about the culture and economy of the town readily available to almost any knowledgeable adult, a committee of interested citizens can supervise its government satisfactorily, but as the town becomes larger and the volume of business increases, the reins of administrative authority must be centralized in the hands of a full-time professional executive if city government is not to fall apart at the seams.

If this presumption is correct and if people recognize and act upon it, centralized executive authority will be more prevalent in large towns than in small ones. Under California law, administrative responsibility can be centralized either in a city manager or a strong mayor. Since general-law cities cannot have a popularly elected mayor, the establishment of a strong mayor requires the city to secure a charter. Save for the two largest municipalities in California, very few cities have adopted this device. Instead, most of the larger ones have preferred to acquire a city manager.

The relationship between city size and type of government is summarized in Table 2.3. The evidence indicates that small cities (arbitrarily classified as those under 5,000 population) prefer the mayor-council form, while large cities prefer the council-manager form. Size, of course, is only one of the factors that influence a city's pattern of governmental organization. But size and organization are closely related.

Table 2.3. Governmental Type and City Size in California: 1958

Population of City	Type of Government		
	Mayor-Council	Council-Manager	Total
(a)	(b)	(c)	(d)
(1) Under 5,000	126	23	149
(2) Over 5,000	55	147	202
(3) Total	181	170	351

Source: Table 2.a

If size were not a factor, the 181 cities employing the mayor-council form would be divided into small and large communities in roughly the same proportion as cities in general: in the proportion 149/202 = 42/58. Thus 42% of these 181 towns (or 77) would fall into the small class and 58% (or 104) would fall into the large class. This contrasts with the actual division of 126 to 55. Similarly, if size were

not a factor, 42% (or 72) of the 170 towns employing the council-manager form of government would fall into the small group and 58% (or
98) would fall into the large class. This contrasts with the actual division of 23 to 147. In light of these magnitudes, the likelihood.that
the data would deceive us — i.e., indicate that size and type were related when they were actually independent — is less than 1 in 1,000.[11]

If we equate centralized administration with the council-manager
plan and decentralized administration with the mayor-council form —
ignoring the presence of a few charter cities with popularly elected
mayors — the large number of cases concentrated in boxes 1-b and 2-c
of Table 2.3 is consistent with the hypothesis that big towns have more
centralized administration than small ones. Some parts of the data, of
course, are also consistent with another hypothesis, namely, that
small towns cannot afford a city manager, a high-priced specialist
whose talents must be extensively used in order to be economically
employed. (For similar reasons, a small town cannot use an elaborate
IBM recording system or set up a radio station for its police department.) Only 23 towns under 5,000 population employed a manager. But
if the diseconomies of employing managers for small towns were the
only factor that influenced the relation between city size and type of
government, we should expect a somewhat different distribution of
cities and governments than in fact prevails. We should, that is, expect
the mayor-council form to be randomly distributed by city size, and
large cities to be randomly distributed by forms of government. The
relatively small number of large cities in the mayor-council category
fails to square with these expectations.

In full generality, then, the relation between city ize and governmental type probably runs as follows: it is not economical for
small towns to centralize administrative responsibility by employing
a full-time executive. A part-time committee composed of the city
council and an honorary mayor as chairman can accomplish the city's
business with the requisite degree of economy. But beyond some critical mass — which varies with the type of community, the economic
base of the region, the distance from metropolitan centers, and the
services provided by other units of government — centralization of
administrative responsibility in a unified executive branch becomes
both economical and indispensable. Beyond this critical mass, furthermore, the diseconomies of fragmenting administration and of mix-

ing legislative with executive responsibility probably increase   as
cities increase in size.

CALIFORNIA'S ECONOMY

The rich and varied economy of the principality of California
turns out a wide variety of specialized industrial and agricultural products. Though Californians, like Texans, have never been overly reti-
cent about touting the virtues of their native state, reality lends cre-
dence to rhetoric. In its great metropolitan centers, its fertile farms,
its spacious forests, and its abundant oil fields, a labor force of about
5.7 million people, working in some 360 to 370 thousand business firms
(plus several thousand nonprofit and governmental enterprises), produced $34.5 billion in personal income in 1957. During the first quar-
ter of 1958 personal income ran at the rate of $34.8 billion, about 10.2%
of the national total. [12]

Among the states, California's relative position in retail sales
and services is higher than its relative position in manufacturing, according to the latest complete tabulation reported by the 1954 Censuses
of Business and Manufactures. With $15.6 billion in value of retail
sales transacted in 131 thousand establishments, California contributed
9.1% of the U.S. total, a magnitude exceeded by only one other state.
California also ranked second in the nation in receipts of service establishments, its 78 thousand garages, beauty shops, hotels, amuse-
ment enterprises, TV repair shops, and so on, having received $2.5
billion or $10.7% of the national total. But the state earned sixth rank
in value added by manufacture. With 1.05 million industrial employees
working in 24.5 thousand establishments, California's $8.6 billion was
7.4% of the national total.

Despite the onward march of the bulldozer and the fertile crop of
homes and highways, which take an increasing toll of California's agricultural lands, the state retains its lead in value of farm products
sold, its 123 thousand farms (surveyed by the 1954 Census of Agriculture) having produced $2.3 million in food and fiber or 9.3% of the
national total. Data on cash recipts from farming for 1957 again put
California in first place with $2.8 billion, Iowa in second with $2.1
billion, and Illinois and Texas trailing with $1.9 billion, out of a na-
tional total of $30.0 billion. [13]

Economic Growth

Manufacturing. The economic growth of California has created

a populous regional market in which a number of large-scale activities
the region was formerly too small to support have now become feasible
and profitable. It has created a pool of skilled labor whose living and
working conditions foster high productivity and efficiency. The wage
differential between the western states and the rest of the nation has
narrowed considerably with the passage of time and improved the competitive position of California producers. It has created a resource base
with adequate supplies of some of the primary metals and other basic
raw materials. It has created a power base with abundant supplies of
electricity, natural gas, and fuel oil; even water, the Achilles' heel
of economic development in the southern portion of the state, will be
available in generous quantities, at present prices, for some tome to
come.[14]

The development of a large-scale regional center sets two contrary tendencies in motion. On the one hand, the region develops
manufacturing capacity to supply commodities it formerly "imported"
from other sections of the country. On the other hand, the region develops specialized types of production whose output is "exported" to
the rest of the country and to the world at large. As a result it must,
in turn. "import" some of the producers' goods and raw material required for specialized manufacture.

Examples of the first tendency are the establishment of automobile assembly plants, which now take care of a significant fraction of
the West Coast market, and the erection of branch factories by eastern
breweries. Examples of the second tendency are the growth of the
California aircraft industry and its related branches, missiles and
electronic equipment, or the development of the canned and frozen
food industry, a logical extension of California's existing specialization in quality fruits and vegetables.

Table 2.4 draws together data on California manufacturing from
the 1954 Census of Manufactures. A rough idea of some of the outstanding specialties of California and of the balance of trade and production
between this region and the economy as a whole can be gleaned by an
examination of the last column of that table.

With California producing 34.0% of the nation's canned and frozen
foods and 29.1% of its aircraft and parts — a noticeable decrease, by
the way, from the 1947 figure of 37.1 — the bulk of this output is now
shipped to markets outside the state. On the other hand, 15.5% of value
added in the production of lumber and basic products is credited to

Table 2.4. Value Added by Manufacture in California, 1954 (in thousands)

Industry	Los Angeles-Long Beach	San Francisco-Oakland Metropolitan Areas	San Diego	Total	Percent Change 1947-54	Percentage of U.S. Value Added, 1947
Food & Kindred Products	442,431	399,609	390,218	1,400,857	44.4	10.5
Canned & Frozen Foods	(D)	(D)		(374,361)	(47.0)	(34.0)
Tobacco Manufacture				1,453	---	0.15
Textile Mill Products	26,570	10,217		39,302	21.5	0.8
Apparel & Related Products	207,257	57,360	3,666	279,351	48.4	5.4
Womens & Misses Outerwear				(125,311)	(39.8)	(7.2)
Lumber & Wood Products	45,067	13,185	1,207	422,036	68.1	13.2
Lumber & Basic Products				(247,943)	(58.7)	(15.5)
Furniture & Fixtures	112,538	32,583	2,357	153,651	67.8	7.8
Pulp, Paper & Products	92,821	63,889	(D)	182,701	126.3	4.0
Printing & Publishing	203,282	97,102	15,812	416,442	59.5	6.7
Chemicals & Products	211,977	152,452	6,091	424,136	51.4	4.5
Petroleum & Coal Products	127,059	128,946	(D)	275,705	29.1	10.7
Rubber Products	122,278	(D)	(D)	135,273	---	7.1
Leather & Leather Goods	28,718	4,801	(D)	35,166	38.5	3.0
Stone, Clay, & Glass Prod.	146,578	49,288	1,903	297,934	92.7	7.8
Primary Metal Industry	177,157	103,831	(D)	355,083	92.3	3.8
Fabricated Metal Products	380,786	144,474	3,912	578,995	104.7	7.6
Machinery, exc. Electrical	407,984	121,839	3,407	580,306	133.2	4.7
Electrical Machinery	259,827	73,291	1,679	409,623	284.1	5.5
Transportation Equipment	1,794,182	126,650	299,679	2,263,882	308.8	16.3
Motor Vehicle & Equip.				(246,436)	(195.1)	(3.8)
Aircraft & Parts	(1,579,499)	(241,428)		(1,830,450)	(416.8)	(29.1)
Instruments & Related Prod.	96,264	9,023	4,804	112,243	---	5.2
Miscellaneous Manufactures	266,129	30,841	3,052	334,304	43.8	7.5
All Industries-Total	5,041,546	1,673,825	390,218	8,597,453	115.2	7.4

Source: U.S. Bureau of the Census, U.S. Census of Manufacturers: 1954 State Bulletin, MC-104; California (Washington: U.S. Government Printing Office, 1957).

D- Data withheld to avoid disclosing figures for individual companies.

California, but California's own construction industry also accounts for about 15% of the value of building in the U.S. If we make the rough and ready assumption that the proportion between lumber and other material is the same in the local construction industry as in the country at large, California either expends the bulk of this output on homes and buildings erected within the state or else its exports to the rest of the economy are balanced by a corresponding volume of imports.

In apparel and related products California produces 5.4% of the national total, but accounts for only 0.8% of the textiles. Presumably, therefore, raw materials for the expanding California garment industry are imported from other areas. Though around 10% of the nation's cars are registered in California — 6.5 million out of a national total of 64.4 in 1956 — California plants assembled only 3.8%, by value, of the motor vehicles produced, indicating another area where sizeable imports occur.

As would be anticipated, California's share of value added by manufacture has increased steadily as the territory gradually transformed itself from a raw material producer to a manufacturing center. Beginning with 2.0% of the U.S. total in 1899, the state advanced to 2.5 in 1909, 3.1 in 1919, 4.4 in 1929, 4.6 in 1939, 5.4 in 1947, and 7.4 in 1954.

Agriculture and Land Use. The rich agricultural economy of California is highly specialized, producing a large amount of citrus and other fruits, nuts, vegetables, hops, barley, honey, turkeys, wine, and sugar beets for "export" to the rest of the U.S. In fact, California turns out more than one-third of the commercial fruits, and about one-fourth of the commercial vegetables produced in the U.S. On the other hand, it produces comparatively little of the major staples such as corn, wheat, oats, and tobacco, and is relatively low in livestock such as beef cattle, hogs, chickens, and horses.

With an average of 307 acres per farm, California's 123,000 farms were worth about $8.6 billion, or $70,000 apiece, in 1954. While methods of cultivation are fairly intensive, the value per acre in the state — $226 — is far below the $343 or the $291 figure found in the rich truck and tobacco lands of Rhode Island and Connecticut and slightly lower than the figure for the grain and livestock farms of Illinois ($231).

Of the state's agricultural domain, only about 2/9 or 8.3 million acres comprise harvested cropland, the remainder being pasture, wood-

land and fallow land. Given the uneven distribution of rainfall in the
state, varying from 100 inches a year in the northwestern redwood
belt to less than 3 inches a year in the southeastern desert (where
most of it is concentrated in three to five months during the winter and
the spring) California farmers must irrigate or perish. Accordingly,
some eight million acres have been placed under irrigation during the
last three-quarters of a century and more can be added if prices and
costs are favorable.

At the edges of the metropolitan hinterland, agriculture and urban development wage a ceaseless struggle for the scarce supply of
land. One writer has described the enveloping tactics of urbanism in
the following graphic passage:

> Flying from Los Angeles to San Bernardino — an unnerving
> lesson in man's infinite capacity to mess up his environment —
> the traveler can see a legion of bulldozers gnawing into the
> last remaining tract of green between the two cities, and from
> San Bernardino another legion of bulldozers gnawing westward.[15]

New irrigation and reclamation projects, however, work in the opposite direction and, to date at least, hold a commanding lead in the race,
inasmuch as farm acreage in California rose from 30.5 million in 1940
to 36.6 in 1950 and 37.8 in 1954. While the urban tide may have en-
gulfed some extremely fertile patches of farm real estate, the amount
of harvested cropland rose by about the same proportion as total acreage.

The rising tide of urbanism, though marooning an occasional
farmer amid a sea of houses and factories, is bound to raise the value
of rural property in two distinctly different ways: (1) It puts him nearer the market and lowers his transportation costs, an advantage, admittedly, only to those who raise garden truck for local sale. (2) It
creates a profitable market for his land. But the second advantage is
a dubious blessing for the man who stands in the zone of uncertainty
between continued operation of the farm and surrender to the urban
subdivider. For the higher the alternative value of his land, the greater
his assessments and his taxes, and the lower his income from agriculture until, eventually, the combination of falling income and rising
prices for his assets pushes him into the waiting arms of the subdivider.
While surrender is ultimately profitable, the continued threat of rising
property taxes during the interval represents an inducement that many
farmers would willingly do without.

Farm groups, accordingly, have attempted to persuade county

officials to assess farm lands at their agricultural value only, an attempt which, if successful, would diminish the incentive for farmers to sell their land and retard (slightly) the rate of urban development in a number of borderline areas.

Income

For a variety of reasons, California's per capita income has long exceeded the national average. Earnings being a function of age, sex, occupation, race, and education, differences in the composition of the state's population together with variations in property owner- ship account for some of this excess; but the remainder must be credited to a fortunate accident of western economic development — namely, that during the state's formative years the demand for labor moved ahead even more rapidly than the supply of labor. That is, the expansion of population, rapid as it has been, proceeded somewhat less rapidly than the expansion of agriculture and industry and its accompanying opportunities for employment.

As a result of this balance of forces we find in 1929, the first year for which reliable statistics of these magnitudes were collected, that state per capita income, at $995, was 42% above the U.S. average and remained between 37% and 45% greater all during the decade of the thirties. Beginning in 1940, however, the growth of population and the supply of labor apparently moved ahead somewhat more rapidly than the phenomenal growth of industry and its accompanying demand for labor, with the result that California's commanding lead in per capita earnings and income began to be eroded away. The percentage excess over the U.S. retreated steadily from 41% in 1940 to 24% in 1950 and 18% in 1957. (See Table 2.5, Part One, col. f.)

This particular statistic, of course, reflects a host of other factors besides the ratio of capital to labor, and changes over time in the supply and demand for labor services. Since labor receives two- thirds to three-quarters of the entire national dividend, the level of personal earnings plays the dominant role in the ratio, but the distri- bution of property incomes has an important supporting role in the drama of economic change. California has a different occupational distribution than the remainder of the U.S. economy, so that even if comparable lines of work were paid exactly equivalent wages in differ- ent areas of the economy, the somewhat higher concentration of skilled and professional workers in California would account for higher incomes per person during the initial period of development. In turn,

Table 2.5 Part One: Personal Income, California and the U.S.: 1929-58

	U.S. and California Income Current Dollars					California Income 1947-49 Dollars	
	Total Personal Income (millions of dollars)		Per Capita Personal Income			Total Income (millions of dollars)	Per Capita Income
Years	U.S.	Calif.	U.S.	Calif.	Calif. as % of U.S.		
(a)	(b)	(c)	(d)	(e)	(f)	(g)	(h)
1929	85,661	5,502	703	995	142	7,631	1,380
1930	76,780	5,079	624	889	142	7,256	1,270
1931	65,597	4,347	529	746	141	6,846	1,175
1932	50,022	3,381	401	574	143	5,829	990
1933	47,122	3,227	375	541	144	5,846	980
1934	53,482	3,590	423	592	140	6,388	1,053
1935	60,104	4,020	472	651	138	6,967	1,128
1936	68,363	4,817	534	760	142	8,319	1,313
1937	73,803	5,132	573	786	137	8,455	1,295
1938	68,433	5,088	527	746	145	8,466	1,271
1939	72,753	5,257	556	775	139	8,835	1,303
1940	78,522	5,839	595	840	141	9,797	1,409
1941	95,953	7,331	719	1,009	140	11,673	1,607
1942	122,417	10,010	909	1,281	141	14,198	1,817
1943	148,409	13,281	1,102	1,540	140	17,803	2,064
1944	160,118	14,653	1,194	1,582	132	19,255	2,079
1945	164,549	15,194	1,234	1,580	128	19,405	2,018
1946	175,701	16,084	1,249	1,654	132	19,034	1,957
1947	189,077	16,638	1,316	1,678	128	17,421	1,757
1948	207,414	17,610	1,420	1,750	123	17,197	1,709
1949	205,452	17,835	1,382	1,725	125	17,468	1,690
1950	225,473	19,627	1,491	1,848	124	19,148	1,803
1951	252,960	22,726	1,649	2,051	124	20,474	1,848
1952	269,050	25,089	1,727	2,144	124	21,912	1,872
1953	283,140	26,642	1,788	2,196	123	22,987	1,895
1954	284,747	27,148	1,767	2,170	123	23,403	1,871
1955	303,391	29,438	1,847	2,271	123	25,465	1,965
1956	330,500	32,501	1,940	2,419	125	27,566	2,051
1957	347,900	34,517	2,016	2,380	118	28,269	1,949
1958	347,100	34,785	2,006	2,334	116	30,467	1,879

Source: Col. a-e U.S. Dept. of Commerce, Office of Business Economics, Personal Income by States Since 1929, 1957, pp. 47-48.

U.S. Dept. of Commerce, Office of Business Economics, Survey of Current Business, February -July 1958.

f = e ÷ d g = b ÷ col. d, Table 2.6; h = e ÷ col. d, Table 2.6

Table 2.5 Part Two: Disposable Income,
California and the U.S.: Selected Years 1929-58

Current Dollars   (1947-49 Dollars)

Years	Total Disposable Personal Income (in millions) U.S.	Calif.	Per Capita Disposable Personal Income U.S.	Calif.	Calif. as % of U.S.	Total Income (in millions)	Per Capita Income
1929	83,020	5,349	682	967	142	7,419	$1,341
1940	75,924	5,649	575	813	141	9,478	1,364
1946	157,003	14,153	1,116	1,455	130	16,749	1,721
1950	204,729	17,615	1,354	1,659	123	17,185	1,619
1953	204,752	23,046	1,656	1,899	121	19,884	1,638
1954	256,885						
1955	274,448	Continuation:					
1956	290,454	1957 305,149	1958 300,100				

Source: Personal Income by States Since 1929. Department of
Commerce, Office of Business Economics, 1956, pp. 47-58, and
Survey of Current Business, February-July, 1958.

Table 2.6

BLS Consumer Price Index, All Items, Selected Years 1917-57
1947-49 = 100

Published data for Los Angeles and San Francisco averaged to derive
state figure for calendar year. Computed state calendar year figures
for adjacent years averaged to derive school (fiscal) year figure.

Calendar Year	Los Angeles	San Francisco	LA-SF Avg.	Two Year Avg.	School (Fiscal) Year
1917	52.4	50.6	51.5	48.1	16-17
1927	76.3	69.2	72.8	73.3	26-27
1937	61.7	59.6	60.7	59.3	36-37
1940	60.5	58.7	59.6	59.6	39-40
1947	95.5	95.6	95.5	90.0	46-47
1948	102.4	102.3	102.4	99.0	47-48
1949	102.1	102.1	102.1	102.2	48-49
1950	102.8	102.2	102.5	102.3	49-50
1951	111.5	110.4	111.0	106.8	50-51
1952	114.7	114.3	114.5	112.8	51-52
1953	115.7	116.2	115.9	115.2	52-53
1954	115.6	116.4	116.0	116.0	53-54
1955	115.6	115.6	115.6	115.8	54-55
1956	117.4	118.4	117.9	116.8	55-56
1957	121.2	123.1	122.1	120.0	56-57

Source: U.S. Dept. of Labor, Bureau of Labor Statistics, Consumer
Price Index: All Items, Series A-11. Compilations for year 1917 through
1957 for Los Angeles and San Francisco supplied by the office of the regional
director, 630 Sansome St., San Francisco 11. Data for years not shown in
the table are available in the basic reference. Notes regarding the rounding
of computed averages: LA-SF Average rounded toward the Los Angeles
figure; two year average rounded toward the later year figure.

as the distribution of California's labor force began to approximate that
of the U.S., the differences in income per head would begin to disap-
pear. Similar observations apply to the age and sex distribution of California's population. Racial and educational composition of the labor
force, plus changes therein, play a part in the picture since the people
of California, according to the 1950 Census, had the highest number of
years of school completed of any state in the nation. (City size and
cost of living differentials are also pertinent.)

When all these factors are taken into account, however, the prime
mover in the relation between California income and U.S. income is
the relative growth of capital and population.

The last column of Table 2.5 (Part One) contains some surprises.
Real income per person, income in dollars of constant value, has not
risen appreciably in California for over a decade and a half, but has
fluctuated slightly between $2,079 (achieved in the war year 1944) and
$1,690 (during the gold-plated recession of 1949) over the entire inter-
val. The price index used to convert current dollars into constant
(1947-49) dollars may overstate the rise in cost of living and thus un-
derstate the change in real income during these decades. (We have used
a combination of the Los Angeles and San Francisco Consumer Price
Indexes, as computed by the Bureau of Labor Statistics. See Table 2.6.)
But while price indexes are a weak reed at best, we have reasonable
confidence in the results depicted.

The causes of this situation are not difficult to decipher. Even
though industry is growing at an enormous rate and capital is accumu-
lating rapidly, the amenity value of living in California attracted such
a horde of people during the postwar era that real earnings scarcely
increased at all.

Employment and the Community

In terms of the relation between the number of people who live in
the city and the number who work in the city, the communities of California fall into three broad classes: (1) balanced cities where the resident labor force approximately equals the number at work in the city;
(2) dormitory cities where most of the resident labor force works outside the city; and (3) employing or central cities where the number of
people who work in the city far exceeds the resident labor force.

For cities over 10,000 population in 1950, this information is
shown in col. b of Table 2.b (Appendix), while col. c shows the ratio
of employed workers to residential labor force. The breakdown of this
group is shown in Table 2.7.

Table 2.7 Employment Patterns among California
Cities Over 10,000 Population: 1950

Type of City	Number	Ratio: Employed Workers to Resident Labor Force
1. Balanced	24	85-115
2. Dormitory	35	Under 85
3. Employing	49	Over 115

Source: Table 2.b (Appendix)

Costs and Benefits of Industrialization. The employment category
into which a city falls is the joint result of underlying economic forces
and the accident of municipal boundaries. In a number of metropolitan
centers the link between the employment type and the tax base of a city
arouses prolonged and partisan controversy, which, in many instances,
is based upon a set of ancient misconceptions that have embittered
metropolitan relations for well over half a century. Misconception
number one is the belief that inhabitants of dormitory communities are
parasitical consumers of government services in the central city in
which they enjoy the benefits of employment, transportation, and police
protection without the accompanying burdens of property taxation. Sometimes a central city tries to reach these peripatetic consumers by a
gross earnings tax. But surely the fact that these people work and shop
in the central (employing) city raises its property values and increases
its tax base. While it is difficult to establish precise equivalence, such
increases go far to compensate for the cost of additional services which
their presence requires.

Misconception number two, a reverse image of number one, is the
belief that dormitory cities can "broaden the tax base" and relieve the
burden on home owners by attracting industry and commerce within
their borders. In some cases, true, this policy pays high dividends if
two special conditions are met: (1) new industrial and commercial
development must not demand more in services than it supplies in taxes,
and (2) the new industrial or commercial enterprises must complement,
rather than compete with, high-quality residential development which
forms the existing tax base of the community. A shopping center is a
good example of a type of development that, all things considered, is
probably advantageous on both counts.

The net direct "profit" the community secures from commerce and
industry that locates within its borders depends upon the kinds of enter-

prises it attracts, the fire and crime hazards they create, and the
amount of unused overhead that exists in city services. The direct effect may be either positive or negative. But the effect upon residential
development in the great majority of cases is bound to be negative in
the long run. For the residential character of a city is linked with its
industrial development. Industrial and commercial activity tends to
raise population density, reduce the size and value of residential
homes — allowing time for adjustment, of course — and attract lower
income families to the community. While the rising tide can be held in
check for a time by stringent zoning laws, the dike springs too many
leaks for this method to be long effective.

On balance, then, how does industrial and commercial development
affect the tax base of the community as measured by property values
per capita? Industry per se raises the base; the indirect effect of industrial development upon residential development lowers it. Which
predominates? Available evidence, drawn from a recent study of the
San Francisco metropolitan area, suggests that industrialization and
commercialization reduce per capita values inasmuch as the amount
of property per person in central and balanced cities is lower than the
amount in dormitory communities.[16] Add to this the cost-increasing
potentialities of factories, stores, and offices upon the services provided by government and the case for suburban industrialization becomes very dubious indeed.

The Economic Base. The commercial and industrial life of each
city has a unique color and flavor that is difficult to distill into stand-
ardized labels. But a clue to the economic character of the city is
provided by data on the distribution of employment. Taken from a recent edition of the Municipal Year Book, and supplemented by Census
data, a tabulation of the economic base of 209 California cities is presented in col. a of Table 2.b and summarized in Table 2.8.

Wealth

Wealth is the capitalized value of the income streams created by
a group of assets. The tangible wealth of an area includes the value of
its physical assets, its land, buildings, equipment, and inventory used
by business enterprise in the production of goods and services, together with the homes, cars, and durable consumer goods used by private households, plus the land and facilities used by government and
nonprofit organizations.

Valuing this aggregation poses a knotty problem because no two
pieces of wealth are exactly alike and many of them have no ascer-

Table 2.8. The Economic Base of California Communities

Label Used in Table 2.b (a)	Description (b)	Number of Cities (c)
1. G	Government Center: 15% or more of the resident labor force employed by a governmental unit.	8
2. Mg	Mining town: 15% or more of the resident labor force employed in mining.	1
3. Mm	Manufacturing city: employment in manufacturing at least 50%, and employment in retail trade less than 30%, of aggregate employment in manufacturing, trade, and service.	12
4. M	Industrial city: employment in manufacturing more than 50%, and in retail trade at least 30%, of aggregate employment.	2
5. Mr	Diversified city: manufacturing employment dominant but less than 50%.	30
6. Rm	Diversified city: employment in retail trade dominant, manufacturing employment at least 20% of aggregate.	38
7. Rr	Retail trade center: employment in retail trade greater than in wholesale trade, service or manufacturing, and manufacturing employment less than 20%.	84
8. Ed	Education center: college enrollment totals 20% or more of city population.	6
9. T	Transportation center: 25% or more of resident labor force employed in transportation.	4
10. W	Wholesale trade center: employment in wholesale trade at least 25% of aggregate.	22
11. X	Resort or retirement town: manufacturing employment less than 15%, and 10% or more of resident labor force employed in eating places, hotels, or places of amusement and recreation.	12

Source: Table 2.b (Appendix).

tainable market price so that the investigator can make only the rough-
est and crudest estimates of their worth. As is well known, assessors,
who must resolve the unresolvable, operate with a standard set of formulas by which each attribute of the property is estimated and evaluated
by a uniform set of weights. While this method is unlikely to yield market value, it is often defended on the grounds that every piece of property is subject to an equal degree of error.

But inability to ascertain the market price of physical assets is by
no means the worst of our difficulties. For a going business concern
is ordinarily worth more than the breakup value of its physical plant
and equipment. The efficiency of its organization, its connections with
suppliers and dealers (which would be valueless in a static economy
but which take time and effort to create in a dynamic and uncertain one),
and the good will (if any) which consumers attach to its products — all
contribute to its value and deserve inclusion in a complete tabulation
of wealth.

Now the market does place a value upon the firm as a going concern, a value which reflects the judgment of the investment market on
the capitalized worth of the income stream the firm creates. This estimate is the market value of its stock (price per share times number
of shares outstanding). If the company has bonds and other debts outstanding, these must be added to its equity (stocks) to get the going
value of the enterprise.

For incorporated enterprises, then — unfortunately, this measure is not available for partnerships and proprietorships, roughly one-
third of the nonfarm sector of business enterprise — the valuation by
stocks and bonds instead of by buildings and equipment can be very
persuasively supported.[17] Over the long pull, the aggregate value of
stocks is nearly half again as great as the book value of assets for
U.S. corporations as a whole.[18]

We may enumerate the wealth of an area, such as the City of San
Francisco or the State of California, from two different points of view.
One is the value of the physical assets that are located in the territory,
and another is the value of the wealth that is owned by the people who
live there. From the first point of view, California's wealth is the
market value of the tangible property located in the state. From the
other point of view, California's wealth includes the market value of
the tangible assets and financial investments — stocks, bonds, and
mortgages, commonly known as "intangibles" — owned by its residents.

Table 2.9. Inventory of California Wealth: 1957
(A in thousands, C, D and E in millions)

		(A) Quantity	(B) Average Value	(C) Assessed Value	(D) Market Value	(E) Total Market Value
1	Property					
2	City and County Assessed					$ 90,139
3	Land			$ 6,984	$ 27,937	
4	Personal			4,248	16,992	
5	Improvements			11,303	45,210	
6	State Assessed					6,205
7	Land			231	462	
8	Improvements			1,739	3,478	
9	Personal			1,132	2,265	
10	Inventories					
11	Retailers				2,150	
12	Wholesalers				1,268	
13	Manufacturers				3,978	
14	Livestock					402
15	Cattle	2,843	$118.00		336	
16	Milk Cows	927	190.00		18	
17	Sheep & Lambs	1,632	18.60		30	
18	Hogs	438	23.60		10	
19	Horses & Mules	70	108.00		8	
20	Poultry					41
21	Chickens	28,994	1.20		35	
22	Turkeys	1,152	5.50		6	
23	Unclassified Private Wealth					6,717
24	Automobiles	6,800	900.00		6,120	
25	Private Cars (Railway)				597	
26	Total Tangible Private Wealth					($110,900)
27	Cash, Deposits and Savings Bonds					22,069
28	Total Private Wealth					($132,969)
29	Publicly Owned Property					$ 13,747
30	Federal	46,855	$4,787	$ 2,217	$ 4,434	
31	State	2,269	7,986	181	362	
32	City			2,749	5,468	
33	County			530	1,060	
34	School Districts			1,212	2,423	
35	Total Wealth					$146,716

Sources: See Appendix to Chapter 2.

From the second point of view, for example, the properties of the movie industry that are in hock to New York bankers would be excluded from its wealth and pieces of property in other states and nations owned by California capitalists would be included.

An Inventory of Wealth in California. Since data on ownership of intangibles are difficult to unearth and since property taxation in California is based on the area rather than on the ownership concept of wealth, we have attempted to enumerate the value of the assets that lie within the borders of the state. For land, buildings, equipment, and personal property, local or state assessments were used as a point of departure. We have assumed — based on data provided by the State Board of Equalization, and cited elsewhere in this study — that assessed value is about a half for state assessed utilities. To get market values, in col. $\underline{d}$ of Table 2.9, the local assessor's figures were multiplied by 4, and the state assessor's by 2.

In the table, a separate evaluation is presented for livestock and business inventory. Although the local assessor is supposed to catch these items, we suspect that they go virtually uncounted in most jurisdictions. The doubling-up involved in adding about half a billion dollars for farm animals and around $7 billion for manufacturing, retail, and wholesale inventories to the existing total of $90 billion (market value) in locally assessed real and personal property is, therefore, rather slight.

In the absence of exact data, the computation of inventory values for 1957 involved extending the estimates of the 1954 census of manufactures by the aid of some rather tricky assumptions, set out fully in the notes to the table.

Since the inclusion of solvent credits (except bank deposits) involves double counting, we have ignored the $4,976 millions reported for "intangible property" in 1957 by local and state assessors and have substituted an independent estimate of the volume of money, bank deposits, and savings bonds in California based on Federal Reserve Board data.

With about half the land in the state owned or controlled by government agencies — the government owns 46 million acres or 46% of California while the state owns about 3% — the value of public property is bound to be a statistic of no little interest. Our estimate, $13.7 billion, is extremely conjectural and must be taken with a considerable grain of salt. We took a detailed study made for a few counties by the Senate

Interim Committee on Public Lands and expanded the data to cover the state as a whole.

Our estimate of the sum total of California's wealth in 1957 is $146.7 billion, of private wealth $133 billion, and of private tangible wealth $110.9 billion. While this, too, must be generously salted before taken, a margin of error of at least 25% being recommended, the gross order of magnitude agrees fairly closely with our initial expectations as detailed below.

Wealth, Taxation and Policy. Armed with this batch of statistics we are in position to calculate an answer to a question of great importance: What is the true tax rate borne by the wealth of California? Comprising some 46% of the revenue of all local governments in the state — the state government has been out of the property tax business since the adoption of Amendment No. 1 in 1910, save for a few million dollars collected from 1912 through 1915 to finance the Panama Pacific Exposition, plus a few thousand dollars of delinquent taxes that continue to dribble in from year to year [19] — $1,438 million in property taxes were collected in fiscal 1957. To this add $106 million in property taxes on automobiles collected under the nom de plume of vehicle license fees, "in lieu" of local property taxes, at a rate equal to 2% of the sale value of the car. [20]

With total property taxes of $1,544 million, the true rate, figured on the basis of total private wealth (including cars and money), was 1.2%; with private tangible wealth (money excluded) as the base, the true rate for 1957 figures out at 1.4%.

While this rate or these amounts appear to be a fairly modest fraction of the value of the state's wealth, they are a substantial portion of the income from property, taxes of $1,544 million being 19.3% of $8 billion,[*] the approximate income from tangible wealth in California (as computed below). To the extent that property taxes are borne by owners of capital the present level represents, roughly, a 20% income tax on receipts from capital investment, about equal, in other words, to the first bracket rate of the Federal Income Tax. Since commercial property receipts are also subject to federal tax, the total rate paid by the owner (neglecting exemptions and deductions allowed by the federal tax) is at least 40%. While schools and streets and parks and policemen are all good and valuable things in their way, the load-

[*]Property income includes monetary receipts plus the estimated use value of owner-occupied homes.

ing of half the cost of local government on a quarter of the social income and taxing commercial property at twice the rate that other sources pay represents a fiscal policy of very dubious equity. Surely, if better alternatives are available, alternatives that tap the whole income of the community instead of the fraction generated by property, they should be explored and adopted, political factors and administrative considerations permitting.

Income and Assets. An alternative method of computing the value of property is to "capitalize" the income it produces at the going rate of interest. With interest at 6%, an asset yielding a dollar a year (after allowing for maintenance and periodic replacement of capital so that the income stream is, in effect, perpetual) can be sold for $16-2/3. One dollar is 6% of the asset value; alternatively, the price of the asset times the rate of interest equals the annual yield. [21]

What is the income of property in the State of California? If the state is representative of the economy at large, about one-quarter of its annual receipts represents monetary and imputed returns to tangible private capital. [22] With income in 1957 running in the neighborhood of $34 billion, about $8 billion (rounding off for convenience) represented the return to land, buildings, inventory, machinery, and other instruments of production. Depreciation and maintenance costs have been subtracted from this amount but property taxes at $1.5 billion (rounding off from 1.544) have not. Assuming that levies on property are borne by owners of capital, net returns to investment were about $6.5 billion.

What is the value of a pile of assets yielding $6.5 billion per year? Assuming for purposes of this problem that the income stream continues indefinitely, the net worth of the assets that create it depends upon the rate of interest. High-grade home mortgages (without benefit of government subsidy) command a rate of 6%, and the earnings/price ratios of many leading common stocks are not too far from that figure. Capitalizing at 6%, accordingly, we get $108 billion as the value of California's tangible wealth. [23]

One hundred eight billion dollars, our conjectural estimate of privately owned tangible capital, is within easy walking distance of the $110.9 billion estimated in Table 2.9 by direct enumeration of asset prices. This happy accident depends very importantly, however, on the fraction of the state's income imputed to tangible capital and on the rate of interest at which returns are capitalized. Larger (or smaller) fractions of income going to capital and lower (or higher) rates of interest yield larger (or smaller) asset values.

In comparing the magnitude enumerated in the table ($110.9 billion of tangible private capital) with the $108 billion conjured up by our capitalized income estimate, several minor qualifications are appropriate. The former magnitude refers to assets located in the state, the latter to assets owned by the state's inhabitants, and the difference between them depends upon the (unknown) distribution of asset ownership. The former includes a billion dollars or so of nonprofit institutions, such as colleges, churches, private schools, and orphanages,[24] whereas the latter excludes this item because the use value of the property does not appear in personal income. The latter also excludes durable consumer goods, since their use value is not included in measured income.

In conclusion, note that all wealth produces an income but that not all the services wealth produces are included in statistical measures of income. National and state figures on personal income include the estimated use value of owner-occupied homes but not the use value of government capital nor the service value of cash and checking accounts. For this reason the capitalized income estimate of asset values must be compared with tangible private wealth rather than with all private wealth (which includes money) or with total wealth (which includes government capital).

GOVERNMENT EMPLOYMENT

With an employed labor force of about 5.4 million in 1957 (out of a total labor force of perhaps 5.7 million) nearly one out of every 13 workers was employed in local government. Slightly less than one out of every 50 was employed by the state while the federal government provided jobs for about one out of every 20 employees. In round numbers, local employees amounted to 411,000, state employees 103,000, and federal 240,000.[25]

Elementary and secondary education was by far the largest component of local government employment, at 185,000 with another 9,000 employed in the local system of junior colleges. Next come cities (106,000), counties (90,000), and, far down on the list, special districts (22,000), all figures being rounded off.

Higher education, with 32,000 people employed on the sprawling campuses of the University of California and the state colleges, was the largest single component of state employment. Within the field of municipal employment the leading areas were public utilities (20,000) and police (18,000), while hospitals (25,000) dominated the scene on the county level.

With an annual payroll of about $1.8 billion in 1957, the services of employees constituted just about half of the resource-using expenditures of local government. The average annual earnings of full-time employees of local government were $6,000 for teachers (including junior college instructors) and $4,500 for others. Elementary and secondary teachers earned around $5,400. All employees of the state government drew about $5,000. Reflecting the relatively high wage standards of the state, the earnings of California's grade and high school teachers are the second highest in the nation, those of other local government employees are the highest, and earnings of state employees are highest by a wide margin — except for Alaska, where special cost of living factors are present.

Government employee and government payrolls have a material impact on the economy of California. The combined state and local payroll is about $200 million a month or from $2.2 to $2.4 billion a year while the federal payroll is between $90 to $100 million a month or $1.08 to $1.2 billion a year. California, incidentally, has far more federal civilian employees than any other state in the union, its 240,000 outranking the second place-state, New York (189,000), by a wide margin, and surpassing even the District of Columbia (233,000). Though the vicissitudes of national and local policy create minor ripples in the trend, government employment is apt to be a good deal more resistant to downturns in business activity than private employment, and its large volume of jobs and payrolls lends an element of stability to the state's economy.

The growth of public employment in California offers a striking confirmation of Parkinson's Law, a recently formulated but widely heralded principle of public administration — enunciated by one of the leading authorities on the subject, the British economic historian, C. Northcote Parkinson — which states, in brief, that regardless of the nature of the tasks to be performed and of the volume of business to be handled, public employment will (a) increase, and (b) increase at approximately 4% per annum. Since this "law" admits of no exception, it is obvious that the population of the state or territory or nation that the government serves must rise by at least 4% per year, otherwise the entire population will eventually be enrolled in the government

Table 2.10. Government Employment in California:
1944-57

(thousands)

Year (a)	State (b)	Local (c)	Total (d)	Percentage Change (e)
1944	34.1	166.6	200.7	--
1945	32.6	167.4	200.0	- .035%
1946	39	207	246.0	23.0%
1947	51	230	281.0	14.2%
1948	66.9	245.4	312.3	11.1%
1949	72.7	263.4	336.1	7.6%
1950	74.5	282.2	356.7	6.1%
1952	73.0	288.3	361.3	1.3%
1953	77.3	301.9	379.2	4.9%
1954	81.6	319.4	401.0	5.7%
1955	87.5	332.9	420.4	4.8%
1956	94.1	357.1	451.2	7.3%
1957	98.2	356.4	454.6	0.75%

a. For 1944-47, figures pertain to the month of April; for 1948-50, figures appear to be annual averages; no 1951 data available; for 1952-56, October estimates are used; 1957 figure pertains to April.

b, c. For 1944-50, the number of "all public employees" is given; for 1952-57, the number of "full time equivalents" is enumerated. For 1944-47, the breakdown between state and local employees was estimated by the authors on the basis of various fragments of data provided in the original sources.

Sources: 1944-47, Statistical Abstract of the U.S. for selected years; 1948-50 and 1952-56, U.S. Bureau of the Census, State Distribution of Public Employment, published in April of 1949 and 1950, March, 1951, and March of 1953-57; 1957, U.S. Bureau of the Census, Summary of Public Employment, April, 1958.

bureaucracy. For if California were to stop growing at this moment and if state and local employment, now at 370 per 10,000 population, were to continue increasing at its predestined rate of 4%, everyone in the state will be working for the government by the middle of the next century — in 84.2 years or by 2042, to be exact.[26] Table 2.10 sums up the growth of public employment in the state.

NOTES TO CHAPTER 2

[1] Exact area 158,693 of which 1,953 is inland water; does not include water surfaces or oceans or bays lying within the territorial jurisdiction of the state. Statistical Abstract of the U.S. 1958, p. 160.

[2] The exact figure tabulated by the Census Bureau for 1850 was 92,597. Statistical Abstract 1957, p. 6.

[3] Data on sources of migration are taken from Robert A. Walker and Floyd A. Cave, How California Is Governed (New York: The Dryden Press, 1953), pp. 3-8. Numbers and percentages are taken from Table 2.1.

[4] Estimated by the State Department of Finance, as reported in The Sacramento Bee, June 20, 1958.

[5] Birth and death rates of 24.5 and 8.8 per thousand were applied to the January 1 population of 14,445 thousand to yield 353,903 births and 127,116 deaths from July 1957 to July 1958. The resulting differential, 226,787, rounded off to 127,000 and subtracted from the total increase in population yielded the estimated data on migration.

[6] Population of New York State on July 1, 1957, was 15,888 thousand; 1958 figure is a rough estimate. For European countries 1956 figures were used. Statistical Abstract 1958, pp. 10, 927-28.

[7] The Board of Equalization's February 1, 1958 figure was contained in a detailed tabulation forwarded to the authors on September 16, 1958 by Mr. David Jacobson, Assistant Statistician, Divison of Research and Statistics. Note that the school district total — consisting of 1,424 elementary, 234 high schools, 104 unified, 27 junior colleges, and 1 college district — does not precisely agree with the July 1, 1957 estimate of the Superintendent of Public Instruction (1818) used elsewhere in this book. The 120 districts that collected their own taxes and the 150 that did not use their tax-levying powers in 1957 were reported in the California State Board of Equalization, Annual Report 1956-57 (Sacramento: California State Printing Office, 1957), p. 10, note to table. The breakdown of the 120 districts was provided by Mr. Jacobson's letter.

[8] Assembly Interim Committee on Municipal and County Government, Incorporations, Transcript of Proceedings July 1, 1958 (Mimeographed), Statement of John M. Johnson, pp. 104-5.

[9] Ibid., Statement of County Supervisor John Anson Ford, pp. 75-76. In order to attain a population of 500, the mandatory minimum for incorporation under California law, 126 inmates of a mental institution were included among the inhabitants of the city.

[10] Edwin A. Cottrell and Helen Jones, Characteristics of the Metropolis, Vol. I of Metropolitan Los Angeles: A Study in Integration (Los Angeles: The Haynes Foundation, 1952), p. 70.

[11] In columns b and c of Table 2.4 the difference between actual and hypothetical values, i.e., those that would have been observed if size were not a factor, can be analyzed by the chi-square test, a statistical formula which indexes the probability that chance alone could have distributed the numbers in this fashion. Applying the chi-

square formula for a 2 x 2 table we get 112.9, a value that would be achieved by chance in far less than 1 out of 1,000 cases.

[12] On the basis of the labor force participation rate for California shown at the end of Table 2.b, the 1957 labor force was estimated as 40% of state population in July of that year. Business firms in 1954 were estimated at 342.9 thousand by the Office of Business Economics in the Survey of Current Business, November 1954. Extrapolation on the basis of past trends yields a figure in the neighborhood of 365,000 for 1957. Since a self-employed person is counted as a "firm" if he has an established place of business, the above enumeration presumably includes most of the family farms, as well as all the farms using hired labor, in the state. It excludes nonprofit organizations. For personal income, see Table 2.5, Part One.

[13] Agricultural Marketing Service, U.S. Dept. of Agriculture, The Farm Income Situation (February 1958), p. 16. These data exclude the value of home consumed foodstuffs and government payments, the latter amounting to $31.6 million out of a U.S. total of $1 billion in 1957.

[14] For background material see the "Economic Survey of California and Its Counties" prepared by the Research Department of the California Chamber of Commerce in the 1958 Blue Book, a concise and insightful summary of economic trends and prospects (published every four years by the State Printer).

[15] William H. Whyte, Jr., "Urban Sprawl," Fortune, LVII (January 1958), 103.

[16] Julius Margolis, "Municipal Fiscal Structure in a Metropolitan Region," Journal of Political Economy, LXV (June 1957), 225-36.

[17] John F. Due, Government Finance: An Economic Analysis (Homewood, Ill.: Richard D. Irwin, Inc., 1954), pp. 375, 380, 393.

[18] Theodore O. Yntema, Statement: Before the Subcommittee on Antitrust and Monopoly of the Committee on the Judiciary, U.S. Senate. Reprinted by the Ford Motor Company (Detroit [1957]), pp. 60, 61. The stocks in question are those included in the Dow-Jones Industrial Index. The research on which this observation is based was apparently done by the finance department of the company.

[19] Tax Digest (November 1952), pp. 378-79.

[20] Property taxes, Table 5.3, chapter 5 below. Motor Vehicle "in lieu" taxes, State of California Budget for the fiscal year July 1, 1958 to June 30, 1959, a summary booklet prepared by the Director of Finance (Sacramento: California State Printing Office, 1958), p. A-6. Of this amount, $101 million (p. A-36) was returned to cities and counties.

[21] For an asset yielding Y dollars per year, at rate of interest i, asset value A, can be derived from the formula:

$$Y = i\,A, \quad \text{so that} \quad A = \frac{Y}{i}$$

When Y is $1, and i is 6/100, A is $16-2/3.

[22] George J. Stigler, The Theory of Price (Rev. ed.; New York: The Macmillan Co., 1952), p. 272.

[23] Using the formula $A = \dfrac{Y}{i}$,

when $Y = 6.5$ and $i = 6/100$, $A = 108\text{-}1/3$

[24] According to the Annual Report, 1956-57 of the State Board of Equalization, pp. 60-61, these properties which are exempt from taxation but included in our estimate are assessed at $394 million and, at the 1 to 4 ratio would be worth $1,576 million.

[25] Data on government employees and payrolls comes from U.S. Bureau of the Census, U.S. Census of Governments: 1957, Vol. II, No. 1, Summary of Public Employment (Washington: U.S. Government Printing Office). Figures on numbers of workers include a great many part-time employees; the "full time equivalent" of the 411,178 people employed by the localities is 356,387. Payroll and earning data apply only to the month of April, 1957; annual figures were presumed to be 12 times these monthly magnitudes, a presumption which, admittedly, yields a biased estimate of annual payrolls since April is not neces-sarily a typical month. The error involved in annual earnings is rela-tively small since most teachers and most local employees are on a 12-month rather than a 9-month basis. The estimate for California's federal payroll was derived by multiplying the number of federal ci-vilian workers by the average earnings of state employees. It is probably a bit on the high side since not all the enumerated federal employees worked full time and about 30% of the state's employees worked in colleges and universities so that the average level of educa-tion of state workers would doubtless exceed that of federal employees.

[26] Solving for n in the formula $\dfrac{(370)}{10,000}(1.04)^{n} = 1$; $n = 84.24$.

FOOTNOTE TO TABLE 2.9 — SOURCES:

[3c], [4c], [5c] California State Board of Equalization, Annual Report 1956-57 (Sacramento State Printing Office, 1957), p. 76.

[7c], [8c], [9c] Ibid.

[11D] U.S. Bureau of the Census, Census of Business-Retail Trade, 1954, Vol. II, pt. 1 (Washington: Government Printing Office, 1955), pp. 40-49.

U.S. Office of Business Economics, Survey of Current Business (February 1958), p. 42 (1957 Sales and Inventories).

Assumption: That California's Percentage of Sales in 1957 was the same as in 1954; that inventories in California are the same per-centage of sales as are national inventories. Data compiled:
    (i)   Total inventories as percentage of sales (1957) 11.7%
    (ii) California sales as percentage of national sales (1954) 9.2%
    (iii) 1957 Total U.S. Sales $200 billion
    (iv) 1957 Total U.S. Inventories $23.4 billion

[12D] U.S. Bureau of the Census, Census of Business: 1954 — Whole-sale Trade. Vol. IV (Washington: Government Printing Office, 1955), pp. 4-48.

U.S. Office of Business Statistics, Current Survey of Business (February 1958), p. 42 (1957 Sales and Inventory).

Assumption: That California's sales and inventory will bear the same relationship to U.S. sales as they did in 1954. Data compiled:

    (i) California sales as percentage of national sales (1954) 15.9%

    (ii) California inventories as percentage of California sales (1954) 5.9%

    (iii) 1957 U.S. Sales $135.2 billion

[13D] U.S. Bureau of the Census, Census of Manufacturers: 1954 — Area Statistics, Vol. III (Washington: Government Printing Office, 1955), pp. 35-104.

U.S. Office of Business Statistics, Current Survey of Business (February 1958), p. 42 (1957 Sales and Inventories).

Assumption: That the California 1954 value added percentage of total U.S. value added will be in the same relationship as California's 1957 share of total U.S. inventories. Data compiled:

    (i) California share as a percentage of total value added (1954) 7.4%

    (ii) 1957 Total manufacturers' inventory $53.7 billion

[14-22] California Department of Agriculture, Annual Livestock Report: 1957 (Sacramento: State Printing Office, 1958), pp. 5-25.

[24A] Statistical Abstract 1957, p. 554.

[24B] Estimated.

[25D] California Board of Equalization, Annual Report 1956-57 (Sacramento: State Printing Office, 1957), pp. 73-74.

[27E] Board of Governors, Federal Reserve System, Federal Reserve Bulletin (Washington: Government Printing Office, May 1958), pp. 944, 960.

[30A] Statistical Abstract 1957, p. 181.

[30B] California, Senate, Committee on Public Land, Public Ownership of State Lands (Sacramento: State Printing Office, 1951), p. 65. Method of computation:

$$\frac{\text{Four County Total Federal (State) Land Value}}{\text{Four County Total Federal (State) Acreage}} = 1950 \text{ value per acre}$$

$$1950 \text{ value per acre} \times \frac{1957 \text{ Wholesale Price Index}}{1950 \text{ Wholesale Price Index}} = 1957 \text{ value}$$

[31A] California, Senate, Committee on Public Lands, State Land Ownership, Sec. 2 (Sacramento: State Printing Office, 1955), p. 67.

[31B] Ibid.

[32-4C] California State Controller, Annual Reports of Financial Transactions Concerning (a) Cities of California, 1956-57, p. 197, (b) Counties of California 1956-57, p. 101, (c) Cities and Counties of California 1952-53, p. 276, and (d) School Districts of California 1956-57, Adjusted for new construction and price changes.

PART II

LOCAL EXPENDITURES: TRENDS AND CONTROLS

JOHN P. SHELTON

Assisted by Bruce F. Davie

For most citizens of California the core of their knowledge about local finance is this: Our taxes are higher today than ever before. Then they proceed to the conclusion, "The reason taxes are so high is because government spending is so high." This train of thought is exemplified in the following statement mailed by the California Taxpayers Association on November 14, 1957. The letter also evidences the fact that recent protests against taxes have far exceeded the usual griping over taxes.

> Property owners in Los Angeles are sizzling — and rightly so — because their local property tax bills are higher this year than they were last year.

> Most people are maddest at the County Assessor — whose representative knocks at every door about once a year.

> Nothing much can be expected from "cussing out" the County Assessor. He is not responsible for the size of anyone's tax bill.

> The key to the whole problem of higher local property tax bills in Los Angeles this year is WHAT THE LOCAL GOVERNMENTS DECIDED TO SPEND DURING THE YEAR.

> This is no whitewash of the County Assessor.

> It is an attempt to direct the flames of indignation of property owners where the responsibility lies and where their protests will do some good for the future — to their local governing boards.

> Our local governing boards for the most part are conscientious men and women. They want to do what the people who have elected them want them to do. They want good, efficient government at a reasonable cost to the people.

> They are subjected to a wide variety of pressures — from enthusiasts for one or another government activity, from employees, from citizens who want more services of one kind or another.

Both this chapter and the next focus on government expenditures, raising such questions as: What are the levels of local expenditures? How do they compare with the past? What factors determine such expenditures? Are local expenditures too high? If so, what can be done about them? At the outset it should be noted that this analysis is concerned solely with local expenditures. Relatively, such expenditures have not risen during the past two decades, but what concerns most people is the size of the total tax burden, which has increased its relative demand on the family budgets during the past three decades, largely because of the greater cost of national defense. To some extent, the reaction to this heavier total burden begets a feeling, largely unwarranted, that local taxes are also increasing in real economic terms.

Before launching into a study of local expenditures, it may clarify

understanding to note a specific example of the kind of problem that
cities, counties, school districts, and other local governmental units
are facing today. Here is an item from The Sacramento Bee of June 27,
1958:

> An $11,000,000 three-year county road construction pro-
> gram was approved yesterday by the board of supervisors along
> with a tax rate increase of 10 cents to help finance the projects.
>
> The tax boost of 10 cents on each $100 assessed valuation
> will raise approximately $1,380,800 in the three-year period.
>
> A requirement for property owners on residential streets to
> build their own roads was the second part of the major policy
> change adopted by the supervisors.
>
> Tax money presently used for residential streets construc-
> tion will be diverted into building primary county roads and major
> traffic ways. In the three year period approximately $1,300,000
> is expected from this source.
>
> The balance of the $11,000,000 proposed expenditure is to
> come from state gasoline taxes and from other state and federal
> funds.

This typical news story offers several points relevant to our study:
(1) Increased expenditures mean extra taxes. (2) The total cost of an
undertaking may not be revealed in the adjusted tax bill alone: it may
also include a shift of costs to other areas. Here part of the cost will
be met by increased taxes, some from less adequate maintenance of
residential streets, and the bulk from federal or state funds. (3) The
decision by the Sacramento County Board of Supervisors raises, im-
plicitly, such questions as these: Will the citizens get $11,000,000
worth of benefit from the construction and improvement of these roads?
Which citizens should be considered — only those residing (or voting?)
in Sacramento County, or all persons who may use the roads, regardless of what county or state they come from? How do the supervisors
determine the needs of the people — whatever their geographical de-
limitations — in a matter like this? Does the county need $11,000,000
in road construction over the next three years, or could it get along
on $7,000,000 — or should it really be spending $15,000,000? Are the
people better served by having more money spent on primary county
roads than on residential streets?

One of the questions most frequently asked concerning the level of
California's local government outlays is whether expenditures are too
high. Unfortunately, there is no objective way of arriving at a defini-
tive answer to this crucial question, but it is so important that it merits

serious consideration even though any answer depends on value judgments that are beyond objective appraisal.

THE IMPRECISE SCALES FOR JUDGING PUBLIC EXPENDITURES

Many people seem to fall into the error of assuming that the question "Are expenditures too high?" is the same as the question "Can
expenditures be cut?" The answer to the second question will nearly
always be "Yes," but this has almost no bearing upon the first. A
parallel in the field of household budgeting will make the distinction
clear. Can a family's rental costs be reduced? Almost certainly they
can: the family could move to a smaller or older house or to a less
desirable neighborhood. But does this mean that the family is paying
too much for housing? Nor necessarily. If the benefits lost in moving
to a cheaper house would outweight the value of the money saved — or
the value of the other things that could be purchased with it — then it
would be a poor decision to move to less expensive housing.

Social Benefits Should Match Social Costs

The point to the analogy is simply this: one cannot answer the
question "Are expenditures too high?" without referring to the benefits
received from the expenditures. The real question is whether the social
cost of the final dollars spent for local government exceeds the social
benefit to be gained from that expenditure. Expenditures are too high
if, for the last dollar in the local budget, social costs exceed social
benefits; expenditures are too low if social benefits exceed social costs.
This is a valid yardstick for determining whether expenditures are too
high, but unfortunately it is not easy to apply. The trouble arises in
trying to measure social costs and social benefits, especially the latter.
The social costs of government expenditures can be approximated by
the dollar cost, but no operational formula exists for measuring social
benefits, though in a few circumstances, where government service
can be placed on an individual-fee basis, benefits can be measured
with some precision.

How the Private Economy Operates

To many people the whole concept of social costs and social benefits may seem too vague to serve as a guide for decisions concerning
the use of resources. However, for the private sector of the economy
(i.e., households and business firms) the yardstick of net gain or loss
of utility is thoroughly sensible. If, for example, a consumer decides
to spend fifteen dollars on a sweater instead of on a fishing pole, presumably he gets more utility from the sweater than from the fishing

pole. This illustrates one of the millions of consumer decisions made daily. Through this simple mechanism — and granted certain assumptions about pure competition, consumer knowledge, and some technical matters regarding the way costs behave as volume changes — the market place automatically determines the optimum allocation of resources for any given distribution of wealth. Adam Smith described the concept in his widely known reference to "the invisible hand." The market guarantees that resources will be used in a way that increases social welfare in the sense that people could not, by using resources differently, get any more immediate satisfaction. (There is no connotation here, however, that this will be the best for people either in the long run or in any moralistic sense.)

Admittedly, even in the private sector of the economy the assumptions necessary to realize this classic picture of the benefits of competition are not completely satisfied. The important thing is that the optimum allocation of resources can be determined, at least theoretically, and that it is approximated in actual practice.

Difficulty of Optimizing in the Governmental Sector

So far as the governmental sector of the economy is concerned, however, there is no market-type solution for determining the proper level of expenditure. No competition exists among suppliers; the taxpayer-consumer cannot choose among several police departments with different "tax costs." He may be able to choose between cities offering a different range of services and tax costs, but only to a limited extent. Essentially there is no competition on the producer where governmental services are concerned.

When it comes to the consumption of governmental services there is little direct buying. Typically, the taxpayer-consumer does not pay for his police, fire, legal, or health protection as he consumes it. He "buys" all the services of government in a block and has almost no option on whether he wants to buy the particular services offered at the price quoted. Furthermore, since many governmental goods and services are consumed by the collective citizenry — for example, police, fire, and legal protection, highways, and public health clinics — there is no reason why one person should indicate his own particular preference for a service of government: the service exists for all to use. In the private sector where goods are consumed individually (if one consumer buys a sweater it cannot also be owned by another), a consumer's preference for a good is revealed by the auction nature of the market place. In the governmental sector there is no institutional arrangement that compels a taxpayer to indicate how much utility he receives from governmental services shared by all.

In the terse language of economics, this may be summarized as follows. Government expenditures should be at such a level that the utility received by all citizens for the marginal dollar of governmental expenditure matches the marginal utility of the private goods that the various citizen-taxpayers are obliged to forego because of their tax payments. In short, the basic principle that to maximize his gains one should spend where he gets the most for his dollar applies to public as well as to private expenditures. The difficulty is that there is virtually no way of getting taxpayers to indicate how much utility they receive from various governmental expenditures. Furthermore, since public expenditures serve (and taxes fall on) the whole community, the problem of government spending is uniquely involved in comparisons of interpersonal utility. As of now, no accurate way has been found to measure the benefit citizen $\underline{A}$ would receive from a redistribution of resources against the loss suffered by citizen $\underline{B}$ and arrive at any grand social welfare summation. Consequently, there is no operational way to determine the optimum level of government expenditures.

The preceding remarks about the greater difficulty of achieving, even theoretically, an optimum allocation of resources in the governmental as compared with the private economy do not mean (we hasten to add) that the private economy in practice operates perfectly. Consumer ignorance, monopolistic practices, and many other frictions in the machinery of private enterprise may actually cause results that are no better than those obtained in government. Furthermore, it should be made clear that, despite the inherent difficulty of allocating public funds optimally, there are many functions that simply must be performed by government. Where a service must be available to everyone if it is to be available to anyone (so called indivisible services such as defense, roads, or police protection), or where there are external economies (e. g. , benefits to society beyond those to the individual as, for example, in education or tuberculosis innoculation) government is clearly the appropriate agency to provide this service.

Furthermore, the fact that there is no accurate meter for measuring citizens' preferences does not imply that there is no basis for evaluating the service of a governmental unit. It is obvious, for instance, that under any value structure it is preferable to get the same service at less cost, or more service without increasing the cost. By their devotion to duty, many government officials serve the citizenry well; others, less capable or devoted, serve society indifferently. Some of the techniques by which local governments in California can achieve greater efficiency are described in the next chapter.

Illustrative Example

Perhaps the preceding points can be illustrated by a hypothetical example of a county supervisors' budget meeting. Let us imagine that they are considering expenditures for (a) public parks, complete with tennis courts, (b) expanding hospital facilities, (c) improving roads, (d) new radio facilities for the sheriff's office, and (e) increasing the funds allocated to the county superintendent of schools. A citizen attending the hearing might question whether some of those functions are proper activities of government, since he could point in almost every case to a counterpart in private business. If people need more recreation facilities let private enterprise provide the service as it does at Disneyland, at the numerous private golf courses, full-scale or miniature, or at private tennis courts. Even the question of what services should be provided by government and what should be handled in the realm of private enterprise is not easily answered.*

*It is interesting to note that government goes further in providing services that can be handled by private enterprise at the local level (a criterion that some might equate with creeping socialism) than at the national or state level. Nationally, about 70% of the budget is spent on defense (including veterans' benefits), 10% for interest on the debt, and 5% for conservation of natural resources and the cost of general government. Most of the remaining 15% is spent on regulatory and charitable functions so only a small percentage could possibly be identified as federal "business-type activities."

The State of California's 1957 budget showed more than 56% of current expenditures going to functions clearly governmental, leaving less than 44% representing "business-type" activities, even if education and mental hygiene are classified as business-type services.

But at the city-county level a large number of activities exist with counterparts in the private economy: garbage collection, public utilities, recreation, education, and hospitals — to mention only the most prominent. It is noteworthy that within the past year the City of Los Angeles forbade private collection of garbage and substituted muncipal service because of racketeering in the garbage-collection industry. Why the decision was to get rid of the industry rather than the racketeering is not precisely clear!

Of the $2,500,000 spent in fiscal 1957 on current expenditures by the various school districts, counties, and cities in California, 53% was for education, public service enterprises (mostly municipal power, water, and bus systems), recreation, and hospitals — all of which have counterparts in private enterprise.

Actually the question of whether business-type activities play a larger relative role in local than in state or federal government is hardly answerable by the statistical measurements cited because there is no basis for determining what functions government would provide

Assume, however, that the items to be considered at the budget session constitute appropriate functions of county government. The question still faces the supervisors: How much shall be spent on each item? The answer, in theory, is clear: the total benefits received by the public from an extra $1,000 spent on roads should match the total benefits from the final $1,000 spent on hospitals or other alternatives.

But this formula, though clear, is not operational. First, there is no counterpart of the market place wherein the benefits people receive can be measured by the prices they are willing to pay. It is difficult to place a dollar value on schools, highways, or recreational facilities. Furthermore, even if people were asked to indicate how much they would be willing to pay for such services, a taxpayer (motivated by self-interest) might indicate the value of the road or the park at less than its real utility to him since he could thereby shift a larger portion of its cost (assuming taxation were on the benefit principle) to other taxpayers. Yet once a road or park is built, its services are equally available to all, regardless of the amount paid by any one person.

Finally, even if some device could be found for measuring the social benefits of various public expenditures, the board of supervisors would still be plagued by the problem of interpersonal comparisons. The aged and infirm who have spent long hours sitting on wooden benches at the hospital waiting their turn for medical attention would like to have hospital facilities expanded. On the other hand, the healthy teen-agers who spend long hours sitting on wooden benches waiting to play on crowded tennis courts would gain little from an improved hospital but would benefit greatly from more money spent on recreational facilities. Citizens who spend two hours a day driving to and from work would prefer to have the money spent on highways. Thus, even if the board were blessed with the power to measure the social benefits arising from expenditures on various functions, it would still have no "scientific" criteria for deciding whose welfare should be served.

In some cases citizens may vote directly on issues of government expenditure. This gives officials a clearer idea of social benefits in comparison with social costs, but the procedure can be used for only

---

in an extreme laissez-faire economy. Perhaps the point should be limited to the observation that where public utilities and transportation systems, which have been socialized in many countries, are owned by governmental units in the United States, it is mostly at the local level.

a small percentage of the decisions about local expenditures and even then it is not a sufficient basis for really comparing social benefits and costs. The following news story from The Sacramento Bee illustrates the inadequacy of voting as a means of determining the level of government expenditures.

ROSEVILLE, Placer Co.

A. Teichert and Son of Sacramento submitted the low bid on the proposed Roseville Heights drainage and street improvement project.

The company bid $216,700 for the portion of the work which will be assessed against the property owners.

The total bid, which included paving of Church Street, was $248,153. The Church Street project is to be paid from gas tax funds.

Mayor Paul J. Lunardi continued the public hearing on the project until July 2nd. As of last night, owners of 54 per cent of the property in the district had signed protests against the project.

Lunardi stated this means the project will be killed unless 25 to 50 owners withdraw their protests.

City Engineer Ken Thompson said assessments based on the bid price will be $373.94 for a 50 by 125 foot interior lot and $670.09 for a corner lot of the same size.

Attorney F. H. Bowers, representing 191 owners of 320 lots, said the assessments in some cases exceed the value of the property and would amount to virtual confiscation.

J. A. Deal, speaking in favor of the project, charged some of the written protests were obtained under false pretenses.

Approximately 85 persons attended the public hearing on the project last night.

Here one can see, among other things, the collective nature of most government expenditures. A consumer of private goods can buy an automobile whether or not his neighbor wishes to buy one; but a consumer of governmental services cannot buy street improvements unless his neighbors also want them. This is proper since the road, once paved, can be used collectively by all, whereas a car remains private property. But a vote, even though it may be the best way for a community to weigh the benefits against the costs, does not really compare them. The reason is because we have no way of comparing the satisfaction or displeasure of one person with that of another.

Voting does this only if we assume that the satisfactions and displeasures of all people are exactly equal in magnitude except that the former are positive and the latter negative. When consumers can act individually, as in the market place, this extreme assumption is not

needed. Specifically, the 46% of the property owners who favor the
drainage and street project may live at the low end of Roseville Heights
and desperately want the improvements proposed because they are
likely to suffer $1,000 damage each during the next heavy rainfall,
whereas the 54% who oppose the expenditure may be rather indifferent
but feel that the cost would probably exceed the probable benefits to
them. Thus, the social benefits would not be represented by a majority
vote.

One other point is also illustrated. How broadly is social benefit
to be defined? Should the decision be made solely by the 350 property
owners on or adjacent to Church Street, or should the postman, dairy-
man, and casual citizen — all of whom may have occasion to use the
street — be considered? This is a most important consideration in connection with education. Who suffers if the students in school district
X are badly educated — only the citizens of that school district, or all
the citizens of California and even the world?

Questions such as these lead economists to believe that government expenditures can be at best determined in a way that gives only
partial assurance that resources are optimally allocated. In short, our
economic and political institutions provide no mechanism for determining precisely — even in theory — whether government expenditures are
optimal in the sense of allocating support correctly between private and
public services or of determining whether the amount spent in the public
sector of the economy is allocated correctly among its various functions.

THE OPERATIONAL METHOD OF DETERMINING GOVERNMENTAL
EXPENDITURES

The foregoing discussion shows why it is virtually impossible to
answer the question "Are government expenditures too high?" As a
matter of practical decision-making it is through his voting, or through
communication or pressure on elected officials, that the consumer-tax-
payer expresses his opinion about the proper level of government expenditure. Thus the answer to the question boils down to this: Government expenditures are too high when a majority either votes against
bond issues, against candidates favoring increased spending, and
against further expansion of government, or puts enough pressure on
elected officials to make them reduce expenses. Even then, because
the majority rules, expenditures may still be too high to suit some and
too low to please others.

The importance of political action as a practical determinant of the

level of government expenditures is clearly apparent in the following
excerpts from a press release of February 11, 1958, by Glenn E.
Coolidge, then Chairman of the Assembly Ways and Means Committee
of the Legislature. Though it happens to refer to state expenditures,
it illustrates the people's attitude toward local government expenditures quite as well.

> Sacramento. February 11:
>
> A call for an "awareness of California's financial plight" was
> made today by Assemblyman Glenn E. Coolidge (R - Santa Cruz),
> chairman of the ways and means committee of the lower house.
>
> The 28-man committee, with the senate finance committee,
> is studying the state's proposed $2.2 billion budget for 1958-59.
>
> Coolidge said that in the face of a tight financial squeeze,
> the committee members have been "flooded with letters, telegrams
> and even personal phone calls" from people disapproving every
> proposed cut in the budget the committee has considered.
>
> "In fact," he said, "large numbers of groups and individuals
> have even demanded various augmentations of the budget."
>
> Coolidge said those demanding maintenance or expansion of
> the budget advanced "logical reasons" for the requests in which
> they have a special interest. However, he said, "it seems to be
> the same old story of everyone wanting to cut the budget, so long
> as it is someone else who bears the cut."
>
> Coolidge said tax-conscious citizens have been "far in the
> minority" in supporting the committee in its efforts to hold the line
> on state expenditures.

FOUR POLICY IMPLICATIONS

Four important policy implications stem from the preceding analysis. Because of the vagueness of the formulas available for determining
either the proper functions of government or the best allocation of public expenditures it is essential, first, that citizens be as fully informed
on public matters as possible. Since the most important yardstick for
determining whether governmental expenditures are at the desired level
lies in the response of the voters, it is vital that citizens be informed
as fully as possible about both the extent of government spending and
what they receive in services for their taxes.

Second, it is essential that maximum use be made of private enterprise wherever practicable. Because there is reason to believe that
economic forces can do less to induce optimum allocation of resources
in the governmental than in the private sector of the economy, it is
preferable, all other things being equal, that the private economy be
utilized to provide as many services as possible. This does not mean
that any function necessary for social welfare should be dropped but

simply that it is preferable, where practical, for these service functions to be carried on within the framework of a private enterprise system.

Conversely, however, the third policy implication is that government must assume those functions that are not adequately performed by private enterprise. People who feel that taxes are rising too high and that government activity is continually encroaching on the field of business should consider the forces that determine which functions remain within the framework of private enterprise and which are transferred to the governmental sector of the economy. Many theories are offered to explain why some functions are handled by business and others by government, but probably the soundest is this: sooner or later government assumes responsibility for a service when private business either cannot, or will not, perform to the satisfaction of the public. To elaborate: individual pricing is impossible for national defense and hardly feasible for police protection. Where the technical nature of a service makes anything other than a monopoly inefficient (e.g., the postal, telephone, or rail services); government will either perform the function directly or supervise it closely. Though many risks can be offset by private insurance, the risk of unemployment is too large and unpredictable for any agency less than the government itself to underwrite. Good schools can certainly be provided by private enterprise but not at a cost most parents could pay; this is the reason education has become largely a government responsibility. Or take garbage collection: Los Angeles shifted to public collection a few years ago because racketeering made private collection unsatisfactory. In brief, government assumption of responsibility is occasioned mainly by deficiencies in service under private enterprise.

The policy implication is clear: if people want to prevent government expenditures from rising and want to keep the government from taking over more and more of the functions of business, they must make sure that the private economy provides the services still entrusted to it in a manner satisfactory to the electorate. When private business fails to produce an optimum solution — whether because of monopolistic tendencies, failure to provide adequate information, or failure to price in a way that provides wide distribution — government will often be asked, indeed compelled, to step in. What is called "creeping socialism" is frequently no more than a pragmatic reaction to "inadequate capitalism."

Fourth, and finally, the standards used in appraising government

operations must necessarily be "political" rather than "economic."
Since there is no precise way to measure the social benefits received
from government services, and no way, furthermore, to decide how
to distribute them, there is no objective way to compute such quantities
as the optimum acreage of parks per capita, the proper number of policemen per thousand inhabitants, or any similar standard for other
functions of government. Many people are familiar with bench marks
or standards used in business operations. Some of them are in the
form of financial and operating analyses. Dun and Bradstreet report
periodically, for example, on fourteen important ratios for more than
one hundred different lines of manufacturing and retailing. Is it not
reasonable to expect cities and counties to be analyzed in a similar
manner? Could not ratios be established that would indicate the proper
budgetary allocation between parks, police, and planning commissions?
Some authorities say that a city should have a public nurse for every
25,000 inhabitants and a school should have a teacher for every twenty-
five pupils. Yet who can say that these, or any other standards, are
optimal, in the sense that marginal costs match marginal benefits?
The conclusion is obvious: it is impossible to develop standards other
than by collecting the judgments of intelligent and well-trained observers.

LIMITATIONS INHERENT IN THE DATA

Despite the fact that there is no market place criterion for evaluating governmental expenditures and consequently no way of measuring
social benefits, it is still possible to say something useful about cost
levels. A careful analysis of the expenditures of a single locality over
many years or of those of similar governmental units for the same
years, can provide comparative bench marks of great value. However,
there are three pitfalls that must be avoided before such data can be
accurately interpreted.

Inadequacy of Governmental Accounting. One of the warnings to
be sounded arises from the nature of governmental accounting. Unlike
business firms, local governmental units do not prepare balance sheets
and income statements. This has many implications regarding the
nature of municipal reports: there are usually no estimates of the value
of land, buildings, or equipment; no depreciation is reported; and —
possibly worst of all — the distinction between capital outlays and
current costs is frequently neglected or made without much precision.
From what has been learned during this study it appears that separation
of capital and current expenses is done most carefully in school financing; in contrast, the reported expenditures for streets and bridges sel-

dom provide an accurate basis for determining how much has been
spent for current maintenance and how much for new additions to the
highway network.

An illustration of the fact that governmental accounting lumps all
expenditures, whether for nonrecurring capital outlays or annual operating costs, in the same budget is afforded by the following story
from The Sacramento Bee.

> Chico, Butte Co.
>
> City budget proposals totaling $1,208,388 are undergoing
> council scrutiny this week.
>
> Principal capital outlays called for in the tentative budget
> include $60,000 for the construction of a second fire station,
> $15,000 to install curbs along the Esplanade and $123,585 to link
> Mangrove Avenue and Pine Street with a bridge over Big Chico
> Creek.
>
> Among requests the council will consider are those for a
> wage raise for police officers.

All uses of funds tend to be treated alike, whether they are for
bridges or policemen's wages. Yet comparisons of cost become vastly
more meaningful if capital outlays are separated from current expenditures because capital expenditures, by their very nature, occur only
infrequently; because of their "lumpiness" they invariably distort annual comparisons. For this study considerable time and effort were
spent making these adjustments even where this involved consulting
the basic reports of counties or cities. However, because of the inherent difficulty of distinguishing capital from current outlays, not to
mention the inadequacy of governmental accounting, it is possible that
they may still be mixed to some extent.

Partial Analysis. A second caveat concerning conclusions to be
drawn from the data of this chapter and the next derives from the fact
of partial economic analysis. Do the figures show real economic phenomena or would the trends and differences noted be canceled out if
the whole economy were considered? There could be a shift of expenditures between local government and the private sector of the economy,
e.g., the cost of fire protection might have risen, but if this resulted
in lower fire insurance rates, the total spent by the citizenry for fire
protection might actually have declined. The same situation applies to
expenditures for better roads versus automobile insurance. Grass in
the school play yard may cost the school district more to maintain
than black top (asphalt), but according to one school principal, the
wear and tear on boys' sneakers and jeans is so much greater with
black top than with grass that it really costs the parents more.

There may also be shifts between levels of government. Analysis could show that expenditures on public health at the local level have not increased materially over the years. Yet a study of larger scope might reveal an increasing share of the public health expenditures borne by the state or federal government, which would mean that tax-supported services for public health in California might have increased substantially.

No Provision for Measuring Service. The final warning is that comparison of governmental costs per citizen between various cities and counties can be accurate only when due allowance is made for differences in the "level of services" provided. One city might be 10% more expensive than another yet offer 20% more service to its citizens, and consequently be more "efficient" than its less expensive counterpart. Analysis of expenditures alone is thus subject to the limitation that differences in cost may be explained solely by differences in services.

CALIFORNIA LOCAL EXPENDITURES: 1956-57

It would be an error, however, to assume that nothing can be learned from analyzing what has happened to California local expenditures. On the contrary, the warnings given should help the reader think through the reasons that so little has yet been done to develop optimum patterns of governmental expenditure. He should also be less likely to draw unwarranted conclusions from this or any other study of governmental costs. All things considered, an analysis of the patterns of local expenditure in California can yield insights of real importance to students of public finance.

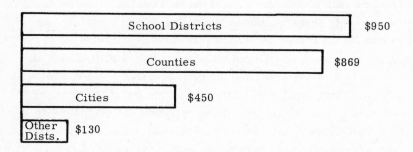

Figure 3.1 Bar Chart Showing Total Current Operating Expenses for Local Units: 1957 (in millions of dollars, San Francisco excluded)

Operating Costs of Local Governments. Expenditures by cities, counties, schools, and other districts in California during fiscal 1956- 57 are summarized in the charts and tables of this chapter. Figure 3.1 shows current operating expenses for all four categories. School ex- penses constitute the major part of local public expenditures, Califor- nia's current operating cost per pupil being sixth highest of all states in the nation. Since there is reason to believe that the quality and quan- tity of mass education have much to do with raising living standards, the fact that education looms large in the California local budget — as it does in all states — should not be a matter of concern. County ser- vices cost nearly as much as the public schools, but municipal expen- ditures amount to little more than half the cost of county government. As for special districts, they comprise slightly less than 6% of all local expenditures.

Local Costs Compared with State and Federal Expenditures. Total local expenditures amounted to approximately 7% of personal in- come earned by Californians during fiscal 1957, as shown by Figure 3.2. This affords a fair measure of the economic burden of local gov- ernment. The comparative magnitude of local expenditures may also be seen from another point of reference in Figure 3.3. California local governments spend nearly three times as much as the state and pro- portionately slightly more than half as much as the federal government. (The data for Figure 3.3 are computed on a basis slightly different from those for the other charts in this chapter. Both current expendi- tures and capital outlays are lumped together in measuring expenditures at the separate levels of government. This has been done because the federal and state data available did not distinguish between current and capital outlays. To make the sums comparable it was considered best to take total local expenditures rather than only those relating to cur- rent operations. Furthermore, the estimate of California's share of federal expenditures is rough at best. It is impossible, for example,

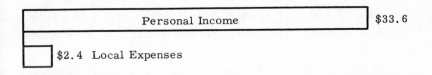

Figure 3.2. Bar Chart Comparison of Local Government Operating Costs and Personal Income Earned by Californians: 1957 (in billions of dollars)

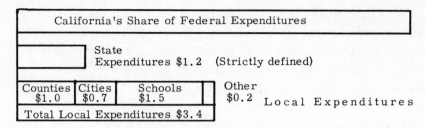

Figure 3.3. Comparison of Federal, State, and Local Expenditures for California: 1957. Note: State allocations to local governments have been excluded from the state total and assigned to the appropriate Local Governments. (Current and capital expenditures in billions of dollars.)

to determine accurately how much California shares in expenditures for defense throughout the world.)

Functional Distribution of Expenses. Having obtained some idea of the magnitude of expenditures by the various types of local government, it is now in order to note how the money is used and what relative amounts are allocated to each function. Figure 3.4 shows the functional division of expenses for cities, counties, and schools. School money is spent mostly for teachers' salaries. County budgets are almost as heavily dominated by charities and corrections. The biggest single item in city budgets is for police and fire protection.

Per Capita Operating Costs. The story of expenditures — their magnitude and their purposes — by local governments in California during fiscal 1957 has been briefly summarized in the four charts shown. Even more may be learned, however, by studying the operating costs incurred during fiscal 1957 by each of the cities and counties after expenses have been adjusted for population differences. Table 3.a and 3.b (See Appendix) show per capita operating costs during 1957 for each of California's 57 counties and 335 cities (San Francisco is treated separately since it is a consolidated city-county). Because such a table makes for arduous reading, the data are summarized below in Tables 3.1 and 3.2. Probably the most striking feature to be noted is the wide range that exists in per capita operating costs among various cities and counties of the state.

Capital Investments. To complete the record of California local expenditures during fiscal 1957, the amount of capital investment made by each of the four types of local units is shown in Figure 3.5. It re-

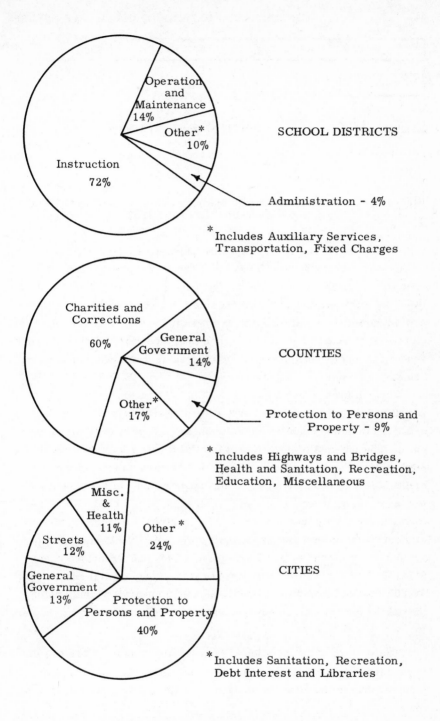

SCHOOL DISTRICTS

Operation and Maintenance 14%

Other* 10%

Instruction 72%

Administration - 4%

*Includes Auxiliary Services, Transportation, Fixed Charges

COUNTIES

Charities and Corrections 60%

General Government 14%

Other* 17%

Protection to Persons and Property - 9%

*Includes Highways and Bridges, Health and Sanitation, Recreation, Education, Miscellaneous

CITIES

Misc. & Health 11%

Streets 12%

Other* 24%

General Government 13%

Protection to Persons and Property 40%

*Includes Sanitation, Recreation, Debt Interest and Libraries

Figure 3.4.   Functional Distribution of Expenditures for Cities, Counties, and School Districts: 1959

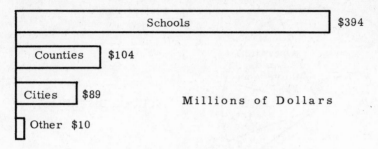

Figure 3.5. Capital Investments Made by Different Levels of Local
Government in California: 1957

veals three major facts: (1) Capital expenditures at the local level
amounted to nearly $600 million. (2) School districts spent more on
capital investment, as they did for operating expenses, than the other
levels of local government. (3) Schools were relatively more dominant in capital expenditures than in operating costs. School capital
outlays were nearly four times larger than those for counties whereas
school running expenses were only 9% greater than country operating
costs.

Expenditures in San Francisco. One other item should be mentioned to fill in the last detail on California local expenditures. The
data for cities and counties listed thus far (except in Figure 3.3) do
not include the cost of government for California's only consolidated
city-county, San Francisco. Any attempt to split its expenditures
artificially into county and city components would run the risk of dis-
torting results. It cannot properly be treated as a city since it per-
forms many county functions — or as a county since it also provides
city services. In this chapter it must suffice merely to state the total
amount of its expenditures. During fiscal 1957 San Francisco spent
$115,589,000 for operating expenses ($142.70 per capita) and
$4,851,000 for capital investment. A brief comparative analysis of
the cost of San Francisco government will be given in the next chapter.

SUMMARY

The answer to the question of how services and functions are divided between government and private enterprise lies more in the
political than in the economic sphere. Similarly, the question of how
much should be spent on each of the various functions allocated to
government is less susceptible of settlement by economic than by
political criteria.

A study of local expenditures is subject to three limitations — the inadequacy of government accounting, the difficulty of comparing services rendered, and the possibility that a more general analysis might cancel out some of the trends observed. With these qualifications in mind, the basic data regarding expenditures of local governments in California have been presented.

Table 3.1. Summary Data on Per Capita Operating Costs for
Counties During Fiscal 1957

	Amount	County or Counties
Median	$87.61	Sutter
Lowest	44.61	Orange
Highest	432.50	Alpine
Range that includes half the counties	$71.38 to $113.65	Imperial to Butte

Table 3.2. Summary Data on Per Capita Operating Costs for
Cities During Fiscal 1957

	Amount	City or Cities
Median	$37.16	Placerville
Lowest	13.19[1]	Lakewood
Highest	165.23[2]	Huntington Beach
Range that includes half the cities	$28.04 to $47.91	Fairfax to Azusa

[1] This was not actually the lowest cost city, for there were 16 with lower per capita costs during 1956-57. However, all of these were newly incorporated and therefore were generally not comparable with other cities.

[2] This was not the highest cost city; Emeryville ($166.49) and Vernon ($3,650.26) both had higher costs but these are industrial enclaves and quite untypical.

Source: Tables 3.a and 3.b (see Appendix) list per capita operating costs for each county and city, respectively.

The stage is thus set for considering in the next chapter such questions as these: How do the expenditures of California's local government in 1957 compare with previous years? What factors explain the difference in current expenses per capita between various cities and also between different counties? How do operating costs per capita compare between cities and counties of different size? How do capital outlays for local government compare with those of prior years? How do total local expenditures in California compare with total local expenditures in other states? What is the outlook for local expenditures in the future?

In order to set the problem of controlling local expenditures in correct perspective it is essential first to discover how the costs of local government in California during fiscal 1957 compare with those of previous years. As a preliminary step, it is necessary to segregate capital outlays from current expenditures because capital outlays are sporadic and dependent on special factors, such as the rate of population growth and the availability of funds. Year-to-year comparisons are, therefore, more meaningful when the analysis is limited to regular operating costs. Unfortunately, operating costs and capital investments are usually lumped together in the annual reports of the financial transactions of local governments published by the State Controller. Thus it has been necessary in this study to go to the complete reports submitted by the cities and counties to get the raw data with respect to each.

COMPARISON OF CURRENT AND PREVIOUS COSTS

The earliest year for which the basic documents were still available was 1937 and the task was so time-consuming that detailed separation of capital from current costs for every city and county were made only for 1937, 1947, and 1957. These years were chosen partly because they spanned two decades, partly because 1957 was the latest fiscal year for which data were available and partly because 1937 was a reasonably typical year prior to World War II; 1947 was a representative postwar year, and 1957 would bring the story up to date. The picture of current operating expenses for cities and counties during these three bench mark years is presented in Figures 4.1 and 4.2.

Real Costs Per Capita Nearly Constant

Figure 4.1 shows that total current operating expenses for cities rose from less than $100 million in 1937 to $450 million 20 years later. Current operating expenses for counties jumped even more — from $116 million to nearly $900 million. On the surface these tremendous increases would seem to justify the claim that local government in California is brewing itself a financial crisis by spending ever increasing amounts of money. It is clear that in 1957 the running expenses of local government exceeded those of any previous year. Apparently, each year during the past decade has seen the cost of local government in California reach a new peak. The trend seems inexorable — higher each year. Yet if one should be tempted to conclude from this review that local governments are spending without restraint, he should recall two important factors: California's population has grown every year for

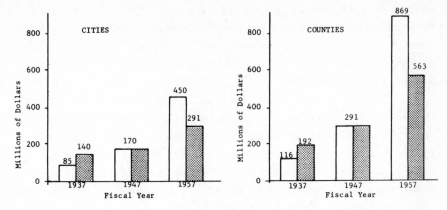

Figure 4.1.   Total Operating Expenses for Cities and Counties both in
Current Prices and Adjusted for Changes in the Price
Level

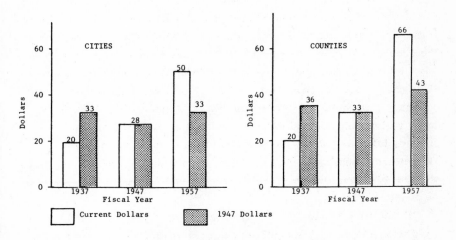

Figure 4.2.   Per Capita Operating Expenses for Cities and Counties
both in Current Prices and Adjusted for Changes in the
Price Level

Sources: Data on expenses came from reports submitted to State
Controller (San Francisco excluded).   The Department of Commerce
Price Index for state and local government purchases of goods and services as reported in THE ECONOMIC REPORT OF THE PRESIDENT,
1958, p. 122, was used to equate '37 and '57 expenditures to the 1947
price level.

several decades, and the price level has risen with almost equal regularity. Naturally the cost of local government has climbed and, given these two trends, it seems likely to continue rising. The influence of both these factors — population growth and inflation — is shown in Figures 4.1 and 4.2.

In Figure 4.1 total running expenses of cities and counties during the three bench mark years are adjusted to show what costs would have been without inflation, the dark bars revealing the diminished rate of increase. In Figure 4.2 costs are further adjusted by removing the element of population growth. Here we see that, in constant dollars, California's city governments spent $32.23 per person (on the average) in 1937 and $32.51 per person in 1957 — virtually no increase at all. County government, however, reveals a different picture. In stabilized dollars, costs per capita rose over the two decades from $33.57 to $42.94, an increase of about 1% a year.

The story revealed by these charts is probably the most important fact developed in this chapter. The cost of local government in California has risen constantly since the end of World War II; it rose during the 1930's, and before that in the 1920's. But when absolute costs are adjusted for inflation and the growth of population, the figures show little change over the past two decades. This pattern has emerged in too many separate studies to be mistaken. It applies both to cities as large as Los Angeles and to those as small as Claremont. It is confirmed, for example, by the analysis of the costs of operating Berkeley's garbage, police, and fire departments in 1947-48 compared to 1939-40.[1] It is true for schools (see Figure 8.6, page 310), as well as counties.

Bradford Trenham, formerly executive vice president of the California Taxpayers' Association, served in 1957-58 as chairman of a Citizens Advisory Committee on Efficiency and Economy to study the financial problems of the City of Los Angeles. One of the major projects undertaken by the Committee was a comparison of taxes paid during selected years over the past three decades. Although the Trenham study related to tax revenue, we can draw inferences from it regarding expenditures if we make these two reasonable assumptions: first, that the cash balances of the City of Los Angeles were approximately the same at the beginning of this 30-year period as at the end; second, that tax revenues were used largely to support current operating expenses and not to finance capital improvements. (Its capital in-

vestments have been financed largely by bond issues.) These two assumptions allow us generally to equate taxable revenue with current
operating expenses.

What are the results of such comparisons? The evidence shows
that in 1927, total taxes collected by the City of Los Angeles amounted
to $54.51 per resident in terms of a constant 1947 dollar. In 1930,
they were $59.50; in 1937, $55.22. During the war years they declined
as low as $36.77; by 1947, they had risen to $44.23; by 1956, to $51.18;
and by 1957, to $51.90. The details of this study are shown in Table
4.1. To see if the pattern of stable per capita costs, in constant dollars,
applied to a small city as well as to Los Angeles, a partial check was
made by analyzing the operating expenses of the City of Claremont for
the past two decades. The results followed the pattern for cities generally — per capita costs in constant dollars fell during most of the 1940's
as a result of war and postwar shortages, then rose in the late 40's
and early 1950's and nearly returned to the level of two decades earlier. Specifically, per capita operating costs for Claremont, after deflation by the Department of Commerce price index for state and local
governments, were $26.21 in 1936-37; $20.75 in 1946-47, and $22.90
in 1956-57.

Inflation, Influx, Improvements

The Committee's analysis prompted Chairman Trenham to summarize the history of Los Angeles municipal finance in an apt and al-
literative phrase that may well apply to all local governments in California. "Gentlemen," he said, as he presented the Committee's summary findings to the Los Angeles City Council, "the history of the
cost of local government here is summed up in three I's — inflation,
influx, and improvements." Actually, most of the growth in cost of
local government in California can be accounted for by inflation and
influx alone. The question of improvement is debatable since it is so
difficult, as shown in the previous chapter, to measure the quality of
government service; such as it is, however, the evidence supports
the belief that there have beem improvements in local government service.

Because the quality of public services is almost incapable of measurement, any attempt to show that California's local governments are
currently giving better (or poorer) service than they did 20 years ago
is bound to be inconclusive. One function of local government, viz.,
fire protection, is, however, especially susceptible to objective evalu-

Table 4.1 Comparison of Los Angeles City Tax Revenue for Selected
Years with Related Population and Price Level Data

Years	Total City Revenue (in millions)	Per Capita Total (Current Dollars)	Adjusted to Constant Dollar (1947 Base)*
1927-28	$43.3	$37.59	$54.51
1928-29	$45.6	$37.80	$55.57
1929-30	$47.0	$37.94	$59.57
1931-32	$47.5	$37.02	$62.93
1934-35	$33.4	$26.22	$44.84
1935-36	$40.0	$30.72	$51.92
1936-37	$44.3	$32.29	$55.22
1937-38	$48.5	$34.25	$56.51
1941-42	$45.9	$21.54	$44.52
1943-44	$46.4	$27.44	$36.77
1945-46	$53.6	$29.73	$36.27
1947-48	$84.4	$44.23	$44.23
1950-51	102.4	$51.89	$45.14
1953-54	130.4	$61.67	$45.64
1955-56	147.0	$66.46	$47.19
1956-57	172.8	$75.26	$51.18
1957-58	184.7	$78.63	$51.90

*State and Local Government Price Index, Department of Commerce

Source: Special Study made for Citizens Advisory Committee on
Efficiency and Economy. Appointed December 1957 by the Los Angeles
City Council.

Table 4.2 Comparison of Fire Department Ratings and Total Fire
Insurance Class for 17 California Cities: 1937 and 1957

City	1937			1957		
	Total Insurance Class	Fire Dept. Deficiency Points	Year of Rating	Total Insurance Class	Fire Dept. Deficiency Points	Year of Rating
Los Angeles	3	212	1935	3	138	1947
San Francisco	3	185	1932	2	185	1951
Oakland	4	229	1933	3	212	1950
Long Beach	4	399	1933	3	394	1944
San Diego	3	371	1938	3	448	1956
Alameda	4	392	1931	3	353	1944
Berkeley	4	355	1932	3	296	1951
Fresno	3	187	1933	3	120	1955
Glendale	3	343	1937	3	367	1946
Pasadena	3	244	1936	3	161	1957
Sacramento	3	340	1937	3	426	1956
San Bernardino	5	779	1937	4	473	1955
San Jose	5	588	1937	4	344	1956
Santa Ana	5	851	1937	3	421	1954
Santa Barbara	4	565	1937	3	359	1955
Santa Monica	5	697	1937	3	345	1950
Stockton	4	535	1935	3	303	1952

The 17 cities in this table include all California cities with population exceeding 30,000 in 1930 and were consequently listed in the 1938
Municipal Year Book published by the International City Managers
Association. The 1957 ratings for the same cities were taken from the
1958 Municipal Year Book.

ation. The National Board of Fire Underwriters recurrently makes an
engineering appraisal of fire-protection facilities in each city and as-
sesses deficiency points for any aspect that does not match the Board's
exacting standards. The fire deficiency points for 17 California cities
with populations in excess of 30,000 in 1937, as published in the 1938
Municipal Year Book, show a range of deficiency points running from
851 to 185, the average deficiency score being 428. (The worst score
possible is 1,500.) By way of contrast, the 1958 Year Book shows
lower scores (i.e., improved fire service) for 13 of these 17 cities,
with one the same, and 3 higher. The scores ranged from 473 to 120
(Fresno was the possessor of this near-perfect rating) and the average
deficiency tally was 314. By 1958, 11 of the cities were ranked in a
more favorable insurance class (meaning lower fire insurance rates)
while 6 remained unchanged from their standing 20 years ago. Since

the standards used by the Board of Fire Underwriters are continually raised as new equipment and techniques are developed, the deficiency-score decrease, if anything, understates the improvements made in those 17 cities since 1938. The details are shown in Table 4.2.

Another objective measure of fire protection is furnished by records indicating the number of building fires per thousand inhabitants. Data for this statistic are not available by cities, consequently California municipalities cannot be evaluated separately, but Table 4.3 shows the comparison for all U.S. cities between 1940 and 1957, and there is no reason to expect that California's cities did not share in this reduced fire loss.

The point of this section is so important for a clear perspective on local expenditures in California that it bears repetition: when the current operating costs of cities, counties, and schools are adjusted for inflation and population growth, they show very little increase during the past two decades, and what there is, is probably the result of giving more or better service.

Table 4.3 Incidence of Building Fires, 1940 and 1957

Size of City (population)	Median Value for Number of Building Fires per 1000 Population	
	1940	1957
Over 500,000	3.3	3.0
250,000 - 500,000	3.7	3.5
100,000 - 250,000	4.3	3.5
50,000 - 100,000	4.2	3.7
25,000 - 50,000	4.5	3.7

Trends in Total Expenditures

Even when adjusted for changes in population and the value of the dollar, however, total expenditures (running expenses plus capital outlays) for local governments have clearly risen since 1930, as is shown in Figure 4.3. This is true of counties and school districts especially; cities and special districts show no increase in terms of per capita constant dollars. Since schools and counties account for the major part of local expenditures, however, their increase means that total expenditures showed a slight increase. On the other hand, the expansion in per capita constant-dollar outlays (combining operating expenses, bond redemption, and capital investment) that has occurred since 1930 approximately matches the growth in the personal income of the people of California. This is revealed in Figure 4.4, which shows that income has grown faster than all local expenditures since

the 1930's and at about the same rate as state outlays. The retrench-
ment of state and local expenditures during World War II and the war
in Korea is also revealed.

Almost the entire increase in constant-dollar outlays per citizen
can be explained by the greater volume of capital improvements made
during the 1950's compared to the 1930's. Table 4.4 shows the ratio
of capital improvements to current expenses for the base years 1937,
1947, and 1957. It points up the fact that, as a percentage of operating
costs, capital outlays are much greater in fiscal 1957 than they were
in 1937 (twice as much for counties, three times greater for cities).
Since capital outlays are influenced to some extent by the rate of population growth, it is understandable that they would call for a larger
share of total expenditures in 1957.

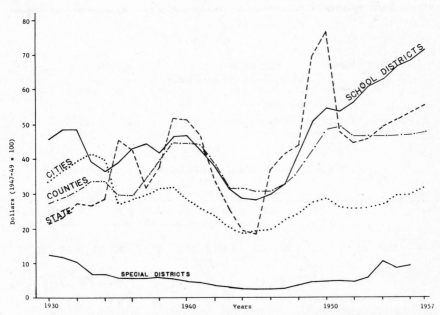

Figure 4.3. California State and Local Expenditures (including operating expenses and capital investments) Adjusted for Changes
in Population and the Value of the Dollar (1947-49 -- 100).

Sources: Expenditure Data came from THE TAX DIGEST, Nov.
1950, p. 376; March 1956, p. 78; and from communication with staff of
the California Taxpayers Association. Population Data is based on
estimates of the Department of Finance, State of California. Price De-
flator is the Department of Commerce Price Index for State and Local
Governments.

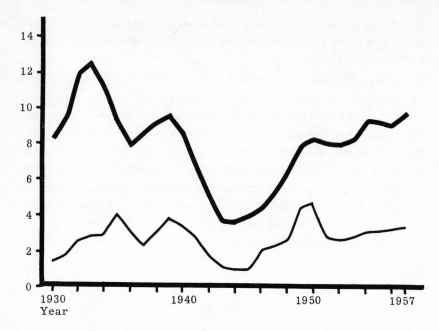

Figure 4.4 ▬▬▬ Local and state expenditures in California as percentages of personal income.
▬▬ State expenditures as a per cent of personal income in California.

Sources: Expenditure data same as Fig. 4.3; personal income data from U.S. Department of Commerce.

Table 4.4. Capital Outlays for Counties and Cities

| | Counties | | | Cities | | |
	1937	1947	1957	1937	1947	1957
Actual (000 omitted)	$6,485	12,313	103,507	5,665	13,799	89,205
Per Capita						
a) Current Dollars	$1.13	1.37	7.90	1.29	2.25	9.91
b) Constant Dollars (1947 = 100)	$1.86	1.37	5.12	2.13	2.25	6.42
As a Percent of Current Operating Costs	6%	4%	12%	7%	8%	20%

Source: Annual Reports of Financial Transactions of Counties and Cities, published by the State Controller's Office, adjusted by detailed analysis of basic documents submitted by each county and city.

This may be all good and well, but what of the taxpayer who says, "The distinction between capital investment and current costs may seem important to an economist or to an accountant, but to me all outflow of governmental funds means a tax bite, so why should I care whether the money is spent for one thing or the other?" The answer is that capital investments are likely to represent improved services of a rather permanent nature; consequently, it would be misleading to charge all their cost against the year of installation. Because of the nonrecurring and lumpy nature of capital investment, and the fact that its value is not used up — as are a policeman's services — during the period it is paid for, the true basis for comparing costs from year to year is the annual operating cost, including depreciation on capital investments. Unfortunately, the latter figure is not provided by governmental accounting.

A comparison of local government costs as adjusted for inflation and population growth thus suggests an answer to the important question raised in the previous chapter, "Are local expenditures in California too high?" They are not significantly higher than they were 20 years ago. Anyone who claims that they are too high today must show either that they have been excessive for the past 20 years or that the need for local services is now considerably less than it used to be.

Operating Costs as a Per Cent of Income

Perhaps a better way to measure the real economic burden of local government is to compare its cost against the income earned by Californians. This analysis differs from the one shown in Figure 4.4, since it excludes capital investment and bond redemption from the cost of government. Again the same picture appears: the operating costs of local government, in relation to personal income, have been remarkably constant for the past two decades. The details are shown in Table 4.5, but the important point is simply that total expenses of local government in California amounted to approximately 6.5% of personal income in 1937 and 6.7% in 1957.

Table 4.5 Current Operating Expenses as a Percentage of Personal
Income

	1937	1947	1957
Cities	1.71%	1.04%	1.34%
Counties	2.34	1.78	2.58
Schools	2.49	1.49	2.82
Total	6.54%	4.31%	6.74%

Annual Costs of the Ten Largest Cities and Counties

Comparisons based on bench mark years are revealing, but it is
also useful to see the trends from year to year without having to hop
across a decade. Since the job of separating capital outlays from annual operating expenses required an analysis of the basic data filed
with the State Controller by each city and county, consecutive annual
comparisons were made for only the ten largest counties and cities
(as of 1957) spanning the 11-year period from 1947 to 1957, inclusive.
The top ten counties contained 77% of California's population (excluding
San Francisco) as of July 1957, and the ten largest cities (not including
San Francisco) comprised 30%.

This time-series analysis for the past 11 years showed essentially
the same pattern as that revealed by the bench mark years (see Figure
4.5). Per capita costs in constant dollars rose 26% for cities and 30%
for counties. It should be remembered that local government expenses
in 1947 were still held down by restrictions and shortages resulting
from the war period and therefore were lower than per capita costs in
real terms in the late 1930's; consequently, much of the increase shown
in the time-series analysis since 1947 represents a return to the pre-
war level of expenses. The study of the ten biggest cities and counties
shows increases in per capita expenses adjusted for constant dollars
that approximate the results observed for all cities during the same
period (17% increase) and all counties (32% gain). This suggests that
essentially similar factors influence changes in operating costs for
large cities and counties as well as for the smaller ones. But there is
one thing the annual series reveals that could not be seen by comparisons across the decade: most of the increase came between 1947 and
1950, when it became possible to catch up after the war. In real terms,
the cost of city and county government in California has apparently remained almost constant since the beginning of the 1950's if the experience of the ten largest cities and counties is indicative.

Schools and Other Special Districts

When adjusted for inflation and increased enrollment, the annual
trend in school expenses, as shown by Figure 8.6, resembles the
pattern for cities and counties, though the increase in adjusted costs
is greater. Since no basis is available for adjusting expenditures for
special districts by population changes (their boundaries do not coincide
with census areas) annual comparisons of their expenditures in terms
of per capita constant dollars could not be made. Yet there is little

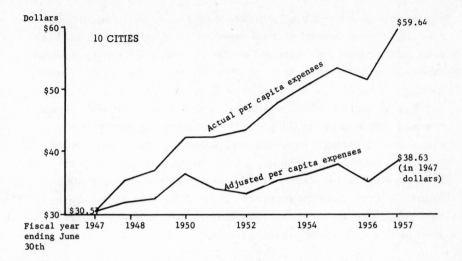

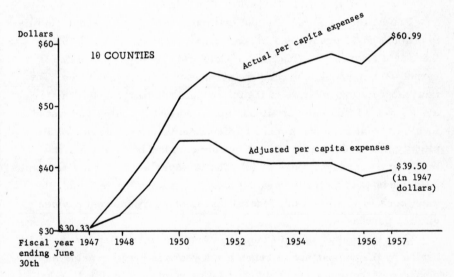

Figure 4.5. Per Capita Operating Expenses of the Ten Largest Cities
and Counties (actual amounts and amounts adjusted for
changes in the price level)

Sources: Annual Reports submitted to the State Controller by each
of the Cities and Counties, adjusted to remove capital
investment. Population Estimates: Department of Finance,
State of California. Price Adjustment: U.S. Dept. of
Commerce, State and Local Government Index.

reason to suppose that the exclusion of special districts distorts the
final conclusion. Special district expenses form only a small part of
total local government costs and the factors influencing their expenditures are no different from those affecting other units of local government.

Every piece of evidence tells the same story. When adjustments
are made for changes in California's population and the effect of inflation, local government expenditures, especially when capital investment is excluded, appear to be running only moderately above the rate
that prevailed in the 1930's. The absolute totals show a startling
growth, but this does not represent any real increase in the economic
burden because the cost of local government has remained fairly constant as a percentage of personal income.

IMPLICATIONS AND OBSERVATIONS

Policy Implications. One policy implication of the 20-year stability of local government costs in real terms is clear: if, as of 1958,
there is a crisis in the financing of California local governments, it
cannot be blamed on an exceesive increase in local expenditures. The
fault must lie in a mixture of the following three factors: (a) The tax
system is so inequitable or ill-administered that it causes the cost of
local government to seem more burdensome than it really is. (b) The
slightly increased cost of capital investments has become the straw
breaking the taxpayer's back. (c) The taxpayer is venting his economic
uneasiness and frustration against local taxes when the real fault lies
elsewhere — with inflation, federal taxes, or heavy interest payments
on time purchases.

Growing Importance of Counties. Another interesting fact revealed by the comparison of bench mark years is the increasing importance of the operating costs of counties compared to cities. Total
expenditures for both operating expenses and capital investment by
counties were less than total city expenditures until 1935; since then,
county expenditures have increasingly surpassed city outlays. In
terms of per capita annual operating expenses, counties and cities were
almost even in 1937 (each costing approximately $20 per citizen). As
of 1957, counties were spending 32% more per person than cities ($66
compared to $50). *

*The growing importance of county over city is also revealed in
the time series for the big ten cities and counties. In 1947, the per
capita running cost for the ten counties was slightly less than for the
ten cities ($30.33 vs. $30.57) whereas by 1957, the counties' actual

The Increasing Burden of Charity. Another way to learn what has been happening to the cost of running California's local governments during the past two decades is to look at comparative functional breakdowns. Are local units of government spending their money on the various functions in the same proportion today as they did 20 years ago? If not, which items are demanding relatively more of the taxpayer's dollars and which have decreased in importance?

The functional breakdown of school expenses is detailed in Table 8.28, so the following analysis will focus on city and county expenses. Tables 4.6 and 4.7 reveal some interesting cross currents in local government expense. For both cities and counties, the cost of maintaining streets, highways, and bridges has declined in constant dollars per capita. This results, in all probability, from the fact that our highway network is being used closer to its capacity than it was in 1937, the cost of maintenance probably being determined more by highway mileage use than by the number of people using the highways. For cities and counties, there has also been a decrease in the per capita carrying cost of debt, especially when deflated. This results, among other things, from the fact that, at least until recently, interest rates — especially for local governments — were one of the few prices that have not risen since the late 1930's.

If highway expenses and debt carrying costs have fallen, in a real sense, since 1937, what items have increased? For cities, the cost of general government and police and fire protection have grown almost enough to offset reductions in the other two items. For counties the biggest growth has been in the amount spent on charities and corrections. This jump, even after adjustments, is so great that by itself it accounts for virtually all the increase in the adjusted cost of local governments, other than for schools during the past two decades.

The details for these observations are shown in Tables 4.6 and 4.7. In 20 years, per capita city costs in constant dollars for general government rose $1.31 while fire and police protection increased $2.15;

---

per capita expenses were slightly greater ($60.99 vs. $59.64). This comparison really points up another factor: the annual per capita operating costs of the big cities are higher than the costs of other cities. This will be discussed in more detail later, but since it is already partly revealed by the tables and charts, it is worth noting here. Interestingly enough, though the ten largest cities had on the average higher per capita operating costs than other cities, the tendency for the ten largest counties was to have lower per capita operating costs than other counties.

Table 4.6 Functional Distribution of Operating Expenses
of California Cities -- 1937, 1947, 1957

Function	Per-Capita Costs in 1947 Dollars			Change in Per-Capita Costs 1957-1937	Percentage Distribution of Costs		
	1937	1947	1957		1937	1947	1957
General Government	$2.83	$2.90	$4.14	$+1.31	9%	10%	13%
Protection of Persons & Property	10.77	9.98	12.92	+2.15	33	36	40
Conservation of Health	.51	.53	.53	+ .02	2	2	2
Sanitation and Promotion of Cleanliness	1.62	2.01	2.39	+ .77	5	7	7
Streets	6.20	4.22	4.01	-2.19	19	15	12
Charities and Correction	.44	.20	.02	- .42	1	1	0
Education and Libraries	1.38	.99	1.19	- .19	4	3	4
Recreation	2.17	2.28	2.99	+ .82	7	8	9
Miscellaneous	1.41	2.91	2.91	+1.50	4	11	9
Interest on Debt	4.89	1.73	1.40	-3.49	15	6	4
TOTAL	$32.23	$27.75	$32.51	$+0.28	100%	100%	100%

Sources: Expenses from State Controller's Annual Reports Concerning
Financial Transactions of Cities and Counties, adjusted to eliminate
capital investments and bond redemption. Population and price index
as in previous tables and figures. The functional categories are those
used by the State Controller. San Francisco is excluded.

Table 4.7 Functional Distribution of Operating Expenses
of California Counties -- 1937, 1947, 1957

Function	Per-Capita Costs in 1947 Dollars			Change in Per-Capita Costs 1957-1937	Percentage Distribution of Costs		
	1937	1947	1957		1937	1947	1957
General Government	$5.76	$4.10	$6.07	$ +.31	17%	13%	14%
Protection to Persons and Property	3.04	2.96	3.78	+.74	9	9	9
Health and Sanitation	1.10	1.04	1.27	+.17	3	3	3
Highways and Bridges	9.80	2.85	3.08	- 1.72	14	9	7
Recreation	.44	.34	.57	+.13	1	1	1
Charities and Correction	16.72	19.93	25.58	+ 8.86	50	61	60
Miscellaneous	.56	.88	2.05	+ 1.49	2	3	5
Education	.63	.43	.48	- .15	2	1	1
Debt Interest	.52	.05	.05	+ .47	2	0	0
TOTAL	$33.57	$32.58	$42.94	+$9.37	100%	100%	100%

Sources: Same as Table 4.6.

on the other hand, a decline of $2.19 was registered for streets and $3.49 for interest on debt. When all items were included, total city costs remained almost constant, changing only from $32.23 to $32.51.

Counties experienced a similar decline in highway and debt costs ($1.72 and $0.47, respectively) while general government and fire and police protection rose ($0.31 and $0.74, respectively). Counties, however, were subject to one pressure that did not fall on city governments: the deflated per capita cost of charities and corrections rose by $8.86 during the period 1937 to 1957. When these costs are put under the microscope, as in Table 4.8, the increased expenses are seen to come almost entirely from two activites: aid to dependent children and support for the needy aged. There have also been increases in the cost of operating county hospitals, welfare administration, and probation expenses.

The essential points revealed by the analysis thus far are these: (1) in items of constant dollars, the per capita cost of local government in California has risen only slightly since 1937; (2) whatever real increase has occurred has come almost entirely from improved teachers' salaries (representing the market response to the shortage of qualified instructors) and from the greater amount spent on the needy aged, needy children, and medical care for the indigent — all of which latter functions are handled by county government.

Change in Voters' Attitudes. The foregoing analysis carries with it an important policy implication. Aside from increased teachers' pay, there is virtually no evidence that local governments in California are spending money more lavishly than they did twenty years ago, except in one area — aid to the needy, be they children, aged, or ill. Thus there is little hope in that simple solution to the problem of mounting local government expenditures for which both the naive and the cynical clamor, namely the elimination of graft and inefficiency. The only way to reduce costs substantially would be to adopt a different set of values regarding the obligation of society to help its less fortunate members. This is a matter of philosophy, not an issue of governmental efficiency. Judging from trends throughout the United States and the world, it is unlikely that the voters of California would be willing to slice the costs of local government by returning to 1937 standards for aid to the indigent. But whether this political prognosis is correct is immaterial. The important thing is to realize that this is the major issue on which people should focus their thinking if they

Table 4.8 Functional Analysis of County Expenses Connected
with Charities and Correction -- 1937 and 1957

Classification	Per Capita Costs in 1947 Dollars		Change in Per-Capita Costs	Percentage Distribution of Costs	
	1937	1957	1957-1937	1937	1957
Hospitals and Medical Care	$3.66	$4.86	$ + 1.20	22%	19%
Home for Aged	.58	.50	- .08	3	2
Welfare Administration	1.14	1.73	+ .59	7	7
Aid to Needy Children	1.02	4.19	+ 3.17	6	16
Aid to Needy Blind	.51	.69	+ .18	3	3
Aid to Needy Aged	6.24	10.98	+ 4.74	37	43
General Relief	2.57	1.08	- 1.49	15	4
Probation Expenses	.58	1.14	+ .56	3	4
State Institutional Accounts					
Correctional Charges	.07	.05	- .02		
Homes for Feeble-Minded	.20	.08	- .12	2	1
Other State Institutions	.02	.03	+ .01		
Special Welfare & Misc.	.15	.27	+ .12	1	1
TOTAL	$16.72	$25.58	$ + 8.86	100%	100%

Source: Same as tables 4.6 and 4.7

are concerned over the gradual increase in the real costs of local government: Have Californians gone too far toward the "welfare state,"
or should a prosperous society deal generously with those citizens less
capable of supporting themselves in the hope that this will improve the
health of the whole body politic?

A parallel situation exists regarding federal expenditures. Many
people feel, with some justification, that the federal government is
wasting money through inefficiency. The Hoover Commission, after
diligent combing, came up with recommendations which it claimed
would achieve savings of $2 billion annually. This amount, approximately
3 per cent of the federal budget, could be saved, they argued, simply
by better management. But the point to be stressed is this: the most
America can hope for through economies in management is trivial compared to the amount spent on national defense. The threat of war and
the prospects of peace are the vital determinants of the level of federal

expenditures, not waste and bureaucracy. A similar situation exists
for California's counties: the major determinants of expenditures are
public attitudes toward education and supporting the indigent, not slip-
shod administration.

FACTORS INFLUENCING COST OF LOCAL GOVERNMENT

Local governments are clearly spending not much more in stable
dollars per capita than they did twenty years ago, and the functions on
which they are spending more reflect the voters' values rather than
governmental inefficiency. This does not mean, however, that local
governments should not, or could not, get more service for their
money. Even the casual student of local government might well ponder
the range of per capita operating costs for cities and counties during
fiscal 1957 as revealed in Table 3.1 and 3.2. Is it possible for the
high-cost cities and counties to reduce their costs closer to the level
of their economical counterparts? One approach to this question is to
explore the factors that are associated with different levels of operating expenses per citizen. Before proceeding on this line of investigation, however, a caveat mentioned in the previous chapter needs re-
peating: the analysis that follows makes no adjustment for the fact that
different cities provide different mixtures of service.

Correlation Analysis

The most precise way to determine what factors are associated
with variation in local expenses is by correlating per capita operating
costs with a variety of factors that may influence those costs. This is
what is called correlation analysis and its virtue is that it both gives
precise numerical values for the relationships investigated and provides
a means for testing which relationships are so strong that they are not
likely to have occurred by random chance. Even so, correlation analysis has the limitation of assuming the observations being analyzed are
homogeneous and distributed in the pattern of a normal, bell-shaped
curve. This assumption is often belied to some extent by the data, including those of the present study. Consequently, such conclusions as
may be drawn are subject to qualification. Another limitation is that
correlation analysis, like any tool of statistical research, can be applied only to data that are available in quantitative form. Finally,
correlation analysis reveals only associations: causal relations must
be discerned from the logic of the situation. If as one factor changes,
another changes proportionately and systematically, the correlation is
perfect and is scored 1.0. (If the relationship is one-for-one, but the

two elements move in opposite directions, the score is -1.0). If one set of observations bears no observable relation to another set, the correlation is 0. This technique may be used to obtain evidence on such questions as: Are county and city expenses influenced by the number of residents? By the average wealth of the community? By per capita income? By the extent of industrialization?

Cities

For the purpose of analyzing municipal expenditures, operating costs per capita for 1957 were related by multiple linear correlation to three independent variables: population, assessed value per capita, and the ratio of nonretail taxable sales to all taxable sales. Because recently incorporated cities reported abnormally low operating costs (the reason appears to be that services in these cities are either limited or still being provided by the county) all cities incorporated since 1952 were eliminated.

For the 303 cities analyzed, the relation between per capita operating costs and the variables indicated is summarized by a multiple correlation coefficient of .77, a statistically significant figure. It means that about 60% of the variance in per capita costs can be explained by the combined independent variables. Another measure of the relation between cost per capita and the associated variables lies in the fact that the actual expenditures of approximately two-thirds of the cities fall within $9.99 of the amount estimated for them by the equation discovered through multiple regression analysis.

Some of the questions that prompted the multiple regression analysis were these: Did the per capita cost of cities rise or fall as the city population increased? Did industrialization increase municipal costs? Do cities that have higher average assessed value or taxable sales spend more? The analysis showed that municipal costs were most closely related to assessed value per capita: this factor was approximately six times as dominant as the second most important factor, retail sales per capita.

The index of industrialization, interestingly enough, showed a slightly negative relation to operating costs, i.e., increasing industrialization was generally associated with lower costs. As the population of cities increased, per capita operating costs also rose very slightly. The coefficients of multiple regression were all found to be statistically significant. (A detailed analysis of the results for cities and counties may be found at the end of this chapter.)

Other Studies of Cities Show Similar Results

The findings of the present analysis of municipal operating costs are reinforced, incidentally, by the results of three similar studies. In 1957 Stanley Scott and Edward L. Feder analyzed per capita expenditures for 196 California cities with more than 2,500 population.[1] Using expenditures for 1950, a census year, they were able to obtain quantitative data on many more variables; consequently, they tested the relations between per capita municipal expenditures and 12 factors: population, retail sales per capita, population density, number of persons per dwelling unit, population growth during the previous decade, assessed value per capita, median family income, median monthly rent, per cent of labor force engaged in manufacturing, labor force as a percentage of total population, median value of one-dwelling structures, and distance from nearest metropolitan center.

Preliminary investigation indicated that only the first six factors had enough bearing on municipal expenditures to warrant the labor involved in linear and curvilinear multiple correlation analysis. The Scott-Feder study differed in several aspects from the present one: capital expenditures were not separated from current expenses; assessed value was slightly adjusted; both the list of cities and the operating period studied were different; and somewhat different variables were used. Yet the results were strikingly similar. Both studies found that per capita property value was by far the most important determinant of municipal expenditures, accounting for nearly 80% of the explained variation. Per capita retail sales constituted the next most important factor. The others were either of limited or of no value at all.

Though the influence of population was found to be negligible in both studies, it was in each case shown to be positively correlated with city costs. This fact is of considerable interest. Until fairly recently it has often been assumed that large cities would achieve "economies of scale" by spreading the overhead of municipal administration among more people and also by using efficient record-keeping machines that would not be feasible for small cities. The evidence, however, suggests that the costs of metropolitanism largely offset the administrative gains to be found in larger units.

The statistical evidence that city costs rise slightly (or at least do not fall) as city size increases is also supported by Lyle C. Fitch in a recent report entitled "Metropolitan Financial Problems."[3]

Results of two recent, as yet unpublished, studies indicate
that the unit costs of government services may be less affected by
the scale of operations than has been popularly supposed. Harvey
Brazer's study (sponsored by the National Bureau of Economic
Research) of general government expenditures in larger cities
(over 25,000) in 1950 finds little correlation between per capita
costs of local government functions and city size. Werner Hirsch's
study of municipal expenditures in St. Louis County, for the
St. Louis Metropolitan Survey, shows similar results for some
80 municipalities, most of them under 25,000 population.

Despite the statistical results of these four studies, it would be
incorrect to conclude there are no economies of scale in municipal
government. The explanation lies in the fact that urban services, the
quality of which is almost unmeasurable, may be better in larger cities.
If such is actually the case, the residents of such cities must receive
better service for virtually no extra cost. This would clearly add up to
economies of scale. As indicated before, however, there is little that
can be said for sure about the quality of municipal government, with
the possible exception of fire protection. Judged by this limited criterion, the larger the city the better the service. The Municipal Year
Book for 1957 shows the following information. (See Table 4.9.)

Table 4.9 Quality of Fire Protection by City Size
1957

City Population	Median Number of Building Fires per 1000 Population	Modal Fire Insurance Classification*
Over 500,000	3.0	2
250 - 500,000	3.5	3
100 - 250,000	3.5	3
50 - 100,000	3.7	3
25 - 50,000	3.7	4
10 - 25,000	Not Available	6

*Lower classification represents less fire hazard

Source: The Municipal Year Book, 1957

The fire insurance classification, determined by the National
Board of Fire Underwriters, reflects an evaluation of the over-all
fire hazard. Regarding fire departments alone, 61% of the cities over
25,000 were in classes 3, 4, or 5. Among cities between 10,000 and
25,000 only 26% had fire departments classified as high as 3, 4 or 5.
Since fire protection is only one of many municipal responsibilities,
however, it would be unwarranted to conclude that larger cities provide, in toto better service than small cities. The data regarding fire

protection simply illustrate the caution that must be applied to most
analyses of government expenditures. Until a better way is found to
measure the quality of government service, it may be assumed that
there is little if any reduction in per capita costs as city size increases.

Counties

A similar multiple regression analysis was made for counties.
Because more statistical data exist for counties than for cities, this
analysis related seven independent variables to 1957 per capita operating costs for 57 counties, all except San Francisco. These were considered to have a possible bearing on per capita county expenses: population, assessed value per capita, average personal income for 1957,
percentage of county population living outside incorporated cities,
ratio of manufacturing wages to personal income, the density of population per square mile, and retail sales per capita.

As with cities, a fairly high multiple correlation coefficient (.79)
was found and it was statistically significant. This means that 63% of
the variation in county costs was explainable in terms of these variables.
Actually, only three of the seven were closely enough related to county
costs to be statistically significant, and only two of these were important in determining county expenses. About 60% of the explained variation in county operating costs could be related to per capita assessed
value. About 37% was associated with the percentage of population residing outside incorporated areas. The only other significant factor
was the volume of taxable sales per capita, and this, surprisingly, had
a negative correlation: the higher the volume, the lower the cost per
capita of county government.

The standard error of estimate was $22.03, which means that
approximately two-thirds of the actual per capita costs would be expected to fall within $22.00 of the amount estimated for them by the
multiple regression equation. (A detailed statement of the results is
included in the appendix to this chapter.) So far as is known, this is
the first time a multiple regression analysis of county operating costs
has been made so there are no other studies by which the results of
this one may be either confirmed or challenged.

Interpreting Relationships

Comparing the correlation analysis for counties and cities is revealing. In both cases, assessed value per capita is the factor most
closely associated with per capita operating costs. For cities, taxable
sales are the next most closely associated characteristic; though for

counties, this relation is slightly negative. For neither cities nor counties does size of population or degree of industrialization appear to be influential in determining the level of operating costs. It is interesting to speculate on the significance of these differences and similarities. The economic characteristics that appear to have the most influence on operating costs of local governments in California are clearly those connected with availability of revenue. As shown in Tables 5.7 and 5.8, during fiscal 1957, counties received only 38.6% of their revenue from the property tax, none from sales tax, and 46.4% through grants or shared revenue, mostly from the state. Cities, however, received 40.3% of their income from the property tax and 19.8% from the sales tax; only 17.6% came from the state or federal government. The most likely interpretation is this: because assessed valuation and retail sales play a much more significant revenue role for cities than for counties, they are more important in determining the operating expenses of cities.

Are Government Expenditures Determined by Need or Availability of Funds?

In theory, high per capita assessed valuation should have little influence on expenditures for the actual taxes collected are determined by assessed valuations multiplied by the tax rate. But the evidence given above obliges one to ask: Why is it that cities, counties, and school districts seem to spend primarily in relation to their ability to get funds?

The answer probably lies in the fact that the needs for local government services, like the demands on the householder's budget, are expansible. The ordinary consumer spends about 90 cents of every extra dollar he receives; as his income rises he finds his needs expanding. Thus, it is not unreasonable to expect local governments to behave in a similar fashion: if more money is available they find they need another park, or better streets, or more police protection. And this will be especially true when, as explained in the previous chapter, the scales for evaluating outlays are anything but precise.

Local governments should, therefore, be extra careful to justify their expenditures on the basis of service provided. More so than agencies in the private sector, governmental units have an obligation to show that they are using their funds in efficient and useful ways, and not spending simply because the money is available. Among other things this means (1) that a much better system of governmental record-keeping, more like performance or managerial accounting instead of the present fund accounting, is required to provide a check on the efficiency of government units, and (2) that citizens need to realize the proper amount of governmental expenditures can never be determined by any automatic governing device such as the struggle for profit or the risk of bankruptcy that faces a private concern. Their only safeguard lies in maintaining a constant interest in the affairs of government in order to see that expenditures are justified both by need and by services actually rendered.

Determinants of Capital Investment

Thus far, this analysis has explored solely the factors associated with operating costs. Yet capital outlays represented 12% of county and 20% of city expenditures in 1957. What light can be cast on the factors that explain capital investment in our local governments?

A reasonable a priori assumption is that capital investment is most closely related to population growth. As a gross check on this assumption, the data for the ten largest counties and cities during the past 11 years were examined. The counties were ranked by two criteria: the amount spent per capita on capital investment from 1947 to 1957, and the percentage of population growth during the period. The two rankings were correlated and it was discovered that there was a negative relation: $(r = -.09)$. The ten largest cities were also ranked in order of capital investment per capita and percentage growth in population during the 11 years. For them the correlation between the two factors was positive $(.52)$.

Admittedly, rank correlation is a crude measure of relationship. Ten is a small number of observations, the relationship was not very close, and it may not be the best test to compare capital expenditures over 11 years against growth in population for the same period. Perhaps a shorter period should have been used — but the results suggest two things: (a) the relationship between capital expenditures and population growth is not as definite as might be assumed, and (b) cities, being able to finance capital investments by bond issues, did so during the period 1947-57 as the pressure of population growth required, but counties (which in California float almost no bonds) were not able to respond to those pressures so easily. Both these observations are consistent with the previous hypothesis that revenue capacity comprises the major determinant of local expenditures.

San Francisco City-County

Because the City-County of San Francisco is unique among California local governments and there is no accurate way of allocating costs between the city and the county portion of this Siamese-twin government, it has been excluded from all the foregoing city or county analyses. However, there is one approach that would seem to make comparisons between San Francisco and other local governments possible. This calls for treating other counties as if they were one large city-county unit: add the operating expenses for all cities within its borders to the county costs and divide the sum by the county's population. The result should give per capita operating cost of all municipal and county functions in the county. That figure would seem directly comparable to the per capita operating cost of the government of San Francisco.

For this purpose San Francisco was matched against the four adjacent counties that are most heavily urbanized. Then, because central cities may experience certain costs that urbanized, but noncentral, local governments can avoid, Los Angeles County was also treated as a city-county and its consolidated per capita costs were included in the table. Finally, since the multiple regression analysis showed that both city and county operating costs were most closely related to assessed value per capita, this figure was also included. (See Table 4.10.)

Table 4.10 San Francisco City-County Per Capita Operating Costs
Compared to Per Capita Costs for Five Combined
County-City "Governments": 1957

	Assessed Value [1] Per Capita	City-County [2] Costs Per Capita	City-County [3] + Special District Costs Per Capita
San Francisco	$1675	$148.28	$150.10
Alameda	1434	112.22	127.57
Contra Costa	2005	95.59	115.40
Los Angeles	1792	105.56	112.69
San Mateo	1716	76.58	95.54
Santa Clara	1702	89.94	93.99

[1] Total assessed valuation divided by county population.

[2] Summation of county and city operating expenses divided by county population.

[3] Same as 2 with special district expenses added.

The results show that San Francisco's per capita operating costs are higher by a considerable margin than those of any of its five simulated counterparts, even though four of the comparative units had higher assessed value per capita. There remains the possibility, however, that this difference may be more apparent than real because the artificially constructed counterparts might have chosen to perform more of their local functions through special districts than was the case for San Francisco. Consequently, all special-district (other than school-district) operating costs for the six counties were added and divided by total county population. The result still showed San Francisco's per capita costs to be the highest by a wide margin.

Two hypotheses are suggested by this result (though unfortunately the statistical analysis is not discriminating enough to show which has the greater merit): (1) Where city and county boundaries completely overlap, the consolidated city-county form of government causes an expensive duplication of services. (2) The cost of metropolitan government is greatly influenced by what might be called the "degree of compactness" or, in other words, by the ratio of total metropolitan population served to the population of the central city. The Los Angeles metropolitan region is larger than the San Francisco region, but San Francisco City-County is a much smaller portion of its region than Los Angeles County is of its region. According to the second hypothesis, San Francisco would be expected to have higher costs than Los Angeles because it comprises a smaller portion of the metropolitan region which it serves as a central city.

PROSPECTIVE EXPENDITURES, 1965

Having reviewed the history of local finance in California and compared the costs and other characteristics of different cities and counties for the year 1957, it is provocative to speculate about the prospects for the not too distant future, say 1965.

Underlying Assumptions. Obviously, any estimate of this type can be no better than the assumptions underlying it. Let us suppose:

1. The operating costs of counties will remain close to the present level of 2.6% of personal income.

2. The costs of running schools will rise from their current 2.8% of income to approximately 3.3%. This increase is based on the belief that as a society prospers it will choose to devote relatively more of its income to education, and also that by 1965 there will be a greater proportion of students in high school and junior college (which cost more than elementary grades) than at present.

3. City operating expenses will remain constant when adjusted for growth in population and changes in the value of the dollar. Furthermore, total city population will constitute approximately 72% of the state's population.

4. Special districts other than schools will have operating costs approximately 7% as large as those for schools, counties and cities combined.

5. Between 1957 and 1965 the prices of things that Californians, particularly their local governments, buy will rise at the rate of 4% a year. (This is somewhat less than the rate of inflation the local governments have had to contend with during the past decade.)

6. Between 1957 and 1965, real income (i.e., income in constant dollars) will rise by 3% per year.

7. Capital investment for all levels of local government will average 20% of operating expenses — in comparison to the 25% in 1957.

8. California's population will be 17.5 million in 1965. (The best estimates range from 16.3 to 19.6 million.)

These assumptions, which seem reasonable in light of past trends, produce a forecast that the total cost of California local government by 1965 will exceed $7 billion. The amounts in each category are indicated in Table 4.11 but each is subject to a margin of error approximating 25%. In other words, one can expect that by 1965 California's local governments will be spending, in 1965 dollars, somewhere between $5-1/4 and $8-3/4 billion. This compares with total local government expenditures in California during 1957 of approximately $3 billion.

Table 4.11 Prospective Local Expenditures in California: 1965

	Operating Expenses	Capital Investment	Total
Schools	$2,581,250,000	$516,250,000	$3,097,500,000
Counties	2,033,713,000	406,742,000	2,440,455,000
Cities	866,375,000	173,270,000	1,039,645,000
Other Districts	383,692,000	76,738,000	460,430,000
Total (in 1965 dollars)	5,865,030,000	1,173,000,000	7,038,030,000
Total (in 1957 dollars)	4,281,046,000	856,204,000	5,137,351,000

Independent Estimate of County Capital Outlays. The deductive estimate given above can be checked in one category, county capital expenditures, by summing the data that have been prepared for various legislative committees. Early in 1957, the Senate Interim Committee on Public Works reviewed the building-construction programs of all California counties for the five-year period, October 1956 to October 1961 and concluded that county needs for capital improvements during this period, excluding roads, would be as shown on page 110.

Meanwhile, the Joint Interim Committee on Transportation Problems, presented to the Legislature on June 12, 1957, its estimate of the county road and city street deficiencies as of October 1956. Its study noted increasing pressure on our highways as revealed by the

42% increase in population during the previous decade and the even
more impressive 99% increase in motor vehicle registrations as of
1956 compared to 10 years earlier (3.53 million then, 7.03 million in
1956). They concluded that 17,900 miles, or 26% of total county road
mileage, were deficient as of the end of 1956, that 2,586 bridges were
inadequate, and that a total investment of $812 million would be neces-
sary to bring county highways up to the standard needed for present
traffic. For the cities, 5,700 miles, or 22% of the total city street
system was deficient, nearly 1,200 bridges or culverts needed to be
built or improved, and 374 grade separations were required, all of
which would cost approximately $1 billion.

	$ (millions)
General government buildings	
(e.g., courthouses, office buildings)	146
Detention facilities	54
Health and welfare facilities	
(e.g., hospitals, nurses' homes, etc.)	124
Garages	4
Recreational facilities	68
Airport facilities	13
Fire stations	1
Miscellaneous	2
Total $	413

The Committee also compared the total cost of estimated deficiencies as of October 1956 with the situation revealed by the previous
state-wide survey made in 1954. Though the counties and cities spent
almost $200 million annually on roads and streets during those two
years, the backlog of need actually increased. A report in August 1957
told the same kind of a story: the county road commissioners, reporting to the State Division of Highways in compliance with the Federal
Highway Act, urged that the mileage of county-maintained roads should
be increased from 67,000 to 96,000 by 1971 and said the total investment needed over the next 15 years for improving county roads sufficiently to handle 1971 traffic would be $9.4 billion. Still another esti-
mate of highway needs was made in August 1958: the State Division of
Highways presented to the Joint Legislative Committee on Highways a
report visualizing by 1990 a 12,241 mile network of freeways linking
every California city of a population of 5,000 or more that would require an investment of $10.5 billion.

Highway planners, like business planners and private families,
are, of course, fallible in their forecasts. Their estimates, therefore,

can be taken with a grain or two of caution. But it would be rash to assume that their estimates of need are biased on the grandiose side.
Who, for example, would claim that the highway engineers who planned
the principal (Spring Street) underpass of the Los Angeles freeway system have overbuilt? Demand far exceeds capacity at that point, resulting in traffic jams of monumental size, especially around 8 A.M. and
5 P.M. Therefore, one can assume that while the above statements of
future highway needs are not precise, they are as likely to underestimate as to overestimate the expenditures that will be required.

These statements of need provide a rough check on the estimate
for county capital expenditures in 1965. If the $413 million projected
for county capital investment other than roads from 1956 to 1961 is
converted to an annual rate, it amounts to approximately $80 million
a year at 1957 prices. If the counties were to spend $9.4 billion (not
the highest estimate) on highways and bridges in the 15 years between
1956 and 1971, this would amount to an annual rate of $620 million.
The sum of these annual estimates for county capital outlay is $700
million compared to the deduced estimate of $400 million for 1965.
This independent check on one aspect of the problem suggests that
the forecast that total local expenditures will reach an annual rate of
$7 billion by 1965 is on the low rather than the high side.

MEASURES FOR INCREASING EFFICIENCY

In any event, the figure will be large enough to demand serious
thought: How can local governments operate more efficiently, reducing
costs without reducing service?

Though the theory of public finance shows that the mechanism of
government does not insure a rigorously adequate answer to the question of how much the government should spend, or how much it should
allocate to various functions, this should not be interpreted as meaning
that there is no basis for applying sound management principles to government operations — the lack of any market place testing — means
that there be even more room to improve the efficiency of performance
in government operations than in the business sector. The available
evidence — e.g., the case study of garbage, police, and fire services
in the City of Berkeley mentioned above and the various time series
analyses adjusted for inflation and population changes as cited earlier
in this chapter — suggests that government service is scarcely more
efficient than it was 20 years ago. This fact supports the belief that
there may be more opportunity to increase efficiency in government

than in business for the private economy has averaged an increase in
real income of approximately 3% per year.

Thus, it is not enough for local government to be performing the
same job at the same real cost that it did twenty years ago; if living
standards are to be raised, both the public and the private sectors of
the economy must become increasingly efficient. Because there is no
precise way to measure the quality of government service, because
government does not have to meet the operational test of survival in
the market place, and because many citizens suspect that government
is inefficient, government officials at all levels should strive vigor-
ously to provide conclusive, convincing, and dramatic evidence that
public employees are just as devoted, just as hard-working, and just
as ingenious at finding better ways to do their jobs as profit- or wage-
motivated private businessmen are.

Better Accounting Methods

Understandably, there are considerable political pressures in
government that may militate against efficiency. The most devoted and
economical public official will achieve little if he cannot be re-elected,
and victory at the polls may require a more liberal attitude vis-à-vis
the public exchequer than a private firm would tolerate. However,
many students of government management, especially at the state and
local levels, have been struck by the archaic quality of government
record-keeping. Probably the most important tool in modern scientific
business management is the use of operating reports to increase management efficiency. This is reflected especially in the evolution of
accounting. Accounting was once largely a matter of providing safeguards for managing cash and property; it was a device to prevent and
to double check the prevention of embezzlement and theft. Gradually,
in response to demands of modern business management, accounting
has developed into the much broader concept of managerial accounting.
Today it provides management with data on the efficiency of each operation. Cost accounting — with its emphasis on standards and complete
reporting of any variations from these standards — is a vital tool in
management control.

If private business has found it necessary to get increasingly more
and better information from its controller's department for greater
efficiency, how can government administrators hope to become more
efficient when the type of information that flows through a modern accounting system is not available to them? Consider the following ex-

amples of how accounting in California's local governments fails to provide the information necessary for efficient management. Would a businessman be content to count as his income or expenses in a certain period the inflows and outflows of cash? Certainly not. He would realize that some income is earned and some expenses are incurred in adjoining periods but the transfer of cash may be advanced or deferred without regard to the time when the income and the expenses are incurred. Yet the vast majority of California's local governments keep their records on a cash, not an accrual, basis.

Would a businessman consider that he had balanced his budget (or in business terminology "broken even") if he neglected to consider the depreciation on his capital investment? No. But governmental accounting never includes depreciation. Consider how difficult it would be for a business manager to make performance comparisons over different periods of time if his accounting system lumped operating expenses with capital investments. Yet municipal and county accounting treats all cash outflows in the same way. Essentially, government accounting is fund accounting, that is, keeping records of cash outflows. It focuses on the prevention of embezzlement. Accounting as practiced in local governments, not only in California but almost everywhere, has not yet embraced the concepts of managerial accounting. The improvements in accounting records recommended by the League of California Cities and the California Society of Certified Public Accountants in March 1956, June 1957 and September 1958 — entitled, respectively, Checklist for the Audit of Financial Records for a California City, Chart of Accounts for California Cities, and Typical Financial Statement for California Cities — are all to the good. They recommend standardization of municipal accounting and would thereby provide more information on which intercity comparisons might be made, but they do not go nearly far enough.

Accounting has become, in the best operated business firms, far more than a double check against embezzlement or a technique for recording stockholders' equities. It helps management to know how the various departments operate and when and where the firm is ahead or behind its targets. Fund accounting, which is the heart of local government record-keeping, provides city managers, county administrative officers, hospital managers, and other executives with virtually no assistance in this respect.

It is easier, however, to point out that governmental accounting provides little basis for measuring efficiency than it is to show how the accounting methods of public agencies should be changed. This latter problem calls for a book in itself — a book that, unfortunately, must still be written. But at least it is possible to indicate some of the directions governmental accounting must take if it is to advance from its present role as a recorder of funds to become a stimulant to greater efficiency. Just as a business firm may have standard costs for every manufacturing operation, and also for many sales or administrative functions, so a city or county should have standards for such activities as garbage collection, hospital operation, and road maintenance. No special study should be needed to find out whether the City of Berkeley is handling its garbage as efficiently today as it did twenty years ago. Every city that collects garbage should have a standard cost for garbage ton-miles hauled, or garbage collections made, so that it could tell at any time whether this function is being performed as well as in the past and whether new methods would improve efficiency. This could also provide bench marks for intracity or -county comparisons that would be stepping stones to increased effectiveness.

Fortunately, many local government officials in California are interested in better data for accounting and reporting and are taking steps in this direction. Here, for instance, is an excerpt from the Alameda County Administrator's budget message, May 1956:

> Workload Measurements: Various kinds of measurements are needed for management purposes — for management improvement in general, for performance budgeting, for program planning, work scheduling, manpower programing, employee motivation, and for accounting and cost control. One kind of measurement that can contribute to all of these purposes and at all levels of county government is work measurement. Work measurement is a method of establishing an equitable relationship between the volume of work performed and the manpower utilized in completing that volume. It will be obvious to your Board that this budget message contains the beginnings of a work measurement program. This will be a matter of continuing study and refinement as time goes on.

Similarly, the county executive of Ventura County stated in his budget report for 1958-59:

> We are pleased to be able to offer more and more departmental workload data each successive year; thus we are approaching the day when we may give greater emphasis to performance budgeting. The term means different things to different people but essentially it is a program of budgeting on the basis of the amount of work to be done. . . . Such projections cannot be made until the work performed is measured in basic and comprehensive units.

New York is also trying to move in this direction as a result of the studies of its Temporary Commission on the Fiscal Affairs of State

Government.[4] The results were published in two volumes in February 1955, under the title A Program for Continued Progress in Fiscal Management. As one part of its study the Commission investigated the possibility of improving governmental accounting, budgeting, and reporting:

> The preparation of a budget depends for its success on how well the accounting system provides the data on costs and expenditures that have to be used as "building blocks." Planning, control, and appraisal — key functions of budgeting — cannot be fully effective unless a system of operational reports provides the administrator with the information he needs.

The Commission observed that the system of accounting used by local governments in New York in 1955 had been installed in 1935 and acknowledged that while it prevented fraud or embezzlement, it did not "provide cost information in a form that is most useful in planning and controlling the many functions undertaken by the state." To show that governmental accounting could be improved, the Commission installed a system of "program accounting" at a state hospital and in a county health department. On the basis of a pilot study of the new system operating in these two agencies, it concluded:

> The program accounting system has proved to be inexpensive to install and operate . . . the system appears to be generally applicable within the state government. . . [it] retains the advantages of the present system and supplements it with unit costs, costs of activities, and costs of programs. In addition, it relates all these financial terms to work produced and activities performed, programs achieved, and, ultimately, services to the public.

The program accounting system adopted in New York relies heavily on techniques developed in industrial cost accounting. Among these are a separation of costs into fixed and variable components and the establishment of standards supplemented by variance analysis to explain any differences between standard and actual costs. It was found that program accounting not only aided the departmental management in controlling costs but it also provided an excellent basis for budgeting future needs and for reporting past performance. The Health Commissioner of the county where the program accounting system was initially installed said that for the first time he "now knows the actual costs of programs and work units under his jurisdiction."

This hasty review of the accounting procedures tried on a limited basis in New York during 1955 does not mean that California local governments should immediately copy the New York accounting system, but it does show that others are also concerned with the inadequacy of governmental accounting and that improved accounting techniques applicable to local government can be developed. It is of the highest priority, if local expenditures are to be intelligently controlled, that California's local governments take steps to adopt accounting procedures similar to those now being introduced in New York.

Cooperation and Consolidation

Improving the municipal accounting techniques is not only one of the most important steps to be taken in achieving greater efficiency, it is also one of the few steps that is not directly linked with politics. There are many other actions that California local governments could take to lower the cost of public service, but virtually all of them impinge on politics or local independence. Yet if the pressure for efficiency grows great enough, even problems closely linked with politics may be tackled.

Elimination of Duplicate Assessments. Many of the steps toward greater efficiency that could be taken by local governments can be described by one general phrase — consolidation of overlapping functions. Consider this example: it is obviously inefficient for cities and counties to assess the same property separately. In 30 of the 50 states there is no overlapping assessment between counties and cities, but in 1956 some 128 California cities out of 325 prepared their own property tax rolls instead of having the county extend city taxes on its rolls. This means that thousands of dollars are being spent by local governments in California to have two different values placed on the same property. Separate valuation by cities, it has been claimed, continues primarily because a city feels that the legal debt or tax limit that would result from accepting county valuations would be too low. To the extent this is true it points up one of the many inefficient results that flow from the essentially irrational nature of the property tax. The tax-rate ceiling justification did not apply, however, to 65 California cities that were, at least nominally, doing their own assessing, according to a cumbersome and expensive operation. In 1955, 58% of the cities theoretically doing their own assessing simply asked the county to supply them with a copy of the relevant portion of the county tax roll. This was then multiplied by some factor to push the valuation high enough to allow the city tax rate of $1 (or whatever the city's statutory or traditional tax limit was) to provide the funds necesary for the city budget. But even this modified form of assessment involved the city in all the problems of collecting and recording taxes, plus some clerical work in billing. For example, suppose a city has an 80 cent tax rate. From a homeowner whose property was assessed at $2,500 (this would probably mean the market value was slightly over $10,000), the tax collection would be $20. It will be necessary for a city that does its own assessing, even in name only, to enter this assessment on its own city-prepared roll, extend the tax, type the tax bill, insert it in an envelope, stamp and mail it, account for the receipt of the tax payments, and follow up on delinquent taxes. All this processing will almost certainly cost the city from $1 to $2 in clerical and office costs. The county would merely need to add the 80 cent city rate to the county and school district rates applicable to the property, extend the total tax as a single lump sum, collect the taxes of the three governmental units as a single amount, and separate out the city tax by a single multiplication of the total amount of tax paid in a given period of time by all persons owning property in the city. For these relatively inexpensive county activities, the city would be charged not more than 20 cents for the tax bill used in this example, which represents a saving of 50-90%. The higher percentage saving described in this theoretical example is very close to the amount found in some actual studies conducted by the State Board of Equalization in 1955. Eighteen cities that transferred their tax administration to the respective counties in recent years listed their estimated annual cost for self-assessing versus the cost of county assessment. The average percentage saving was 83%. Here are some selected examples:

City	1st Year of County Assessment	Est. Annual Cost Prior to Transfer	Actual Cost in 1954-1955	Estimated Annual Savings	Percentage Savings
Anaheim	1951	$ 7,377	$ 1,266	$ 6,111	83%
Azusa	1950	4,000	904	3,096	78
Carmel	1949	3,169 *	430	2,739	86
Chula Vista	1953	5,000 *	1,434	3,566	71
Hayward	1950	17,150	1,564	15,586	91
Salinas	1951	5,000	2,171	2,829	57

*Cost of collection only

For cities that are larger than those shown above, the cost savings naturally are larger (and the cost estimates are probably more accurate). For example, in 1954, Stockton made a study that showed it was spending nearly $78,000 for self-assessing against $12,570 that it would cost to have the county do it. And in 1955, Long Beach spent $224,000 for self-assessing, a job that would have been done by the county for $15,000.

Consolidation of Health, Personnel, Fire and Police Services. Whereas most cities accept the wisdom of using county facilities for assessment, they seem less willing to use county services for many other functions. Eleven cities in California operate their own health departments even though substantial economies could be achieved by having all health services handled by the county. In July 1957, the Ontario Health Department was abolished after 50 years of operation on the basis of a contract for health services with San Bernardino County as reported in the Pomona Progress-Bulletin for July 2:

> The motion for abolishment came from Councilman Mike Kelber. It carried 4 to 1 with Councilman C. E. Petersen dissenting.
>
> Kelber said his move was one of economy, since it would cut about $30,000 from city costs. Kelber argued that Ontario taxpayers helped support the county health department but received no services.

Burbank made a similar decision effective September 15, 1958. On the recommendation of City Manager Herman R. Bennett, the functions of the health department (and four employees) were transferred by contract to Los Angeles County. Burbank had formed its health department in 1946 to enforce city health ordinances. Thereafter various health regulations were enforced by both city and county officials. The decision to use the county's facilities arose from the belief that a more uniform enforcement of health codes would result and the duplication of services would be eliminated.

If many cities have found it efficient to use county assessment and health facilities, why don't all cities follow this procedure? Are there other ways in which well-planned consolidation of services would benefit both cities and counties? The recruitment and selection of good personnel is difficult under the best of circumstances, yet few cities are large enough to put personnel selection and training on any but a haphazard basis. However, by contracting with the county, cities could (and nearly a dozen do) utilize a skilled personnel department to assist in screening potential employees. This is especially important where civil-service-type employment rules make it difficult to fire employees, once hired, for anything less than gross dereliction.

Most of the expense of operating fire departments is connected with "stand-by time." If the city is to have any fire department at all, most of the costs are incurred whether they fight one fire a day or one a year. By more extensive use of agreements to share fire-fighting facilities between cities and the county, or across city boundaries, increased fire protection could be obtained with no additional equipment and expense, in fact, probably less. To a lesser extent, the sharing of radio communication equipment by neighboring towns and the coordination of county and city traffic patrols illustrate ways by which police efficiency and cooperation might be improved. Similar possibilities of cooperation exist in the field of education.

Two basic difficulties must be faced, however, by anyone advocating greater intergovernmental consolidation. The first is the fact that areas differ in per capita wealth or income. This means that the organization of territory in larger units has the effect of sharing wealth or, depending on one's point of view, of sharing poverty. Areas with greater than average wealth contribute more than their per capita share in taxes while areas of less than average wealth reap corresponding benefits. It is only when the efficiency and economy of a service are sufficiently increased by larger-scale operations that the wealthier components of the combination benefit too. This is one reason why functional consolidation comes slowly. This difficulty, however, does not apply when only cooperation between governmental units is involved. Another reason is the desire of people to keep government responsive and local in nature. Taxpayers may be willing to pay more for service just to have it close and presumably more responsive to their requests.

Can a small city enjoy home rule and still avoid the inefficiencies and handicaps that a small operation often entails? Mr. Richard Winter, Director of Local Activities for the California Taxpayers Association, examined this question with respect to police service in a speech to the metropolitan governments symposium in April 1958:

> The question "why 61 chiefs of police in Los Angeles County today?" has been frequently and eloquently raised by ardent advocates of functional consolidation. Over many years, studies and plans have pointed out the goal of a large and efficient police force coordinated in all parts of the county. [Since] crime is no respecter of municipal boundary lines, [cannot] some way be devised to gain at least some of the advantages of the big police force and at the same time preserve the cherished values of home rule? [Why not combine the] 61 chiefs of police and the home control that goes with them [with] a central records bureau so that every police department has the advantage of broad knowledge? . . . Central crime laboratories, . . . homicide investigators, and other experts [should be] available to help the smaller departments meet the technical sides of their problems. In all probability for economy reasons, we would need to contemplate centralized incarceration of all sentenced prisoners. Further, some official, perhaps from a State level, should have the authority and the responsibility to insist on minimum standards for police personnel

such as are now required for professional workers in county welfare departments.

Pooled Funds. Since cities and counties receive property tax
payments twice a year and sales tax payments quarterly but incur expenses at a generally uniform rate during the year, there is an understandable tendency to build cash reserves large enough to meet the
unforeseen needs that may occur between receipts of revenue. This
practice is augmented by the custom of meeting different expenses
from funds that are separately earmarked, e.g., street improvements
paid out of a street fund, or park expenses from a recreation fund.

Though the saving and the carrying cost of money would not be
large compared to expenditures, even small savings should be actively
sought. The following item from the Berkeley Gazette, October 29,
1958, illustrates the problem when each individual city has to maintain
separate funds where temporary surpluses and deficits might counterbalance each other.

> Contra Costa County has been forced into a deficit finance
> system for the first time in 17 years, it was reported today by
> the county Board of Supervisors.
>
> The supervisors announced that the county has sold
> $5,000,000 in tax anticipation notes to finance the county gov-
> ernments for 51 days until new tax receipts begin to roll in.
>
> The notes went to the Bank of America National Trust and
> Savings Association at an annual interest rate of 1.9558%, low-
> est of three bids submitted. The loan will cost the county
> $13,664 for the seven-plus week period.
>
> The county has a bank balance of $40,000,000, according
> to County Auditor Eugene V. Waring, but the money is earmarked
> for special use.

Contracting for Services. Contracting for services offers another
possibility for significant reductions in cost. Speaking recently before
a sub-committee of the Assembly Interim Committee on Municipal and
County Government, John Leach, Assistant Administrative Officer of
Los Angeles County, summarized the services that huge county was
then providing under contract:

> As of 1956, Los Angeles County assessed property and
> collected taxes for 46 of the 48 municipalities within its boun-
> daries; performed health services for 43 cities; recruited and
> examined personnel for 16 municipalities through the county
> Civil Service Commission; provided prisoner service for 36
> municipalities; and performed building inspection service for
> 8 cities.
>
> For Lakewood, a city of nearly 80,000, the county per-
> forms virtually all the municipal functions. Lakewood has ten

five-year contracts with the county to perform 16 services. The contracts are made on a cost basis, computed by the county auditor. All costs, both direct and indirect, are computed in the contract price and both parties are satisifed with the prices.

Later the committee concluded that water supply, sanitation, health service, training of firemen and policemen, and centralized purchasing of supplies and equipment were functions particularly adaptable to consolidation or contractual arrangements.

Cooperative Purchasing. Centralized purchasing procedures offer another effective means of enlarging the buying power of the tax dollar. By eliminating duplication of materials and personnel and by securing the economies of quantity prices, pooled purchasing could significantly benefit local governments in California. Joint buying is common in industry: large corporations typically centralize their purchasing for separate plants, and unrelated firms even create organizations, like the Independent Grocers of America, to centralize purchasing for small, independent, retail outlets. Higher standards of service at lower costs have resulted from intergovernmental cooperation in many fields but few positive achievements have yet been recorded in the field of cooperative public purchasing. This is partly because governmental buying is hedged by prescribed rules and procedures; however, legislative action could surmount this hurdle. Probably one of the simplest steps the state could take to help local governments cut their costs would be that proposed by Assemblyman Ronald E. Cameron of Whittier as reported in the Sacramento Bee, February 9, 1959. Under his plan, bids for supplies sent out by state purchasing agents would contain this provision: "It is understood and agreed that in addition to state agencies, political subdivisions or districts therein may also participate in this contract."

In Cincinnati, the city, the county, and the Board of Education experimented in 1931 by combining coal purchases. The savings on the first order amounted to $50,000. Subsequently, these three units of local government have continued pooled purchasing and extended it to other commodities. In Milwaukee, the city, county, schools, and sewage commission likewise have a pooled buying arrangement: the agencies can buy directly from a vendor or through the City of Milwaukee, whichever is more advantageous. The estimated annual savings exceed $100,000. In Seattle, the school district, county, hospital system, Port of Seattle, and Housing Authority can all participate with the city in contracts. In 1930, six cities in Michigan pooled their fire-hose

requirements and purchased 5,200 feet of hose through their joint organization, the municipal purchasing service, at 64 cents per foot.
This was less than half the average price being paid for fire hose of
similar size by other Michigan cities. By 1950, over 100 cities had
joined the service, and the same technique had spread to Montana where
many cities were pooling their purchase of fire hose.

Joint Planning. Local governments, by their very independence,
often make it difficult to achieve the best allocation of resources between city, county and schools. If possible, proposed expenditures
should be laid out at the same time and examined in relation to each
other. An illustration of the benefits that can be achieved by such cross-
agency planning is the building of a swimming pool as part of a school
facility, using both city and school funds. During the summer, the pool
may then easily serve as part of the city's recreation program.

On-the-Job Improvements

Better accounting methods and prudent intergovernmental cooperation or consolidation should lead to considerable economies for
California local government, but these are long-range improvements,
some of which could not be installed without a change in the city or
county charter. What can localities do to become more efficient within
the framework of their present organizations? Actually, there are many
steps they can adopt to provide the same service at less cost. Clearly,
specific actions depend on particular conditions and it is difficult to
generalize about on-the-job improvements. For example, the clerical,
billing, purchasing, payroll, and other administrative routines of Los
Angeles County are large enough that the impending installation of a
large electronic data-processing machine will bring clerical savings
estimated at approximately $1,000,000 a year. Though Los Angeles
County may be one of the few counties that can justify a large computing machine, it seems almost certain that many other cities and counties
could reduce clerical costs by using smaller data-processing equipment.
Almost certainly this development will take place in the future, but ag-
gressive, cost-conscious local governments should investigate it now
and bring closer the day of clerical saving.

Riverside's Example. The City of Riverside provides a notable
example of how local government can take steps to increase the efficiency of its operations. In March 1956, the City Manager's office presented to the city council and interested citizens a booklet entitled
"Master Plan for Administration — 101 Ways Riverside Plans to Cut

Costs." Riverside's self-analysis was guided by the Check List on How Cities Can Cut Costs published by the International City Managers' Association, but the city manager also received ideas from outside experts and solicited suggestions from his own city's employees.

The report was divided into two parts: administrative organization and administrative management. Because of its growth from 34,000 population in 1940 to 66,000 in 1955, Riverside then had 700 city employees and its organizational structure needed streamlining to reduce duplication, improve coordination, and concentrate responsibility. As an example of one way that the proposed administrative reorganization would help, Riverside, at the time of the study, owned 260 pieces of automotive equipment — cars, trucks, motorcycles, street sweepers, bulldozers, and the like, which cost $250,000 annually to operate and maintain, with another $150,000 to spend on replacement in recent years. Five departments maintained their own garage and maintenance facilities, other departments depending on them for minor servicing. But all departments also sent certain work to outside repair shops since each was left to its own devices for maintenance. Despite the fact that the City of Riverside employed 13 men for vehicle repairs and servicing, at a salary cost of $57,000, more than half its garage work was handled by outside shops. The proposed reorganization provided the city with a central automotive equipment section to repair and service all city-owned vehicles.

In addition to administrative reorganization, City Manager Oren L. King, who was largely responsible for the cost-cutting study, recommended certain improvements in day-to-day administration that could be adopted without reorganization. His first recommendation in this category was that his own office, "in cooperation with the various operating departments, should develop standard units of measurement for as many governmental operations as possible and establish standards of performance for each unit." This idea was based on the conviction that "the work standard is one of the most important tools management has for increasing productivity . . . and through the setting of specific standards of production, much can be accomplished to raise the levels of performance in our offices and shops."

As a corollary to the recommendation for establishing standards, the city manager's office "should prepare and review budgets on the basis of analyses of departmental services and work programs, with an eye toward achieving performance budgeting for municipal departments." The report also recommended that a "genuine cost-accounting system should be established and integrated with the general accounting system as a basis for (1) preparing budgets, (2) determining the degree of efficiency with which service is rendered, (3) determining whether work can be done more cheaply by contract or existing city employees." This recommendation is strikingly similar to the one New York recently developed.

A brief sample of other recommendations will give even more of the flavor of the report:

> Property accounting should be mechanized throughout the city.

> Billing functions including those relating to commercial sanitation, should be centralized.

> A system of performance ratings should be installed to assist in determining employee fitness for promotions and merited salary increases.

> Employees and equipment should be shifted between departments and offices to meet peak loads that cannot be eliminated.

> The city should initiate a well defined and practical records destruction program . . . to make urgently needed space available in all sections of city activity.

> All motors and other equipment as well as city tools should be stamped and painted a distinctive color to discourage theft and reduce loss.

> A larger proportion of fire department activities, appropriations, and manpower should be directed toward fire prevention activities . . . At present less than 4% of the entire fire department is used directly for fire prevention purposes. Uniformed firemen should serve as fire inspectors in districts in the vicinity of their stations. They will inspect dwellings — a practice not now followed. They will become better acquainted with surrounding buildings while at once fostering the removal of fire hazards.

> The Fire Department should study the feasibility of assessing charges for the cost of extinguishing fire caused by negligence or by violation of fire laws for which notice has been duly issued.

> The city on its own initiative should endeavor to cooperate more closely with school recreation authorities in the joint planning of recreation programs on school grounds and in school buildings under provisions of the California Recreation Enabling Law.

These extensive quotations from Riverside's excellent study on how to cut costs do not imply that it is the only California municipality striving to become more efficient; in fact many Riverside ideas are based on long-established practices in other cities. But the study is an excellent example of how a municipality can find ways to hold down expenses without reducing services. Any Californian who is worried about the mounting cost of local government should not put the blame else-

where until he has at least made an effort to ascertain if his community
has adopted a plan such as Riverside's, and if not, why not.

County Economies. To indicate that counties can also find ways
to economize, here are some plans outlined by the Alameda County Administrator in his 1956-1957 budget message:

> Property Management: Alameda County does not have at
> this time a fully coordinated property management program. . . .

> Duplicating Equipment: Numerous items of capital outlay
> for additional or replacement duplicating equipment have been
> eliminated from the 1956-57 budget recommendations. The pos-
> sibility of establishing a central service [agency], incorporating
> the duplicating operations, is considered a part of this study.

> Records Management and Forms Control: A number of
> departments have requested our cooperation in making studies
> in their department on forms control. . . . A coordinated records
> management program will result in the saving of office space,
> storage space, filing equipment, and paper work.

> Standardization: The department heads have unanimously
> pledged cooperation to develop a standardization program for
> the purchasing of material supplies and capital outlay items for
> various county agencies.

Other possibilities lie in the substantial portion of the county
welfare budget that is absorbed by support of children whose fathers
have deserted their families. Though legally responsible for such support, many "absent fathers" escape this responsibility by departing
without leaving a forwarding address. More vigorous searching could
often trace these delinquent fathers and make them assume the payments that otherwise have to come from county charitable agencies.

Finally, the State Bar Association has made several studies and
recommendations concerning the loose and easy pace many judges set
in county courts (some spending only a few hours a day on the bench),
and considerable criticism has been leveled at the self-serving, extra-
curricular activities of a number of "marrying judges" who use public
facilities and capitalize on their official titles for extra income. This
indicates that, at the judicial level, too, the county taxpayer can
reasonably expect to obtain more for his dollar.

Elimination of Property Tax on Household Furnishings

Another economy could be achieved in connection with the personal property tax on household furnishings. This tax has been eliminated in New York and many other states for reasons that are extremely persuasive. The valuation of household furnishings depend on
the crudest estimate of true value, since the people who perform this
task have virtually no training and often come no closer to the furnish-

ings than the front porch. This inevitably creates distrust in the whole process. Since the individual appraisals correlate closely with assessments on the house itself (because people living in expensive homes usually have valuable furniture and vice versa), almost exactly the same tax burden would be borne by all citizens if the household-furnishings tax were eliminated, with real property valuations increased to compensate for the tax loss. Superficially, it might seem that this would benefit tenants of unfurnished apartments and houses (who now pay a small tax on their furnishings) by shifting the burden to their landlords. In a short time, however, the landlords would pass the higher real property tax on to the tenants by raising rents and the tax burden would be right back where it was before.

Yet if this plan raises no further revenue and distributes the property tax burden just as it was before, why adopt it? Aside from the virtue of eliminating a tax that tends to mock the assessment practice and thus belittle the whole tax-collecting process, the plan would save considerable money by eliminating the expenses involved in hiring "assessors" of household furnishings and in the administration and bookkeeping connected with it. In Los Angeles County alone it has been estimated that this might save $250,000 annually.

Appointment of Non-policy-Making Officials

Many cities in California still elect their treasurers, nearly half a dozen elect their police chiefs, a few provide for the election of their city attorneys, and almost all of them have elected clerks. Without doubt, all of these officials are necessary in city government but since none of them have policy-making functions it is almost certain that governmental efficiency is hampered by having such officers elected instead of appointed. Both in California and elsewhere the practice of electing administrative officials is more prevalent at the local than at higher levels of government. Elimination of this custom would increase the efficiency of local government in a variety of ways: better qualified personnel could be obtained, the cost of conducting elections would be reduced, and most of all, a clear administrative chain-of-command would be effected.

Several volumes and man-years of study could profitably be devoted to the problem of how to provide the same services of local government at lower cost. Only a summary view has been presented here, but it has served to indicate that there are distinct possibilities for getting greater efficiency in local governments — in fact there is probably more opportunity for economy in local governments than in state or federal operations.

Curtailing Services

The cost of local government could also be reduced by eliminating some services and reducing others such as welfare programs, highway improvements, and hospital expansion. Many discussions of how to cut the costs of local government focus on this aspect — cut the cost by eliminating the service. As indicated in the previous chapter, however, there really is no objective basis for deciding where to draw the line in this approach; it is a matter of values. Consequently, this chapter has carefully avoided suggesting that the cost of local governments be lowered by reducing governmental functions. That is a matter the voter must settle. It is tempting, however, to suggest that by almost any reasonable value structure the State of California seems to devote more money to county fairs than it does to education, health, sanitation, highways, and parks. Even without searching for activities that should be curtailed, there is ample opportunity here for reductions of 10-15% in local expenditures simply by insisting on greater efficiency.

SUMMARY

This chapter has shown that the real costs of California local government have remained almost constant during the past two decades even though nominal costs have risen more than six times. Analysis of the economic characteristics associated with city and county expenses show that tax-paying capacity, especially assessed value, is the factor most closely related to variations in per capita costs. The best estimate of how great California's total local expenditures will be in 1965 is $7 billion, more than twice as high as those for 1957. The magnitude of these amounts makes it increasingly important that steps be taken to increase efficiency, and several have been suggested. Chief among them are: better accounting, intergovernmental cooperation and consolidation, better management of day-to-day operations, elimination of the property tax on household furnishings, and appointment rather than election of all non-policy-making officials.

NOTES TO CHAPTER 4

[1] John C. Bollens and Stanley Scott, Effect of Inflation and Growth on City Costs and Services: Case Study of Berkeley, California; University of California, Bureau of Public Administration (1949).

[2] Stanley Scott and Edward L. Feder, Factors Associated with Variations in Municipal Expenditure Levels. Bureau of Public Administration, University of California, Berkeley, February 1957.

[3] L. C. Fitch, "Metropolitan Financial Problems," Annals of the American Academy of Political and Social Science, November 1957, pp. 66-73.

[4] Temporary Commission on the Fiscal Affairs of State Government, A Program for Continued Progress in Fiscal Management, State of New York. February 1955.

[5] The problems of duplicate assessment are discussed in two pamphlets issued by the State Board of Equalization: "Assessment and Collection of City Property Taxes in California" (January 1956) and "Are Separate City Property Tax Assessment and Collection Necessary?" (December 1956).

Note: The Municipal Year Book, which is quoted several times in this chapter, is published by the International City Managers' Association, Chicago 37, Illinois.

STATISTICAL APPENDIX

Detailed results of the linear multiple correlation analysis of per capita expenses for cities and counties is presented below.

COUNTIES

x_1 = Per capita operating costs during fiscal 1957.

x_2 = Population as estimated by State Department of Finance. Figure used is average of 1956 and 1957.

x_3 = Assessed value per capita.

x_4 = Mean personal income. Income estimate for counties supplied by California State Chamber of Commerce. Figure used is average of 1956 and 1957.

x_5 = Percentage of county population not living in incorporated cities.

x_6 = The ratio of manufacturing wages to personal income. Source: California State Chamber of Commerce.

x_7 = Population per square mile.

x_8 = Taxable retail sales per capita. Source: State Board of Equalization.

Coefficient of Multiple Correlation = R = .793

Coefficient of Determination = R^2 = .628

Standard Error of Estimate = $22.03

Multiple Regression Equation:

$$x_1 = -\$57.63 + .0000116\ x_2 + .025987\ x_3$$
$$+ .0185514\ x_4 + .1.1596478\ x_5 + .1481192\ x_6$$
$$+ .0001464\ x_7 - .0028268\ x_8$$

Independent Variable	Multiple Regression Coefficient	Standard Error	Significant at the 1% Level	Beta Coefficient
x_2	.0000116	±.0010669	No	.00143
x_3	.0259871	±.0051157	Yes	.52760
x_4	.0185514	±.0156904	No	.11204
x_5	1.1596478	±.3601466	Yes	.40006
x_6	.1481192	±.5047218	No	.02903
x_7	.0001464	±.0006239	No	.00066
x_8	-.0028268	±.0005090	Yes	.04947

Partial Correlation Coefficients

$r_{12.345678} = .0016$

$r_{13.245678} = .5873$

$r_{14.235678} = .1665$

$r_{15.234678} = .4178$

$r_{16.234578} = .0419$

$r_{17.234568} = .0006$

$r_{18.234567} = -.0079$

Matrix of Simple Correlation Coefficients: For Counties

		x_1	x_2	x_3	x_4	x_5	x_6	x_7	x_8
Per Capita Costs	(x_1)	1.0	-.19	.70	.03	.63	-.07	-.32	-.08
Population	(x_2)	-.19	1.0	-.13	.20	-.38	.16	.74	.04
Assessed Value Per Capita	(x_3)	.70	-.13	1.0	-.05	.46	-.20	-.22	-.08
Mean Income	(x_4)	.03	.20	-.05	1.0	-.10	-.23	.25	.13
Percent Living in Unincorporated Areas	(x_5)	.63	-.38	.46	-.10	1.0	.08	-.58	.00
Mfr. Wages ÷ Income	(x_6)	-.07	.16	-.20	-.23	.08	1.0	.10	-.11
Population Per Square Mile	(x_7)	-.32	.74	-.22	.25	-.58	.10	1.0	.04
Retail Sales	(x_8)	-.08	.04	-.08	.13	.00	-.11	.04	1.0

From the above table one can read the simple correlation coefficients between each variable and every other variable.

CITIES

x_1 = Per capita operating costs during fiscal 1957.

x_2 = Population as estimated by State Department of Finance.

x_3 = Assessed value per capita.

x_4 = Taxable retail sales per capita during second quarter of 1957. Source: State Board of Equalization.

x_5 = Taxable non-retail sales divided by total retail sales. Source: State Board of Equalization.

Coefficient of Multiple Correlation = R = .772

Coefficient of Determination = R^2 = .596

Standard Error of Estimate = \$9.99

Multiple Regression Equation:

$$x_1 = \$28.35 + .000017\ x_2 + .008459\ x_3$$

$$+ .013269\ x_4 - .002218\ x_5$$

Independent Variable	Multiple Regression Coefficient	Standard Error	Significant at the 1% Level	Beta Coefficient
x_2	.000017	±.0000005	Yes	.13564
x_3	.008459	±.000071	Yes	.62434
x_4	.013269	±.000232	Yes	.27270
x_5	-.002218	±.000003	Yes	.18693

Partial Correlation Coefficients

$r_{12.345}$ = .208

$r_{13.245}$ = .566

$r_{14.235}$ = .314

$r_{15.234}$ = - .249

Matrix of Simple Correlation Coefficients: For Cities

		x_1	x_2	x_3	x_4	x_5
Per Capita Costs	(x_1)	1.0	.13	.71	.63	.18
Population	(x_2)	.13	1.0	.01	.02	.09
Assessed Value Per Capita	(x_3)	.71	.01	1.0	.63	.47
Retail Sales	(x_4)	.63	.02	.63	1.0	.23
Non-retail Sales ÷ Total Sales	(x_5)	.18	.09	.47	.23	1.0

From the table above one can read the simple correlation coefficients between each variable and every other variable.

The above report of the multiple linear correlation analyses is presented for those who want to scrutinize the results in detail. The findings should be interpreted with an awareness that few economic statistics, these included, meet the requirements for rigorous application of
multiple correlation. To be specific: the relationships here may be
curvilinear instead of linear; the distribution of at least some of the
variables is considerably skewed (non-normal), and both the dependent
and some of the independent variables are in per capita terms. The last
qualification was incorporated knowingly as perhaps the lesser of two
evils. Otherwise the assessed value, the income, and the taxable sales
of large cities or counties (e.g., 42% of the assessed value in the State
of California is found in Los Angeles County alone) would tend to distort the regression line and other results unduly. It might have been
better to perform a logarithmic transformation on all data before analyzing it, but the results would not have been so easy to interpret.

PART III

TOWARD A MORE EQUITABLE REVENUE SYSTEM

GERHARD N. ROSTVOLD

Assisted by William N. Littlefield

> "Governments existing by the will of the governed are destined to be confronted with fiscal problems, since free peoples seem to have both a large appetite for governmental services and the means of expressing their instinctive aversion to taxes." — Report of the Commission on Intergovernmental Relations, June 1955, p. 91.

Local units of government in California face a revenue crisis. This is the working hypothesis underlying the discussion in the next two chapters. Upon whom should the responsibility for meeting this crisis rest ? The answer is simple. Article IV, Section 1, of the California Constitution provides that the taxing power shall be vested in "the Legislature" and in "the people." An enlightened legislature and an informed people can provide the key to the solution of the crisis in local finance. The main purpose of this chapter is to make explicit the nature of the crisis.

THE ROLE OF TAXATION IN A PRIVATE ENTERPRISE SYSTEM

A private enterprise system operates on the premise that as many of society's wants as possible should be satisfied through private initiative. Under this system, privately owned resources are allocated by the market price mechanism toward the production of consumption and investment goods. The motive force behind private production is pecuniary gain: only when goods and services promise a profit to the producer will they be made available to satisfy private wants.

There are, however, as the two preceding chapters have revealed, certain socially valuable goods and services that government is expected to provide in the common interest. Adam Smith, in developing the laissez-faire doctrine concerning the functions of government, assigned three main duties to the sovereign: (1) to protect the society from the violence and invasion of other independent societies; (2) to protect, as far as possible, every member of society from the injustice or oppression of every other member of it, i.e., to establish an exact administration of justice; and (3) to erect and maintain certain public works and institutions, whose profits could never repay the expense to any individual or small number of individuals, though they may frequently do much more than repay it to a great society.[1] The laissez-faire doctrine assigns to government the role of providing external and internal protection, and promoting those aspects of social welfare — e.g., poor relief — not provided by the market place.

People in every society demand and consume both private and public goods. Both types are indispensable. Consumer-citizens, however, tend to apply different values to private and to public goods. In a market economy, privately produced goods are valued in terms of the price the buyer is willing to pay. Price is simply the value of a good expressed in money terms. One should note further that private goods are generally applied to the <u>direct</u> satisfaction of a person's wants.

In contrast with private goods, public goods — e.g., education — seldom carry an explicit market price and, generally speaking, their benefits are broadly distributed. As a consequence, the individual citizen rarely thinks of public services in terms of their direct value. Paradoxically, however, publicly produced goods and services may be more valuable to the welfare of the citizen than many privately produced goods which carry an explicit market price. There is a tendency, in short, for the consumer-citizen to take for granted the continuous availability of public goods and services. At the same time, privately produced and consumed goods monopolize the value orientation of the individual. This phenomenon is crucial to an understanding of and an intelligent discussion of the revenue plight of the local unit of government.

The traditional roles of government under democratic capitalism have been to provide protection and promote social welfare. If these functions are entrusted to government, some means must be provided to finance the expenditures involved. Several financing alternatives are available. Taxation aside, government might simply develop an appropriate system of service charges and fees. For various reasons it would not be practical to use this technique in "pricing" all government services. The armed forces, for example, provide widely diffused benefits. It would be difficult to define and collect the price of such protection from each citizen since the benefits are so general in nature. In the field of public assistance or poor relief, the reasons that a system of charges and fees would not be workable are even more obvious. Such a scheme of public finance would be feasible only where it is possible to measure directly the benefit a person derives from the service and when he also has the ability to pay for it. The postal service offers an illustration of the service charge or fee approach.

Capital levies provide a second potential source of public revenue. Resort to them would, however, violate the basic premises of public finance in a private enterprise system because they would involve the direct appropriation of private capital, the means of income generation. Such fiscal action would be inappropriate because it would undermine the institution of private property itself. Thus only in the direct cir-

cumstances would it be practicable to consider using the capital levy to
finance public services.

As a third source, government might conceivably borrow from citizens and business firms in the private sector. Short- and long-term borrowing have a definite place in government finance, though for practical
purposes this source must clearly be reserved for major capital improvements and for emergencies.

As a fourth technique — and one much used historically — governments may finance expenditures merely by printing new money. It goes
without saying that the inflationary consequences of such action make
this form of public finance highly undesirable. In addition, state and
local governments, lacking full sovereignty, would find it impossible
to utilize this device.

To summarize the analysis to this point: of the four sources of
revenue mentioned thus far — fees and charges, the capital levy, borrowing, and resorting to the printing press — the first and third have
a role to play in financing public services, but the other two are inherently impractical. Basically, however, a case cannot be made for financing all government services through a system of fees and charges
and/or through borrowing. Excessive application of the fee or service
charge approach would violate the equity criterion of a model revenue
system. The ability of government to borrow, moreover, presumes
the availability of an alternative income source to underwrite the servicing and retirement of the government debt. Thus, taxation becomes
the real key to public finance under democratic capitalism, and it is
essential that the general philosophy of taxation in a free society be
understood.

Conceivably one might argue that taxation is incompatible with the
basic precepts of a private enterprise system. This is not the case,
however, and for several reasons. First, even in Adam Smith's laissez-
faire model the performance of essential social services is assigned to
the public sector of the economy. Second, in the pure laissez-faire
system, property rights in economic resources rest not in public but
in private hands. Economic resources, when combined in production,
provide additions to the social product, or income. The primary claim
to this income accrues to the private individual or business holding title
to the resources that generated the income. This income represents
dollar votes which may be cast in the market place to bid for privately
produced goods and services.

It follows accordingly that if private citizens and business firms demand services from government they incur corresponding obligations. These demands require a diversion of resources from the private to the public sector of the economy, which can be achieved only if the government has at its disposal a share of the social income or dollar votes. Essentially, taxation in a private enterprise system is the appropriation of private income without a direct quid pro quo so that the government may bid for the private resources necessary to provide privately demanded public goods and services of general social value. Taxation is therefore perfectly compatible with democratic capitalism, and, in view of the limitations and disadvantages of alternative sources of revenue, it must play the leading role in financing government services. It follows that as the demand for services increases, so must the level of taxes. Failure to recognize the inextricable relationship between government spending and taxing programs provides one of the reasons for the threat of a crisis in local finance. As the people of California learn to appreciate how heavy demands for government services lead inevitably to higher taxes, their psychology regarding local finance will change and the crisis will be considerably mitigated. The real aspects of the crisis turn on other factors and it is to these that most of the subsequent sections of the study are devoted.

FISCAL CHARACTER OF THE AMERICAN FEDERAL SYSTEM
Division of the Taxing Power

The American system of government — a federal system — is characterized by a division of power between a national or central government and the governments of the several states. The national or federal government has only delegated powers — those enumerated in the Constitution — and such implied powers as have been sanctioned by the courts to make the express powers effective. The respective states possess inherent or reserved powers, the broadest of which is the police power. State governments may exercise any powers that have not been vested in the federal government and are not denied to them either by the federal constitution or their own. Local governments — counties, municipalities, school districts, and other districts — operate under powers delegated to them by the states. These local units are not sovereign but rather legal subdivisions of the state.

A federal division of power attempts to promote maximum responsibility on the part of state and local government units in the performance of public functions. Yet in actual practice local governments, op-

erating under powers delegated by the states, no longer appear to be
equal to the task of financing their traditional functions. A brief review
of the revenue sources utilized at each level of government will provide
useful background for a discussion of the fiscal inadequacies of the
existing local government revenue structure.

Development of the Federal Revenue Structure

During the fiscal year 1956-57, 72.3% of total federal revenues
were derived from personal and corporate income taxes. (See Table 5.1.)
The heavy reliance upon these two forms of income taxation is a relatively recent development and, as such, merits brief attention. With
few exceptions, customs duties and excises provided the bulk of federal
revenues up through the early 1900's. The income tax was used as a
source of revenue during the Civil War, but was repealed in 1872. A
subsequent attempt, in 1894, to incorporate the income tax into the
federal revenue system was declared unconstitutional. Continued pressure for the adoption of a federal income tax led to the passage of the
Corporation Excise Tax of 1909. The tax constituted a levy on the privilege of conducting business as a corporate entity and a tax rate of 1%
on net income above $5,000 was applicable.

The corporate excise tax of 1909 comprised, in a sense, an interim
"income" tax measure preceding the passage of the Sixteenth Amendment
in 1913. This significant amendment to the Constitution granted the
federal government the power to "lay and collect taxes on income from
whatever source derived, without apportionment among the several
states, and without regard to any census or enumeration." Viewed in
historical perspective, these two measures represent the two most important developments in federal finance in the 20th century.

In 1913, approximately 95% of all federal revenues came from customs and excises. The corporate excise tax yielded the remainder. By
1930, personal and corporate income taxes produced 57.7% of total
federal revenues, and fiscal developments during the great depression,
World War II, and the cold war, have further established the income
tax as the main source of federal fiscal support.

Development of State Finance in the United States

In striking contrast with the federal system, at least 50% of all
state revenue in 1957 was produced by general sales, gasoline, tobacco,
beverage, and motor vehicle taxes and licenses. (See Table 5.2.) Income taxes yielded only 11%, and the property tax was of relatively
minor significance. In other words, the several types of sales and ex-

Table 5.1. Federal Revenue Structure, by Source: 1930, 1940, and 1952-57

(billions of dollars)

	1930		1940		1950		1952		1953		1954		1955		1956		1957	
	Amount	%	Amount	%	Amount	%	Amount	%	Amount	%	Amount	%	Amount	%	Amount	%	Amount	%
Personal Income Tax	$1.1	27.4	$1.0	16.6	$17.2	41.5	$29.3	43.1	$32.5	44.8	$32.8	44.8	$31.7	45.6	$35.3	44.8	$39.0	46.6
Corporate Income Tax[1]	1.3	30.3	1.1	19.5	10.9	26.4	21.5	31.6	21.6	29.7	21.5	29.5	18.3	26.3	21.3	27.1	21.5	25.7
Other Taxes[2]	.6	15.1	3.2	54.5	10.9	26.4	14.2	21.0	15.6	21.4	15.6	21.3	16.3	23.5	18.5	23.4	19.6	23.5
Total Tax Revenues	$3.0	72.8	$5.3	90.6	$39.0	94.3	$65.0	95.7	$69.7	95.9	$69.9	95.6	$66.3	95.4	$75.1	95.3	$80.1	95.8
Non-Tax Revenues[3]	1.2	27.2	.6	9.4	2.3	5.7	3.0	4.3	2.9	4.1	3.3	4.4	3.2	4.6	3.7	4.7	3.5	4.2
Total Revenues	$4.2		$5.9		$41.3		$68.0		$72.6		$73.2		$69.5		$78.8		$83.6	
Less: Transfers, etc.[4]	0.0		.7		4.8		6.6		7.8		8.5		9.1		10.6		12.6	
Net Revenues	$4.2	100%	$5.2	100%	$36.5	100%	$61.4	100%	$64.8	100%	$64.7	100%	$60.4	100%	$68.2	100%	$71.0	100%

[1] Includes excess profits taxes in years when tax applies.

[2] Includes excises, gift, estate, employment taxes, and miscellaneous.

[3] Includes repayment of investments, sale of property, Indian moneys, all District of Columbia receipts, customs and miscellaneous.

[4] Includes transfers or apportionments to Social Security and tax refunds.

Source: Annual Report of the Secretary of the Treasury, 1958.

Table 5.2. Revenue Structure, by Source, of the Forty-Eight States: 1930, 1940, 1950, 1952-57

(millions of dollars)

Fiscal Year Source	1930 Amount	%	1940 Amount	%	1950 Amount	%	1952 Amount	%	1953 Amount	%	1954 Amount	%	1955 Amount	%	1956 Amount	%	1957 Amount	%
Sales Taxes	$ 1	0.0	$ 499	10.7	$ 1,670	13.8	$ 2,229	15.4	$ 2,433	15.7	$ 2,540	15.6	$ 2,637	15.4	$ 3,036	15.6	$ 3,373	15.7
Gas Tax	495	22.1	839	18.0	1,544	12.8	1,870	12.9	2,019	13.0	2,218	13.6	2,353	13.7	2,687	13.8	2,828	13.2
Tobacco & Alcohol Tax	12	.5	352	7.6	911	7.5	1,068	7.4	1,013	6.5	1,006	6.2	1,009	5.9	1,061	5.5	1,125	5.3
Motor Vehicle and Operators Licenses	356	15.9	387	8.3	755	6.3	924	6.4	1,012	6.5	1,098	6.8	1,184	6.9	1,290	6.6	1,370	6.4
Personal Income Tax	233	10.4	206	4.4	724	6.0	913	6.3	969	6.3	1,004	6.2	1,094	6.4	1,374	7.1	1,563	7.3
Corporate Income Tax			155	3.3	586	4.9	838	5.8	810	5.3	772	4.7	737	4.3	890	4.6	984	4.6
Property Tax	345	15.4	260	5.6	307	2.6	370	2.6	365	2.4	391	2.4	412	2.4	467	2.4	479	2.2
Others	665	29.7	615	13.2	1,432	11.9	1,744	12.1	1,932	12.5	2,061	12.7	2,167	12.6	2,572	13.3	2,807	13.1
Total Tax Revenues	$2,108	94.0	$3,313	71.1	$7,930	65.7	$9,956	68.9	$10,552	68.2	$11,089	68.2	$11,597	67.6	$13,377	68.9	$14,529	67.8
Non-Tax Revenues **	15	.7	625	13.4	1,719	14.2	2,011	13.9	2,165	14.0	2,302	14.1	2,570	15.0	2,737	14.1	2,988	13.9
Intergovernmental Revenues	120	5.3	725	15.5	2,423	20.1	2,485	17.2	2,761	17.8	2,882	17.7	2,989	17.4	3,296	17.0	3,928	18.3
Total Revenues	$2,243	100%	$4,663	100%	$12,072	100%	$14,452	100%	$15,478	100%	$16,273	100%	$17,156	100%	$19,410	100%	$21,445	100%

*Includes: death, gift, and miscellaneous taxes.

**Includes: charges, liquor store revenue, and miscellaneous.

Sources: Facts and Figures on Government Finance. 9th edition, 1956-57. New York: The Tax Foundation, 1956 and Bureau of the Census, Financial Statistics of States, 1930.

cise taxes provide by far the largest share of revenue at the state level. Intergovernmental transfers in the form of grants and nontax revenues provided, respectively, 18.3 and 13.9% of total revenue in 1957.

In tracing historical developments in the pattern of state finance, it is significant to note that in 1900 over 50% of all state revenues came from the property tax. General sales taxes and income taxes were non-existent. Since 1900, most of the states have made a serious effort to reserve the property tax to local units and this has been accomplished to a considerable degree.

During the 1920's, the states began to make nominal use of individual and corporate income taxes. The way for expanding the personal income tax had been opened up by significant tax legislative reform in Wisconsin in 1911. By 1956, 31 states and the District of Columbia were using the individual income tax. Some 10.7% of total state tax collections were derived from this source in 1957.

The depression decade of the 1930's brought further significant changes. Although state use of the property tax had already begun to decline, in 1927, 23% of all state tax collections came from this source. The decrease in property values and incomes during the early stages of the depression, coupled with the necessity to reserve the property tax for local use, forced the states to seek other tax sources. The sales tax provided the answer. In 1932, less than one-half of one percent of total state tax revenues were derived from general sales, use, or gross receipts taxes, but by 1956, 23% of total state tax revenues came from these sources.

Recent developments in state finance have involved: (1) the elimination in large part of the property tax; (2) an increased reliance upon sales taxes;[*] (3) the expanded use of corporate and personal income taxes; and (4) a marked growth in the relative importance of intergovernmental revenues and nontax revenues.[**]

Financing Local Government

The traditional financial mainstay for local government in the United States has been the general property tax. In 1902, 89.5% of all

[*] Thirty-three states had enacted some form of general retail sales tax legislation by 1958.

[**] For a more detailed summary of recent state tax legislation, see L. Laszlo Ecker-Racz, "State Taxes After the 1956-1957 Legislative Sessions," National Tax Journal, X, No. 4, December 1957, pp. 289-97.

local tax revenue was produced by the property tax, and 68.3% of total revenues came from this source. The relative importance of the property tax in the local revenue structure was maintained through 1930. In that year, 68% of total local revenue and 95.3% of all local taxes were derived from property tax sources. [*]

With the collapse of property values during the 1930's, the financing of local functions was placed in serious jeopardy. Subsequent developments in local finance may be summarized as follows: (1) a decline in the relative importance of the property tax; (2) a marked growth in state aid to local governments; (3) an increased reliance upon nontax revenue sources, e.g., service charges, utility, and liquor store revenues; and (4) the entry of local governments into new tax fields such as the general sales tax. By 1957, taxes accounted for 50%, nontax sources for 23.4%, and intergovernmental grants-in-aid for 26.6% of total local government revenue. (See Table 5.3.) One of the leading questions in local finance is to determine what role the general property tax should play in the future.

Summary of Federal, State, and Local Revenue Sources

Further insight into the revenue crisis at the local level of government may be gained from an examination of the over-all tax structure. In 1930, local units of government collected 46.2% of all taxes; the federal government ranked second, collecting 31.6%, while the states shared 22.2% of total tax revenues. The federal government's dominance in the field of taxation has been established as a result of the severe depression of the 1930's, World War II, the Korean War, and the chronic uncertainties associated with the cold war. This is borne out by the fact that in 1957, 71.8% of total governmental tax revenues in the United States accrued to the federal government, while the state and local levels received 14.4% and 13.8%, respectively. (See Table 5.4 and Figure 5.1.) Any discussion of the plight of the local unit must take cognizance of this significant change in the relative importance of the federal government vis-à-vis state and local government in the taxation area of public finance. There can be no question that the heavy growth in federal spending and taxation has complicated the task of local finance.

---

[*] For an excellent discussion of the role of the property tax in local finance, see Mabel Newcomer, "The Decline of the General Property Tax," National Tax Journal, VI, No. 1, March 1953, pp. 38-51.

Table 5.3. Revenue Sources of All U.S. Government Units: 1930, 1940, 1950, and 1952-57

(millions of dollars)

Fiscal Year Source	1930 Amount	%	1940 Amount	%	1950 Amount	%	1952 Amount	%	1953 Amount	%	1954 Amount	%	1955 Amount	%	1956 Amount	%	1957 Amount	%
Revenue from Own Sources																		
Tax Revenues:																		
Property	$4,259	68.0	$4,170	54.5	$7,042	44.3	$8,282	43.3	$8,890	43.2	$9,577	43.3	$10,324	43.3	$11,282	43.4	$12,152	43.4
Sales	26	.4	130	1.7	484	3.0	627	3.3	713	3.5	703	3.2	779	3.3	889	3.4	952	3.4
Individual Income			18	{.3	64	{.4	85	{.5	96	{.5	122	{.6	143	{.6	164	{.6	168	{.6
Corp. Net Income			1	{	7	{	8	{	7	{	7	{	7	{	7	{	7	{
License and Other*	92	1.5	178	2.3	387	2.5	465	2.4	508	2.5	569	2.6	633	2.7	657	2.6	728	2.6
Total Tax Revenue	$4,377	69.9	$4,497	58.8	$7,984	50.2	$9,467	49.5	$10,214	49.7	$10,978	49.9	$11,886	49.9	$12,992	50.0	$14,000	50.0
Non-tax Revenues																		
Charges and Miscellaneous	$ 712	11.4	$ 510	6.6	$1,602	10.1	$2,205	11.5	$2,285	11.1	$2,651	12.0	$2,851	12.0	$3,246	12.5	$3,528	12.6
Liquor Store and Utility Revenue	430	6.8	717	9.4	1,902	11.9	2,184	11.4	2,381	11.6	2,522	11.4	2,726	11.4	2,835	10.9	3,024	10.8
Total Non-tax Revenue	$1,142	18.2	$1,227	16.0	$3,504	22.0	$4,389	22.9	$4,666	22.7	$5,173	23.4	$5,577	23.4	$6,081	23.4	$6,552	23.4
Total Revenue from Own Sources	$5,519	88.1	$5,724	74.8	$11,488	72.2	$13,856	72.4	$14,880	72.4	$16,151	73.1	$17,463	73.3	$19,073	73.4	$20,552	73.4
Intergovernmental Revenue from States	$ 699	11.2	$1,654	21.6	$4,217	26.5	$5,044	26.4	$5,384	26.2	$5,635	25.5	$5,987	25.1	$6,590	25.4	$7,056	25.2
from Federal Government	45	.7	278	3.6	211	1.3	237	1.2	300	1.4	298	1.4	368	1.6	309	1.2	392	1.4
Total Intergovernmental Revenue	$ 744	11.9	$1,932	25.2	$4,428	27.8	$5,281	27.6	$5,684	27.6	$5,934	26.9	$6,355	26.7	$6,899	26.6	$7,448	26.6
Total Revenue from All Sources	$6,263	100%	$7,656	100%	$15,916	100%	$19,137	100%	$20,564	100%	$22,085	100%	$23,818	100%	$25,972	100%	$28,000	100%

* Excludes: Insurance Trust Revenue and Taxes

Sources: Bureau of the Census. Historical Statistics on State and Local Government Finances, 1902-1953. Bureau of the Census. Summary of Governmental Finances.

Table 5.4. Total Tax Revenues,[1] by Level of Government: 1930, 1940, 1950, 1957

(millions of dollars)

Fiscal Year Source	1930 Amount	%	1940 Amount	%	1950 Amount	%	1957 Amount	%
Federal	$3,000.0	31.6	$4,500.0	36.6	$36,400.0	69.6	$72,500.0	71.8
State	2,108.0	22.2	3,313.0	26.9	7,930.0	15.2	14,529.0[2]	14.4
Local	4,377.0	46.2	4,497.0	36.5	7,984.0	15.2	14,000.0[2]	13.8
	$ 9,485.0	100%	$12,310.0	100%	$52,314.0	100%	$101,029.0	100%

[1]Excludes unemployment compensation taxes and other tax-trust items.

[2]Estimated.

Source: Tables 5.1, 5.1, 5.3

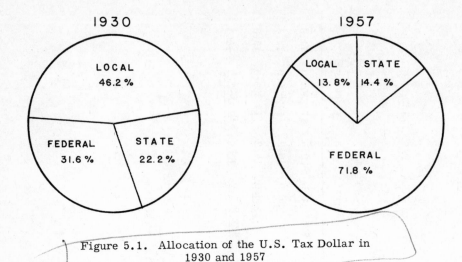

Figure 5.1. Allocation of the U.S. Tax Dollar in
1930 and 1957

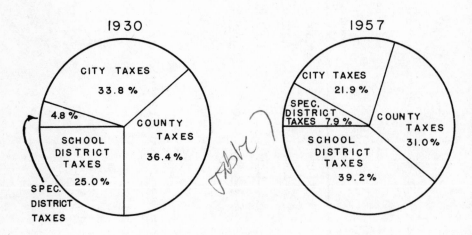

Figure 5.2. The 1930 and the 1957 California Local
Government Tax Dollar

FINANCING LOCAL GOVERNMENT IN CALIFORNIA

Any analysis of the local revenue structure in California must begin with an examination of the pattern of local government itself. The pattern is of considerable complexity, including, as it does, 57 counties and one city-county, over 350 cities, some 1,818 school districts, and 2,780 other districts. Numerically as well as financially the counties, cities, school districts, and other special districts bulk large in the picture of California public finance. Table 5.5 summarizes the receipts of all local governments in the state by source for selected years, and Figure 5.2 shows the allocation of the California local tax dollar in 1930 and 1957.

Financing County Government in California

In terms of tax sources, the counties have traditionally relied heavily upon the property tax. In 1930, for example, the property tax furnished 100% of all county tax revenues and 76.5% of total revenues. Nontax receipts (11.6%) and grants-in-aid and shared revenues (11.9%) provided the balance. The drastic decline in property values during the early 1930's gave impetus to the decline in the relative importance of the property tax in the revenue structure of California counties. By 1957, property taxes yielded only 39% of total county revenue. The decline in the property tax as a source of revenue has been compensated by a moderate increase in the relative importance of nontax county receipts (12.4% of total revenues in 1957), and a marked increase in state grants and shared revenues. The latter sources provided 46.4% of all California county revenue in 1957.

County governments entered the sales and use tax fields for the first time in 1956. This development has been described by the State Board of Equalization as follows:

> The Bradley-Burns Uniform Sales and Use Tax Law, passed at the 1955 Legislative Session, enabled counties to levy sales and use taxes for the first time, provided they contracted with the State Board of Equalization for administration. Counties were given no choice of tax rates or bases; only a 1 percent rate was allowed, and, with minor exceptions, the tax base had to be the State's tax base. Each city in a county that exercised this option could then levy a state-administered city tax with the same tax base and a rate of 1 percent or less which would be credited against the county tax. The credit device had the practical effect of forcing cities into the program whenever their counties entered it. To levy no city sales and use tax would deprive a city of revenue without improving the lot of its retailers, who would pay a 1 percent county tax in any event. To levy a city sales and use tax outside the Bradley-Burns program would be to superimpose the city tax upon the 1 percent county tax, for only a city tax imposed under the Bradley-Burns law qualifies as a credit against the county tax.[2]

Table 5.5.   Receipts of California Local Governments, by Source: 1930, 1937, 1947, 1957

(millions of dollars)

Source	1930		1937		1947		1957	
	Amount	%	Amount	%	Amount	%	Amount	%
Property Taxes	$351.6	78.8	$261.7	60.9	$492.1	54.4	$1,433.8	46.1
Other Taxes[1]	4.4	1.0	4.3	1.0	26.3	2.9	183.5	5.9
Non-tax Receipts	43.0	9.6	30.0	7.0	101.2	11.2	417.9	13.4
Grants-in-aid and Shared Revenues	47.5	10.6	133.5	31.1	284.5	31.5	1,076.0	34.6
Total Receipts	$446.5	100%	$429.5	100%	$904.1	100%	$3,111.2	100%

[1]Includes sales and use taxes and city business licenses (all other city licenses and permits are included in non-tax receipts as are all county licenses and permits).

Source: State Controller, Annual Reports.

During 1957, the 34 counties participating in the program realized $24.7 million in sales and use tax revenue. By January 1, 1958, 47 counties had contracted for state administration of a 1% county sales tax. Division of the revenue between a county and its cities is worked out locally. Table 5.6 summarizes the revenue structure of California counties for selected years between 1930 and 1957.

Financing California's Cities

Property taxes have traditionally provided the main source of revenue for California's cities. In 1930, 96% of all tax revenues and 78.2% of total revenues were derived from this source. Nontax revenues (15.1%) and grants-in-aid and shared revenues (3.4%) made up the balance of city receipts in 1930. Several significant developments have taken place since then. First, the pattern of taxation has undergone changes and the relative importance of taxes in the total city revenue pciture has declined drastically. Second, nontax revenues, especially service charges, have expanded. Third, grants-in-aid and shared revenues have assumed a more important place in the revenue structure of California cities. Each of these developments will be examined in turn.

Perhaps one of the most significant changes has been the drastic decline in the relative importance of the property tax. Whereas in 1930 this tax yielded 96% of total tax revenues, in 1957 it provided 62.4% of tax revenues, and 40.3% of total revenues. The entry of California cities into the sales tax field in 1945 represented a concurrent development in the area of finance. As mentioned earlier, the sales tax found wide acceptance at the state level during and following the depression decade of the 1930's. San Bernardino levied the first city sales tax in California, effective January 1, 1945. By the end of 1946, various other cities had incorporated the sales tax into their revenue structures, and by June 1953, 162 of the state's then 310 cities were levying sales taxes.[3] Sales and use taxes yielded $14 million in 60 cities in 1947; by 1957, they were producing $134.9 million, or 19.8%, of total city revenues. As of January 1, 1958, more than 90% of California cities were realizing revenue from locally imposed sales taxes. The sales tax has become an integral part of California's municipal revenue structure.

The business license tax is the third most important source of tax revenue for California cities. Various formulas are used in establishing the amount of the tax, and its relative importance as a source of revenue varies considerably from city to city. Los Angeles, for example, reported 39.1% of the total license tax receipts realized by

Table 5.6. Amount and Percentages of Aggregate Revenues, by Major Source, of all California Counties:
1930, 1937, 1947, 1952-57

(millions of dollars)

Fiscal Year Source	1930 Amount	%	1937 Amount	%	1947 Amount	%	1952 Amount	%	1953 Amount	%	1954 Amount	%	1955 Amount	%	1956 Amount	%	1957 Amount	%
Property Taxes	$115.1	76.5	$ 76.5	61.3	$152.9	48.2	$259.9	40.4	$280.7	39.0	$302.1	39.5	$337.7	41.5	$338.6	40.0	$372.9	38.6
Sales Taxes																	24.8	2.6
Non-Tax Receipts and Licenses*	17.4	11.6	8.9	7.1	25.3	8.0	46.7	7.2	57.2	8.0	66.2	8.6	74.7	9.2	87.0	10.4	120.0	12.4
Grants and Shared Revenue	17.9	11.9	39.4	31.6	138.9	43.8	336.8	52.4	380.9	53.0	397.7	51.9	400.8	49.6	420.1	49.6	448.0	46.4
Total Receipts	$150.4	100%	$124.8	100%	$317.1	100%	$643.4	100%	$718.8	100%	$766.0	100%	$813.2	100%	$845.7	100%	$965.7	100%

*Includes: Licenses and permits, fines and penalties, fees and commission,s privileges, fees for special services rendered, rent from property, gifts and miscellaneous.

Excludes: Sale of property, bond sales, public service enterprises and social insurance receipts.

Source: California State Controller, Annual Report of Financial Transactions of Cities and Counties.

all cities in California in 1956-57. Two years earlier, in fiscal 1955, the proportion of current revenue derived from the business license tax ranged from 1/10 of 1% in the lowest city to a high of 23.2%; per capita yields ranged from $0.07 to $18.37. Although aggregate dollar yields from the business license tax have increased in the postwar period, they have declined in relative importance. In 1947, 4.7% of total municipal revenues were derived from this source, whereas in 1957 only 3.5% of total revenues came from business licenses. The introduction of the general sales tax into the municipal revenue system has diverted attention away from the business license tax.[*]

City-collected nontax receipts yielded 15.1% of total municipal revenues in 1930. Included in this category are the proceeds from permits, fines, privileges, rent, sale of municipal property, interest, fees and charges for services, parking meters, and miscellaneous charges for sewage disposal and garbage collection. Nontax revenue sources yielded 17.9% of total city revenues in 1957. Faced with growing revenue needs, cities have been inclined to resort to nontax revenue sources whenever it has been feasible to do so.

State and federal subventions and grants provided only 2.4 and 1%, respectively, of total revenue for California municipalities in 1930. By 1957, however, state grants-in-aid and shared revenues amounted to $102.4 million, and represented 15.1% of total city revenues. The funds received from the state consisted of three shared license taxes and fees: (a) motor vehicle fuel and license taxes and motor vehicle license "in lieu" fees, (b) liquor license fees, and (c) grants to cities for public health assistance and other miscellaneous purposes. Federal grants to California cities have remained fairly stable, providing approximately 2.5% of total revenues in 1957. In the main, these were payments in lieu of ad valorem taxes on public housing and federal property of other types.

Table 5.7 summarizes in detail recent and contemporary developments in California municipal finance.

Financing California's School Districts

Prior to 1930, the largest share of the cost of public education in California was borne by the locally levied property tax. Although of lesser relative importance, state and county grants-in-aid had histori-

[*]The 1954-55 data in this section have been derived from League of California Cities, Business License Taxes, June 1957, pp. 1-2.

Table 5.7. Amount and Percentages of Aggregate Revenues, by Major Source, for all California Municipalities: 1930, 1937, 1947, and 1952-57

(millions of dollars)

Fiscal Year Source	1930 Amount	%	1937 Amount	%	1947 Amount	%	1952 Amount	%	1953 Amount	%	1954 Amount	%	1955 Amount	%	1956 Amount	%	1957 Amount	%
Tax Revenues																		
General Property	$126.8	78.2	$92.0	65.6	$140.3	53.9	$211.1	45.6	$220.0	45.4	$216.9	44.6	$241.2	44.8	$257.1	43.0	$274.2	40.3
Sales Tax					14.0	5.4	41.7	9.0	48.2	9.9	49.7	10.2	66.0	12.3	87.2	14.6	134.9	19.8
Licenses & Permits																		
Business	4.4	2.7	4.3	3.1	12.3	4.7	17.7	3.9	18.9	3.9	19.8	4.1	20.7	3.8	22.1	3.7	23.8	3.5
Other*	1.0	.6	1.3	.9	3.0	1.2	4.2	.9	5.0	1.0	5.2	1.1	6.5	1.2	6.5	1.1	6.3	.9
Total Tax Revenues	$132.2	81.5	$97.6	69.6	$169.6	65.2	$274.7	59.4	$291.1	60.2	$291.6	60.0	$334.4	62.1	$372.9	62.4	$439.2	64.5
Non-Tax Revenue **	24.6	15.1	15.2	10.8	49.8	19.1	75.2	16.1	82.9	17.2	89.4	18.4	100.5	18.6	114.2	19.1	121.6	17.9
Grants-in-aid and Shared Revenues																		
State	3.7	2.4	19.0	13.6	32.3	12.4	94.8	20.5	87.6	18.1	87.1	17.9	86.3	16.0	94.0	15.7	102.4	15.1
Federal & County	1.7	1.0	8.4	6.0	8.7	3.3	18.3	4.0	21.6	4.5	17.9	3.7	17.6	3.3	16.9	2.8	17.1	2.5
Total Receipts	$162.2	100%	$140.2	100%	$260.4	100%	$463.0	100%	$484.2	100%	$486.0	100%	$538.8	100%	$598.0	100%	$680.3	100%

*Includes: dog licenses and department permits

**Includes: Fines and penalties, privileges, fees and charges for services and minor departmental sales, rent from property.

Excludes: Sale of property, bond sales, public service receipts and trust monies.

Source: State Controller, Annual Report of Financial Transactions Concerning Cities and Counties of California.

cally represented the second largest source of public school finance. In the first year of the depression, 72.4% of all school district revenues were produced by local property taxes. State subventions and grants accounted for 23.6%, nontax revenues 3.3%, and federal grants 7/10 of 1% of the revenue total. Like other local units, school districts faced a financial problem as a result of the precipitous decline in the property tax base during the 1930's. State grants-in-aid and subventions were required to fill the gap.

In recent years the State of California has provided approximately 40% of all school district funds while the local property tax continues to supply about half the total financial support for public education. Table 5.8 presents a summary of school district finance for selected years between 1930 and 1957.

Financing Special Districts in California

As the name might suggest, some 2,780 special districts have been organized in California as more or less autonomous units of government to perform certain specific functions beyond the legal scope or geographic boundaries of other local units of government. These districts perform a variety of services including, among others, air pollution control, airport facilities, fire protection, flood control, hospital and library service, mosquito abatement, reclamation, sanitation, sewage disposal, storm drainage, electric power, and metropolitan water supply.

The most significant development in special district financing in recent years has been the trend toward greater reliance upon nontax revenue sources, mainly upon service charges. Whereas in 1930, 100% of all special district financing was derived from property taxation, it is estimated that for the fiscal year 1956-57, no more than 56% of their revenues will be provided by this tax source. Nontax revenues provided an estimated 38.6% of total special district revenues while subventions contribute 5% of the total. (See Table 5.9.)

The increased reliance on service charges may be said to be consistent with many of the functions performed by special districts. Such financing is in accord with the benefit principle, under which the direct recipients of a service are charged a fee that conforms, at least in part, to the value of the service. This principle has substantial merit when the value of the service to the citizen-consumer is measurable, and when he has the ability to pay. Since many special district functions are of this kind, it is appropriate that service charges should play an increasing role in their support.

Table 5.8. Amount and Percentages of Aggregate Revenues, by Major Source, for California School Districts: 1930, 1937, 1947, 1952-57

(millions of dollars)

Fiscal Year Source	1930 Amount	%	1937 Amount	%	1947 Amount	%	1952 Amount	%	1953 Amount	%	1954 Amount	%	1955 Amount	%	1956 Amount	%	1957 Amount	%
Property Taxes	$ 86.6	78.2	$ 78.0	52.2	$175.8	61.7	$359.3	55.0	$406.4	54.2	$439.0	50.4	$476.1	49.8	$533.2	50.6	$647.7	53.1
Non-tax Revenues			4.6	311	4.9	1.7	37.8	5.8	44.0	5.9	49.4	5.7	54.9	5.7	62.1	5.9	75.0	6.1
Subventions and Grants-in-aid:																		
State	24.2	21.8	66.7	44.7	104.3	36.6	239.7	36.7	279.8	37.3	363.4	41.7	394.5	41.2	425.7	40.4	455.8	37.4
Federal							16.7	2.5	19.7	2.6	19.0	2.2	23.4	2.5	24.1	2.3	30.4	2.5
County													8.1	.8	8.9	.8	10.3	.9
Total Receipts	$110.8	100%	$149.3	100%	$285.0	100%	$653.1	100%	$749.9	100%	$870.8	100%	$957.0	100%	$1054.0	100%	$1219.2	100%

Sources: State Controller, Annual Report of Financial Transactions Concerning School Districts of California, and Annual Report of Financial Transactions of Cities and Counties.

Table 5. 9.   Amount and Percentages of Aggregate Revenues, by Major Source, for California Special Districts*:
1930, 1937, 1947, 1952-57

(millions of dollars)

Fiscal Year Source	1930 Amount	%	1937 Amount	%	1947 Amount	%	1952 Amount	%	1953 Amount	%	1954 Amount	%	1955 Amount	%	1956 Amount	%	1957 Amount	%
Property Taxes	$23.1	100	$15.2	100	$23.1	55.5	$52.3	53.5	$ 61.6	52.4	$105.3	60.3	$ 93.8	53.7	$113.4	53.7	$139.0*	56.5
Non-tax Revenues**					18.2	43.8	43.0*	44.0	52.0*	44.2	63.3	36.2	72.7	41.6	87.6	41.4	95.0*	38.6
Grants-in-aid					.3	.7	2.5*	2.5	4.0*	3.4	6.2	3.5	8.0	4.7	10.9	5.1	12.0*	4.9
Total Receipts	$23.1	100%	$15.2	100%	$41.6	100%	$97.8	100%	$117.6	100%	$174.8	100%	$174.6	100%	$211.9	100%	$246.0*	100%

* County only, city is reported as part of city property tax.

** Non-tax revenues include charges for services rendered, donations, interest on monies and receipts from activities not directly connected with operation of the district, such as work performed for services rendered to other governmental agencies.

* Estimated

Sources: State Controller, Annual Report of Financial Transactions of Cities and Counties, and, "Income and Expenditures of Government in California, 1910 to 1950," The Tax Digest, V. 28, No. 11 (November, 1950).

THE REVENUE DILEMMA OF LOCAL GOVERNMENTS TODAY

Paradoxically, during World War II local governments in California lived in a fiscal utopia. Many cities and counties deferred spending programs in order to release men and materials for the war effort. Between 1940 and 1944, total local expenditures in California increased by only $50 million, as contrasted with an increase of $172 million between 1946 and 1947. On a per capita basis, city, school district, and special district expenditures actually declined between 1940 and 1944, and county (per capita) expenditures increased nominally. The state of full employment enabled local units to curtail expenditures in the public welfare and assistance area. As incomes increased, tax monies flowed rapidly into local governmental coffers. In many instances, citizens volunteered payment of taxes delinquent since the depression. In brief, the pressures of finance at the local government level were at a minimum during the war period. Most local units, assured of revenues in excess of their current expenditures, were able to reduce their indebtedness substantially.

With the end of World War II, however, the wheels of fiscal fortune were reversed. Cities, counties, school districts, and special districts faced a situation in which demands for expenditure simply exceeded existing revenue capacity. Local government, in short, faced a revenue crisis, and the crisis persists. This situation is due to a multitude of forces and developments, each of which will be discussed in turn.

First, local units emerged from World War II with a considerable backlog of essential public works projects that had been postponed in some cases since the 1930's. Extensive programs of street repair, school building, water and sewage disposal system development had to be undertaken without delay.

A second factor that placed pressure upon the local unit of government was the unprecedented growth in California's population in the postwar period. This striking development has been a function of (1) the doubling of the birth rate in the state (25 live births per 1,000 population, as against 12.6 live births per 1,000 population in 1933), and (2) a sustained level of immigration from other states. In 1945, the population of the state, including armed forces stationed within its borders, totaled 9,344,000 persons. In 1958, total population was fast approaching 15 million, with little prospect that the surge would diminish significantly.

Sheer growth alone creates heavy pressure for increased expen-

ditures by local units. A related development contributing to the financial plight of the local unit, especially the school district, has been the
change in the age distribution of the population in California in the postwar period. In 1930, approximately 15.5% of the state's population fell
into the 0 - 9 age group; in 1950, this same age group accounted for
over 18%. This third factor has translated itself directly into increased
school enrollments. Whereas in 1947, 1,091,167 elementary pupils
were enrolled in the California public school system, projected elementary enrollment for 1959 is 2,392,300. For school districts these
enrollment increases mean a higher level of expenditures for classrooms and teachers; for cities and counties this phenomenon demands
increased expenditures for parks and recreation programs. Population
growth carries with it inescapable social responsibilities.

A fourth factor contributing to the financial plight of local government is the high degree of population mobility in the postwar period.
Perhaps the clearest evidence of this social change is represented by
the sustained rate of migration into the state. Yet perhaps even more
significant in relation to the financial responsibilities of local units has
been the mass movement to the suburbs. The emergence of suburbia as
a way of life has served more than any other social development to compound the emerging crisis in local finance. The geographic expansion
of cities and the concentration of population growth in so-called "fringe"
areas inevitably produces the need for new schools, roads, water, sewage and waste disposal systems, police and fire protection, flood control, and recreation areas. All of these must be financed in the main
from local revenue sources.

Even when properly planned the transformation of an orange grove
into a new suburb or subdivision proves costly. Unfortunately, many
new subdivisions were developed under lax zoning laws. The result was
inadequate water, drainage and sewage systems, all of which are tremendously costly to rebuild once the community has been established.
Annexation on many occasions involved the assumption of heavy expenditure responsibilities by cities. Rarely were new school-building plans
linked to subdivision developments. Many a new home owner has had
the enthusiasm of home ownership dampened within a year or two as
tax rates have been increased to meet the hard social realities associated with the establishment of new communities. There was, in short,
a lagged relationship between the creation of new living areas and recognition of the fiscal problems inherent in the process of suburban
development.

The movement to the suburbs has created other types of fiscal problems, especially for the central cities. Many of the families that have moved to the suburbs have been of relatively high income status. In many instances, lower income groups assumed the residence location of those who moved to the suburbs. The postwar period has also witnessed considerable movement of industry and commerce to outlying areas. Core cities thus lost property tax potential at a time when heavy demands for mass transportation, street widening, expanded police and fire protection, and urban rehabilitation became inescapable. The direct result has been a chronic imbalance between the expenditure programs and the traditional source of revenue, namely, the property tax.

Competition from private industry, relentless inflation, higher standards, and the expanded demands of the citizen have also served to increase costs of local government. In order to hold well-qualified personnel, local governments have had to raise salary schedules, shorten the work week, and offer pensions and other fringe benefits to employees. The prices of materials needed for streets, buildings, flood-control facilities, and the like, have risen dramatically. In a word, the local revenue dollar has felt, with a vengeance, the attrition of inflation. The taxpayer, meanwhile, has been demanding more and better street cleaning, more and better police and fire protection, more and better recreation and health services. All of these translate themselves into a higher level of local expenditures.

The crisis in local finance is mainly a function of the growth of public needs and desires at a rate exceeding the revenue-generating capacity of the local unit. The balance of the problem is explained by factors that condition the revenue side of the budget. Local revenues have lagged behind expenditure demands for a number of reasons. One might suggest, first, that local units have been overly tradition-bound in their approach to finance. They have placed excessive reliance upon the property tax. Unfortunately, it is a hard, cold, fiscal fact of life that this tax incorporates certain inherent shortcomings in an economic setting where government expenditures must increase at a rapid rate.

The shortcomings of the property tax as a source of increased revenue under growth conditions are the following:

1. Although market values of property increase substantially during periods of growth, assessed valuations — the tax base — increase less in proportion to the increases in market value because of lags in the assessment process.

2. Variations in the fiscal capacity of the property tax within dif-

ferent local units create problems. The most rapid growth area, for
example, may have the least fiscal capacity under the property tax base.
There is no necessary correlation, in other words, between the rate of
growth of a community and the rate of increase in the revenue-generating
capacity of the property tax. The process of community growth, which
produces virtually a "bedroom city," unquestionably generates dollar
demands on the expenditure side which are greater than the property
tax dollars it is feasible to produce on the revenue side.

3. The manner in which the property tax is levied militates
against smooth taxpayer acceptance. The federal income tax is paid in
large part through payroll withholding and quarterly installments; sales
and excise taxes, which provide the largest share of state revenues,
are paid in numerous small "installments"; the property tax bill, on the
other hand, is a lump-sum affair allowing only two payments. Little
wonder that the taxpayer is more conscious of his property tax burden
and resists strenuously increases thereof!

4. Local officials who are responsible for setting the actual
property tax rates (per $100 assessed valuation), i.e., city councils,
school board trustees, and boards of supervisors, have been caught in
the vise of the citizen's ambivalent attitude toward the two related aspects of local finance, namely, spending and taxing. Citizens, on the
one hand, have demanded higher standards and expanded public services.
But many of these same citizens, on the other hand, have been most
vocal in expressing their displeasure with the tax rate increases that
must inevitably follow the increased demand for services. Local officials
have been exceedingly gun shy in the matter of proposing either new
taxes or increased rates. It is too easy for the taxpayer to harangue his
councilman or school board trustee on the subject of "holding the tax
line." Indeed, more direct mass pressure is exerted against local property tax increases than against tax changes at the other levels of gover-
ment.

5. The flexibility of the local government fiscal structure is
restricted by state constitutional and statutory provisions that limit the
local officials' power to tax. Particularly restrictive under growth conditions is the provision that places maximum limits on local tax rates.
At the beginning of the postwar period of growth in 1945 and 1946, 85%
of all California cities were at or within 10% of their statutory tax limits.
This obviously provided little leeway for increases in local property tax
rates without time-consuming statutory or constitutional changes. Once

property tax rate ceilings are approached the destiny of local government finance is largely tied to the assessment process. In other words, the inflexibility of legal property tax rates and the lag of assessed valuations behind market values severely limit the productivity of the property tax during a period of growth.

6. The heavy reliance on the property tax as expenditure demands increase accentuates the burden of the tax. It is generally agreed that, on balance, the property tax places a proportionately higher burden on lower income groups. As such, the tax violates the equity criterion of a good tax system. The degree of inequity in taxation at the local level of government has grown in the postwar period. When the magnitude of the tax burden becomes great enough to arouse the ire of the mass of the tax-paying public, it becomes increasingly difficult (at least from the point of view of political expediency) for local officials to lead the way toward increased property taxes.

By way of summary, certain administrative aspects, differences in the property tax base, the pattern of community growth, and the "politics" of local tax administration limit the fiscal efficacy of the local property tax in a period of dynamic growth.

Aside from the limitations of the property tax as a source of revenue to local government, other factors have contributed to the revenue deficiencies of the local tax structure. First, local and state government officials have failed to take a comprehensive view of the local finance situation and to develop a more diversified tax structure. To be sure, the sales tax has become a part of the local revenue system in the postwar period. In many instances, however, the adoption of the local sales tax represented a desperation measure, and in no sense was related to a thoroughgoing study of the available tax alternatives.

The sheer weight of the total federal, state, and local tax burden on the average family unit is bound to generate taxpayer resistance. Unfortunately, from the point of view of local finance, the citizen's aversion to higher taxes is most conveniently expressed at the local level. A letter sent to Washington protesting high taxes may be much less effective than vocal resistance in the local council or school board meeting. The property tax, in particular, generates mass tax consciousness.

The sources of the financial plight of the local unit of government are therefore many and varied. The essence of the problem stems from the overwhelming expenditure pressures associated with growth and the inadequacies of a tradition-bound local revenue structure which has not been adapted to the needs of a dynamic economy. The end result is increased pressure for state and federal underwriting of many traditional functions of local government.

THE CALIFORNIA STATE REVENUE STRUCTURE: PAST AND PRESENT

The discussion in the preceding sections has revealed that local government units in California derive considerable amounts of financial support from state subventions or grants-in-aid. It follows, therefore, that the fiscal well-being of the local unit is inextricably bound up with the fiscal capacity of the state. The purpose of this section is to develop briefly the nature of the California revenue structure.

Historical Developments in California State Finance

In 1900, total tax collections by the State of California amounted to $7,915,165. In that year 89.4% of all California state taxes were derived from ad valorem property taxes. For the fiscal year 1958-59, tax revenues for the state are estimated at $1.86 billion. Given the importance of taxes in the over-all California state revenue picture, it is appropriate to examine the state tax structure in some detail.

Although the property tax provided the largest share of state revenue in 1900, this form of taxation yielded less than one percent of total state funds by 1920. Utility gross receipts taxes and motor vehicle licenses yielded 31.3 and 12.5%, respectively, and nontax sources accounted for 33.4% of the 1920 revenue total. The depression decade of the 1930's brought drastic pressures for changes. Two main pressures are worthy of mention: (1) As early as 1930, it was apparent that the existing tax system was unequal to the task of financing growing state expenditures. (2) The advent of the depression, and the consequent decline in property tax values and income, served to compound the already emerging crisis. Local governmental units, faced with a virtual collapse of their main source of support, the property tax, turned in desperation to the state for assistance.

One of the results of the depression crisis in California state and local finance was the "Riley-Stewart Plan," which took the form of Senate Constitutional Amendment No. 30, adopted on June 27, 1933.* This amendment transferred to the state the counties' share of school

---

*The discussion of the Riley-Stewart Act has been adapted from Report of the Senate Interim Committee on State and Local Taxation, Part III - State and Local Taxes in California: A Comparative Analysis. Sacramento: California Legislature, 1951 Regular Session, April 1951, pp. 35-36.

costs with the provision that the state raise the necessary revenue from sources other than taxes on property. The implication to be drawn from the Riley-Stewart Act was that the state should adopt either a sales tax or a personal income tax or both to meet its newly acquired responsibilities. The Legislature subsequently passed bills providing for both; however, the income tax bill was vetoed by the Governor. A 2-1/2% general sales tax became a part of the California General Fund revenue structure in 1933; by 1934, 16.6% of all state revenues were being derived from this source. By this time the constitutionality of the tax had been established and the sales tax has assumed an increasingly important place in the state revenue system.

Pressures on the California state revenue structure continued through 1934. On July 1, 1935, the following basic changes in the sales tax law became effective: (1) retail sales of food products were exempted, (2) leases and rentals were added to the list of taxable transactions, and (3) the rate of the tax was increased to 3%.

Another potentially significant development in California finance was the passage of the Personal Income Tax Law, effective June 13, 1935, against income received on or after January 1, 1935. The personal income tax emerged as a part of the state revenue structure as a result of the exigencies of the depression. Under the following rate structure, the tax yielded 6.9% of all state revenues in fiscal 1957:[*]

Taxable Income	% Tax Rate
$ 0 to $ 5,000	1
5,000 to 10,000	2
10,000 to 15,000	3
15,000 to 20,000	4
20,000 to 25,000	5
Over 25,000	6

Corporate income in California is taxed under either the bank and corporation franchise tax or the corporation income tax. The franchise tax was first levied in 1929. Important changes were effected in the Franchise Tax Act in 1935 when the tax rate was raised to 4%. Railroads and public utilities were brought under the law with the repeal of the utility gross receipts tax. The base for the franchise tax is measured by net income, and the current rate ranges from 4 to 8%, with a minimum tax per annum of $25.

[*] The original rate structure ranged from 1 through 15 but the rates were reduced to these levels during World War II. They were raised again in 1959.

The corporation income tax was established by statute in 1937. This tax is designed to supplement the Bank and Corporation Franchise Tax Act since it relates to certain corporations, e.g., "foreign" corporations doing business in California, which are not subject to the franchise tax. The corporation income tax is imposed at a rate of 4% on a net tax basis. Together, the franchise and corporate income taxes yielded 9% of state revenue in 1957, the proceeds going to the General Fund.

The Insurance Premium Tax is levied at a rate of 2.35% on gross premiums collected in California. The tax dating back to 1862 yielded about 2% of total state revenues in 1957. Special rules and rates apply to title insurance and ocean marine insurance companies.

The Alcoholic Beverage Control Act, effective July 1, 1935, provided for a system of liquor license fees and a series of excise taxes on distilled spirits, beer, and wine sold in California. Fees range from $11 per year for retail package off-sale beer and wine licenses to $825 per year for a beer manufacturer's license. The excises are set at varying rates per gallon, as follows:

```
Beer...................................... $0.02
Natural dry wine .......................    .01
All other still wine ....................   .02
Distilled spirits of proof strength ........ 1.50
(Champagne or sparkling wine is taxed from 24 cents
to 30 cents per gallon.)
```

Prior to July 1, 1954, all revenues from liquor license fees were apportioned to cities and counties. On the basis of legislation in 1954 and 1955, liquor license fees were increased by 10%, with the proceeds from the increase earmarked for the General Fund. In 1955, the excise on distilled spirits was increased from 80 cents to $1.50 per gallon; at the same time, the excise on champagne and sparkling wine was increased to the present rates. Alcoholic beverage excise tax revenues are also credited to the General Fund. Liquor licenses and excise taxes yielded 2.4% of state revenue in 1957.

Since 1933, the state has levied what are generally labeled "horse-racing fees." These "fees" might more accurately be defined as a tax on pari-mutuel pool wagering. The tax rate ranges from 4% on any amount in the pari-mutuel wagering pool to $10 million to 6% on any amount over $20 million. The pari-mutuel tax, along with a system of license fees on trainers, jockeys, and others, yielded $5.6 million during fiscal year 1957. Well over three-fourths of this revenue is allocated to the Fair and Exposition and the State College Funds; the proceeds from pari-mutuel taxes in excess of 4% of the wagering pool for each racing meet accrue to the General Fund.

Subsequent to 1930, inheritance and gift taxes declined relatively as a source of state General Fund revenue. Four different sets of rates apply depending upon the recipient's relationship to the decedent or donor. The inheritance and gift tax rates range from 2% to 16%. A combination of low rates and lenient exemptions reduces the revenue potential of these two tax sources.

Motor vehicle license and registration fees and the 6 cents per gallon state gasoline tax yielded, respectively, 10.6 and 14.1% of total California state revenues in 1957. Proceeds from the former taxes are used for the administration and enforcement of motor vehicle laws, and for street and highway maintenance; gasoline excise revenues are shared with counties and cities, and are earmarked specifically for highway and street construction and improvements. Vehicle licenses and gasoline excises combined represent the second most important source of revenue to the State of California.

Table 5.10 presents the total revenue picture for the State of California for selected fiscal years between 1930 and 1957. One should note that in recent years taxes have provided at least 75% of total revenues; nontax sources and federal grants-in-aid have made up the balance, with grants providing 17% of 1957 revenues. For the forty-eight states, collectively, 67.8% of total 1957 revenues were derived from tax sources. California places heavier reliance on tax sources than do the majority of states.

One further summary observation with respect to the California structure appears in order at this point. During fiscal year 1957, at least $1.0 billion of the state's revenue was derived from tax sources which can accurately be placed under the "sales" or "excise" categories. These tax sources were: the 3% general sales and use tax, which yielded approximately 30% of the state's total revenue, gasoline, motor vehicle (licenses), liquor, and pari-mutuel pool wagering taxes. In other words, 62.5% of all tax revenues, and 48.5% of total state revenues in 1957 were derived from tax sources which, generally speaking, place a proportionately higher burden on lower income groups. (See Figures 5.3 and 5.4.) These tax revenues, in turn, finance a considerable portion of locally-administered governmental functions of which public education is clearly the most important.

Table 5.10. California State Revenues, by Major Source: 1930, 1937, 1947, 1952-57

(Millions of dollars)

Fiscal Year Source	1930 Amount	%	1937 Amount	%	1947 Amount	%	1952 Amount	%	1953 Amount	%	1954 Amount	%	1955 Amount	%	1956 Amount	%	1957 Amount	%
Tax Revenues																		
Sales & Use Tax			$ 84.6	31.4	$241.5	34.2	$417.7	33.1	$460.1	33.1	$465.1	30.6	$492.9	29.1	$564.2	30.3	$600.1	29.1
Gasoline & Diesel Fuel Tax	$ 33.9	29.5	44.2	16.4	75.5	10.7	162.1	12.8	170.9	12.3	234.4	15.4	244.6	14.5	273.1	14.7	291.4	14.1
Motor Vehicle Taxes and Licenses*	10.9	9.5	26.4	9.8	60.0	8.5	139.7	11.1	153.2	11.0	184.3	12.1	199.8	11.8	228.2	12.3	236.8	11.5
Franchises & Corporate Income Tax	6.8	5.9	17.4	6.5	59.2	8.4	120.1	9.5	119.2	8.6	125.0	8.2	133.7	7.9	157.1	8.4	167.4	8.1
Personal Income Tax			16.8	6.3	51.2	7.2	90.9	7.2	94.6	6.8	96.2	6.3	106.7	6.3	127.8	6.9	143.3	6.9
Liquor Tax & Licenses			16.4	6.1	28.8	4.1	26.0	2.1	28.4	2.0	28.1	1.8	29.5	1.7	48.0	2.6	49.9	2.4
Gift & Inheritance Tax	11.6	10.1	5.7	2.1	20.1	2.8	29.2	2.3	23.5	1.7	24.1	1.6	30.3	1.8	36.3	1.9	38.5	1.9
Other Taxes**	40.4	35.2	8.6	3.2	36.0	5.1	48.3	3.8	52.9	3.9	59.7	4.0	64.7	3.9	65.4	3.5	70.3	3.4
Total Tax Receipts	$130.6	90.2	$220.1	81.8	$572.3	81.0	$1034.0	81.9	$1102.8	79.4	$1216.9	80.0	$1302.2	77.0	$1500.1	80.6	$1597.7	77.4
Non-tax Receipts***	6.4	5.6	15.6	5.8	37.3	5.3	52.0	4.1	49.3	3.5	54.1	3.5	131.6	7.8	77.9	4.2	114.9	5.6
Receipts from the Federal Government	4.8	4.2	33.4	12.4	96.8	13.7	176.7	14.0	237.5	17.1	251.0	16.5	257.8	15.2	284.0	15.2	352.0	17.0
Total Receipts	$114.8	100%	$269.1	100%	$706.4	100%	$1262.7	100%	$1389.6	100%	$1522.0	100%	$1691.6	100%	$1862.0	100%	$2064.6	100%

* Includes: Motor vehicle license tax, motor vehicle in lieu tax, motor vehicle registration, motor transportation tax.

** Includes: Insurance premium tax, race track revenues, ad valorem taxes, utility gross receipts tax (1930 only) and regulatory taxes and penalties, private car tax.

*** Excludes: Unemployment and workmen's compensation taxes.

Includes: Departmental and miscellaneous revenues.

Additional receipts of $122.3 million were received from Long Beach Tidelands Case.

Source: State Controller, Annual Reports.

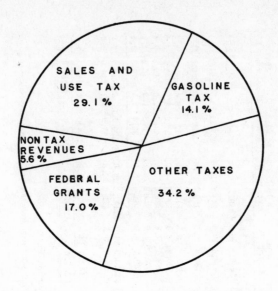

Figure 5.3. The 1957 California State Revenue Dollar

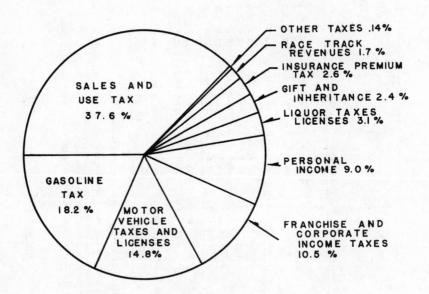

Figure 5.4. The 1957 California State Tax Dollar

THE STATE OF CALIFORNIA FACES ITS OWN REVENUE CRISIS

Proceeding on the assumption that a solution of the existing crisis in California local finance is functionally related to the revenue adequacies or inadequacies of the state itself, it is appropriate to inquire into the state's own current fiscal state-of-affairs. Unfortunately, there is much evidence to support the position that the State of California faces a fiscal crisis. It becomes apparent, therefore, that a long-run solution to the state's current fiscal dilemma must be developed if the crisis in local finance is to be met. The alternatives are, (1) a deterioration in a number of socially necessary expenditure programs at the state and local levels, e.g., public education, or (2) increased reliance on federal grants-in-aid.

Facts Supporting the Crisis Thesis

What evidence supports the position that a crisis in finance actually exists at the state level? Recognition of the crisis has manifested itself in a number of ways. One has but to examine the Governor's 1958-59 Budget Message to find "official" recognition of the state's dilemma. The following excerpt from this message highlights the predicament the state is now facing:[4]

> You will see from the summary tabulation of the General Fund shown below that estimated expenditure requirements through the 1958-59 Fiscal Year exceed available current funds by $94,463,762.

Condition of the General Fund - Estimates in Millions of Dollars

	1957-58	1958-59
Surplus July 1	$ 109,694,825	$ 8,482,620
Revenues	1,144,524,507	1,183,487,986
Expenditures:		
State Operations	398,384,622	431,982,463
Capital Outlay	86,925,076	30,204,836
Local Assistance	772,302,005	831,979,109
	$1,257,611,703	$1,294,166,408
Deficiency of Current Income	113,087,196	110,678,422
Transfers from Other Funds*	11,874,991	7,732,040
Surplus June 30, 1958	8,482,620	
Accumulated Deficiency June 30, 1959	----	94,463,762

*Includes transfers from School Bond Retirement Fund in accordance with Chapter 1073/1957.

> I recommend the following means of meeting this deficiency as a budget balancing plan which does not require additional taxes:

1. Transfer the Revenue Deficiency Reserve Fund to the
    General Fund $75,000,000
2. Repay to the General Fund an advance made
    to the School Building Aid Fund in 1952 of   20,000,000

        Total to be made available $95,000,000
        Estimated deficiency   94,463,762

        Estimated working surplus $ 536,238

Several sobering facts emerge from a scrutiny of the statistics
Governor Knight presented in this message. First, during fiscal year
1957-58, the $113,087,196 current income deficiency in the General
Fund was met in large part using surpluses accumulated during previous years, with interfund transfers making up the balance.[*] Second,
for the fiscal year 1958-59, a General Fund revenue deficiency of
$110,678,422 is indicated. This deficiency was to be covered largely
by using the Revenue Deficiency Reserve, or "Rainy Day," Fund of
$75 million which was set aside at the close of World War II. Third,
the existing tax structure is not geared to meet the present fiscal
needs of the state. Perhaps the most salient observation to be drawn
from these data is the fact that, to date (November 1958), little or no
positive action has been taken to meet the state's fiscal dilemma. Both
the governor and the Legislature have chosen to rely upon bookkeeping
interfund transfers as a short-run delaying action. That this approach
has not provided a long-run solution to the state's budgetary problems
is revealed in a statement by the State Controller on June 23, 1958:
"We have bridged this gap between revenue and expenditures [in the
1957-58 State budget] by making transfers from reserves, and by using
surplus money accumulated in prior years. But at the close of the next
fiscal year [1958-59], the surplus will have evaporated and the State
cupboard will be bare of all but a pittance of reserve funds."[**] The
State of California, indeed, faces a fiscal crisis.

Factors Underlying California's Financial Crisis

The development of a proper perspective with respect to the current crisis in California state finance depends on clarifying the underlying forces that have placed the state in its present fiscal dilemma.

_____

[*] Actually, in the last weeks of the 1957-58 fiscal year, the state
found it necessary to use approximately $20 million of the $75 million
Revenue Deficiency Reserve Fund.

[**] Release from State Controller, dated June 23, 1958. The statement had specific reference to the $50 million revenue losses to the
state associated with Proposition No. 17 which appeared on the state
ballot in November 1958.

Isolating the specific factors involved allows one to fix responsibility, and provides a framework within which to develop an appropriate set of recommendations. The following factors account in large part for California's fiscal difficulties:

1. The state emerged from World War II with huge expenditure needs, e.g., schools and highways, related to the effects of the depression as well as to the drastic curtailment of state construction programs during World War II.

2. The rapid population growth involves heavy expenditures for schools, highways, public health, mental hygeine, and corrections, to mention but a few areas of pressure at the state level. In-migration has added to school enrollment totals and has accentuated the pressures for higher expenditures in the field of public education at all levels from kindergarten to college.

3. The related phenomenon of population mobility, particularly the postwar exodus from city to suburbia, has placed heavy pressures on the state budget. Population mobility involves, among other things, new schools, streets, and highways, all of which involve sizeable expenditures.

4. Inflation has worked its relentless attrition on the state's expenditure dollar. The U.S. Bureau of Public Roads highway construction cost index (per standard mile) increased from a monthly average of 91.6 in 1945 (1946 = 100), to 142.9 in 1947. This increase is typical of the price inflation that has plagued the state in the postwar period. Inflation serves to compound the pressures on the revenue side of the budget.

5. Another factor heightening the existing revenue dilemma is the fact that approximately 70% of the state's expenditures are fixed either by the Constitution or by existing statutes. The basic grants to school districts, for example, are fixed by constitutional provision. Financial assistance to the aged and aid to dependent children comprise additional commitments fixed by existing laws. Only about one-third of the state's expenditures are variable and subject to revision as each annual appropriation bill is passed upon.[*] The preponderance of fixed outlays in the state budget can alone create periodic short-run crises in local finance if revenues fluctuate in response to cyclical variations in the economy.

[*] As state college and university enrollments expand, even this portion of the budget is subject to encroachment.

6. California's revenue structure is geared closely to the over-all level of business volume and income. Thus, whenever recessions occur, the state tax revenue stream slows down and narrows. Deficits become the obvious result in the face of the inability to cut expenditures. This is certainly one of the causes of the deficit in the budget for 1958-59. The severe fluctuations in state revenues may be considerably miti-gated by achieving greater diversity in tax sources. California utilizes most traditional state tax sources, but tends to rely most upon three major sources: the general sales tax, auto fees, and the gasoline tax. The danger of running a deficit on General Fund account may also be reduced by implementing a sounder counter-cyclical policy on the revenue side. To be sure, pressures on the expenditure side of the budget have been great in the postwar period. A lengthening of the state's fiscal planning horizon, however, would have promoted a size-able General Fund surplus to be carried over on a year-to-year basis to meet revenue demands during periodic business recessions.

7. Related to the previous point is the fact that the state is com-mitted, in many instances by statute, to share tax revenues with local units of government. As a result, the state faces a degree of fixity with respect to the revenue dollar it collects. This reduces its ability to operate within the framework of the existing revenue structure when General Fund expenditures are increasing at a rapid rate.

8. Perhaps one of the less obvious factors contributing to the state's current fiscal dilemma has been the existence of the $75 million "Rainy Day" Fund, built up during World War II. As long as this fund existed both the Executive and Legislative branches played the line closely in the matter of new taxation. These funds were always con-sidered adequate to bridge the gap when the existing revenue structure faltered under the pressures of a cyclical downturn. The mere exist-ence of the fund, in other words, generated a false sense of fiscal security, jolted rudely during the 1957-58 recession.

9. The current embarrassing state of fiscal affairs is largely a result of one factor implied in the preceding paragraph: Californians, in the postwar period, have faced to face up to the tax question. In a period of unprecedented growth in state expenditures, both qualitative-ly and quantitatively, "the State's tax structure has remained virtually unchanged for more than 20 years."[5] Herein lies a fundamental cause of the current plight of California state finance. Aside from the in-creases in excises on distilled spirits voted by the Legislature in 1955,

no significant piece of tax legislation has been enacted in the postwar period. The 1957 Legislature enacted tax measures producing an estimated $4 million over-all <u>reduction</u> in General and Special Fund tax receipts. The principal piece of legislation reduced the motor transportation tax from 3 to 1.5% (and deleted weight fee credit); the revenue loss due to this change was estimated to be $7,625,000 per year.

The failure to enact new tax levies and the reluctance to revise the existing tax structure provide key explanations of the revenue inadequacies of the California tax structure. A fiscal show-down is imminent, and the state's tax <u>status quo</u> favoring a variety of interest groups <u>must</u> receive a thorough reappraisal.

NOTES TO CHAPTER 5

[1] Adam Smith, Wealth of Nations, New York: Random House, Inc., 1937, Book V, Chapter I.

[2] California State Board of Equalization, <u>Annual Report,</u> 1956-57, p. 22.

[3] Dixwell L. Pierce, "California Has a Sales Tax Headache," <u>National Tax Journal,</u> VI, No. 2, June 1953, pp. 168-75.

[4] <u>Budget Message of Goodwin J. Knight,</u> Governor of California, 1958-59 Budget. Transmitted to the California Legislature Monday, February 3, 1958, p. 9.

[5] Ibid., p. 11.

> There is in America no important disagreement as to the proper objectives of economic policy — larger real income, greater regularity of production and employment, reduction of inequality, preservation of democratic institutions. The real issues have to do merely with means, not with ends (or intentions); but the future of our civilization hangs in balance as these issues are decided. Henry Simons, Economic Policy for a Free Society, Chicago: University of Chicago Press, 1948, p. 40.

What can be done to meet the impending crisis in California state and local finance? The answer to this question calls for an evaluation of the present revenue system, and the development of specific recommendations as well as the outline of a program through which these may be effected.

EVALUATION OF THE LOCAL REVENUE SYSTEM

Property, sales, and business license taxes produced 100% of local tax revenues and 52% of total receipts, including grants and shared revenues, in the fiscal year 1957. Since the property tax continues, and will continue, to play a dominant role in local finance (46.1% of total receipts in 1957) evaluation of the local revenue system must concentrate heavily on this tax.

The General Property Tax

Constitutional and Statutory Provisions. Of crucial importance to the ultimate social equity and fiscal effects of the property tax are the constitutional and statutory provisions that are applicable to it. Section 1 of Article XIII of the state Constitution provides:

> All property in the State except as otherwise in this Constitution provided, not exempt under the laws of the United States, shall be taxed in proportion to its value, to be ascertained as provided by law, or as hereinafter provided. The word "property," as used in this article and section, is hereby declared to include moneys, credits, bonds, stocks, dues, franchises, and all other matters and things, real, personal, and mixed, capable of private ownership.

By action of the Legislature, two classes of property are identified for tax purposes. Section 104 of the Revenue and Taxation Code defines the first class, real estate, or property, to include: (a) The possession of, claim to, ownership of, or right to the possession of land. (b) All mines, minerals, and quarries in the land, all standing timber whether or not belonging to the owner of the land, and all rights and privileges appertaining thereto. (c) Improvements, defined in Section 105, include all buildings, structures, fixtures, and fences erected on or affixed to the land, except telephone and telegraph lines, and all fruit, nut-bearing, or ornamental trees and vines, not of natural growth, and not exempt from taxation, except date palms under eight years of age.

Section 106 of the Code defines the second category, personal property, to include all property except real estate, and Section 14 of Article XIII of the Constitution provides that:

> The Legislature shall have the power to provide for the assessment, levy and collection of taxes upon all forms of tangible personal property, all notes, debentures, shares of capital stock, bonds, solvent credits, deeds of trust, mortgages, and any legal or equitable interest therein, not exempt from taxation under the provisions of this Constitution, in such manner, and at such rates, as may be provided by law, and in pursuance of the exercise of such power the Legislature, two-thirds of all the members elected to each of the two houses voting in favor thereof, may classify any and all kinds of personal property for the purposes of assessment and taxation in a manner and at a rate or rates in proportion to value different from any other property in this State subject to taxation and may exempt entirely from taxation any or all forms, types or classes of personal property.

> The total tax imposed on notes, debentures, shares of capital stock, bonds, solvent credits, deeds of trust, mortgages and any legal or equitable interest therein in pursuance of the provisions of this section shall not be at a rate in excess of four-tenths of 1 percent of the actual value of such property and no tax burden shall be imposed upon any personal property either tangible or intangible which shall exceed the tax burden on real property in the same taxing jurisdiction in proportion to the actual value of such property.

Intangible personal property is defined in Section 111 to include only notes, debentures, shares of capital stock, bonds, solvent credits, deeds of trust, and mortgages. Article XIII, Section 14 of the Constitution provides, however, for the exemption from taxation of notes, debentures, shares of capital stock, bonds, deeds of trust, mortgages, and any interest therein. In other words, only two kinds of intangible personal property are now taxable in California — solvent credits and franchises.*

Exclusions from the Property Tax Base. The definition of the property tax base as set forth in Section 1 of Article XIII of the Constitution has been appreciably narrowed through time by a series of amendments and statutory changes. Reference has already been made to the provision for the exemption of certain types of intangible property. In addition, the specific exemptions currently operative are listed on the following page.

---

*Solvent credits are defined by Section 113 of the Code to include all credits, except notes, bonds, debentures, and intercorporation advances or deposits. By action of the State Legislature a tax limit of one-tenth of 1% is applicable to the actual value of solvent credits and any interest therein, and is in lieu of all other property taxes levied on intangibles. Typical examples of solvent credits are accounts receivable, deposits in commercial banks (excluding savings accounts), trust receipts, and United States checks.

1. Growing crops (Article XIII, Section 1).
2. Property used for free public libraries and free museums (Article XIII, Section 1).
3. Property used exclusively for public schools (Article XIII, Section 1).
4. Property belonging to this state, a county, or a city (Article XIII, Section 1).
5. Property exempt under the laws of the United States (Article XIII, Section 1).
6. State colleges; use of certain personal property (added by Stats. 1957).
7. Property used by nonprofit educational institution of collegiate grade (Article XIII, Section 1a).
8. Nonprofit cemeteries (Article XIII, Section 1b).
9. $1,000 of the assessed value of the property of all U.S. military veterans not owning property exceeding $5,000 in assessed value (Article XIII, Section 1-1/4).
10. Church property (Article XIII, Section 1-1/2).
11. Orphanages (Article XIII, Section 1-1/2a).
12. State, County, Municipal, and District Bonds (Article XIII, Section 1-3/4).
13. Vessels (Article XIII, Section 4).
14. Householder's exemption (Article XIII, Section 10-1/2).
15. Trees and vines (Article XIII, Section 12-3/4).
16. Exhibits (Revenue and Taxation Code, Section 213).
17. Property used exclusively for religious, hospital, scientific, or charitable purposes owned and operated by community chests, funds, foundations or corporations organized and operated for religious, hospital, scientific, or charitable purposes, if certain conditions are met (added by Stats. 1945, 1949, 1951, 1953, 1955).
18. Property of veterans organizations (added by Stats. 1945).
19. Vending stands of blind operators (added by Stats. 1955).
20. Aircraft being repaired in California (added by Stats. 1955).

Sources and Limitations on Local Taxing Power. Local units of government possess no inherent power of taxation. Article XI, Section 12 of the State Constitution authorizes the Legislature to make specific grants of taxing power to cities, counties, school districts, and other districts:

> Except as otherwise provided in this Constitution, the Legislature shall have no power to impose taxes upon counties, cities, towns or other public or municipal corporations, or upon the inhabitants or property thereof, for county, city, town, or other municipal purposes, but may, by general laws, vest in the corporate authorities thereof the power to assess and collect taxes for such purposes.

> All property subject to taxation shall be assessed for taxation at its full cash value. (Amendment adopted June 27, 1933.)

The conditions governing taxation of property by California counties are set forth in Title 2 of the Political Code, Sections 4000 to 4348, or in the respective county charters. California cities derive their power to tax property from the general laws of the state, or from their own

charters. The statutes contain numerous provisions relating to the
processes of assessment and collection.* Local units are subject to
maximum tax rate provisions, as follows:

> Maximum tax rates, which may be exceeded only by vote of
> the people, are established by law for certain political subdivi-
> sions. Sixth class cities in California may not levy for general
> purposes more than $1.00 per $100 of assessed valuation, except
> by vote and for specific programs, such as retirement, debt ser-
> vice, and certain expenditures for park, recreation, and library
> activities. In a fifth class city the tax rate may be raised to $1.25
> by unanimous vote of the municipality's board of trustees. Char-
> tered cities in many instances have tax rate limits in their char-
> ters. For some special districts tax rate limits have no over-all
> tax rate limits but the law restricts spending for such things as
> publicity and advertising.

> Tax rate limits for school districts, which may be exceeded
> by vote of the people, include for example, for elementary school
> districts with kindergarten, 90 cents, without kindergarten, 80
> cents. High school districts may levy up to 75 cents for high
> school purposes; if junior college classes are maintained up to
> $1.10. Junior college districts may levy up to 35 cents for oper-
> ation. Unified districts which are combined elementary and high
> school may levy up to $1.55; high school and junior college may
> levy up to $1.90; with kindergarten $2. Where a high school dis-
> trict and a junior college district are coterminous, the maximum
> rate is $1.10.[1]

The actual tax rates for the various local jurisdictions are reviewed annually by local officials.

Provisions Relating to Property Tax Administration. Central to
the administration of the local property tax is the process of assessment. In California, three agencies are principally responsible for assessing property. These are the State Board of Equalization, the 58
county assessors, and city assessors. Under Article XIII, Section 14
of the Constitution, the State Board of Equalization is required to assess
railroad, public utility, and certain other properties. The assessment
rolls are transmitted for taxation purposes to the units in which such
property is located. County assessors assess all other property for
county, school district, and most special district purposes. By 1958,
nearly two-thirds of the state's municipalities were relying upon county
assessment and collection of their property taxes. In these instances a
single assessment roll suffices for both city and county purposes. Some
119 cities, however, were still preparing their own assessment rolls and

* For an excellent discussion of the details surrounding the taxation
power of local government in California, see Report of Senate Interim
Committee on State and Local Taxation, State and Local Government
Finance in California, January 1947, Ch. II and III, and State and Local
Taxes in California: A Comparative Analysis, April 1951, pp. 497-512.

collecting their own property taxes. Certain special districts also have statutory authority to prepare their own assessment rolls and collect their own taxes.[2]

The annual chronology of property tax assessment and equalization in California runs as follows:[3]

Between the first Mondays in March and July, the county assessor is required to assess all taxable common property in the county to the person owning, claiming, possessing, or controlling it as of noon of the first Monday in March; and on or before the first Monday in August, the State Board of Equalization must assess all public utility and other property assessable by it to the owner, likewise as of noon of the first Monday in March.

On or before the first Monday in July, the county assessor is required to complete a portion of the assessment roll known as the "local roll," which lists all the property that the assessor is required to assess, the values of such property, the names of the assessees, and other required information; and upon its completion must deliver it to the clerk of the board of supervisors.

Immediately after the third Monday in August, the State Board of Equalization must transmit to each county auditor an assessment roll, known as the "board roll, " showing the assessments made by it of state-assessed property in the county. (Property on the board roll is also part of the 'secured roll', as is property on the local roll the taxes on which are a lien on real property sufficient, in the opinion of the assessor, to secure the payment after taxes. The local roll also consists of "unsecured property, " which is property the taxes on which are not such a lien. Such property makes up the "unsecured roll." Such property is thereafter subject to local taxation to the same extent and in the same manner as property assessed by the county assessor.

From the first Monday in July to a date not later than the third Monday in July, the county board of supervisors sits as a county board of equalization to equalize the assessment of property shown on the local roll. To that end, it may increase or lower individual assessments, but cannot raise or lower the entire roll. Following such equalization, the local roll, as corrected by such process, is delivered by the clerk of the board to the county auditor. The latter then totals up the valuations, prepares duplicate valuation statements, one of which must be sent to the State Board of Equalization and the other to the State Controller, and, for collection purposes, transmits that portion of the local roll showing unsecured property either to the assessor or, if designated to collect taxes on such property to the tax collector.

From the third Monday in July to the third Monday in August, the State Board of Equalization meets at Sacramento for the purpose of equalizing the assessments of county assessed property. On the completion of equalization, the board's secretary transmits a statement of changes to the county auditor of each county whose roll the board changes. It is then the duty of the auditor to make appropriate entries on the assessment roll.

Evaluation of the General Property Tax. When matched against the criteria generally attributed to a model tax, the property tax fails badly. Its main shortcomings, each of which will be discussed in some detail, are as follows:[*]

1. It is highly discriminatory in its application to different forms of wealth as a result of existing classification and exemption provisions.

2. It is inherently regressive.

3. When recognition is given to tax shifting, the incidence of the tax tends to be concentrated on those with the least ability to pay.

4. The use of an ad valorem base for tax purposes places an excessive burden on persons with small current cash income.

5. Though levied against a real property base, the actual tax is paid in large part from income earned from nonproperty sources, primarily wages, and not from wealth sources.

6. It is levied on a "gross" rather than on a "net" valuation basis and thus places a tax burden upon "phantom" property rights.

7. It is a poor index or measure of benefits received.

8. It is cumbersome and fails to adjust to the changing economic conditions of a highly industrialized economy.

9. It is difficult to administer.

10. It produces undersirable resource allocation effects.

Discriminatory aspects. Legislative action under Article XIII of the Constitution, Section 14, has produced highly discriminatory results in terms of the manner in which the property tax affects different forms of wealth in California. A sample review of the taxable status of various types of property under existing law reveals the following:

Type of Property	Taxable Status	
	Yes	No
1. Land	X	
2. Improvements	X	
3. Household goods	X	
4. Personal effects	X	
5. Automobiles	X	
6. Cash	X	
7. Business inventories	X	
8. Notes Receivable		X
9. Shares of Stock		X
10. Bonds		X
11. Mortgages		X
12. Deeds of Trust		X
13. Accounts Receivable	X	
14. Demand Deposits	X	

The greatest burden of the tax falls upon the owner of real property and improvements. (See Table 6.1.) This principle of taxation is

[*] For an excellent discussion of the property tax see John F. Due, Government Finance, Homewood, Ill.: Richard D. Irwin, Inc: 1954), Ch. 21.

defensible in an agrarian economy in which land is the main productive
source of income. Today, however, the tax falls heavily upon one particular type of noncash income-producing real property — the family
residence. In other words, it discriminates heavily against the homeowner vis-à-vis owners of other forms of wealth.

Table 6.1 Total Valuation of County Assessed Tangible
Property in California, by Class of Property: 1958 *

(billions)

Type of Property	1958	
	Assessed Valuation**	% of Total
Land	$ 7.472	31.2
Improvements	12.075	50.4
Personal Property	4.415	18.4
	$23.962	100.4

* Before reflecting exemptions.
** State Board of Equalization, Annual Reports for fiscal year
ended June 30, 1958.

The property tax is also discriminatory in terms of its treatment
of real versus personal property.[4] Personal property of considerable
value escapes assessment, whereas most real property appears on assess
sessment rolls. Some have suggested that personal property be exempted
from taxation in order to eliminate this form of discrimination. This
would be unwise for several reasons. First, personal property represented 18.4% of all county-assessed tangible property in California in
1958 (see Table 6.1). Local units of government cannot afford to relinquish such a large part of their property tax base. Second, the discriminatory effects of personal property taxation can be mitigated through
improved administration. Application of a uniform state-wide assessment ratio would constitute a step in the right direction. Beyond this
increased efforts toward placing all items of taxable personal property
on the tax rolls could eliminate most of the existing inequities in this
area.

The policy of assessing business inventories as of the first Monday
in March allows some enterprises to work their stocks down to a nominal
level as of the assessment date. Those firms that cannot take such
evasive action pay a proportionately higher personal property tax on their
inventories. Substituting a monthly or quarterly average inventory figure
would eliminate this form of discrimination.

One final aspect of personal property taxation — namely, the taxation of household furnishings — demands brief reference. The laxity with which the tax on household furnishings and personal effects is administered has a demoralizing effect on both the taxpayer and the assessor. On grounds of administrative feasibility as well as productivity, a strong case can be made for the elimination of the tax on these items of personal property. Local officials, of course, resist such action, since every dollar of property tax revenue counts. If the tax on household furnishings is to be retained, drastic improvement in assessment procedure is essential.

As between tangible and intangible personal property, the action of the Legislature has eliminated entirely the tax on certain forms of intangibles, i.e., notes, debentures, shares of capital stock, bonds, deeds of trust, and mortgages. The existing classification and exemption system, and the discrimination that inevitably results, is of serious social consequence. The exemption of intangibles, such as stocks and bonds, is predicated on the reasoning that income from these forms of wealth should be taxed under the state personal or corporate income tax. Apparently, the Legislature assumes that equity will thereby obtain, yet a simple example will reveal that this is anything but the case.

Assume that A has $10,000 invested in his own home. Assume, further, that the home is assessed at $2,500. With a tax rate of $8 per $100 of assessed valuation, A pays an annual property tax of $200. Let B, on the other hand, invest his $10,000 in the form of corporate securities. With an annual rate of return of, say, 7% he realizes $700 of taxable dividend income each year. If one assumes that B is subject to the top marginal rate of 6% under the California personal income tax statute, his tax liability would be $42. This can hardly be termed equity. Let us assume further that the imputed rental value of A's home is $80 a month. On an annual basis he realizes — in real terms — $960 worth of rental services from his investment. Under the property tax A pays a tax of 20.8% on this imputed income ($200 ÷ $960). Even when the taxable status of A and B is reduced to income terms, it becomes clear that the legislative action exempting intangibles from property taxation is highly discriminatory. Given the concentration of the ownership of intangible forms of property in the hands of higher income groups, the exemption discriminates in favor of those with greatest ability to pay. The gross discrimination associated with the exemption of intangibles thus produces highly inequitable results in property taxation. The responsibility for correcting this inequity rests with the California Legislature.

Critics may argue that to tax intangibles such as stocks and bonds is to place a double burden on the same property. This, of course, was the argument behind the Legislature's action in providing for the exemption. The "double taxation" argument cannot, however, justify complete exemption of the intangibles in question for it ignores entirely the separation between ownership and control in the modern corporate enterprise system. Although a share of stock or a bond may represent a legal interest in the property of a corporation, the realities of the relationship between the intangible property right and real property may be quite different. Share values bear no necessary relationship to book values. The stockholder, in the matter of liquidating his ownership share, has recourse not to the corporate entity, but to a financial intermediary, the securities market. In short, the modern corporate entity exists in its own right as a separate and distinct unit, apart from its legal owners. When recognition is given to the realities of the separateness of the corporation and the holder of intangible property rights therein, the double taxation argument loses much of its significance. We suggest, further, that to the extent that shares of stock are held against foreign corporations, no double taxation of property under the local property tax occurs in California. The exemption of these intangibles represents the grossest type of discrimination.

Other exemptions. No single rationale governs the other exemptions from the property tax base. The $100 exemption for household furnishings, for example, is based upon administrative expediency. The veteran's exemption represents a reward for services, and is in lieu of a direct bonus payment. Federal property is exempt under the "immunity doctrine." The exemption of religious, charitable, educational, and social service organizations is attributed to the fact that these institutions perform socially valuable services that would otherwise have to be performed by government at the taxpayer's expense. State and local government bonds are exempt supposedly to encourage and promote the purchase of these securities at low rates of interest. Unquestionably, many of these exemptions have considerable merit. One cannot ignore the fact, however, that certain exemptions from property taxation are not grounded upon a socially oriented rationale but are simply the result of the pressures of interest groups.

County and state assessed valuations have increased from $7.1 billion in 1937 to $25.6 billion in 1957. Property tax exemptions in the former year carried an assessed valuation of $170.8 million. In 1957, they totaled $1.3 billion, 5.4% of taxable property. The exemptions granted to 1,090,859 veterans equaled $930,057,000, or approximately 70% of total property exclusions in California during 1957. (See Table 6.2.) What is the approximate revenue loss associated with the veterans' exemption? By multiplying the value of the veterans' property exemption in each county by the average tax rate for that county we find that in 1957 the revenue loss associated with this exclusion totaled $59,430,642.* This represented an average property tax concession of about $54.48 for each eligible veteran. The revenue loss for each local unit depends, of course, upon the number of eligible veterans located therein. Los Angeles County, for example, sustained a revenue loss of $26,140,604 under the veterans' exemption during 1957, while Alpine County suffered a loss of $290.

Whatever merits underlie each exclusion from the property tax base, the facts are that exemptions narrow the base and necessarily involve a transfer of the tax burden to other property owners. Exemptions due mainly to the pressure of interest groups certainly violate the maxim of equal treatment of equals.[5] There is a need, in our opinion, for a comprehensive review of all exemptions from the property tax. We recommend in particular the eventual elimination of the veterans' exemption.

The exemption of federal- and state-owned property under the immunity doctrine is of crucial significance to local finance. Roughly 47,174,500 acres, or 47.1% of the state's total area of 100,353,920 acres, is currently owned by the government.** The largest portion of this land consists of the nearly 16,500,000 acres of unappropriated public domain under the jurisdiction of the Bureau of Land Management and 19,977,000 acres held by the U.S. Forest Service. The military services hold 4,119,827 acres with the Navy having 2,179,852 acres, mostly arid desert land used for gunnery training. It is apparent, in other words, that certain federally owned lands do not currently undermine the effective property tax base of local governments in the state. And, fair recognition should be given to the economic benefits that military payrolls and other types of expenditures bring to the localities in question. It must be remembered, however, that privately owned business enterprises bring similar economic advantages to a community.

---

*The revenue loss for 1944-45 was approximately $6.6 million. By 1946-47 the loss had increased to $15.2 million.

** The State of California owns over 2,268,000 acres, roughly 2.2% of the land area.

Table 6.2. Total Assessed Value of Property Tax
Exemptions in California: 1957

	Amount	% of Total
Veterans	$930,057,000	70.2
Churches	155,614,000	11.8
Colleges	66,251,000	5.0
Schools below college grade	53,225,000	4.0
Hospitals	68,000,000	5.1
Other (e.g., orphanages)	51,031,000	3.9
	$1,324,178,000	100.0

Source: Annual Report of the State Board of Equalization for the
fiscal year ended June 30, 1957, pp. 60-61.

Of direct significance to the problem of local finance in California
is the fact that in a number of counties federal property exemptions
have considerably narrowed the effective tax base. In San Diego County,
for instance, the federal government owns over 30% and the state owns
17.2% of the total land area. We must hastily add, however, that the
state-owned land consists of beach and park lands, most of which is
desert land of little value for property tax purposes. It is true, nonetheless, that the heavy concentration of military establishments in the
San Diego area significantly narrows the property tax base. Together,
the federal and state governments own one-third of the land area in Los
Angeles County. Table 6.3 summarizes the relative importance of such
ownership in California's 58 counties.

Partial recognition has been given to the problems of local finance
created by extensive federal ownership of property by the passage of
Public Law 815 (1950) amended by P. L. 246 (1953) and Public Law 874
(1950) amended by P. L. 248 (1953). Public Law 815 provides for federal assistance for school construction in districts where school enrollments have increased as a result of "federal activity," e.g., the
establishment of a new military installation. Public Law 874 provides
assistance for school operation and maintenance in federally affected

Table 6.3. Percentage of Land Area in California Counties Owned
by Federal and State Governments, 1957

County	State Ownership as a % of Total	Federal Ownership as a % of Total	Total Government Ownership as a % of Total
Alameda	2.65	2.34	4.09
Alpine	0.22	97.77	97.99
Amador	1.05	20.35	21.40
Butte	0.89	14.10	14.99
Calaveras	1.08	18.83	19.91
Colusa	0.62	15.15	15.77
Contra Costa	1.14	2.31	3.45
Del Norte	2.95	67.88	70.83
El Dorado	0.60	45.70	46.30
Fresno	0.92	38.85	39.77
Glenn	0.26	24.41	24.67
Humboldt	1.83	19.21	21.04
Imperial	6.54	63.76	70.30
Inyo	2.32	95.15	97.47
Kern	1.75	25.95	27.70
Kings	0.26	0.64	.90
Lake	1.72	43.78	45.50
Lassen	3.37	47.42	50.79
LOS ANGELES	0.88	32.43	33.31
Madera	0.13	36.95	37.08
Marin	2.04	1.62	3.66
Mariposa	0.37	48.10	48.47
Mendocino	3.49	14.46	17.95
Merced	0.54	1.09	1.63
Modoc	0.96	66.77	67.73
Mono	1.09	79.84	80.93
Monterey	0.60	32.45	33.05
Napa	2.16	12.76	14.92
Nevada	0.99	39.79	40.78
ORANGE	0.78	11.59	12.37
Placer	0.53	32.09	32.62
Plumas	0.53	71.22	71.75
Riverside	3.69	53.18	56.87
Sacramento	0.98	1.91	2.89
San Benito	0.89	14.35	15.24
San Bernardino	3.75	74.22	77.97
San Diego	17.23	30.54	47.77
SAN FRANCISCO	3.46	12.63	16.09
San Joaquin	0.56	0.53	1.09
San Luis Obispo	1.11	15.89	17.00
San Mateo	1.66	0.35	2.01
Santa Barbara	0.37	43.24	43.61
Santa Clara	0.92	2.81	3.73
Santa Cruz	5.90	0.03	5.93
Shasta	1.26	39.68	40.94
Sierra	1.04	60.54	61.58
Siskiyou	0.52	62.14	62.66
Solano	3.17	2.37	5.54
Sonoma	1.61	2.41	4.02
Stanislaus	0.27	2.31	2.58
Sutter	1.37	0.33	1.70
Tehama	2.78	22.91	25.69
Trinity	0.76	71.35	72.10
Tulare	0.45	49.96	50.41
Tuolumne	0.33	75.03	75.36
Ventura	0.56	48.67	49.02
Yolo	0.93	5.16	6.09
Yuba	0.65	28.99	29.64
Totals	2.26%	46.14%	48.40%

Source: Senate Interim Committee on Public Land, Public Lands and Resource
Development, 1957, p. 12

areas. During 1957, California school districts received $17,671,297 under Public Law 874 and $469,544 under Public Law 815. Other forms of school aid amounted to $3,439,782. These "in lieu" payments and grants are helpful to be sure, but it is unlikely that federal payments of this type fully underwrite the costs of "federal ownership" in many communities.* Moreover, it is likely that the in lieu payments actually made to local units fall far below the revenue yields which might be gained by placing the federally owned property on the local tax roll.** The latter approach to a determination of the enormity of the in lieu payments made to the respective local units commends itself to serious consideration. Full recognition must be given to the immunity doctrine, but this should not preclude their following the generally accepted procedures for property taxation as a formula for determining the amount of such payments. Revision along these lines would have the effect of transferring part of the local revenue burden to a more equitable form of taxation, namely, the income tax.

Regressivity Aspects. Aside from the inequities which emerge from the assessment process, the proportional general property tax tends to be seriously regressive when related to the incomes of the persons bearing the burden of the tax. Thus, although the tax is proportional per the statute in relation to the tax base — assessed value — it places a disproportionate burden on lower income groups. A simple example illustrates the point. In a given subdivision (in which all houses are of equal value) family unit income may range from, say,

*Federal grants to California counties during 1957 amounted to $180,998,380. These amounts were actually direct grants to the state which were apportioned to counties for such purposes as civil defense, vocational education, mental hygiene, hospital construction, social welfare programs, water pollution control, and veterans affairs.

**Federally owned land in the City-County of San Francisco, if assessed and taxed as private property, would have yielded approximately $15 million in 1956-57. Federal grants and subventions and payments under Public Law 874 amounted to $9,065,951 and $402,000, respectively, for the same year. Based on original cost data, a federally owned facility located adjacent to a Southern California community that has undergone dramatic growth within the past 10 years would yield at least one million dollars in property taxes if privately owned. If privately owned, the proprderty and improvements in question would add at least $12.5 million of assessed value to the city's current $75 million assessed valuation. It is no coincidence that the school district in this community is under constant pressure to raise its lagging instructional salary scale while the superintendent, operating within budgetary limits, concentrates on hiring the new teachers demanded by the growth of enrollment. Federal "in lieu" payments to school districts in surrounding communities amounted to approximately $175,000 in 1957.

$4,000 to $10,000. The assessor will follow, and rightly so, the procedure of assigning equal values to each residence. Assuming that each
home has a market value of $12,000, and that the assessor assigns
a $3,000 valuation for tax purposes, each taxpayer under an $8 rate per
$100 of assessed value pays a tax of $240. (Veterans' exemptions are
disregarded at this point.) The effective property tax burden on the
person with an income of $4,000 is 6% (240 ÷ $4,000), whereas the
effective rate on the person earning $10,000 is 2.4%. Regressivity is
inherent in property taxation even when the criterion of uniform assessment is met. "This results in a miscarriage of justice in taxation."[6]

The regressive nature of the property tax in the United States has
been established empirically in the Musgrave study of the distribution
of tax burdens by income class.[7] The results of the study, insofar as
they relate to property tax burdens, are summarized in Figure 6.1.

The property tax is also inequitable as a result of discriminatory
classifications and exemptions and these inequities are further increased
by tax shifting. The incidence of the collective burden of the real property tax tends to be concentrated on the income strata where the least
ability to pay exists. Generally accepted economic theory supports the
position that the tax on the owner-occupied dwelling cannot be shifted.
The incidence, in other words, is on the owner. The property tax on
rental housing tends to shift forward to the tenants, depending upon the
supply-demand conditions. The property tax falling on producer's goods,
such as plant and equipment, is generally treated as a direct expense of
production and, as such, can shift, at least in part, to the consumer.
In summary, the property tax is largely a tax on consumption. It bears
little relationship to the effective wealth of the mass of householders who
ultimately bear the incidence of the tax. The shifting of the tax adds to
its total regressivity.

Burden Aspects. The general property tax places an inordinately
heavy burden upon people with small cash incomes. Since the tax is
levied on an ad valorem base, it often happens, especially in the case of
persons living on retirement income, that its burden bears little relation to the current income of the taxpayer, thus violating the ability
principle. To the extent that the taxpayer must liquidate his wealth in
order to meet property tax obligations, the tax becomes a capital levy.

The original intent of property taxation was to tax those forms of
property yielding spendable income but the tax on residential property
falls mainly on nonproperty sources of income, that is, on wages and

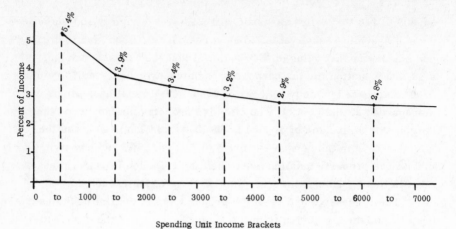

Spending Unit Income Brackets

Figure 6.1 Distribution of Property Tax Burdens, by Income Groups, in the United States, 1948

Source: Musgrave, R. A., Carroll, J. J., Cook, L. D. and Frane, L. "Distribution of Tax Payments by Income Groups: A Case Study for 1948." National Tax Journal, IV, No. 1 (March 1951), p. 36.

salaries. For all practical purposes, property tax liability, though measured against a property base, amounts to a tax on nonproperty income, which is already heavily tapped by the income and sales taxes. The foundation of the local property tax rests, not so much on a real, as on a mythical relationship between property, its income-generating capacity, and its tax-paying ability. The assumption is heroic at best and demands a searching reappraisal of its social equity consequences.

Another serious defect of the local property tax relates to the fact that it is levied on a "gross" rather than on a "net" valuation basis. A person "owning" a $16,000 home may, in the true economic sense, possess a net equity of $4,000 in the home. Yet for property tax purposes it is assumed that the person has full legal title to a property interest amounting to $16,000. In effect, if the property is assessed at $4,000, he pays tax on every single dollar of his true economic interest. The holder of the mortgage, on the other hand, has a legal and economic interest in the property of $12,000. Under the existing statute he pays no tax, yet his economic interest in the property far exceeds that of the "owner" occupant.

The effective tax burden on the property rights of the mortgagor and the mortgagee may be illustrated by assuming that the property in

question is assessed at $4,000. Under an $8 tax rate, the occupant pays
a $320 tax each year. When the tax burden is related to the equity of the
"homeowner," the effective tax on his economic interest is 8% ($320 ÷
$4,000). The mortgage holder, with an interest of $12,000, pays no
property tax but is subject to, say, a marginal rate of 4% under the
California corporate income tax. If the mortgage interest income is 6%
per annum, i.e., $720, the income tax liability is $28.80. The "in
lieu" income tax of $28.80, when related to the economic interest of
$12,000 produces an infinitesimal effective property tax burden. By
way of summary, it is highly inequitable for the "homeowner" to pay
the property tax on the economic interest of the mortgagee. Some
means of apportioning the burden should be initiated. The way the tax
currently operates makes an unwarranted qualitative distinction between the burdens it ultimately places on real property, wage, and
salary income vis-à-vis financial income from intangibles, compounding the existing inequities of the property tax.

No one can deny that every owner of property receives some benefit from local expenditures. It follows that every property owner
should expect to pay his fair share of the costs of fire and police protection, for example. It does not follow, however, that the property
tax provides a proper index of one's ability to pay for public education. One could not hope to support existing property tax burdens purely
on the benefit principle.

The preceding discussion has revealed the many respects in which
the tax violates the ability principle. One might aptly describe the local property tax as being based upon the "inability-to-pay principle of
taxation." In discussing the limitations of the benefit principle as a
basis for supporting the existing property tax burdens, Professor
Harold M. Groves has observed: "Perhaps it would be more realistic
to conclude that local units of government require revenue for public
services; that the property tax is the only important source of local
revenue available; and that therefore we have the property tax."[8]

In the preceding chapter, we pointed up the limitations of the
local property tax as a fiscal device for meeting rapid growth conditions. The tax is simply too cumbersome to adapt to the dynamic and
growing needs of a highly industrialized economy. We do not deny that
assessed valuations and tax rates increase over time. We merely suggest that the tax is inherently cumbersome and that its fiscal efficiency

increases with a lagged response as expenditure needs expand under
growth conditions. The shortcomings of the tax in periods of severe
economic readjustment are well documented in the annals of fiscal
history.

Administrative Shortcomings. Finally, one of the most crucial
shortcomings of the property tax is the difficulty inherent in its administration. It is generally agreed that the assessment process is costly,
that valuations are often tenuous, that uniformity (and thus equalization)
is virtually an impossibility, that some properties escape taxation completely, and that the regressivity of the tax is increased by certain shortcomings of the assessment process. The editor of Tax Policy has observed: "THE SHOCKING INEQUITIES in the administration of the property tax have been known to tax specialists for generations. Oddly
enough, however, citizens have been lethargic in demanding that law-
makers and administrators put property tax administration on an efficient and equitable basis." [9]

A critique of the administrative shortcomings of the property tax,
we would hold, should begin by giving due recognition to county and city
assessors and their staffs and to the State Board of Equalization. These
public servants have the thankless task of enforcing the intent of the
Constitution and the Legislature which, in turn, are supposed to represent the will of the people in the matter of taxation. On paper the job of
the assessor appears to be simple. He has merely to track down every
unit of taxable property in his jurisdiction and assign to it a value for tax
purposes. Land, improvements, and personal property must be assessed separately. The Los Angeles County Assessor's office had -
800,000 parcels of property to appraise in 1958. Appearances notwith-
standing, the task of administering the property tax is not an easy one.
Many of the problems and shortcomings of property tax administration
are inherent in the nature of the tax itself: they are not due to inefficiency in the assessor's office.

One of the most important factors conditioning the assessment
process is the constitutional provision that property shall be taxed "in
proportion to its value." This demands, in other words, uniform assessment of all property subject to taxation. The assessor within a
given tax jurisdiction has the responsibility of assessing all taxable
property uniformly. This constitutional mandate demands that all taxable property within the state shall be assessed uniformly. In short,
the ratio of assessed to full value must be "equalized" among all of

California's 58 counties. Present laws place final responsibility for the equalization of assessments on the State Board of Equalization.*

The State Constitution in Article XI, Section 12, further directs that: "All property subject to taxation shall be assessed at its full cash value." "Full cash value" is defined in Section 110 of the Revenue and Taxation Code in the following words: "Value, full cash value, or cash value means the amount at which property would be taken in payment of a just debt from a solvent debtor." In a recent case, De Luz Homes, Inc. v. County of San Diego (45 A.C. No. 20), the California Supreme Court has further explained this definition by saying:

> It provides, in other words, for an assessment at the price that property would bring to its owner if it were offered for sale on an open market under conditions in which neither buyer nor seller could take advantage of the exigencies of the other. It is a measure of desirability translated into money amounts and might be called the market value of property for use in its present condition.

From the above definitions and opinions the standard of value for assessment purposes has been clearly established as "full cash value," and has also established market value as the basic guide in its estimation.

In a statement dated January 2, 1958, the Los Angeles County Assessor suggested that the following points have been established:

1. The standard of value for assessment purposes is "full cash value."
2. Market value is the basic guide in the estimation of this standard of value.
3. All property subject to taxation shall be assessed by the same standard of valuation.
4. All property subject to taxation must be assessed at a fair and uniform proportion of this same standard of value.

These are the guide lines for the taxation of property in California as set forth in the Constitution, the Revenue and Taxation Code, and in court decisions interpreting constitutional and statutory provisions. They provide the legal background against which an evaluation of the local property tax must be set.

In spite of concerted efforts to achieve uniformity in the valuation of taxable property there is no doubt that inequities continue to exist. Students of public finance are in general agreement that inequities inevitably arise from the following characteristics of the assessment

* The following excerpts have been extracted verbatim from "statement of the Los Angeles County Assessor on the Valuation of Property for Assessment Purposes," January 2, 1958.

process: (1) failure to assess some property; (2) a general (but not uniform) tendency toward undervaluation; (3) a tendency toward competitive undervaluation by different assessors in different taxing districts; (4) a tendency for assessors to value different properties of the same type and value at widely varying ratios to true or exchange values; (5) a tendency for a given assessor to assess low valued properties at a higher ratio to true value than properties of relatively high value. [10]

It is common knowledge that many items of personal property — e.g., jewelry and cash — escape the property tax. Failure to include them is generally defended on grounds of administrative expediency even though they represent real ability to pay. It is argued that the costs of tracing certain types of personal property and/or the general attitude of the taxpayer preclude its being listed on the tax roll. Assessors operating on the principle of "minimum encroachment on the taxpayer's personal property status" inevitably produce discriminatory results in the over-all assessment process. These qualitative distinctions in the assessment of property produce inequities in the distribution of the quantitative burdens of the tax.

The tendency toward general undervaluation of property is an institutionalized feature of the assessment process. Ratios of assessed to true value for the state as a whole for selected years are as follows:[11]

1912 - 45.1%	1926 - 41.7%	1935 - 50.0%	1955 - 22.8%
1916 - 42.0	1928 - 42.0	1936 - 50.0	1956 - 23.2
1922 - 44.8	1930 - 40.0	1937 - 50.0	1957 - 23.7
1924 - 45.5	1932 - 43.2	1951 - 28.0	1958 - 23.7

Underassessment in relation to market value is an empirical fact. If undervaluation represents an inconsistency, then equity will be served as long as the assessor is consistently inconsistent in the valuation of property in relation to its "true" value. In this connection, an official close to the property tax scene in California, when questioned on this point by our group, observed: [12]

> Assessed value is whatever value the assessor puts on the tax roll. The statutes say that this is to be full cash (R. & T.C., sec. 401) or actual (R. & T.C., sec. 75) value, but only lip service, if that much is paid to this directive or its constitutional counterpart (Art. XIII, sec. 1) to tax property "in proportion to its value," which was probably intended to relate only to the tax rate but has been cited as justification for assessment in proportion to value as well. County assessors are believed to have aimed at 50 percent of full value in prewar days and at 25 percent in the last three years, but this statement must be recognized as a broad generalization. Between 1941 and 1956, the aims of different assessors, and indeed their concepts of value which they sought to undershoot, varied somewhat.

City assessors, as you doubtless know, have always had
varying objectives and seem to have little if any statutory guidance.
The terms of Article XI, sec. 12, would seem to be applicable to
them, however.

The State Board of Equalization has, since 1935, assessed
utilities at 50 percent of the staff's market value estimates.

Difficulties inherent in the valuation process and traditional assessment policies result in a lack of uniformity in the ratios of assessed
to true value for different type s of property. According to data published
recently by the U.S. Bureau of the Census, state-wide averages in California for 1956 were as follows:

Non-farm residential properties . . .   19.8%
    Single-family only 19.8
Acreage and farm properties. 12.7
Vacant lots 17.8
Commercial properties. 18.4
Industrial properties 17.8

Clearly, certain types of property bear a proportionately higher assessed
valuation. The tendency to assess lower valued properties at a higher
ratio to true value than properties of relatively higher value adds further
to the regressivity of the property tax. The complexities of administration undeniably increase the inequities of the tax. In short, better
trained personnel, more adequate facilities and records, more frequent reappraisals, and a higher operating budget for the assessor's
office are needed to provide the eventual key to minimizing these inherent inequities.

The duplication of the assessment function by various units of
local government in California further accentuates inequalities in the
ratios of assessed to true values.[13] As early as 1891, the California
Legislature enacted legislation permitting cities to transfer the assessment and collection functions to the county level. By 1957-58, nearly
two-thirds of the state's municipalities had elected to rely upon county
assessment and collection of locally assessed property taxes. In these
instances a single local assessment roll was prepared for both the city
and the county. The remaining 119 cities prepared their own assessment rolls.[14]

Duplication of property assessment by cities and counties is
costly and should be avoided whenever possible. Most of the 90 general-
law cities perform their own assessment, however, from fiscal necessity. Should they contract for county assessment and collection, they
would have to use the county tax base. These cities are subject to a
maximum tax rate of $1 per $100 of assessed valuation. The simple

fact is that the maximum rate, when applied to the county-assessed tax base, would fail in most cases to provide sufficient revenue. Of the 119 cities involved in assessing local property in 1957-58, 94 used an assessed to market value ratio higher than that of the county. Insofar as existing maximum tax rates promote uneconomical duplication in the assessment process, a strong case can be made for lifting these limitations. The uniformity desiderata would undoubtedly be promoted by such action.

The Equalization Program in California. Whether for competitive reasons, as a result of administrative complexity, or as a consequence of the limitations of the human element in the valuation process, it is apparent that similar types of property are assessed at varying rates both in the same and in different counties in California. Since the state laws provide that properties shall be assessed equally in proportion to their value, equalization becomes mandatory. The county assessor and the county supervisors are responsible for intracounty equalization. The State Board of Equalization has the constitutional duty to promote intercounty equalization. County officials unquestionably attempt to achieve uniformity of assessments within their respective jurisdictions. Given the complexity of the task of uniform valuation as between identical and, even more difficult, different types of property, we would not be so optimistic as to say that perfect uniformity in intracounty assessment has been achieved. We commend, however, the diligent efforts of those conscientious county officials who are striving to reduce inequities of this type.

What is the record of intercounty equalization in California?[15] The history of property tax equalization in this state can best be examined in relation to three time periods: 1850 to 1910, 1910 to 1933, and 1933 to the present. During the first period the state had its own property tax but all property was assessed by local officials, which resulted in competitive underassessment in various counties in violation of the constitutional standard of equal and uniform taxation. In consequence, the first State Board of Equalization was created in 1870. Constitutional amendments adopted in 1910, however, resulted in the state's abandonment of the property tax as a source of revenue. The advantages of competitive underassessment were thereby eliminated, and the state-wide intercounty equalization concept became relevant only to the "in lieu" tax on the gross receipts of public utilities. The return of public utility property to local tax rolls in 1935 as a result of the Riley-Stewart Amendment of

1933 was accompanied by the issuance of several equalization orders by
the State Board in 1935, 1936, and 1937. Operating on the assumption
that intracounty equalization was more important than intercounty equalization, no further equalization orders were issued by the State Board of
Equalization until 1955. From 1938 to 1954 it was the Board's considered
judgment "that its efforts should be directed toward the improvement
of the county assessment processes."[16] It concentrated its efforts accordingly on working with local assessors "in an effort to secure better
original assessments and to minimize the necessity for further equalization orders."[17]

Meanwhile, there was good reason to believe that lack of uniformity
in the ratios of assessed value to full value existed on the intracounty as
well as on the intercounty level. One study revealed that the median
ratios of assessed valuation to selling price for 752 properties sold in
32 counties between 1940 and 1949 ranged from a low of 14.8 in Trinity
County to a high of 40.9 in Merced County. The study further revealed
that the ratios of assessed valuations to selling prices declined drastically from 1940-41 to 1948-49. [18]

With the expansion of state aid programs to local governments in
the postwar period — e.g., in the areas of school equalization aid and
assistance to the aged, the blind, and needy children — the need for
improved intercounty equalization of assessments became imperative.
The need for equalization of the ratios of assessed to actual value for
each county stemmed from the fact that state allocation of funds under
these various local aid programs was based in part upon local assessed
valuations. In the absence of either equalization or adjustments in line
with the degree of underassessment in a given county, state funds would
be distributed inequitably. Counties with relatively low assessments
would receive disproportionately large amounts of state aid in relation
to their actual needs and ability.

The Legislature took apparent action to meet this problem by
enacting Chapter 1466 of the California Statutes of 1949.* The basic
provisions of this "Equalization Law" have been summarized as follows:

> The State Board of Equalization was directed to make an
> annual survey in each county to determine the relationship between
> the assessed and market values of property assessed locally. In
> making the survey the board was to use sales and other appraisal

* This legislation became effective on September 2, 1950, but Chapter
1466 has never gone into effect. It has been postponed for successive two-
year intervals and it is currently slated for adoption by the 1959 Legislature.

data relating to representative samples of property subject to local assessment. Using the same data, the board was also to determine the average relationship between the assessed and market values throughout the State of property assessed locally.

Each survey was to be completed by the second Monday in July, and on or before the third Monday in that month a report of the survey, together with a notice of the board's determinations of both the statewide and local ratios was to be transmitted to the clerk of the board of supervisors of each county.

A hearing on the ratios was to be afforded any county affected between the third Mondays in July and August.

In the event of a difference of not more than 10 percent between the local ratio of any county and the state-wide ratio, the board was to equalize the valuation of the taxable property in the county by assessing public utility property in the county at a figure bearing the same ratio to its market value as the ratio between the assessed and market values of locally-assessed property.

Where there was more than a 10 percent difference in ratios, the board was to equalize the valuation of taxable property in the county either as provided in the last paragraph or by raising or lowering the assessed value of locally-assessed property by the percentage necessary to make it conform to the state-wide ratio.

State-assessed property was to be assessed by the board on or before the fourth, rather than the first, Monday in August.

Following its notifying the board of supervisors of its determination of the county-wide and state-wide ratios, the board was to furnish a statement of the ratios, upon request, to any owner or assessee of state-assessed property; and, upon written application filed not later than the first Monday in August, was to hear any objection made by such person to a ratio in any county in which property might be owned by or assessed to him. Any such hearing could be consolidated with any hearing afforded any county on the ratios.

The board was before the first Monday in August to prepare tabulations showing its determination of the values of state-assessed property, and such tabulations were to be open for the inspection of all persons interested.[19]

Proceeding under the provisions of Chapter 1466, the State Board of Equalization conducted a survey to establish the county ratios of assessed to market value and a state-wide average ratio of assessed to market value. These ratios (see Table 6.4) were made a matter of public record on July 16, 1951, and served as a basis for equalization action. On the same day, however, the Governor signed Senate Bill 919 which postponed until 1953 the effective date of Chapter 1466.* The board's equalization action was thereby made ineffective.

*The moratorium on Chapter 1466 was based, first, on the objections of local officials who held that publication of the ratios would produce numerous appeals for equalization from those who had previously been resigned to their assessed values, and, second, on the fear of

Since the effective date of Chapter 1466 has been postponed by legislative action until 1959, the State Board of Equalization has been unable to carry into effect the initial provisions of the Statute of 1949. In the meantime, however, it has carried forward the "new era of intercounty equalization" by operating within the authority set forth in Sections 9 and 14 of Article XIII of the Constitution.[20] The 1951 survey had revealed that 14 California counties were more than 15% below the state-wide ratio of assessed to market value. A similar survey in 1952 revealed that eight of these counties had increased their assessments so they fell within the tolerance range. That is, their ratios of assessed to market value had been raised to within 15% of the 1952 state-wide average. The six remaining counties rated as follows:

County	Percentage below State-wide Average
Humboldt	21
Modoc	36
San Bernardino	26
San Luis Obispo	37
Stanislaus	20
Tulare	25

These counties were directed on July 22, 1952, to show cause why their assessment ratios should not be raised. Hearings were held in Sacramento from August 4, 1952, to August 6, 1952, inclusive, but on August 5, 1952, the Senate adopted a resolution declaring that it had been the intent of the Legislature to postpone until 1953 equalization of assessments by the State Board of Equalization. On August 7, 1952, the board deferred action.[21]

Perplexed, to be sure, but undaunted, the board continued its program and improved the highly complex sampling plan used in establishing assessment ratios. In 1955, this time under the authority of the constitutional directive contained in Sections 9 and 14 of Article XIII, the board issued equalization orders directing 14 California counties to increase locally assessed values by percentages ranging from 19 to 39.

On the basis of its study of the 1955 assessed to market value ratios the board's staff had "tentatively concluded that there were 19 counties whose average assessment levels were between 15 and 19.9 percent of market value, 29 whose levels were between 20 and 24.9

---

local officials and taxpayers that the board's equalization orders would produce reductions in state-assessed property values (of public utilities) and a consequent shift in the tax burden to locally assessed property owners.

Table 6.4. Assessed Value as a Percentage of Market Value
for Each County and for the State as a Whole, as Computed by the
State Board of Equalization: 1951

County	Assessed Value as a Percent of Market Value	County	Assessed Value as a Percent of Market Value
Alameda	25.25	Orange	31.81
Alpine	21.49	Placer	24.01
Amador	29.77	Plumas	27.67
Butte	26.36	Riverside	29.54
Calaveras	31.13	Sacramento	23.68
Colusa	25.34	San Benito	21.45
Contra Costa	23.48	San Bernardino	22.07
Del Norte	25.07	San Diego	26.58
El Dorado	29.27	San Francisco	31.35
Fresno	30.70	San Joaquin	27.74
Glenn	30.70	San Luis Obispo	22.68
Humboldt	22.78	San Mateo	19.47
Imperial	24.61	Santa Barbara	27.94
Inyo	26.21	Santa Clara	26.99
Kern	26.41	Santa Cruz	21.23
Kings	30.54	Shasta	18.81
Lake	28.16	Sierra	24.72
Lassen	22.07	Siskiyou	25.48
Los Angeles	29.88	Solano	25.19
Madera	27.06	Sonoma	28.57
Marin	24.64	Stanislaus	23.09
Mariposa	24.88	Sutter	31.33
Mendocino	28.95	Tehama	27.70
Merced	24.06	Trinity	16.99
Modoc	21.62	Tulare	21.71
Mono	26.56	Tuolumne	31.58
Monterey	27.15	Ventura	25.67
Napa	27.90	Yolo	24.97
Nevada	21.01	Yuba	27.95

State-wide ratio 28.00

Source: State Board of Equalization.

percent, and 10 whose levels were between 25 and 29.9 percent. The
state-wide average level was computed as approximately 22 percent."[24]
The equalization target for 1955 was set at 25 percent. After a preliminary comparison of data with the 19 counties involved, 14 counties were
found to have assessment levels within the 15 to 19.9% range. Officials
from all but one of these counties accepted invitations to appear before
the board for public hearings.

The difficulties of implementing the program of intercounty property tax assessments have been described in these terms:

Although such a hearing has a strong appeal to anyone who
believes in democratic government, it may have the unfortunate

effect of arraying state and local officials as antagonists in an action in which they should be allies — or at least not opponents. In an economy more often characterized by inflation than by deflation, there is a natural and apparently irresistible tendency for assessed values to fall below accepted standards. Hence, equalization orders of the uniform-ratio type commonly result in increases in local assessment rolls, and county officials usually feel obliged to defend their constituents from the loss of state aid, the shift of taxes from state-assessed to locally-assessed property, and the increase in local budgets (presumably those not controlled by the defenders) which may ensue from adoption of a proposed order. Thus the state agency finds the staff which has worked under its direction pitted against the county assessor, who should be happy to have an outside agency perform the distasteful task of raising his values if they are lower than they should be, and against the county supervisors, who should not view a larger local tax base with utter repugnance. No matter how well intentioned the participants, it is difficult to maintain friendly relations throughout the ensuing controversy. [23]

After completing its hearings, the State Board of Equalization in August 1955 issued orders for increases in assessed valuations as follows:

County	Percentage Increase in Assessed Valuation Ordered, August, 1955
Alameda	20
Butte	19
Contra Costa	35
Del Norte	21
Humboldt	39
Imperial	37
Marin	26
Mariposa	29
Mendocino	25
San Bernardino	39
San Luis Obispo	35
Sonoma	19
Stanislaus	28
Tulare	23

Tulare County officials chose not to honor the board's order and petitioned the Superior Court of that county to set it aside. The court subsequently ruled in favor of the county and the decision was not appealed. The following legal principles applicable to intercounty equalization actions of the State Board of Equalization emerged from the decision of the Superior Court: [25]

1. At this time the only power of the Board of Equalization to order changes in valuations on local rolls stems from Article XIII, Section 9, of the California Constitution. The statutory provisions of Sections 1832-1843 of the Revenue and Taxation Code have been suspended. The procedural rules of Sections 2700-2705, Title 18, Administrative Code, prescribe the mode of conducting intercounty equalization hearings.

2. The state board has jurisdiction only to enter orders raising or lowering the entire assessment roll in order to equalize it with the entire assessment rolls of the other 57 counties in the State. The entire roll includes the "secured," "unsecured" and "board roll."

3. That in equalizing the rolls of the several counties it is beyond the power of the state board to "equalize" to an arbitrary 'standard" only a part of the roll of a few of the counties leaving the remaining counties at varying and unequal levels of assessment.

4. In the conduct of equalization hearings observance of due process and equal protection requires there be a reasonable opportunity for the county to study lengthy and involved statistical summaries presented against it, reasonable opportunity to examine and rebut appraisal data used as the basis for the state board summaries, the right to be present during the taking of evidence against it, the right to elicit the state board's findings as to assessment levels of all other counties, the right to elicit facts concerning the determination of a purported "state-wide average level of assessments," the right to reasonable continuances to enable the county to meet evidence not theretofore disclosed to it, the right to sufficient notice to enable it to prepare its case, and the findings and orders of the state board must be supported by competent evidence.

The most recent development in the intercounty equalization program was recorded in the July 23, 1958 edition of The Sacramento Bee (page A-4):

58 COUNTY TAX ASSESSORS AGREE: NO BIG CHANGES
For the first time in many years the state board of equalization and California's 58 county assessors are so close in agreement on assessment for county tax purposes the board this year will not hold the usual equalization hearings.

Table 6.5. summarizes the distribution of assessment ratios for California counties for the year 1955 through 1958.*

The Economic Effects of Property Taxation. Space limitations forbid a detailed treatment of the economic effects of the property tax. In terms of its effect on productivity it is unlikely that the tax has a highly repressive effect on personal efficiency and incentives. The tax does produce, however, adverse resource allocation effects in terms of location and the types of capital goods produced. Property tax yields tend to lag behind general over-all changes in economic activity and thus to accentuate inflationary pressures in periods of prosperity and deflationary pressures during recessions and depressions.

Summary Evaluation and Recommendations for Improvement of Property Tax. When measured against the criteria generally attributed to an ideal tax, the property tax ranks low. A summary evaluation

* The State Board of Equalization has not published individual county ratios since 1951.

Table 6.5 Assessment Ratios for California Counties, 1955-58

Ratio*	1955†	1956†	1957	1958
20	3	3	2	-
20.5	7	3	3	1
21	6	4	5	4
21.5	8	9	9	5
22	2	8	4	8
22.5	14(M)	6(M)	5(M)	6
23	4	5	4	4(M)
23.5	1	4	6	6
24	1	2	2	2
24.5	-	2	3	3
25	3	1	2	5
25.5	2	5	2	3
26	2	-	6	1
26.5	1	4	2	2
27	1	-	3	4
27.5	-	1	-	2
28	1	-	-	-
28.5	1	1	-	-
29	-	-	-	2
29.5	1	-	-	-

* Rounded to the closest half percentage point except that no ratio between 19.5 and 19.9 was rounded upward to 20.

† After giving effect to orders of the State Board.

(M) Median

Source: Letter dated July 31, 1958, from Ronald B. Welch, Chief, Division of Research and Statistics, California State Board of Equalization.

of the tax is presented in Table 6.6.** There is imperative need for its improvement and the following recommendations are offered toward that end:

a) A comprehensive review and appraisal of the existing system of property classification and exemptions is in order, especially with respect to intangibles and the veterans' exemption.

b) Greater flexibility in the matter of tax rate limitations is long overdue.

c) Concerted efforts for improvements in the administration of the tax should receive top priority.

d) Intercounty equalization should be continued in full force. Uniformity in assessment ratios has by no means been achieved.

e) Consideration should be given to a changeover from semi-annual to quarterly installment payment.

f) In the area of personal property taxation, the valuation of business inventories should be placed on a monthly average basis and greater diligence exercised in placing all items of tangible personal property on the assessment rolls.

** The fiscal criteria of "adequacy" and "balance" are not applicable since they relate to a revenue system, not to a particular tax.

g) We recommend the use of a revised formula for determination of "in lieu" payments by the federal government. Specifically, such properties should be valued by conventional methods and current tax rates should be applied. The "in lieu" payments called for by this formula would more closely approximate the burdens placed on local units of government as a result of federal activities.

h) Specific consideration should be directed toward the taxation of the householder on his net economic equity with reallocation of part of the property tax burden to the mortgagee.

i) Finally, we recommend the introduction of a "county-wide" property tax rate for school finance purposes in order to eliminate the tax "oases" that have developed under the existing system. (This proposal is elaborated upon in Chapter 9.)

Local Sales and Use Taxes. In the period since 1945 the sales and use tax has become an integral part of the local revenue structure in California. Chapter 1311 of the Statutes of 1955 provides the basis for uniformity in this field of taxation. During 1957 the tax yielded 19.8% of aggregate municipal revenues. As noted earlier, the tax is administered by the State Board of Equalization, with local units making reimbursement for the costs of such services. *

On the positive side, the sales tax has a number of advantages for purposes of state and local finance. Chief among these are the following:

1. It is convenient from the point of view of the taxpayer as well as the tax collector.

2. It has the capacity of reaching economic units otherwise exempt from income and/or property taxation.

3. It is broadly based. Its fiscal potential, therefore, is high.

4. It involves minimum cost of administration and compliance, estimated at about 2 cents for each dollar of revenue collected.

5. Its base is readily measurable.

6. It provides a relatively stable source of revenue.

7. Its adverse economic effects are minimal. The sales tax produces little, if any, negative effect on incentives and it is unlikely that the tax is highly destructive of income when recognition is given to both the extraction and expenditure processes.

8. Reliance on the local sales-use tax transfers part of increasing tax burdens away from the highly inequitable property tax.

9. By reducing the real demand for private goods in a period of inflation the sales tax mitigates somewhat inflationary pressures on the general price level.

10. Taxpayers are fairly well reconciled to this form of taxation.

Against these advantages, however, the following shortcomings must be acknowledged:

* The Board makes annual revenue estimates on the local sales-use tax to assist local officials in their fiscal planning.

Table 6.6. The Property Tax Measured by the Criteria
of an Ideal Tax

Criteria	(+)	(—)	(0)
Social: Equity		X	
Political Confirmity	X		
Predictable Incidence	X		
Public Acceptance		X	
Convenience of Compliance		X	
Simplicity		X	
Fiscal: Breadth of Base	X		
Stability of Yield		X	
Flexibility		X	
Administrative: Ease of Administration		X	
Economy of Collection		X	
Measurability of Tax Base		X	
Economic: Effects on Productivity			
Increased Incentive			X
Increased Efficiency			X
Effects on Employment			
Encouragement of Consumption		X	
Encouragement of Investment		X	
Encouragement of Saving		X	

(+) Meets the criterion
(—) Fails to meet the criterion
(0) Neutral with respect to criterion

1. With food exempt the tax tends to be proportional in relation to
income over wide ranges of the income scale. It is very probable, however, that in the extremely low income ranges (up to
$2, 000) it is regressive. As such, the tax is inequitable.

2. The exemption of certain items, i.e., services, from the tax
base makes it somewhat capricious. No clear cut rationale
governs specific exclusions and inclusions.

3. The sales tax places an administrative burden on the retailers
who must collect and remit the tax.*

4. In a period of recession, the negative effect of the tax burden
on real private demand accentuates deflationary pressures.

5. Although the yield from the sales-use tax is relatively stable
over the course of the business cycle, its cyclical sensitivity
may force state and local units of government to pursue a
perverse fiscal policy.

Taken separately, each of these positive and negative aspects of

the state-local sales and use tax has some validity. A given tax or

revenue system, however, must be evaluated with balanced perspective

giving due recognition to the social value, fiscal, administrative, and

*This argument has been countered by Ruth Harmer, "California's
Sales Tax and How It Spawns an Annual 20-Billion Penny Steal, "Frontier,
August, 1958, pp. 15-16.

economic criteria of the ideal model. A summary evaluation of the
California sales-use tax is presented in Table 6.7. When viewed within
this broader context the sales tax proves far superior to the property
tax as a source of local revenue. This is not to say that we should move
immediately toward eliminating the property tax and using the sales tax
as the major source of local revenue. Other sources, equally available
to local units of government, may rank even higher on the ideal revenue
system continuum.

Business License Taxes[26]

Business license taxes yielded $23.8 million, or 3.4% of the total
revenues of California cities in 1957. Under existing statutes general-
law cities may impose license taxes* for both <u>regulatory</u> and <u>revenue</u>
purposes upon all lawful business transactions within their jurisdiction.
Charter cities may license for both purposes also unless the charter
itself or the federal and state constitution limits this power. Most
municipalities levy the business license tax on retail firms with a fixed
location within the city limits; about 10% of the cities exclude whole-
salers and 25% exclude manufacturers from license coverage.[27]

Business licensing in unincorporated areas is under the supervision of the county board of supervisors. The authority of the county
to license business stems from the police power, not from the taxing
power. County licensing is, therefore, restricted in the main to regulatory purposes. Section 16100 of the Business and Professions Code
provides:

> The boards of supervisors in their respective counties, may
> in the exercise of their police powers, and for the purpose of
> regulation, as herein provided, and not otherwise, license any
> kind of business not prohibited by law, transacted and carried on
> within the limits of their respective jurisdictions, including all
> shows, exhibitions, and lawful games, and may fix the rate of
> license fee and provide for its collection by suit or otherwise.

County governments may use the business license tax for <u>revenue</u>
purposes only in the case of hawkers, itinerant peddlers and vendors,
merchants other than those having a fixed place of business in the
county, their employees, and farmers selling farm products produced
by them (Section 16101), except that no license tax may be imposed if
the peddler is an ex-serviceman (Section 16102). Since counties lack
the authority to use business licenses for broad revenue purposes,

---

*The constitutional authority for municipal business license tax-
ation is found in Article XI, Sections 6, 8(j), 11, and 12 of the California
Constitution.

Table 6.7. Sales and Use Tax Measured by the Criteria of a Model Tax

Criteria	(+)	(−)	(0)
Social: Equity		X	
Political Conformity	X		
Predictability of Incidence	X		
Public Acceptance	X		
Convenience of Compliance	X		
Simplicity	X		
Fiscal: Breadth of Base	X		
Stability of Yield		X	
Flexibility		X	
Administration: Ease of Administration		X	
Economy of Collection	X		
Measurability of Tax Base	X		
Economic: Effects on Productivity			
Increased Incentive			X
Increased Efficiency			X
Effects on Employment			
Encouragement of Consumption		X	
Encouragement of Investment			X
Encouragement of Saving			X

(+) Meets the criterion
(−) Fails to meet the criterion
(0) Neutral with respect to criterion

the following analysis will evaluate the tax as a potential source of municipal revenue.

At the risk of anticipating our final conclusions with respect to the role which the business license tax should play in municipal finance, we begin by saying that in the absence of expanded use of the shared-tax device, this tax may be the real "sleeping beauty" in the local revenue system. Many California municipalities have simply failed to utilize this source of revenue effectively. The case for more extensive taxation of local business under a revitalized license tax may be stated as follows: (1) Business units possess the ability to make a greater contribution to local finance. (2) Household units pay property as well as sales taxes. Increased business license taxes would serve to correct to a degree the existing imbalance in the allocation of local revenue burdens. (3) Business enterprises receive substantial benefits from local services such as police and fire protection. (4) The business community has a responsibility to contribute to the general welfare.

Of the 287 cities included in a recent survey, 144, or 50.1% used gross receipts as the base for retail license tax purposes. (See Table 6.8.)

Table 6.8. Bases for Business License Taxation:
Retailing of Goods, Wares, or Merchandise

Measure	Number of Cities	% of Total
Gross Receipts	144	50.1
Flat-rate Tax	91	31.7
Average Number of Employees	46	16.0
Gross Receipts - Average Number of Employees	3	1.0
Net Income	1	.3
No License Tax	2	.7
Totals	287	100.0

Source: League of California Cities, Business License Taxes, June,
1957, p.20.

In the case of wholesale establishments 40.4% of the 287 cities surveyed
used the gross receipts base and 29.9% used a flat-rate tax. For ser-
vice-type firms, 57.1% of the cities enumerated used a flat-rate basis
of taxation.

A variety of business license tax rates are currently operative.
The flat-fee structure, of course, calls for the payment of an identical
amount of tax by all firms regardless of sales volume, net income, or
number of employees. And, when applied to a variety of businesses, it
leaves much to be desired. Some cities using a gross-receipts base set
fees in terms of so many mills per dollar or a specified number of
dollars of tax per thousand dollars of gross receipts. The pattern of
rate structures of cities using the gross-receipts base is anything but
uniform. At best these rate structures tend to be erratic and unscien-
tific. A common business license fee schedule is based on a fixed
dollar fee for different brackets of gross receipts. The amount of license tax paid depends upon the gross-receipts bracket into which a
firm falls. Professor Davisson has written: [28]

> Several features of rate schedules based on bracketed gross
> receipts should be noted:
>
> (1) In many cities bracketing is by wide intervals and as a
> consequence differential burdens are imposed within given
> brackets. One ordinance, for instance, provides for a quarterly
> fee of $45 where gross receipts are within the bracket $120,000
> to $150,000 per quarter. A licensee whose gross receipts are at
> the lower extreme of this interval — $120,000 — pays $45, or at
> the rate of 37-1/2 cents per thousand. A licensee whose gross
> receipts are at the upper extreme of this interval — $150,000 —
> also pays $45, but at the rate of 30 cents per thousand.
>
> (2) Many rate schedules extend brackets up to a given level
> of gross receipts, say $100,000 per quarter, with a fixed dollar

fee for all licensees whose gross receipts are above this level irrespective of the amount of the excess.

If the highest bracket is at a level which will include the majority of licenses, this type of rate schedule creates no great difficulty. But if there are a number of licensees whose gross receipts are in excess of the upper limit of the highest bracket, those just above the upper limit pay the same dollar amount as those whose excess above the upper limit is large. One schedule of this type provides varying fees for bracketed gross receipts up to $100,000 and a fee of $98 where gross receipts exceed $100,000. Under this schedule, a licensee whose gross receipts are $101,000 pays $98, or at the rate of 97 cents per thousand. A licensee whose gross receipts are $1,000,00 also pays $98, but at the rate of just under 10 cents per thousand.

This problem is met in some cities by providing that where gross receipts exceed so much (the upper limit of the highest bracket), the license fee shall be a specified amount for each additional $1,000 of gross receipts in excess of the upper limit of the highest bracket. This obviates the necessity of extending brackets to very high levels in which only a few licensees will fall but at the same time requires a larger dollar amount to be paid by the licensee whose excess over the upper limit is large as compared with one just over the line.

(3) Typically the dollar amount of license fee for the various brackets is so set as to result in a progressively lower burden per dollar of gross receipts as gross becomes larger. In one city, for example, a retailer with gross receipts of $10,000 pays at the rate of $1.25 per $1,000; a retailer grossing $1,000,000 pays at the rate of 40 cents per thousand. This means, in effect, that in this city the privilege of selling goods at retail is regarded as worth more than three times as much to the $10,000 licensee as the same privilege is worth to the $1,000,000 licensee.

In spite of its frequent use, the gross-receipts basis for business license taxation has certain distinct limitations. Retailers in different lines of trade, for example, may have identical gross receipts, but their profit margins may differ significantly. To mitigate the inequities traceable to this factor some cities have initiated a system of license taxes based on gross receipts with the amount payable determined in relation to the firm's profit margin. This procedure tends to complicate the process of business license taxation. Although business generally would resist this suggestion, it is possible that a more workable system of license taxes - in terms of revenue capacity and equity - would be promoted by use of the net-receipts base. Currently, only one California city, Fairfax, in Marin County uses the net income base.

Given this lack of uniformity in rate schedules and tax bases, we would expect significant differences in the manner in which different cities tax similar types of businesses. Table 6.9 presents calculations showing the business license payments made by retailers in selected

Table 6.9. License Taxes on Retail Firms for Selected California Cities Using a Gross Receipts Base, 1958.

City	TAX ON GROSS RECEIPTS OF							
	$5,000	$10,000	$25,000	$50,000	$100,000	$200,000	$500,000	$1,000,000
San Luis Obispo	$25	$25	$30	$55	$80	$137.50	$287.50	$462.60
Fontana								
Newport Beach	25	25	25	25	25	25	25	25
Mountain View	30	30	30	30	30	30	30	30
Eureka	20	40	60	60	60	60	60	60
Santa Rosa	12	20	35	55	95	215	525	1000
Ontario	24	24	24	24	24	24	24	24
Vallejo	16	20	30	46	69	93	157	222
Tulare	20	20	30	38	60	80	120	186
Santa Maria	20	20	20	20	20	20	20	20
San Mateo	13	16	25	65	123	180	420	660
Anaheim	25	25	25.40	31	45.50	61.25	99.12	149.50
Gardena	15	15	42	125	250	500	1250	2500

California municipalities under existing (1958) ordinances. It is evident
the business enterprises in California receive anything but uniform
treatment. The social significance of this nonuniformity must be
measured, however, in the light of the fiscal importance of this tax
in the existing local revenue structure. It must be noted, further,
that every dollar of local revenue raised by the business license tax
relieves the pressure on the highly inequitable property tax.

After a recent reading of 280 California municipal business license
ordinances, Professor Davisson concluded:

> About 30 cities have thoroughly revised their ordinances since
> 1950. Ordinances of the other cities date back to the forties,
> thirties, and twenties, and I even found a few of pre-World War I
> vintage. Amendments have been made largely on a piecemeal
> basis and the end product is far from satisfactory. [29]

Aside from the obsolescence factor, Davisson cited three common deficiencies of existing business license ordinances: (1) Inadequate coverage resulting in unwarranted exemptions not defensible on grounds of
public policy. (2) Inequitable measures of license fees working injustice to licensees and preventing cities from sharing in growth in business
volume. (3) Outmoded rate structures which fail to recognize changes
in prices and expansion of the level of economic activity in cities.

As one important step toward meeting the impending crises in
California local finance, we strongly recommend that every municipality undertake a thorough review of its business license ordinance.
Existing exemption provisions should be reevaluated and outmoded provisions deleted, but primary attention should be directed toward adopting
a new rate structure with the aim of increasing local business tax yields
substantially. The rate structure and tax base should be geared to the
particular commercial and industrial characteristics of each community.
In the final analysis the municipal business license tax is levied on the
privilege of carrying on business within a city for profit, and the fiscal
objective is revenue, not regulation.

Nontax Revenue Sources

Local units of government in California derived 13.4% of their
1957 receipts from miscellaneous nontax sources, e.g., from fines,
permits, interest, parking fees, and service charges for sewage and
garbage disposal. Special districts performing specific functions for
a defined area have utilized this revenue source to a considerable
degree and municipalities have made expanded use of this source of

revenue since 1940.* Increased reliance upon nontax sources, especially service charges, is partly related to the inherent inadequacies
of the traditional city tax system. These units of government have
simply been forced to adopt nontax sources of revenue whenever it has
been feasible to do so. Parking fees and charges for sewage and garbage disposal have therefore found expanded use for municipal finance
purposes in the postwar period.

Aside from fines and forfeitures, nontax levies are theoretically
based upon the benefit principle. Selectivity in the system of local
finance is acceptable when (1) the benefits received from a government
service are directly traceable to a particular person or area, (2) the
value of the service is measurable, that is, when a fair price may be
reasonably determined, (3) the service charge is relatively small,
(4) the ability to pay may be assumed to exist, and (5) the costs of administering such charges and fees are low.

It follows that extensive use of nontax sources, especially fees
and service charges, violates the criteria of a model revenue system
when (1) the benefits are widely diffused, (2) the value of the benefit is
difficult to measure, (3) the resulting service charge would be considerably high, (4) there is limited ability to pay, and (5) the costs of administration are high.

Certain nontax sources, e.g., fines and forfeitures, will always
be a part of the local revenue system. To the extent, however, that
the use of flat-rate service charges is expanded beyond the confines of
the benefit principle, the equity criterion is violated. Furthermore,
the service-charge technique can prove administratively costly if
monthly billings are involved. We recommend, therefore, that local
units of government refrain from expanded use of nontax revenue sources
if the action is based upon fiscal expediency alone. Other more efficient
and equitable tax sources are available to meet the expanded revenue
needs of local government.

Shared Revenues

Revenues from the following sources are collected by agencies of
the State of California and are shared, at least in part, with local units:
liquor license fees, motor vehicle fuel taxes (@ 6 cents per gallon on
gasoline and 7 cents per gallon on diesel fuel), motor vehicle registration

_____

*In 1957 California municipalities secured 17.9 percent of their
total receipts from nontax sources.

taxes, motor vehicle in lieu (license) taxes, and the gross receipts tax
on carriers.

Liquor license fees shared with county and city units amounted to
$8,399,805 in 1957. Current statutes provide that 90 percent of such
fees must be allocated to these units of local government; the remaining
10 percent goes into the state General Fund.

Motor vehicle fuel tax collections, less costs of administration,
are transferred to the Highway Users Tax Fund for apportionment to
cities, counties, and the State Highway Fund. The proceeds of the
registration fees, after allowance for costs of maintaining the Department of Motor Vehicles and the California Highway Patrol, are also
transferred to the Highway Users Tax Fund. The "in lieu" tax collections are divided equally between cities and counties in the proportion
the population of each bears to total population, after providing for interest and redemption charges on state highway bonds. The gross receipts tax on carriers, after providing for administration costs, is
also transferred to the Highway Users Tax Fund.

State apportionments to city and county governments in 1957 were
as follows:

Apportionments to counties:

Highway users taxes--for public roads, streets and highways and other related purposes	$72,682,437
Unrefunded taxes on aviation gasoline--for county owned airports	234,552
Motor Vehicle license fees (in lieu tax)--for any state purpose	49,265,173
Trailer coach license fees--for distribution equally between counties, cities and school districts, to be expended for any state purpose	2,218,870
TOTAL APPORTIONMENT TO COUNTIES	$124,401,032

Apportionments to cities:

Highway user taxes--for city streets and other related purposes	$28,738,462
Unrefunded taxes on aviation gasoline--for city-owned airports	115,654
Motor vehicle license fees--for expenditure on law enforcement, regulation, fire protection of highway traffic and for any state purpose	49,396,886
TOTAL APPORTIONMENT TO CITIES	$78,251,002

The shared tax arrangement has several advantages from the
point of view of local finance. First, the administration of the tax is
performed at the state level, thereby relieving each local unit of this
task. Second, these particular shared taxes provide a means of financing needed improvement and expansion in local street and traffic
systems. In our opinion these shared revenues are levied in a manner

consistent with the pure theory of the benefit principle of taxation and, as such, meet the basic criteria of an ideal tax system.

Federal Subventions for Local Assistance Purposes

Federal assistance to local government in California during fiscal year 1957-58 is estimated at $194,242,415. The major share of these subventions (91 percent) were for social welfare purposes, namely, old age security, aid to the needy blind, and aid to needy children. Lesser amounts were granted to assist local units in financing education, public health, and public works (highway) programs. Table 6.10 summarizes federal subventions for 1957-58.

Table 6.10. Estimated Federal Subventions for Local Assistance in California: 1957-58

Purpose	Amount	% of Total
Education	$2,780,000	1.4%
Public Health	6,727,341	3.6
Public Works	7,920,377	4.0
Social Welfare	176,814,697	91.0
TOTAL	$194,242,415	100.0

State-Financed Subventions for Local Assistance

State-financed subventions provide approximately one-fourth of the total local government receipts in California. During 1958, state grants for local assistance amounting to $778,676,910 were financed through the General Fund.* Table 6.11 presents the detail of these grants.

State grants to the counties underwrite aid to the needy aged, needy children, needy blind, tuberculosis sanitoria, public health, and the salaries of superior court judges and certain other public officials. Cities with a population of 50,000 or more receive public health grants on a matching basis. Special districts receive aid in financing various public works programs, e.g., flood control. Subventions for education consist of the basic apportionment for public schools and other payments to finance vocational education, child care centers, debt service on public school building bonds, contributions to teacher retirement, and textbooks.

The nature of the programs involved attests to the importance of state subventions to local units of government. In the light of the

_____

* Reserve funds supplied an additional $9,647,993 for local assistance.

Table 6.11. State Subventions for Local Assistance in
California: 1958

Purpose	Amount	% of Total
Education		
Public Schools-	$530,267,754	
State School Building Aid-		
Debt Service on School		
Building Bonds	9,851,533	
Free Textbooks	5,311,472	
Contributions to Teachers		
Retirement System	27,228,000	
Other Educational Purposes	4,776,181	
Total Education...............	$577,434,940	(74.2)
Public Health-		
Administration of Local Agencies	3,633,261	
Maintenance of Tuberculosis		
Sanatoria	4,985,701	
Services for Physically		
Handicapped Children	3,900,872	
Construction of Hospital		
Facilities	3,997,781	
Other Public Health Purposes	381,226	
Total Public Health...........	$16,898,841	(2.2)
Public Works-Flood Damage and		
Control	$5,475,436	(.7)
Social Welfare-		
Aid to Aged	$117,805,699	
Aid to Blind	7,908,832	
Aid to Children	46,072,774	
Aid to Needy Disabled	877,407	
Other Social Welfare Purposes	2,579,309	
Total Social Welfare..........	$175,244,121	(22.5)
For Other Purposes-		
Salaries of Superior Court Judges	$2,279,799	
Miscellaneous, Other Purposes	1,343,773	
Total Other Purposes..........	$3,623,572	(.4)
TOTAL LOCAL ASSISTANCE	$778,676,910	100.0

Source: State Controller's _Preliminary Annual Report_, July 25, 1958,
p. 5.

limitations and inequities that characterize the existing local revenue
system, subventions will necessarily continue to play a growing role in
local finance in California.

Apropos of the impending crisis in California local finance it is
worthwhile to note that over 98 percent of state subventions to local
government are financed from the General Fund. It is reasonable to
assume, therefore, that the largest part of these state-financed subventions are underwritten by the 3 percent retail sales tax, which produced $603.7 million of General Fund revenue in 1958. Reference has
previously been made to the fact that the State of California faces its
own revenue crisis. The current state of fiscal affairs in California
suggests that (1) the local revenue structure must be bolstered by other
tax sources, and (2) the state revenue system must be revitalized to
meet increasing needs in the areas of state operations, capital outlay,
and local assistance.

IMPROVING THE CALIFORNIA REVENUE SYSTEM
The Local Revenue System

On the basis of the analysis made in the preceding sections of this
chapter, our recommmendations for the improvement of the local revenue
structure in California are as follows:

1. The Ad Valorem Property Tax. We recommend: a critical review of the present system of exemptions and property classification;
provision for greater flexibility in rate limitations; improved administration; elimination of duplicate assessments; continuance of the intercounty equalization program; introduction of quarterly installment
payments; use of an averaging technique in the valuation of business inventories; revision of the "in lieu" formula applicable to federally owned
property; allocation of the property tax burden between the mortgagor
and mortgagee on a net equity basis; introduction of a county-wide
property tax as the basic local source of school revenue, with the existing school district tax being retained as a supplementary source.

2. The Local Retail Sales Tax. We recommend that the 1 percent
local sales tax be retained at its present level. This form of taxation
tends toward regressivity and, in our opinion, lower income groups are
already paying more than their fair share of local (and state) taxes.

3. The Business License Tax. We recommend that every municipality in the state review its business license ordinance with a view
toward greater use of this tax source.

4. Local Nontax Revenue. These sources of revenue are acceptable

in our opinion, when the basic attributes of the benefit principle are
met. Given the inadequacies of the existing local tax system, there is
a growing tendency for local units to exploit nontax revenue sources.
The main danger is that these sources will be extended beyond the scope
of the benefit principle thereby adding to the existing inequities of the
local revenue system. There is no question that existing fee arrangements for certain special administrative services and charges for
sewage and garbage services should be retained as part of the local
revenue system. We recommend a general hold-the-line policy in this
area of local finance.

5. Shared Revenues. In our opinion, the revenue-sharing technique of finance should be extended. Local units of government, on
statutory and administrative grounds, are precluded from entering new
areas of taxation. The solution to both these problems can be met by
the shared-revenue device. This form of state-local finance will promote the diversity and balance currently lacking in the local revenue
system. Simply stated, the local revenue problem in California might
be solved easily by increasing state income tax rates and placing the
tax on a shared basis. (See next section.)

The State Revenue System in Relation to Local Finance

Since two-thirds of the state's General Fund expenditures are
committed to local assistance, the financial well-being of the local unit
of government is inextricably bound up with the fiscal condition of the
state. We have previously noted that the State of California faces its
own revenue problems; we urge legislative action along the following
lines to assure a sound program of state-local finance:

1. We recommend increases in the rates of the personal income
   tax, the corporate franchise and income tax, and the insurance
   premium tax.

2. We recommend use of the severance tax as an integral part of the
   state revenue structure, with the proceeds either earmarked
   for local assistance or shared directly with local units of
   government.

If these proposals were carried into effect, it would be possible
to reduce the state sales and uses tax to 2 percent. In our opinion these
recommendations will make for a more equitable state-local revenue
system, and will provide for meeting the expanded revenue needs of
California government.

The Case for Increasing Personal Income Tax Rates.* In 1957 the

* Taxpayer compliance would be expedited if it were possible to use
adjusted gross income as stipulated on the federal return in computing
state income tax liability.

personal income tax yielded $143.3 million, or 6.9 percent, of the total
state receipts. As presently constituted (1958) the tax makes a relatively minor contribution to state finances. Its low yield is traceable to
the system of exemptions, to the nature of its rate structure, and to the
income-splitting privilege on the joint returns filed by married couples.
Exemptions under the existing statute are: married couple, $3,500; single
person $2,000; and $400 for each dependent. We recommend that this
system of exemptions be retained.

Under California's community property laws it is highly unlikely
that the income-splitting privilege can be denied those filing a joint return. We recommend, however, an increase in the rates since the effective degree of progressivity in the existing rate structure is illusory.
Under the present statute the 1 percent first-bracket rate applies to the
actual net income range between $4,601 and $14,900 in the case of the
married couple with two children, using the standard deduction. The
tax is proportional, in other words, over this wide range of income.
The distribution of taxable income among people in various tax brackets
has been tabulated for 1956 in Table 6.12.

Table 6.12. Distribution of Taxable Personal Income
among Tax Brackets in California: 1956

Tax Rate (in percent)	Taxable Income (All Returns)	Percent
1	$5,458,377,300	61.6
2	1,268,835,581	14.3
3	596,971,445	6.7
4	357,839,700	4.1
5	238,109,603	2.7
6	943,089,981	10.6
	$8,863,223,610	100.0

Source: State of California, Franchise Tax Board, Annual Report
1957, p. 5

These data reveal that 75.9 percent of the tax base is subject to a maximum rate of 2 percent.

We propose the adoption of the personal income tax rate structure
in California listed on the top of the following page.

This rate structure has several advantages. First, it would
obviously yield increased tax revenues. Second, it would promote
greater equity in the California tax system.

Taxable Amount		Tax
Single Person	Joint Return	Rate
$ 0 - $2,000	$ 0 - $4,000	1%
2,000 - 4,000	4,000 - 8,000	2
4,000 - 6,000	8,000 - 12,000	3
6,000 - 8,000	12,000 - 16,000	4
8,000 - 10,000	16,000 - 20,000	5
10,000 - 15,000	20,000 - 30,000	6
15,000 - 20,000	30,000 - 40,000	7
Over $20,000	Over $40,000	8

The Case for Increased Corporate Franchise and Income Taxes.

The corporate franchise and income tax produced $167.4 million in
1957. This represented 8.1 percent of total state receipts. The case
for an increase in the business net income tax rests in part on the relatively small contribution business firms make toward financing state
activities. Other relevant considerations are: (1) The 4 percent rate
has been in effect since 1935. (2) Corporate enterprises possess the
ability to make a greater contribution to state finance. (3) The high
concentration in the ownership of corporate securities — 8 percent of
all stockholders, comprising less than 1 percent of all American families, own over four-fifths of all publicly held stocks individually owned –
makes it apparent that the ability principle will not be violated.[30]
(4) The modern corporate entity exists as an economic end in itself and
as such enjoys the full privileges of protection under the law. (5) The
largest share of the state-local tax burden in California is currently
borne by consumer-citizens. (6) The existing state-local revenue system
tends toward regressivity. (7) Provisions governing the definition of
the corporate net income tax base are lenient compared to the federal
corporate income tax. During 1956, the 40,713 corporations reporting
net income reported $19 billion of net income for federal tax purposes
and $3.6 billion for California franchise tax purposes. Crude petroleum
and natural gas producers reported $659 million for federal income tax
purposes and $233 million for state franchise tax purposes.[31] (8) Eighteen
of the 32 states levying income or franchise taxes on the corporate form
of business have higher rates than California.

We recommend that the bank and corporate franchise and the corporation income tax rates be raised from 4 to at least 6 percent. We
recommend, further, that the provisions governing the definition of the

tax base receive a thorough review to bring the base as defined by the
California statutes into line with the federal corporate income tax base.

The Case for Increasing the Insurance Premiums Tax. The general
limitations of the gross premium basis for the taxation of insurance
companies are recognized, but the development of a more scientific tax
base lies beyond the scope of this study. Consistent with the state's
need for additional revenues and the desire to expand the role of more
equitable forms of taxation, we recommend a tax rate of 3.35 percent on
the gross premiums of insurance companies. The existing 2.35 percent
rate has been in effect since 1948. The tax contributed $42.5 million
to California's General Fund during 1957.[32]

The Case for the Severance Tax. The severance tax is generally
levied as an excise on the privilege of severing or extracting natural resources from the earth itself. Twenty-eight states utilize the tax and
levy it in lieu of or in addition to local property taxes. Resources subject to severance taxes in the various states include petroleum, natural
gas, coal, metallic ores, stone, sand, gravel, timber, salt, and fish.
The tax is ordinarily levied either on the basis of quantity of physical
production or on the value of such production.[33]

At present, California levies nominal severance taxes upon oil
and natural gas, fish, kelp, and agricultural minerals. The proceeds
are used to finance the conservation activities of the Division of Oil
and Gas, the Division of Fish and Game, and the Department of Agriculture. In the case of oil and gas production the rate in 1958 is
$0.002179 per barrel of oil or 10 mcf. of gas sold. Minerals in the
ground and standing timber (with certain exceptions) are taxed under the
ad valorem property tax.[34]

As compared with other states similarly endowed with natural resources, California takes no advantage whatsoever of this potential
source of tax revenue.* California ranks with Texas, Oklahoma, and
Louisiana as one of the top producers of petroleum products and natural
gas in the United States. In 1957, the percentage of severance tax collections on total state tax collections were as follows: Texas, 30.1
percent; Oklahoma, 14.4 percent; Louisiana, 22.2 percent; California,
0.078 percent. (See Table 6.13 for summary of state severance tax
data in 1955.)

*It almost goes without saying that a severance tax on petroleum
products would provide a logical method of finance for meeting the subsidence problem in Long Beach.

Table 6.13. Severance Taxes as a Percentage of Total
Taxes, 1955
(in thousands of dollars)

State	Severance Taxes	Total Taxes	Severance Taxes as % of Total
Alabama	$ 965	$ 163,205	.59%
Arkansas	3,937	107,486	3.66
California	1,168	1,334,391	.09
Colorado	5,586	132,682	4.21
Florida	53	293,783	.02
Idaho	82	38,032	.22
Indiana	308	254,004	.12
Kansas	273	144,523	.19
Kentucky	208	162,189	.13
Louisiana	66,923	303,497	22.05
Michigan	699	645,877	.11
Minnesota	19,040	245,391	7.76
Mississippi	6,533	125,041	5.22
Montana	1,582	41,581	3.80
Nevada	134	20,396	.66
New Hampshire	14	27,554	.05
New Mexico	6,527	80,210	8.14
North Dakota	757	45,935	1.65
Oklahoma	28,999	210,434	13.78
Oregon	741	129,828	.57
South Dakota	682	40,423	1.68
Texas	158,781	489,030	32.47
Utah	1,760	54,964	3.20
Virginia	201	206,324	.10
Wisconsin	148	266,971	.06

Source: Ohio Department of Taxation, Severance Taxation, pp. 22-3.

The revenue yielding capacity of a severance tax will naturally be determined by its rate and its base. The rates and bases applied to different resources in selected states are presented in Table 6.14.

The potential yield of a severance tax on oil, natural gas, timber, cement, and stone production in California during 1956, is presented in Table 6.15. A hypothetical rate of 6 percent on the value of production is applied to the first three products; a rate of 6 cents per barrel is assumed for cement and 4 cents per short ton for stone. At current rates of production severance taxes levied at these rates would yield an estimated $100 million per annum.

Table 6.14. Severance Taxes on Major Resources, Selected States: 1956

State	Kind of Resource	Rate and Measure	Tax in Lieu of Local Property Taxes
Arkansas	Coal	1c per ton	No
	Timber	25-50c per 1,000 ft., board measure, log scale; pulpwood, veneer, 20-25c per cord	No
	Oil	4% of market value + 5 mills per barrel	No
	Natural gas	3/20c per 1,000 cu. ft. + 1/2 mill per 1,000 cu. ft.	No
	Metal Ores	10c per ton – barite, bauxite, titanium, etc.	No
	Other – sulphur, salt	4% of market value	No
	Silica sand, dimension stone	1c per ton	No
	Crushed stone, clay, etc.	1/2c per ton	No
California	Oil and gas	Rates per barrel and per 1,000 ft. determined annually to meet conservation costs	No
Colorado	Coal	7/10c per ton	No
	Oil and gas	2-5% graduated gross income tax + 2 mills per barrel and per 50,000 cu. ft.	No
Louisiana	Coal	10c per ton	No
	Timber	25c-$1.50 per 1,000 ft. log scale 2¼-5% of market value on other than virgin timber	No
		6% of market value on timber grown on reforestation contracts	Yes (Including general severance tax)
	Oil	18-26c per barrel	Yes
	Gas	3/10c per 1,000 cu. ft.	Yes
	Sand, gravel, stone	3c per ton	No
	Ores	10c per ton	No
	Marble	20c per ton	No
	Sulphur	$1.03 per long ton	Yes
	Frogs	2c per lb. dressed	--
	Shrimp	15-50c per barrel (210 lbs.)	--
New Mexico	Coal	1/8% of value	No
	Oil and gas	2½% of value	No
	Copper	½% of value	No
	Other metals	1/8% of value	No
North Carolina	Oil	1/2c per barrel	No
	Gas	1/2 mill per 1,000 cu. ft. $50 well drilling fee	No
Oklahoma	Gas	5% of gross value + 2/100c per 1,000 cu. ft.	Yes
	Oil	5% of gross value + 1/8c per barrel	Yes
	Metal ores	3/4 of 1% of gross value	Yes
Texas	Oil	4.6% of market value or 4.6c per barrel, whichever is greater, + 3/16c per barrel	No
	Gas	8% of market value 7% after Sept. 1, 1956	No
	Sulphur	$1.40 per long ton	No

SOURCE: Ohio Department of Taxation, Severance Taxation, pp. 13-17.

What considerations support the case for the introduction of a severance tax into the California revenue system? First, the potential of the tax as a revenue device is well illustrated by the preceding analysis. Second, the tax is relatively easy to administer and convenient to comply with. The valuation problem is simplified since the market value at the

Table 6.15. Estimated Yield of Severance Tax on 1956
Production of Selected Resources in California

Resource	Basis for Taxation	Revenue Yield
Oil	6% of Sales Value	$49,560,000
Natural Gas	6% of Sales Value	7,383,000
Timber	6% of Sales Value	29,419,540
Cement	6¢ per bbl.	2,160,000
Stone	4¢ per short ton	1,000,000
TOTAL		$89,522,540

time of severance may be used. If the volume-of-production base is
used, no valuation problem is involved. Payment of the tax is geared to
the production and sale of the resource in question. Third, the tax pro-
motes conservation in the use of natural resources. Fourth, the tax
rests against resources which are in a sense the property of all citizens;
therefore, all should benefit from the extraction process. To the extent
that severance tax revenues underwrite expenditures producing widely
diffused social benefits, this result will be realized. Fifth, the regulation costs are minimal. Sixth, the tax burden will fall in large part on a
surplus element of economic return and will tend, therefore, to rest on
the producer. Seventh, the severance tax would provide a flexible source
of state-local revenue over the business cycle. Eighth, the industries in
question create social costs, e.g., land subsidence, which should be
underwritten by a severance tax.

It is unlikely that the severance tax would produce severe disloca-
tion in the industries concerned. The main effect of the tax would be to
redistribute a certain amount of income from the producers to the state's
General Fund, the ultimate benefits being widely diffused over California's growing population.

A Model Tax System for California

We have recommended greater reliance on personal income, corporate income, insurance premium, and severance taxes at the state
level. Income-based taxes, in our opinion, provide a desirable balance
of the social value, fiscal, administrative, and economic criteria of a
model tax system. The next problem is one of determining the relative
importance of each of these taxes in the total revenue structure.

During 1957, the State of California raised $1,598 billion through
taxation. Of this amount, $528 million was produced by so-called "user"
taxes, i.e., gasoline and diesel fuel, motor vehicle taxes and licenses,
the proceeds of which were earmarked in the main for highway and street

financing.* Unrestricted, or general, taxes yielded somewhat over a billion dollars, the 3 percent sales and use tax and various liquor excises producing $640 million, or nearly 60 percent of the General Fund total.

Table 6.16 presents a summary of state General Fund tax revenues for 1957 and our conception of a model tax system for California. The most noteworthy features of this model are: (1) it assigns a relatively greater responsibility to the individual and corporate income taxes; (2) it makes the severance tax an integral part of the state tax system; and (3) it reduces the proportionate and absolute burden of the sales and use tax.

Table 6.16. State of California General Fund Tax Revenues: Actual 1957 Receipts Compared with a Model System (in millions)

| | 1957 | | Model Tax System | |
Type of Tax	Amount	Total	Amount	% of Total
Sales	$640.0*	59.8	$321.0	30.0
Personal Income	143.3	13.4	267.5	25.0
Corporate Income and Franchise	167.4	15.6	267.5	25.0
Severance	---	--	107.0	10.0
Insurance Premium	42.5	4.0	53.5	5.0
Gift and Inheritance	38.5	3.6	40.6	3.8
Other+	38.3	3.6	12.9	1.2
	$1,070.0	100.0	$1,070.0	100.0

*Includes $39.9 million from liquor excises.
+Ad valorem taxes, private car tax.

Although political expediency and fiscal necessity may preclude a reduction of the 3 percent sales and use tax rate, the ultimate realization of a model tax system demands increased rates for the individual and corporate income taxes and also the introduction of severance taxes into the revenue system. The imposition of excises on tobacco, or increases in the rates of existing sales and excises, will tend to work in the oppo-site direction.

In the final analysis, most, if not all, taxes are paid from income. Income, moreover, represents the best measure of ability to pay. Whe-ther or not an "ideal state-local fiscal society" becomes a reality in California depends upon the Legislature and the people. At the moment such a society exists only in the mind of the social scientist.

*In our opinion, highway user taxes should be increased as neces-sary in order to expedite the street and highway program.

NOTES TO CHAPTER 6

[1] The Tax Burden and the California Tax System, " The Tax Digest, March 1956, p. 103.

[2] Annual Report of the State Board of Equalization, fiscal year ended June 30, 1957, p. 11.

[3] Extracted from J. Gould, The California Tax System, pp. 35-38, as reprinted from West's Annotated California Codes, Vol. 59, 1956.

[4] See Report of the Senate Interim Committee on State and Local Taxation, Part Two, The Taxation of Personal Property in California, January 1953.

[5] For a more detailed discussion of tax exemptions see Francis J. Carr, "The Effects of Tax Exemptions, " The Tax Digest, Vol. 29, No. 5, May 1951, pp. 156-59, 173-75.

[6] C. Ward Macy, "The Theory and Practice of Central Assessment, " 1956 Proceedings of the National Tax Association, p. 505.

[7] R. A. Musgrave, J. J. Carroll, L. D. Cook, and L. Frane, "Distribution of Tax Payments by Income Groups: A Case Study for 1948, " National Tax Journal Vol. IV, No. 1, March 1951, pp. 1-53.

[8] Groves, Financing Government (New York: Henry Holt and Company, 4th edition, 1954), p. 50.

[9] Tax Policy, Vol. XVII, May-June 1950, p. 3.

[10] O. H. Brownlee and Edward D. Allen, Economics of Public Finance (New York: Prentice-Hall, Inc., 1954), pp. 340-41.

[11] For information on the mean ratio of assessed to true value for the state as a whole see the Special Report of the California State Board of Equalization on the Relative Burden of State and Local Taxes in 1912, p. 36; Report of the Tax Commission of 1917, p. 253; also see Reports of the California State Board of Equalization for the following years: 1921-22, p. 87; 1923-24, p. 76; 1925-26, p. 74; 1927-28, p. 30; 1929-30, p. 26; 1931-32, p. 30; Senate Interim Committee on State and Local Taxation, Property Assessment and Equalization in California, 1953, p. 280; Minutes of the meeting of the Board of Equalization, July 22, 1957 and July 21, 1958.

[12] Letter dated July 31, 1958 from Ronald B. Welch, Chief, Division of Research and Statistics, California State Board of Equalization.

[13] For a detailed discussion of duplicate assessments see State Board of Equalization, Assessment and Collection of City Property Taxes in California, January 1956 (mimeo).

[14] Annual Report of the State Board of Equalization, fiscal year ended June 30, 1957, p. 11.

[15] For a detailed account see State Interim Committee on Governmental Organization, Equalization of the Ad Valorem Tax Assessments in California, 1957.

[16] Ibid., p. 20.

[17] State Board of Equalization Biennial Report for 1945-46, p. 5.

[18] Harry M. Howell, "Assessment Practices in California Counties and Their Relationship to Measuring Local Ability in Making Contributions to a Foundation Program of Education"(mimeo.), California Cooperative Committee on School Finance, 1948, pp. 7-8, referred to in Report of the Senate Interim Committee on State and Local Taxation, Part Three, State and Local Taxes in California: A Comparative Analysis, April 1951, p. 505.

[19] J. Gould, The California Tax System, Reprinted from West's Annotated California Codes, Vol. 59, 1956, pp. 35-38. See also Malcolm M. Davisson and William K. Schmelzle, "Equalization of Property Tax Assessments in California," National Tax Journal, September 1950, pp. 211-32.

[20] For an excellent detailed summary of the actions of the State Board of Equalization since 1949 see Ronald A. Welch, "Intercounty Equalization in California," National Tax Journal, Vol. X, No. 1, March 1957, pp. 57-65, Vol. X, No. 2, June 1957, pp. 148-57.

[21] Report of the Senate Interim Committee on State and Local Taxation, Part Six, Property Assessments and Equalization in California, March 1953, p. 20.

[22] Welch, Intercounty Equalization, " p. 148.

[23] Ibid., pp. 150-51.

[24] State Interim Committee on Governmental Organization, Equalization of Ad Valorem Tax Assessments in California, p. 32.

[25] Ibid,, pp. 44-45.

[26] Excellent treatments of the business license tax in California may be found in League of California Cities, Business License Taxes, June 1957, and Malcolm M. Davisson, "Trends in Licensing of Businesses, Trades, and Professions in California Cities," an address presented at the Annual Conference, League of California Cities, October 29, 1956.

[27] Davisson, "Trends in Licensing of Business..."

[28] Ibid.

[29] Ibid.

[30] Senate Committee on Banking and Currency, Staff Report, Factors Affecting the Stock Market, Washington, 1955, p. 90.

[31] State of California, Franchise Tax Board, Annual Report 1957, pp. 70-71.

[32] For an expanded discussion of state taxation of insurance companies see Report of the Senate Interim Committee on State and Local Taxation, Part Three, State and Local Taxes in California: A Comparative Analysis, April 1951, pp. 225-55.

[33] Ohio Department of Taxation, Severance Taxation, 1956, p. 1.

[34] See Report of the Senate Interim Committee, Part Three, State and Local Taxes in California, pp. 281-341.

PART IV

MEASUREMENT OF LOCAL INDEBTEDNESS

JOHN A. VIEG

Assisted by Paul R. Kaufman

"I believe·in living within my income even if I have to borrow
to do it."

— Mark Twain

To borrow or not to borrow is a question that confronts all governments, rich as well as poor, those that plan ahead with care as
well as those content merely to muddle along. Statistics on local indebtedness are easy to amass but no one can tell from such data alone
which communities have borrowed wisely and which have not. The
answer depends on all the circumstances involved, though chiefly on
the benefits deriving from the use to which the loans are put.

THE ECONOMICS OF LOCAL BORROWING

Except during a prolonged depression — and even then only if
the national and state governments default on their responsibilities —
borrowing by cities, counties, school and other special districts should
as a general principle be reserved for one prime purpose: to make
possible the immediate construction of a major public improvement of
enduring value which it would be impossible or inadvisable to finance
either out of reserves or current revenues or both combined.

Borrowing for Long-Range Needs

Long-term loans fall properly into three categories: those made
(a) for broad governmental purposes, (b) to finance improvements benefiting specific property owners, and (c) to finance utility-type services.
Each type will be examined in turn, but by way of introduction, certain
things need to be said about the economic logic of local borrowing in
general.

Though borrowing by governmental units is and can be only partially analogous to borrowing by the private sector of the economy,
cities, counties, school districts, and other special units should decide the questions of when and how much to borrow only after giving
due thought to the balance between the prospective costs and prospective benefits of a project or, in other words, what economists call the
efficiency of capital. If $100,000, borrowed and invested in a capital
improvement today, promises during the term of the bonds to yield
benefits clearly exceeding or even equaling the cost of the loan, the
governing board of a locality would be warranted in sponsoring a bond
issue, provided it could not finance the project otherwise. Since the
benefits of most governmental functions are widely diffused, however,
determination of their value will in many cases be more a matter of
judgment than of arithmetic. The expenditure may have to be made

even though gains from the improvement in question may be impossible
to compute in anything like precise dollar amounts. What matters is that
the members of local boards and the voter-taxpayers at least try to ask
the economically pertinent questions before committing the community
to a long-term debt.

General Obligation Bonds. These are the best bonds that local
governmental units can offer the investing public and they should be
used only for lasting improvements benefiting as nearly as possible all
the people of the community. Illustrative of projects appropriately financed in this way are such things as a new city hall or county court-
house, major bridges and underpasses, a new water works or sewage
system. On the other hand, a new fire truck or street sweeper and new
office furniture afford good examples of purchases that ought not to be
financed via long-term bond issues because they do not constitute lasting improvements, also in some cases because they may be too small.

Special or Assessment District Bonds. Both cities and counties,
though more particularly cities, often undertake major outlays so clearly benefiting the owners of property located in one particular area that
it would be unfair to finance the improvements with bonds constituting
a general obligation upon the whole community. In such cases the approved method is to issue bonds backed by special assessments upon
given parcels of property or — what amounts to the same thing — to
form appropriate assessment districts and make such bonds an obligation of those districts exclusively.

Revenue Bonds. In the case of utility-type services, such as municipal gas or electric systems or parking facilities, the theory of borrowing — especially in a private enterprise economy — calls for the
use of revenue rather than general obligation bonds. Such businesslike
or "trading" enterprises (the British term for them) cannot be judged
on their merits unless they compete in the bond market on the same
basis as private utilities. Water systems, however, form an exception
to this rule. By common consent they are so basic to health and survival in the modern urban community that capital outlays for them are
often underwritten by general obligation bonds, even when they will be
paid for out of earnings rather than taxes.

Limited use has been made of revenue bonds in California in the
past because federal regulations prohibit banks from buying them, but
the State Controller reports that there has been a "marked trend"
toward their employment in recent years, especially among cities.

Nearly 38% of municipal indebtedness outstanding on June 30, 1958 was in the form of revenue bonds. "Let the user pay" is a policy that appeals to discriminating voters as well as to elective officials. Investors have sometimes been reluctant to put their money in revenue bonds without the added inducement of higher interest rates, but if the bonds have a sound business footing they are now readily acceptable as "stable, prudent investments." While the proposed $1.75 billion issue of state water bonds on the 1960 ballot will be general obligation in character, they would be repaid out of the earnings of the water system if possible and it is expected that water revenues alone will be adequate for this purpose. [1]

Occasions for Short-Term Borrowing

Far-sighted planning and attentive management will normally obviate any need to borrow for short-term purposes. There are, however, four conditions under which such loans may be both necessary and justifiable.

Tax Anticipation Loans. When, on the one hand, a community is unable to build up a cash reserve or, on the other, its tax revenues do not become available until the fiscal year is well under way, it can hardly escape having to go to a bank and float a short-term loan to pay its bills. Obviously, this is a sorry arrangement for everybody, except possibly the bankers, but it is one under which historically thousands of local governmental units throughout the country have been compelled to operate.

Three simple steps could reduce the need for this kind of borrowing to zero: (a) The first tax delinquency date could be set to coincide with the beginning of the fiscal year. (b) Local governments could be authorized and encouraged to build up working reserves to tide them over the first part of every fiscal year. Using this method, the City of Los Angeles "has not borrowed a dollar or registered a warrant in anticipation of taxes for nearly a generation." [2] (c) With respect to local assistance and shared revenues, the state could remit to the localities several months earlier than it does now, a considerate practice that the State Controller has promoted in recent years.

Bond Anticipation Loans. Because only relatively small amounts of money may be needed in the early stages of a capital improvement for which bonding has been authorized, it may be good management to defer the sale of bonds until major expenditures are required and to defray initial costs via short-term loans. If such a situation arises, a

local board or council would be unwise not to use its credit. Indeed,
the taxpayers would have cause for criticism if they failed to do so.

Disaster Loans. Though every well-planned local budget includes
an item for contingencies, no city council, county board or school board
can be expected to anticipate what the law quaintly calls "acts of God."
Prediction of disaster has not yet been subjected to statistical discipline.
Thus, if a community should suffer a misfortune greatly exceeding the
proportions of its contingency fund (and if it has engaged in prudent
management otherwise), it should not hesitate to cope with the emer-
gency by borrowing. Obviously it might have to borrow anyway, but it
could do so more easily and confidently with a past record of sound administration.

Loans for Initial Relief Projects. By general agreement the prime
responsibility for coping with economic depression and recession rests
on the national and state governments. Should either delay or default by
one or the other threaten hardship on the people of a community beyond
the capacity or ordinary public assistance and private charity, a city or
county board might well be justified in borrowing on a short-term basis
to finance an initial relief program — especially if this would insure
getting ahead with well-planned, long-term capital improvements.

THE LAW ON LOCAL BORROWING

The California Government Code (GC) for counties, cities, and
local agencies and the Education Code for school districts differ on
some points from the carefully formulated Model County and Municipal
Bond Law and the Model Municipal Revenue Bond Law of the National
Municipal League. By and large, however, they afford all four types
of governmental units in this state fair leeway for the wise use of their
respective capacities to borrow. The main fault of the code lies in its
unintentional role as a stimulant for creating special districts, and
perhaps it would be well to begin with this feature.

Limitations on Amount of Indebtedness

Counties are limited in the total amount of their bonded indebtedness for general purposes to 5% of their taxable property as shown by
the last equalized assessment roll. This is increased, however, to a
total of 15% in case bonds are floated for "water conservation, flood
control, irrigation, reclamation, or drainage works" (GC Section
29909).

Cities may bond themselves for improvements up to an aggregate
of "15 per cent of the assessed value of all real and personal property"

within their boundaries. Such improvements include "bridges, water-
works, water rights, sewers, light and power works or plants, buildings
for municipal uses, wharves, breakwaters, jetties, seawalls, school-
houses, fire apparatus, street work, and other works, property or
structures necessary or convenient to carry out the objects, purposes
and powers of the city," such for example as "public golf courses and
related public conveniences," which latter may also be undertaken by
counties or other local agencies (GC Section 43601, 43605, 50701).

In addition to issuing general obligation bonds for the foregoing
purposes, cities may, as indicated above, sell special or assessment
district bonds in the amounts required to improve properties in a
particular location and also sell revenue bonds. The amount of money
that can be raised by revenue bonds is limited only by the earnings of
the enterprise.

It is difficult to describe clearly the limitations on indebtedness
pertaining to special districts because they vary considerably from one
type to another. In terms of percentage of assessed valuation, they
range from 5 to 20%, though some are prohibited from issuing bonds
of any kind. Moreover, unlike the other units of local government,
which have a common maximum redemption period, some special districts can borrow for no longer than 5 years while others may borrow
for 75.[3]

To return to the point made at the beginning of this section, legal
debt limits in the form of 5, 10, or 15% of assessed valuation operate
at times (especially in combination with property assessment at approximately 25% of true or market value) to establish special districts when
either the city or the county, as general purpose governments, could
otherwise have performed the service desired.

The obvious remedy for this situation would be to abolish such
limitations and put officials, voters, and investors on notice that they
must look to the merits of every bond issue rather than rely on mechanical and often deceptive assurances of this kind.

Yet other considerations must be borne in mind in this connection.
There is sufficient merit in the report of the National Municipal League's
Committee on Model Fiscal Legislation for Local Governments accompanying its Model County and Municipal Bond Law to justify retention of
some type of debt limitation, leaving the proliferation of special districts to be dealt with in some other way. The committee recognizes
that any limitation, to be effective, "must be imposed on the composite

local debt which is chargeable against the resources of a given community" and suggests that "where the overlapping situation is complex, utilization of a county board or state agency may be necessary to allocate a composite borrowing power." The model law it proposes, however, advises continued use of the method of limiting indebtedness to a fixed percentage of assessed property values. The committee admits that, as an index of a community's basic economic resources, this yardstick is "far from ideal." Yet it supplies "the only annually necessary measurement standard available for all classes and sizes of local political subdivisions" and, given certain qualifications (along with steady improvement in assessment practices), it can be made increasingly fair and serviceable.[3]

Three stipulations would do a great deal to make this traditional type of debt limitation more acceptable. The first would restrict the base of the property tax to real property. The second would make it perfectly clear, legally, that the ratios stipulated applied to assessed valuation on a full value basis; otherwise, the 15% composite limit proposed — 4% for counties, 6% for cities, and 5% for schools — would be unreasonably low. The third stipulation is that the limit should be computed against the average of assessed real property valuation for three years, namely, the current year and the two immediately preceding.[4] California might well revise its Government Code accordingly, making due allowance however for the rate at which its heavily urban counties are becoming municipalized.

Limitations on Redemption

As recently as 1950, the general maximum time limit on local bonded indebtedness was 20 years, but it has since been fixed at 40 years (GC Sections, 29901 and 43620). Though the Code emphasizes that this is simply the maximum and that bonds should be made redeemable in the minimum time needed for the purpose, California might also weigh the merits of the specific time limits set forth in the Model Bond Law for various types of capital improvements. Such standards would furnish considerable guidance particularly for smaller units with their less highly trained administrative staffs. The proposed limits are set forth in Article V as follows:

1. Water systems	35 years
2. Sewer systems	30 years; replacements 10 years
3. Electric systems and gas plants	30 years; replacements 10 years
4. Incinerator or disposal plants	15 years; replacements 5 years

5.	Docks	30 years
6.	Rapid transit railroads	40 years
7.	Bridges, tunnels, underpasses	30 years
8.	Buildings: Class A (fireproof)	30 years
	Class B (fire-resistant)	20 years
	Class C (all others)	15 years
9.	Conversion of Class B or C into A	20 years
10.	Other building changes re Class A and B	10 years, re Class C, 5 years
11.	Airports	30 years
12.	Parks (including equipment)	20 years
13.	Roads, streets, parkways	5 to 10 years depending on durability
14.	Land acquisition	30 years
15.	Dikes and bulkheads - steel, stone concrete	20 years; earth or wood, 10 years
16.	Sewer and water connections	10 years
17.	Curbs, sidewalks, gutters	5 years
18.	Police and fire alarm systems	10 years
19.	Equipment, apparatus, furnishings	5 years
20.	Apparatus and vehicles; if cost is over $1,000	10 years
21.	All other unspecified objects	5 years

Limitations on Popular Approval

No type of limitation on local indebtedness is more basic than the requirement of popular approval, and the California Code calls for a 2/3 popular vote on county, city, and school district bond issues.[5] Investment bankers apparently believe that this stipulation, as much as any other factor, has contributed to the high credit rating of these three most common types of local governmental units. There is a loophole in the law, however, with regard to special districts. In a progress report submitted to the California Legislature, January 1958 (Assembly Journal, March 10, 1958, pp. 173-85) the Subcommittee on Public Indebtedness of the Assembly Committee on Revenue and Taxation disclosed that because of the loose definition of indebtedness in Article XI, Section 18 of the state constitution, none of California's more than 3,000 special districts can be required to submit bond issues to a popular vote. As a result, the boards in control have committed the taxpayers of many such districts to debt obligations of which they are almost unaware and the credit of local government generally is being impaired. What makes the matter worse, as the subcommittee explained, is that in some instances the debts have been incurred after the voters had rejected the proposed bond issue.

There is, however, another side to this question. Due to the length of the local government ballot and the frequency of elections, the average voter appears to be somewhat overburdened. Even for much-needed and planned capital improvements and with careful and extensive publicity, it is sometimes difficult to secure a 2-1 vote in favor of a bond issue.

Recognizing the hard realities of the situation, the Assembly subcommittee has wisely concluded that although the requirements of a popular vote ought to be extended to cover special districts too, there is nothing inherently sacred about the figure of 66-2/3%. By sponsoring a bill to reduce this requirement to 60% (for which there is a good prospect in the 1959 General Session) several committee members hope to be able not only to "plug this loophole" but to ease the position of certain local school districts as well. Many school officials, including trustees as well as administrators, would apparently welcome a lowering of the requirement from 2/3 to 3/5. It is likely that the measure will also attempt to define public indebtedness to include lease-purchase agreements and revenue bonds, both of which have sometimes been used by special district boards to evade the necessity of getting popular approval.[6]

A good case can be made for departing even farther from the flat requirement of a popular vote. In the judgment of the National Municipal League's Committee on the Model Bond Law, effective notice, hearings, and publicity furnish better safeguards against rash borrowing than the mechanical requirement of a popular vote. Consequently, the Model Law requires approval of a bond resolution by 3/5 of all the members of the governing body after a public hearing and appropriate notice in the press. It does not specify that there must be a popular vote but provides instead that "where a mandatory referendum is not otherwise required" the authorization of bonds shall be "subject to a permissive referendum on petition."[7]

Limitations on Rates of Interest and Down Payments

Among the remaining types of limitations specified by law, actually or potentially, there is space for mention of no more than three. As to the rate of interest at which local governmental units may borrow on general obligation bonds, the California Code sets a limit of 6% (GC Sections 29916 and 43609). This is identical with the limitation embodied in the Model Law.

California has no specific provision regarding a "down payment" out of current revenues on proposed bonded capital improvements, but the Model Law lays considerable stress on such a requirement and there is good logic behind it. Since a local community that finances a capital

project through the sale of its bonds is, in effect, buying the improvement on the installment plan, it is wholly in order to begin with a 5%
down payment as recommended by the League. (Preference should, of
course, be given to serial-type bonds, which California now uses
almost exclusively, rather than to those based on the sinking fund principle.)

The idea of a down payment is anything but rare for "it was established in Massachusetts more than 25 years ago" and has also been
used extensively in New Jersey, New York, and several other states.
As the League explains, principal gain flowing from the requirement
is not that it reduces the amount of borrowing by 5% but that, since the
down payment has to be acquired, the local board or council is thereby
compelled to do at least a little bit of budgeting before it can take on a
capital project.

California does not have such a down payment requirement at the
present time, but it does have a provision, permissive in character,
which looks to somewhat the same end. Sections 53730-37 of the Government Code specifically authorize cities, counties, schools, and
other special districts to accumulate capital outlay funds as follows:

> By ordinance, the legislative body of a local agency may
> provide for the levy and collection of assessments or taxes for
> the creation and accumulation of a fund for capital outlays. . . .
> In a local agency required to adopt a budget, all or part of the
> fund may be shown in the budget as reserves for future expendi-
> tures in subsequent years and when so shown shall be identified
> as to purpose, but need not be itemized. At any time after the
> creation of the fund the legislative body may transfer to the fund
> any unincumbered surplus funds remaining on hand at the end of
> a fiscal year . . . the fund shall remain inviolate for the making
> of any capital outlays and money shall not be disbursed from the
> fund except for such a purpose unless the legislative body submits
> a proposition to the electors . . . . A two-thirds vote of all the
> voters voting at the election is necessary to authorize the expendi-
> ture.

This plan is being used today by many progressive communities
in California to finance their capital improvements. Its possibilities
ought to be exploited by every unit of local government throughout the
state.

Undoubtedly one of the most constructive limitations on borrowing for capital outlays — assuming it is genuine rather than merely pro
forma — would be a requirement that no debt could be incurred except
for a project forming an integral part of a long-term plan of capital improvements. Failure to plan accounts for more of the waste and inefficiency in local borrowing than any other factor. Compulsion has never

been very effective, however, as a means of getting people to exercise imagination and foresight. What needs to be amended is not so much the law as the state of mind that almost dismisses planning as a bothersome waste of time.

TRENDS IN LOCAL INDEBTEDNESS
Current Volume of State-Local Bonded Debt.

Inasmuch as the different bond issues making up the total volume of state-local debt often rest on different people (depending on which city, county, or school district is responsible for each local issue), statistics showing the aggregate amount of such indebtedness chargeable against the people of California are clearly of limited significance. The figures on the total volume of California's current state and local debt obligations do, however, furnish a broad background for the analysis of local indebtedness.

Table 7.1, based on the latest data available at the time of writing, indicates that as of 1957 the grand total of bonded debt in this state amounted to $4,327 million. Of this amount, averaging approximately $300 per capita, state bonds outstanding on December 31, 1957, represented 26.7%; county bonds outstanding on June 30 of that year represented 7.3%; city bonds, 23.6%; school district bonds, 29.6%; and special district bonds (the latest figures available at the time of writing were for June 30, 1956), 12.8%. [*]

How many more millions in potential debt obligations will have been voted before the end of 1958 no one will know for years to come, if ever, for no one is charged (not that anyone should be) with keeping such a record. At the November election, however, four propositions were adopted that authorized the state alone to borrow an additional $780 million.

Trend of County Indebtedness: 1937, 1947, 1957

Four types of data are essential to understanding what has been happening in the last generation in the field of local debt: (1) the absolute amounts of the dollar obligations of local governmental units as corporate entities, (2) the volume of debt per capita for each of the key years, (3) the ratio of bonded debt to the assessed valuation of property, and (4) the ratio of debt service (payments for interest and redemption of principal combined) to the total cost of government.

[*] County indebtedness is small because, though their expenditures are heavy, they receive far more in subventions and grants than do the cities, which taken together also have larger budgets.

Table 7.1 Volume of State and Local Bonded Debt in California: 1957*
(in millions)

	%	Amount	%
State Bonds Outstanding			
December 31, 1957	100.00	$1,157.1	26.7
Highways	.99	11.5	
Sacramento State Buildings	.26	3.0	
San Francisco State Buildings	.01	.2	
University of California Buildings	.03	.3	
Other State and University Buildings	.17	2.0	
Tenth Olympiad	.03	.4	
India Basin	.03	.4	
First Harbor	.28	3.2	
Second Harbor	.37	4.3	
Third Harbor	.74	8.5	
Veterans	56.79	657.1	
School Building Aid	40.29	466.2	
County Bonds Outstanding			
June 30, 1957	100.00	315.3	7.3
General Bonds	21.06	66.4	
Special & Assessment Dist. Bonds	78.94	248.9	
City Bonds Outstanding			
June 30, 1957	100.00	1,022.8	23.6
(includes bonds for revenue- producing enterprises as well as for general governmental functions)			
Local School District Bonds Out- standing June 30, 1957	100.00	1,279.1	29.6
Bonds of Other Districts Out- standing June 30, 1956 **	100.00	552.8	12.8
Grand Total of State and Local Debt: 1957	100.00	$4,327.0	100.0

*Total public bonded debt in California would include, in addition to the amount given here, California's proportionate share (roughly 10%) of the U.S. Government debt of $27,500,000,000, for a super grand total of $31,827,036,027. A somewhat comparable figure for private debt would be California's share of national mortgage debt ($156.3 billion) plus consumer credit ($44.8 billion) or 10% of $201.1 billion. The other side of the picture is that Californians enjoy almost exactly 10% of disposable personal income in the United States or, for 1957, $30,060,000,000.

**Special District indebtedness on June 30, 1957 totaled $588.9 million, which figure became available after this table had been completed.

Table 7.2 gives the absolute figures on total bonded debt, total debt service and total cost of government for all counties (except San Francisco, which, being a consolidated city-county, is in a class by itself) for each of the years 1937, 1947, and 1957.

Table 7.3 (supplemented by Table 7-a in the Appendix) shows variations in bonded indebtedness for every county (except San Francisco) from three different perspectives: (1) per capita, (2) in terms of percentage of assessed valuation, and (3) in terms of debt service in relation to the total cost of government. Perhaps the most pertinent data from the standpoint of the general reader are that median county debt per capita, which stood at $30.14 in 1937, had dropped to $17.17 by 1947, but then increased to $87.48 by 1957. Adjusted for changes of price level (with 1957 taken as the base), the corresponding figures become $78.36, $25.93, and $87.48. Total and inter-quartile ranges are also given for all three years. Another significant fact is that, disregarding such changes as may have occurred in assessment ratios, for the median county, the ratio of bonded debt to assessed valuation changed from 2.6% in 1937, to 1.4% in 1947, and to 4.7% in 1957. That fact should, however, be checked against the following ratios of debt service to the total cost of government. For the median county this percentage stood at 7.7 in 1937; by 1947 it had fallen to 2.5, and by 1957 it had risen again to 3.2. (See Figure 7.1.)

Trend of Municipal Indebtedness: 1937. 1947, 1957

The broad pattern of municipal indebtedness during the past generation resembles that for counties and schools: relatively high in the 1930's as a heritage from the construction of the 1920's, low in the 1940's due to the general deferment of major improvements during the depression and World War II, and advancing to a higher high or a lower low, depending on the point of view, in the 1950's because of the huge backlog of needed facilities and California's tremendous prosperity and population growth. The total amount of municipal bonds outstanding on June 30 of each of the three base years used in this study was as follows: 1937 - $511,299,500; 1947 - $448,328,487; 1957 - $1,022,794,415

Table 7-b in the Appendix presents the basic data on bonded indebtedness for every city in the state (except San Francisco) during the last twenty years, giving figures on the total value of bonds outstanding, total debt service, and total cost of government for 1937, 1947, and 1957, both for each municipality and by county totals.

Probably the most significant general measures of the burden of

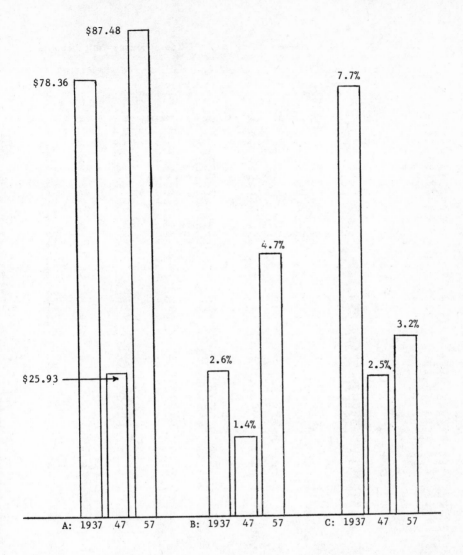

Figure 7.1. Variations in Three Medians as Measures of Local
           Indebtedness Among California Counties *

A: Median total bonded debt per capita (in dollars). **
B: Median total bonded debt as percentage of assessed valuation.
C: Median total debt service as percentage of total cost of government.

    *City-County of San Francisco excluded.

    **Adjusted by U.S. Department of Commerce Construction Cost
Index, 1956.

    Source: Table 7.3.

Table 7.2. Basic Data Relating to Individual County Indebtedness: 1937, 1947, 1957
(for all counties except the City-County of San Francisco)

County	Total Bonded Debt (In thousands)			Total Debt Service (In thousands)			Total Cost of Government (In millions)		
	1937	1947	1957	1937	1947	1957	1937	1947	1957
Alameda	$ 21,972.6	$ 28,776.4	$ 79,247.0	$ 2,194.6	$ 2,359.5	$ 4,939.8	$ 22.1	$ 40.3	$ 148.6
Alpine	3.5	....	....	3.3	....	....	.1	.1	.2
Amador	2.0	7.2	481.7	1.3	1.3	50.7	.5	.9	1.6
Butte	1,748.1	1,189.6	4,846.9	285.5	38.9	451.9	2.5	4.7	16.7
Calaveras	113.0	49.0	1,458.0	14.6	11.9	119.6	.4	.8	2.5
Colusa	3,777.0	320.5	421.5	120.0	84.0	36.8	1.5	1.8	3.6
Contra Costa	4,444.7	5,101.7	64,515.0	647.5	424.6	5,434.3	4.8	13.9	90.8
Del Norte	145.0	....	1,664.4	14.0	....	436.8	.3	.6	4.7
El Dorado	205.5	180.0	1,517.9	21.8	21.6	208.2	.6	1.1	4.7
Fresno	8,442.2	6,311.8	34,971.6	926.8	821.3	3,110.7	8.6	19.0	73.0
Glenn	404.0	254.0	2,200.0	63.1	32.4	116.3	.8	1.5	4.2
Humboldt	422.5	967.5	7,108.5	65.0	56.4	719.6	2.2	4.4	21.8
Imperial	2,718.8	1,960.9	4,317.0	426.9	83.1	545.6	2.5	3.8	14.9
Inyo	224.5	240.5	2,070.5	31.6	29.9	110.8	.5	1.1	3.7
Kern	1,544.9	1,911.6	25,830.4	421.7	302.3	5,008.2	7.4	19.9	79.3
Kings	1,062.9	470.5	2,713.8	131.3	34.8	305.6	1.8	3.9	10.8
Lake	236.0	105.5	452.9	29.8	14.1	56.6	.5	1.2	3.5
Lassen	293.2	202.4	297.4	40.5	50.9	42.4	.8	1.6	3.5
Los Angeles	162,544.6	150,757.0	691,578.5	15,758.6	13,054.8	53,330.9	131.3	260.5	1,030.8
Madera	248.5	360.5	1,173.8	48.6	33.5	119.0	1.1	2.8	9.8
Marin	1,690.4	2,219.0	17,166.0	239.8	192.9	907.5	2.0	4.6	23.6
Mariposa	100.4	67.2	149.5	9.7	7.1	24.2	.3	.5	1.3
Mendocino	371.6	379.7	6,683.9	47.8	43.4	376.4	1.4	2.6	10.5
Merced	1,790.6	531.8	4,895.0	243.4	167.1	515.7	2.3	5.1	16.7
Modoc	219.5	233.0	732.0	46.9	12.5	85.5	.6	.9	2.9
Mono	....	....	30.0	....	....	3.0	.2	.2	1.1
Monterey	2,895.4	3,080.2	23,951.4	385.5	307.6	1,710.5	3.3	7.2	30.7
Napa	641.5	1,112.0	8,323.0	119.9	74.7	528.7	1.1	2.5	21.0
Nevada	400.7	358.9	243.7	38.2	45.2	39.5	.9	1.4	3.6
Orange	6,541.8	5,671.8	78,561.2	922.1	697.7	4,159.6	8.6	14.1	97.4
Placer	474.4	673.1	354.2	75.6	39.0	294.6	1.3	2.6	9.7
Plumas	21.4	308.4	1,288.6	2.5	35.8	196.7	.7	1.3	4.1
Riverside	7,797.3	7,442.8	36,464.3	510.6	438.2	2,039.7	5.1	11.7	50.9
Sacramento	10,839.5	8,633.3	45,380.3	914.5	691.1	3,176.5	7.7	15.0	81.3
San Benito	$ 152.1	$ 22.0	$ 90.0	$ 35.6	$ 4.1	$ 27.2	$ .5	$ 1.0	$ 2.6
San Bernardino	5,230.5	7,721.0	56,956.2	628.2	550.5	3,554.2	7.3	17.6	99.2
San Diego	16,425.7	14,318.9	70,098.5	1,229.5	1,134.5	4,883.1	11.5	29.6	127.1
San Joaquin	2,909.6	5,083.6	25,574.6	340.0	486.1	1,422.4	5.4	12.4	47.1
San Luis Obispo	2,752.4	1,259.8	7,105.1	379.6	68.4	826.4	2.6	4.6	14.3
San Mateo	2,930.1	4,619.8	56,794.4	600.8	366.6	3,946.9	4.4	10.7	67.0
Santa Barbara	3,327.6	917.1	10,127.1	465.2	206.9	737.1	4.4	7.5	23.9
Santa Clara	6,337.0	3,729.0	75,946.4	795.7	455.8	4,166.7	7.5	15.8	96.5
Santa Cruz	1,077.2	788.5	6,944.7	190.2	86.3	565.1	2.0	4.3	15.5
Shasta	324.1	464.1	7,135.1	53.9	22.7	529.8	1.0	2.6	13.2
Sierra	16.0	16.0	21.0	1.3	3.6	1.7	.2	.3	1.0
Siskiyou	198.7	485.8	3,878.4	44.1	18.2	113.2	1.4	2.6	8.7
Solano	976.7	1,681.6	11,973.5	139.1	146.5	947.3	1.6	5.9	23.5
Sonoma	2,471.7	1,594.1	21,016.5	325.9	261.5	1,148.7	3.6	7.6	40.7
Stanislaus	1,779.0	3,880.2	15,887.3	228.3	223.1	1,083.2	3.1	8.4	31.5
Sutter	673.7	302.0	2,091.0	133.8	67.4	167.4	1.7	2.7	7.1
Tehama	575.6	242.3	1,239.0	68.4	45.7	141.6	.9	1.5	4.9
Trinity	7.3	6.0	308.1	.5	6.4	31.6	.3	.5	2.5
Tulare	2,670.7	2,691.1	10,795.6	444.8	277.2	914.6	4.1	10.8	37.6
Tuolumne	70.5	106.0	627.9	8.6	14.9	62.5	.7	1.2	3.6
Ventura	2,752.6	5,453.5	34,677.2	387.8	476.3	2,674.9	3.9	8.1	37.4
Yolo	1,338.8	1,207.6	4,513.7	159.6	127.1	375.4	1.7	3.3	10.8
Yuba	668.1	40.0	2,362.0	34.3	32.0	169.9	.9	2.0	7.1

Source: State Controller's Annual Reports concerning Financial Transactions of Counties for years cited.

Table 7.3. Variation in Bonded Indebtedness Among All Counties (except San Francisco) by Medians, Quartiles and Range: 1937, 1947, 1957

Total County Bonded Debt on June 30 of Base Year[1]

	$ Per Capita[2]			Percentage of Assessed Valuation[3]			Debt Service as % of Total Cost of Government[4]		
	1937 (a)	1947 (b)	1957 (c)	1937 (d)	1947 (e)	1957 (f)	1937 (g)	1947 (h)	1957 (i)
State Aggregate[5]	$ 72.09	$40.92	$125.62	6.7%	3.7%	7.3%	13.2%	5.2%	5.9%
Adjusted[6]	187.43	61.79	125.62						
Counties:									
High	380.94	52.04	212.48	18.2	5.2	12.2	17.1	5.9	9.4
Q3	43.99	26.61	129.32	3.6	2.4	7.6	10.7	3.4	4.2
Median	30.14	17.17	87.48	2.6	1.4	4.7	7.7	2.5	3.2
Q1[1]	16.00	10.08	54.92	1.1	.7	2.2	4.3	1.3	2.4
Low	00.00	00.00	00.00	0.0	0.0	0.0	0.0	0.0	0.0
Median: Adjusted[6]	78.36	25.93	87.48						

[1]All basic data were derived from the State Controller's Annual Reports for Counties. See Table 7.2.

[2]Population estimates used for 1937 were those developed by the California Taxpayer's Association (interpolated for January 1 of that year) and for 1947 and 1957, those of the State Department of Finance.

[3]All indebtedness noted in this table consists of general obligation bonds. Because of changes in reporting practices that for 1957 (under all three headings)* consists of all bonded debt of California's 57 counties plus San Francisco's debt as given in the State Controller's report on Cities plus all school district debt. But for these additions figures for 1957 would not correspond to those for 1937 and 1947.
*for State aggregate only.

[4]Debt service includes both interest payments and redemptions of principal.

[5]It cannot be claimed that these figures on state aggregates are very significant because responsibility for different segments of local indebtedness rests with the taxpayers of the unit which incurred the particular debt, not on the taxpayers of the state as a whole.

[6]These figures have been adjusted through use of the U.S. Department of Commerce Cost-of-Construction Index (1956).

bonded indebtedness consist of these three ratios: (<u>a</u>) bonded debt per
capita, (<u>b</u>) bonded debt as a percentage of assessed property valuation,
and (<u>c</u>) debt service (payments for interest and redemption) as a percentage of the total cost of government.

Appendix Table 7-c presents those ratios for every city in California as of June 30, 1957, the latest year for which figures were available at the time of writing. It also indicates the median for each of
these measures and the total and inter-quartile ranges. Table 7.4 offers
a summary view of these various measures and proportions. In terms
of indebtedness per capita the median among all cities fell at $20.12
(between San Mateo's $20.09, and Hanford's $20.35) with a range extending from zero to $5,839.49 (Vernon). In terms of the ratio of in-
debtedness to assessed valuation the median fell at 1.70% (between
Ripon's 1.69, and Holtville's 1.71), the range extending from zero for
a good many cities to 35.9% for Blue Lake. The figures on debt service
as a percentage of the total cost of government establish Fullerton and
Perris as twin median cities at 3.2, with many at zero and Cypress at
35.8%.

Table 7.4. Summary of Variation in Bonded Indebtedness Among All
Cities (except San Francisco) by Medians, Quartiles, and Range: 1957

Indebtedness Per Capita

High	$5,839.49	Vernon
Q^3	56.89	Gustine
Median	20.22	San Mateo (20.09), Hanford (20.35)
Q^1	.41	Visalia (.33), Benicia (.43)
Low	....	Too numerous to list

Percentage of Assessed Valuation

High	35.90%	Blue Lake
Q^3	4.68	Petaluma
Median	1.70	Ripon (1.69), Holtville (1.71)
Q^1	.06	Inglewood
Low	....	Too numerous to list

Debt Service as Percentage of Total Cost of Government

High	35.8%	Cypress
Q^3	6.3	Port Hueneme, Nevada City
Median	3.2	Fullerton, Perris
Q^1	.4	Gilroy, Hawthorne
Low	....	Too numerous to list

To what extent have the cities of California already used up their borrowing capacity, and under what terms can they borrow today? Perhaps the best answers to those questions are offered by the report on municipal borrowing presented in the International City Managers' Association Municipal Yearbook for 1958. Table 7.5 indicates what net interest rate each California city of more than 10,000 population had to pay on general obligation, revenue, and special assessment bonds issued in 1957, and how much borrowing capacity it still had available.[8]

Trend of School District Bonded Debt: 1940-1957

The problems of local school finance are treated so comprehensively in the two succeeding chapters that a relatively brief examination of the indebtedness of California's school districts will suffice here. School bonds totaled $170.2 million in 1940 but dropped to $125.1 million by the end of the war in 1945. Five years later, the aggregate had mounted to $469.1 million, and by 1957 the figure had increased to $1,279 million.[9]

Meanwhile, however, the fiscal difficulties confronting many districts had become so acute that the state found itself obliged to supplement the assistance it had been giving toward current expenditures by additional aid designed to meet the unprecedented expenditures hundreds of districts had to make for new buildings. Beginning in 1947-48, the Legislature appropriated $55 million for outright grants to school districts for capital outlays used to purchase and improve sites or to construct and furnish buildings. To be eligible for this type of aid, a district was required to be taxing itself within one-half cent of the legal limit (disregarding any overriding of the limit that may have been approved by the voters) and to be bonded up to at least 95% of its limit.

By 1949, it was clear that the scale of such assistance needed to be stepped up enormously. The Legislature then passed a new school building aid law and proposed a $250 million bond issue that was subsequently approved by the voters. Apportionments under this act were made, as before, by a State Allocations Board, but in the form of interest-bearing loans rather than grants. Perhaps the clearest measure of the state's generosity and, by the same token, the urgency of local needs lies in the terms adopted with regard to repayment. No district was to be obligated, in paying off its own bonds and its obligations to the State School Building Fund, to do more than tax itself,

Table 7.5   Municipal Borrowing by California Cities Over 10,000: 1958

| City | General Obligation Bonds | | Revenue Bonds | Special Assessment Bonds |
	Net Interest Rate[1]	Unused Borrowing Capacity (in thousands)	Net Interest Rate[2]	Interest Rate to Property Owners[3]
Over 1,000,000				
Los Angeles	3.68%	$301,438	3.52%	6.0%
500,000 to 1,000,000				
San Francisco	3.13	121,009	...	..
250,000 to 500,000				
Long Beach	3.60	56,327	...	6.0
Oakland	...	67,470	3.30	..
San Diego	3.73	121,468	...	6.0
100,000 to 250,000				
Berkeley	...	....	4.47	..
Fresno	3.33	27,000	...	6.0
Pasadena	...	30,282	3.16	..
Sacramento	...	35,425	...	5.0
San Jose	3.63	22,000	...	5.0
50,000 to 100,000				
Compton	...	11,530	...	6.0
Glendale	...	27,531	3.06	..
Richmond	4.36	14,870	...	..
Riverside	3.54	13,000	...	..
San Bernardino	...	15,428	...	6.0
San Mateo	3.48	21,000	...	6.0
Santa Ana	3.84	8,654	...	6.0
25,000 to 50,000				
Beverly Hills	...	6,000	4.58	..
Fullerton	...	11,963	...	6.0
Lynwood	...	3,500	...	6.0
Manhattan Beach	...	4,092	...	6.0
Monterey Park	4.43	5,000	...	..
Ontario	3.63	5,757	...	..
Oxnard	...	....	...	..
Palo Alto	3.57	....	...	4.6
Pomona	3.46	10,364	3.58	6.0
Redwood City	3.27	15,332	...	6.0
Santa Barbara	2.87	5,000	...	..
Torrance	...	....	...	6.0
10,000 to 25,000				
Antioch	...	....	...	6.0
Burlingame	...	....	...	5.0
Chico	...	....	...	5.8
Colton	4.19	1,641	4.44	..
Concord	...	4,325	...	6.0
El Centro	4.19	3,965	...	..
El Segundo	...	11,817	...	6.0
Hanford	...	3,500	4.01	..
La Mesa	....	3,893	5.75	..
Madera	...	1,391	...	6.0
Menlo Park	2.89	....	...	6.0
Merced	3.52	5,252	...	4.0
Monterey	3.70	2,463	...	5.0
Mountain View	4.25	4,494	...	5.0
Newport Beach	3.97	7,940	...	..
Oceanside	4.25	2,592	...	6.0
Palm Springs	3.75	2,783	...	6.0
Redding	3.68	....	...	..
Redlands	...	4,470	...	6.0
San Bruno	4.20	825	...	6.0
San Carlos	...	4,425	...	4.9
San Gabriel	...	....	...	..
San Luis Obispo	...	3,204	...	5.4
Santa Clara	3.21	7,000	...	..
Santa Cruz	...	5,000	5.13	..
Santa Rosa	...	7,312	4.37	4.9
Sunnyvale	3.52	3,600	4.25	5.5
Tulare	3.50	....	...	..
Upland	4.07	1,800	...	..

1 The average net rate of interest paid by all cities over 10,000 throughout the country for their latest bond issue in 1957 was 3.35%. (This is a simple arithmetic average and is not weighted by the dollar amounts of the various issues.)

2 The average net rate of interest on revenue bonds for all American cities, computed as above, was 3.77%.

3 Special assessment bonds are secured only by license against the properties benefited rather than by the full faith and credit of the municipality. Throughout the United States, the effective interest rate on such bonds to the property owner (as distinguished from the cost of interest to the city government) ranged from a low of 2% to a high of 9%, the median city falling in the bracket, 5.0 to 5.9%.

4 The symbols ... indicate that no bonds were sold during the year, not that the city has no bonds outstanding at the present time.

for these two purposes combined, at a rate of 40 cents per $100 assessed
valuation for 25 years, which has been fixed by statute as the maximum
redemption period for school debts. Moreover, no district was obliged
to levy more than a 30 cent rate to repay its debt to the state. Whatever
might remain unpaid after these requirements had been satisfied would
be canceled.

Even this quarter-billion-dollar fund proved insufficient. Consequently, additional bond issues have since been proposed and approved:
$185 million in 1952, $100 million in 1954, $100 million in 1956, and
$220 million in November 1958. Will this be enough? The answer is
almost certainly no. While it would be rather easy from an economic
standpoint to remake the pattern of school districts so that each local
unit could finance its own needs for sites and buildings, it is difficult
to change long-established habits of thought overnight. Another obstacle
lies in the unintended (and to some extent unforeseeable) effects of the
assistance already given. The status quo is hardening, for the changing
of district boundaries has been "made increasingly difficult by the
pyramiding of district bond issues and state loans."[10]

To illustrate the unintended effects, both the law of 1949 and the
subsequent law of 1952 (under which the last four bond issues have been
authorized) specified that the local district's liability should not exceed
a 40 cent tax levy per $100 of assessed valuation. But because they are
in the form of two separate acts, the repayments required under each
law must be calculated separately. Thus, a district sufficiently impoverished to have been compelled to ask for school building aid under
both laws has a combined tax liability of 70 cents (30 plus 40) on its
construction. On the other hand, a district which has borrowed an
equal amount of money but under only one of the statutes can meet its
obligations without going above the 40 cent level.

As of 1955-56 the net result of the operation of these two laws
was that tax rates for local debt service and repayment of state loans
varied among 377 elementary districts as shown on page 246.[11]

With the prospect of continuing rapid growth, especially among
children of school age, it is evident that California is unlikely to find
an acceptable solution to the problem of school district indebtedness
within the scope of existing legislation. The Assembly Interim Committee on Education received from its Subcommittee on School District
Tax and Bonded Indebtedness in March 1957 a report urging five types
of remedial legislation:[*]

[*]These square substantially with the recommendations offered in
Chapter 9.

Cents	Districts	Per Cent
Less than 40	27	7.2
40 - 49	63	16.7
50 - 59	58	15.4
60 - 69	58	15.4
70 - 79	49	13.0
80 - 89	45	12.0
90 - 99	31	8.2
$1.00 - $1.09	20	5.3
$1.10 - $1.19	12	3.1
Over $1.20	14	3.7
TOTAL	377	100.0

(a) To broaden the tax base — principally by empowering school
    districts to impose property taxes upon publicly owned elec-
    tric or gas utilities within their boundaries.

(b) To reduce interest rates for district bonds — mainly by plac-
    ing the full faith and credit of the state behind all such issues.

(c) To eliminate the inequities caused by the cumulative opera-
    tion of the two school building aid laws of 1949 and 1952 —
    by limiting the liability of all districts to the 40 cent level.

(d) To reduce restriction on district building activities — by re-
    linquishing some measure of the control now exercised by
    the State Allocations Board under the applicable statutes.

(e) To eliminate substantially the inequity arising from dispari-
    ties between the school populations of local districts and their
    proportionate taxable wealth — chiefly by adoption of a con-
    stitutional amendment creating a State School Building Con-
    struction Fund which would thereafter serve as the "source
    of all funds needed . . . for school construction within the
    limits of the austerity program and for service and retirement
    of existing district construction bonds.

No action had been taken on these proposals at the time the present study was completed but they will all deserve careful consideration
from the 1959-60 Legislature. With a bit of imagination and vigorous
leadership, California could solve the problem of borrowing for local
school construction and the riddle of financing the current expense of
education without increasing reliance on state aid.[12]

Trend of Special District Indebtedness: 1940-1957

Anyone trying to analyze systematically the indebtedness of special districts in California (other than school districts) encounters peculiar hazards. The Assembly Interim Committee on Municipal and
County Government found in its final report of March 1957 entitled
Special Districts that there were by conservative estimates "between

5,000 and 6,000 districts of all types" in California today but that there is "no central agency to which all districts are required to report, even as to their existence." For this reason the figures given below must be used with caution.

The aggregate value of special district bonds outstanding in 1940 amounted to $61.2 million dollars. By 1945, at war's end, redemptions had reduced the total to $42.5 million, but by the end of the decade that total had climbed to $77.7 million. Reflecting much the same forces as those influencing other types of local government during the postwar period, special district bonded indebtedness has zoomed in the 1950's, reaching by June 30, 1957, a total of $588.9 million, of which $180 million had been issued by the Metropolitan Water District of Southern California. It is impossible to predict what further borrowing will be needed during the coming decade, but with no complete solutions yet in sight for the problems of water and air pollution — not to mention the baffling questions of metropolitan transit and urban redevelopment — the prospect is for substantial additional bonding.

Though the space that can be allotted to this subject here is sharply limited, the matter is one of tremendous significance, for it is hardly too much to say that California has allowed these special districts to get out of hand. Considering the amounts of indebtedness they have already incurred (in many instances without a popular referendum) and the fact that the higher these "pyramids" grow the harder it will be to consolidate them with general purpose units like a city or county (or for that matter with each other), it is essential that they be brought under closer and more continuous surveillance either by duly elected representatives of the general public or by the citizens of the community themselves.

SUBVENTIONS AND GRANTS

Equality is so integral to the democratic ideal that, with regard to a matter like state aid, the normal assumption is that those local units best able to support themselves should receive the least state aid. Each law providing subventions or grants to the cities, counties, school districts, or other special districts has a certain logic and each has been adopted in conformity with the constitutional processes of the nation and the state. Yet it is interesting to note that the net result of all of them taken together reveals a pattern difficult to justify.

On the assumption that those counties having the highest personal

income per capita should have the least need for state assistance and
hence the lowest total of subventions and grants per capita, all the
counties have been ranked in terms of these two measures and likewise
on the basis of total county bonded debt per capita and all local debt per
capita. (See Table 7.6.)

Comparison between the columns of Table 7.6 reveals a number
of rather striking anomalies. Colusa County has the highest income per
capita; yet, instead of being lowest — or even among the bottom ten
counties — in subventions and grants per capita, it ranked 48th, ten
from the top. The receipt of so much assistance from the state and
federal governments could perhaps be justified if the county had already
made full use of its own credit resources. But, instead of having a large
bonded debt per capita, Colusa ranked 48-49, meaning that only eight
counties had a smaller burden of indebtedness.

At the other extreme, Nevada County, with the lowest per capita
income, was far from enjoying the highest volume of subventions and
grants. Instead of ranking 57th in low-to-high order, it ranked 37th.
The vast difference in its ranking with regard to total bonded debt and
all local debt can be explained by the fact that the former measure pertains to county indebtedness as reported in tables 7.2 and 7.3, meaning
county bonded debt per se, plus school and special district debt as reported by the State Controller in his books on the financial transactions
of counties. All local debt includes, in addition, the bonds of cities and
such other special districts as are not included in the report on counties.

Los Angeles County, to take a third and final illustration, stands
second in per capita income and eighth from the bottom in subventions
and grants per capita. This accords fairly well with logical expectations
as does its position on the other two measures. It ranks sixteenth from
high to low in total bonded debt per capita and sixth when all local indebtedness is considered.

Though these comparisons might be further refined and qualified,
the examples cited, backed by the table as a whole, indicate that the
state must keep its various subventions and grants under continuous
review if it wants to make sure that local assistance is parcelled out in
relation to need.

THE PROSPECTIVE NEED FOR FUTURE BORROWING

Few states, if any, enjoy a more favorable position in America's
"affluent society" than California. Many of her cities, counties, school
districts, and other districts have been able to build their capital im-

Table 7.6. Range and Ranking of All Counties except San Francisco with Respect to (a) Subventions and Grants; (b) Personal Income; (c) Bonded Debt. All Per Capita (pc): 1956-57[1]

County	Subventions-Grants: 1956-57		Per. Inc.: 1956		S&G pc	PBD pc	ALD pc
	Total	pc	pc	Rank H-L*	Rank L-H	Rank H-L*	Rank H-L*
Alameda	$ 54,526,690	$ 62.39	$ 2556	4	9	28	20
Alpine	167,268	41.81	1888	44	1	57	57
Amador	1,055,895	117.32	1867	46	45	44	46
Butte	8,010,747	110.49	2086	25	40	39	38-39
Calaveras	1,156,791	123.06	1891	43	47	4	17-19
Colusa	1,495,172	125.64	3113	1	48	48	48-49
Contra Costa	26,426,767	74.08	1757	51	14	2	7
Del Norte	1,670,960	87.02	1978	36	25	31	42
El Dorado	2,223,841	110.63	1836	47	41	35	41
Fresno	29,861,222	88.66	1987	33	27	24	35
Glenn	1,593,490	92.64	2369	9	29	15	47
Humboldt	9,444,101	95.20	2261	15	31	37	38-39
Imperial	6,522,718	93.31	2171	22	30	40	1
Inyo	1,360,175	113.34	2360	10	44	3	17-19
Kern	23,194,697	84.83	2211	18	23	27	36
Kings	4,158,595	88.10	1745	53	26	41	48-49
Lake	1,745,930	154.50	1756	52	51	46	52
Lassen	2,153,374	146.48	2065	27	49	51	54-55
Los Angeles	346,818,193	61.95	2617	2	8	16	6
Madera	4,550,821	118.51	1933	38	46	50	5
Marin	6,607,153	51.29	2353	11	2	12	12
Mariposa	768,639	170.80	2376	17	54	49	50
Mendocino	4,684,741	84.40	1923	42	22	18	28
Merced	7,071,627	81.37	1928	39	21	42	26
Modoc	9,435,485	1036.86	2170	23	57	32	43-44
Mono	468,279	180.10	1804	49	55	53	56
Monterey	10,238,305	55.97	2172	21	5	13	27
Napa	6,525,708	107.50	1580	56	36	11	13
Nevada	1,969,509	108.21	1515	57	37	52	2
Orange	27,902,327	54.56	1764	50	4	5	14
Placer	4,229,102	85.26	1705	16	24	55	11
Plumas	1,882,305	160.88	2248	55	52	20	30
Riverside	18,953,474	78.54	1986	34	19	6	10
Sacramento	31,681,251	74.17	2372	8	15	23	17-19
San Benito	1,137,040	73.35	2159	24	13	56	53
San Bernardino	32,949,328	75.62	1926	41	17	14	23
San Diego	52,906,273	58.75	2187	20	7	34	22
San Joaquin	18,305,269	76.78	2081	26	18	22	4
San Luis Obispo	5,929,779	96.73	1983	35	32	19	33
San Mateo	19,836,486	52.46	2557	3	3	7	24
Santa Barbara	7,345,654	63.32	2198	19	10	30	32
Santa Clara	30,853,293	58.48	2032	31	6	10	16
Santa Cruz	6,531,160	92.37	1834	48	28	26	31
Shasta	5,141,528	104.92	2050	29	35	9	25
Sierra	647,928	269.97	2266	14	56	54	54-55
Siskiyou	4,704,324	149.81	2288	12	50	17	8
Solano	8,803,845	75.11	2286	13	16	25	21
Sonoma	11,161,184	79.27	1713	54	20	8	16
Stanislaus	14,329,137	96.88	1875	45	33	21	3
Sutter	3,144,253	104.80	2385	6	34	38	37
Tehama	2,427,429	110.33	1928	40	39	43	43-44
Trinity	1,272,241	161.04	2064	28	53	47	34
Tulare	16,557,533	111.64	2034	30	43	36	45
Tuolumne	1,674,572	110.89	2455	5	42	45	51
Ventura	10,531,253	64.53	2029	32	11	1	9
Yolo	4,091,908	72.55	1970	37	12	33	29
Yuba	2,937,442	108.79	2230	17	38	29	40

*Data for the first column, headed Subventions-Grants, represent the sum of the figures listed in the State Controller's report on Counties plus those in his report on School Districts. The second column is derived from the first by using as divisors the population estimates for July 1, 1957, issued by the State Department of Finance. Personal income per capita has been computed by taking the State Chamber of Commerce estimate of income for each county and dividing it by the Department of Finance estimate of population for that same year. The ranking of the counties is from high to low. With regard to S-G per capita, the ranking is from low to high. In the case of total bonded debt per capita, the ranking is again from high to low, the basic data being taken from Table 7.3. Thanks are due for the information supporting the column headed "all local debt per capita" to John B. Marshall of the staff of the State Board of Equalization. Again the ranking is from high to low. The omission of San Francisco from the table is due to the fact that, by virtue of its being a consolidated city-county, it is somewhat difficult to secure comparable figures with regard to it.

provements on a pay-as-you-go basis or very nearly so. Except for
those compelled to deal with problems of explosive growth, many others
could have done the same had they disciplined themselves by long-range
planning and capital budgeting. These two devices plus that of the Cumulative Capital Outlay Fund already described can, if used properly, reduce the need to borrow to a minimum.

Yet to say this is not to suggest, much less insist, that local
governmental units in this state can escape the necessity of increasing
their bonded indebtedness. In many places the growth of population continues at a pace so rapid that, at least for school districts and cities,
there is no possibility of making the capital outlays essential to the
performance of their functions without further resort to borrowing.
Because of their relatively smaller need for capital structures the
counties and special districts appear, on the whole, to be in a somewhat easier situation. Yet they, too, are sometimes compelled to cope
with sudden demands for greatly expanded services and, where these
require substantial capital improvements, they may well have no option but to go to the bond market for funds.

By and large most of the bonded indebtedness existing at the present time has been incurred to finance the more basic type of capital improvements — school buildings, water systems, sewer lines, sewage
treatment plants, streets, roads, and bridges. Some of the works of
this type enacted since 1945 represent the backlog of permanent improvements not built during the war; others reflect the effort, on the
whole remarkably successful, to keep pace with the growth of population since then.

Even if the most crucial needs had now been met everywhere,
hundreds of communities have second-order requirements that will
call for extensive bonding. Large-scale funds are needed for such purposes as these: land for park and recreation sites, secondary roads,
modernized civic centers, swimming pools, conservation and flood
control, libraries, hospitals, and jails. Slum clearance, urban rede-
velopment and public housing will in some cases make additional drafts
on the public credit.

It is being said as this study nears completion that the 1958 election gave unmistakable evidence that the people of California and all of
the nation want more active concern for their needs on the part of all
their governments. If so, this will be in keeping with the quiet "revolu-
tion of rising expectations," which in many ways has been the most remarkable development of the 20th century in this country as well as

abroad. Fortunately, the local governments of California have arrived
at this stage of their history with credit ratings still generally high. It
behooves them, however, to use their credit more wisely than ever in
the years to come, otherwise, they will find themselves inexcusably
dependent on the state or even on the federal government.

NOTES TO CHAPTER 7

[1] State Controller Alan Cranston, News Release, July 16, 1959;
also Interview, August 1958, with Frank Stockbridge, Vice-President
of Municipal Securities, Security First National Bank of Los Angeles
and September 1958, with Alan Bartlett, Director of Research, Bank
of America, San Francisco.

[2] International City Managers' Association, Municipal Finance
Administration, 5th ed., Chicago, 1955, p. 321.

[3] California Taxpayers Association, Comparative Analysis of
Selected California Special District Statutes (1950), p.v. Quoted in
Eugene C. Lee and Stanley Scott, Financing Local Public Works,
University of California, Bureau of Public Administration (1951), p.15.

[4] National Municipal League, Model County and Municipal Bond
Law, New York, 1953, pp. xiii-xvi and Article IV.

[5] See for example the Government Code, Sections 29908 and
43614.

[6] In Los Angeles County, for example, the Subcommittee found
that of approximately $96 million in long-term special district debt,
"$47 million has been incurred without a vote." See California Public
Survey, April 1958, pp. 70-71.

[7] National Municipal League, Model County, pp. viii-ix.

[8] Source of Table 7.5: International City Managers' Association,
Municipal Yearbook (Chicago, 1958), pp. 185-95.

[9] Senate Interim Committee on State and Local Taxation, Local
Government Finance in California: 1940-53 (Sacramento,1955), p. 129,
and State Controller's report of Financial Transactions concerning
School Districts, June 30, 1957.

[10] Much of this section is based on the Report of the Subcommittee
on School District Tax and Bonded Indebtedness (of the Assembly Interim Committee on Education) March 1957. This quotation may be
found on page 7.

[11] Ibid., p. 29.

[12] Readers especially interested in the problem of local indebtedness will find Municipal Finance for August 1957 of great value. The
official magazine of the Municipal Finance Officers Association of the
U.S. and Canada, this number is devoted almost entirely to the subject
of "Municipal Debt Administration in a Period of Rising Interest Rates."

PART V

FINANCIAL SUPPORT FOR PUBLIC EDUCATION

HUBERT C. ARMSTRONG AND FRANK FARNER

Assisted by James Thomas Doyle, Jr.

A general diffusion of knowledge and intelligence being
essential to the preservation of the rights and liberties of the
people, the Legislature shall encourage by all suitable means
the promotion of intellectual, scientific, moral, and agricultural
improvement. — Constitution of the State of California, Article IX,
Section 1

The public schools have been under stress for a long time. The
collapse in 1929, the depression of the thirties, World War II in the
early forties, and the present tidal wave of children have marked a
succession of critical periods during which normalcy has been an
imaginary state of affairs. During the depression, we were like Mother
Hubbard; today, we resemble the Old Woman Who Lived in a Shoe —
and some think we resemble both. But to be under stress is not necessarily to experience a crisis.

CRISIS-PRODUCING FACTORS

Some school districts are facing severe problems while others
are healthy, wealthy, and very well satisfied with things as they are.
Great as some of the problems are in certain districts, we need to
recognize the fact that we are the wealthiest nation, that we are one of
the wealthier states, and that our real income per capita after taxes
has been increasing ever since the end of the depression. What then
can bring about a crisis?

Abnormal Growth

When population growth in a school district exceeds the rate of
5% per year, serious strain is placed upon its economy.[*] Financing
the increased capital outlay for construction, for example, must be
done out of cash reserves or through loans (bonds), the retirement of
which can come only from income. In the period from 1900 to 1940,
California's total population (see Table 8.3) increased at the rate of
3.96% per year; and between 1940 and 1958, the mean annual rate of
increase was 4.17%. During these same two periods school enrollments
increased 3.77 and 5.40% per year, respectively. (See Table 8.4.)
Note that the rate for school enrollment was below that for total population prior to 1940 but has been considerably higher since. Moreover,
when we examine the war and postwar periods in detail, we find that

[*]Note that small differences in rates of growth produce great
differences in effect. If, for example, California's population had
grown at the rate of 5% per year since 1900, our population today
would be approaching 25 million.

the increase in school enrollment was at a low rate of 3.72% per year
from 1940 to 1947, while from 1947 to 1957 it increased to an amazing
6.87% per year. The annual rate of increase predicted by the State
Department of Finance for the period 1958 to 1970 is 4.54%. While this
rate is significantly lower than what we have just experienced, its effect will be quite startling, for it will mean an increase of about 2.5
million students in the public schools, or almost double the present
enrollment.

Rates of increase in some suburban areas are fantastic. The enrollment in the Covina Elementary School District in Los Angeles
County, for example, increased 63% in one year (from 1,665 in 1951-
52 to 2,712 the following year). Furthermore, the average annual rate
of increase for this district between 1949-50 and 1957-58 was 34.7%.
Had the population of California grown at the same rate in the same
eight years, it would now (1958) be over 113 million.

Dependents and Income

A second factor that can precipitate a crisis is an increase in the
relative proportion of the economically dependent as compared with the
wage-earning or productive portion of the population. A convenient
measure of this factor is the percentage of the dependent population as
compared with the 18-64 age group (see Table 8.3). Within the last
eighteen years (1940-58), the percentage of wage earners has declined
from 67.6 to 57.5%. During this same period, the percentage of children (from birth to 18) has increased from 24.4 to 34.3%.

Thus, today, fewer income producers must support more dependents. There were .48 dependents per person in the 18-64 age group in
1940 while in 1958 there are .76 such dependents. But a more remarkable fact is that, in the period from 1939-40 to 1956-57, personal income in constant dollars per capita rose about 50%, and for wage-earn-
ers something over 75%. These simple figures offer rather dramatic
testimony to the fact that our economy is increasingly productive. The
amount of personal income in dollars of constant value per total dependent, however, tells a different story. The income per dependent person
was $4,163 in 1939-40. By 1950-51 it had climbed 19% to $4,968. Since
then, it has remained practically constant as the figures in Table 8.1
indicate.

As the length of the school period increases and as mean life expectancy lengthens, a greater load is placed on the income producers.

And as living costs increase, there is a greater tendency for women to become employed to aid in family support. In an agrarian society this does not take the mother away from the home, whereas in an industrial society such as ours, it does. This, in turn, has important implications for the stability of the family, and indirectly for society. It tends, for example, to throw more responsibility on the public schools.

Table 8.1. Personal Income Per Total Dependent (Birth - 17 plus Age 65 and Over) in Constant Dollars: 1950-51 to 1955-56

Year	Income
1950-51	$4,968
51-52	4,964
52-53	4,924
53-54	4,805
54-55	4,802
1955-56	4,946

Source: See Table 8.31

Champagne Appetites and Limited Income

A third factor lies in the amount of uncommitted income of the tax-paying public. Obviously, this depends not upon the level of income, but rather upon the amounts of income beyond prior commitments. One would expect communities of young parents, whose children are in school, to willingly vote for new facilities, but the amount of their income not already committed to a new house, car, refrigerator, television, or high-fidelity sound system may be so small that any increase in taxes may tip the scales and produce a family crisis. Yet any one of the decisions would have produced the crisis if it were the last one made. Hence, the relationship between the American family's psychological appetite for goods and its ability to balance wants with income is another potential stress factor. It would appear, moreover, that demands for more and better goods and services are almost unlimited and insatiable, and that this is true both in the private and public sectors of the economy. In the private economy, however, the market is selectively competitive in the direction of a one-to-one correspondence between price and product, while in the public economy one dollar in taxes may return to the individual taxpayer either more or less than a dollar's worth of services. Hence, there is less free choice to the individual in the realm of public price and public product and less knowledge of the relation between costs and benefits.

Private Benefits and the Public Dollar

How, then, does the rational citizen judge the desirability of the services he is asked to finance? He may pose several questions: (1) Are tax funds being used in the public interest and thus to some extent in his own? (2) Is every service essential to the public interest? (3) Is every dollar being used efficiently and effectively for the purposes intended? In this regard, we appear to hold a higher ethical standard for government than for private economy, for we impose severe penalties for the misuse of public funds, whereas the use of private funds is subject only to personal evaluation and economic survival. (4) To what degree do benefits justify cost? (5) Do the public services satisfy the citizen-consumer?

Any citizen is virtually certain to be influenced by his personal experience. His degree of satisfaction with a service may become a criterion of money well spent even though the cost of the service is unknown. Thus, the goodness of a school system is likely to be measured by the attitudes and learning of one's children, by impressions gained from casual observation or common talk, and by private reactions to teachers in the local schools. And the degree of satisfaction may be quite unrelated to the amount of taxes an individual pays. For example, a family with three children will in 20 years receive public school benefits amounting to a total of about $15,000. But if the school is unsatisfactory, the fact that the family may pay only a fraction of this amount in taxes will hardly deter complaints.

The dilemma arising from an insatiable desire for governmental services and the lack of correlation between services received and taxes paid may be resolved, at least in part, by considering the public interest rather than the private gain, by judging costs in terms of the value of the benefits received, by assessing the quality of service in terms of consumer satisfaction, and by weighing new services against possible alternative uses of the citizen's dollar. Finally, the efficiency with which the tax dollar is administered is relevant to both the public and the private sectors of the economy, for a dollar wasted is a dollar lost in either case.

Defects in the Fiscal System

Fifth, any system of governmental finance may be generally good yet so defective in certain respects that public funds are wasted or so inadequate in others that the funds are inefficiently used. California's fiscal system for schools must serve districts that have a range of wealth per pupil of 7,000 to 1 and a size-range of from 5 to nearly 500,000 pupils. It must, therefore, be judged by its particular applications as well as by its main characteristics and intent. In this sense the exceptional case will prove the adaptability of the system.

Summary. The several factors that can produce a fiscal crisis for public education have been examined with a view to clarifying some of the problems now facing a number of the school districts and to make clearer the meaning of some of the statistical data to be presented later on. A crisis may develop when rapid increases occur either in general growth or in the ratio of dependents to producers, when either uncommitted income or reserves are low, when the public interest goes unsupported, when school policies, however good, are badly administered, or when the system of collecting and disbursing public funds places inequitable burdens on certain localities. If California's economy is sound but certain local units of government are nevertheless in a critical condition financially, it would appear that something is wrong.

EDUCATIONAL FINANCE — A GENERAL VIEW

The public school system of California is of impressive magnitude. About two and three-quarter million children, young people, and adults are now attending the public schools. The teaching staff numbers upwards of 100,000. It is a matter of common knowledge that the growing population, the shrinking dollar, the teacher shortage, and the need for more classrooms have presented problems hitherto unknown in California. It is not the purpose of this study merely to dissect the past, but rather to analyze the current financial problems on the basis of recent experience with two purposes in mind: first, to anticipate the nature of the fiscal problems of the near future and, second, to raise certain major policy issues bearing upon those fiscal problems with a view to increasing the efficiency of the fiscal system.

The current operating expenses of the public schools were roughly $950 million in 1956-57 (see Table 8.31). This was an increase of over 900% since 1929-30, and about 650% since 1939-40. These figures included the cost of elementary schools, junior high schools, senior high, and junior colleges. In general, the cost per student increases by grade level, in the order indicated above, but differences among districts also vary greatly.

Under present statutes the State School Fund is apportioned to districts and to offices of county superintendents of schools in the ap-

proximate percentages shown below. However, many special provisions
and exceptions, some of them highly complex, have been omitted.

Apportionment of State School Fund: 1956-57
($533,770,662.00 — 100%)

To County Superintendents
2.75%

To Local School Districts
97.25%

For:

Fiscal Services
Supervision
Special Services
Special Schools

Main Apportionment
92.05%

Basic Aid
$125 per ADA
64.3%

Equalization Aid
(According to need)
21.3%

Aid for Rapid
Growth
6.45%

Special Purposes
5.2%

Handicapped
Children
2.65%

Transportation
2.06%

Driver training
0.34%

All Others
0.15%

The principal apportionment (about 85%) of the State School Fund
is made by two separate formulas. The first is based on average daily
attendance[*] of the district and does not depend upon its need for state
aid. This amount, Basic Aid, is equal to $125 multiplied by the ADA of
the district. But no district may receive less than $2,400. The second
method is based primarily on the assessed valuation of the district,
which is taken as a measure of need for state aid. Funds apportioned
by this method are known as Equalization Aid. The calculation of
Equalization Aid requires that as a criterion, a minimum level of support be established. The Foundation Program serves as this criterion.

The Foundation Program is an amount per ADA or, in small
schools, an amount per teacher employed. It differs according to the
size, level, and wealth of a district. Separate Foundation Programs
are established for grades K[**] to 8 and 9 to 12, for junior colleges,
and for small, medium, and large elementary and high school districts.
In addition, poorer districts have different levels of minimal support
from those of moderate wealth. All told, there are eleven Foundation
Programs.

The Foundation Program is jointly supported by state and district
funds. Each district is charged with providing an amount of self-support
known as District Aid, which is calculated by the State Department of
Education by multiplying its assessed valuation by a stipulated compu-

[*]Hereafter the abbreviation ADA will be used for "average daily
attendance."

[**]K stands for kindergarten.

tational tax rate. This rate also differs according to the size, level, and wealth of the district.

If the sum of District Aid as calculated above plus the amount of Basic Aid ($125 per ADA) is less than the amount of the Foundation Program, the difference is made up in the form of Equalization Aid. Thus Equalization Aid is apportioned inversely to wealth. Basic Aid, on the other hand, is apportioned irrespective of wealth.

Table 8.2 illustrates the method of apportionment as it would apply to three elementary districts of varying wealth. Note that while the poorer district receives more than the other districts in absolute terms, it receives relatively less when the tax rate and the Basic Aid amounts are considered. The "overpayment" of $13,000 in Basic Aid to the wealthier district C indicates how the flat-grant may make the total amount of their school funds relatively greater than the amounts available in poorer districts of equal size.

Table 8.2. Example of Apportionments to Three Hypothetical Elementary Districts

	District A	District B	District C
ADA	1,000	1,000	1,000
Assessed Valuation	$6 million	$12 million	$18 million
Foundation Program per ADA	$295	$220	$220
FP x ADA	$295,000	$220,000	$220,000
Basic Aid	$125,000	$125,000	$125,000[*]
Computational Tax Rate for District Aid	$1.35	$.60	$.60
(AV x Tax Rate) District Aid	$ 81,000	$ 72,000	$108,000
Sum of Basic & District Aid	$206,000	$197,000	$233,000[*]
Equalization Aid (FP less above sum)	$ 89,000	$ 23,000	$ none[*]

[*] Basic Aid plus District Aid exceeds the Foundation Program by $13,000.

EFFECTS OF CHANGES IN AMERICAN LIFE

The enormous expansion of California's school population cannot be accounted for by increase in birth rates and migration alone. The normal period of school attendance has increased from grammar school graduation a half-century ago to high school graduation today, and larger numbers of students look forward to going to junior college. In 1900 about 3% of the population graduated from high school. Today about 75% (and much more in many areas) finish the 12th grade — an increase of 25 times. Thus, not only do more people attend school but they start earlier and stay longer.

The ideal of universal rather than compulsory education seems to be a major factor in increasing the span of schooling, for neither the enrollment in the kindergarten and grades one and two (the basic compulsory school age span is 8-16) nor the rapid rise in junior college attendance can be explained by compulsory attendance laws. The marked increase in the percentage of the population attending school and the lengthening of the age span of the population has brought forth two problems hitherto unknown.

The first is a sharp rise in the need for teachers. We now employ as teachers about one person in 80 of the adult population aged 18-64. The higher this percentage becomes, the less selective becomes the process of choosing them and the lower the average level of talent one may expect. This factor is accentuated when the economic rewards of teaching fall relatively below those of competing occupations. On the other hand, California's relatively high salaries, compared to other states, may well attract better teachers from elsewhere.

The second problem arises from the fact that today virtually the entire range of human talent is to be found in the public schools. This was formerly true only of the pre-teen population. The middle 94% of the 15-year-old population varies about nine years in mental ability and the average ability of high school students now approaches that of the total population, whereas under conditions 50 years ago, only the most apt attended. The above fact has resulted in a need for the schools to provide for a very wide range in natural talent. They have, in turn, been criticized for pacing instruction to the central tendency of the population because, with the current emphasis on science, there is now strong insistence on instruction adapted to the more talented. However, there are relatively few of the more able. Only ten per cent of the population have IQ's above 120 and only 3% above 130.[*] One implication for fiscal policy is apparent. Small classes for the more able are inevitable if they are to be taught separately. The schools once limited instruction to the more formal subjects, such as mathematics, history,

[*]Derived from norms as given in Terman and Merrill, Measuring Intelligence, 1937.

grammar, and Latin. Today the comprehensive high school offers not only the college preparatory studies but also commercial subjects, music and art, and a variety of shop work, home-making, and physical education. The high schools are struggling with problems that arise in part from the needs of a complex society and in part from a student body which ranges from brilliant students to those whose ability is low and for whom success is measured more by social than academic achievement.

The desire of many administrators for large high schools obviously stems from an attempt to compromise between a wide diversity of offerings and classes of sufficient size to avoid prohibitively high costs.* As our economy becomes more and more technological, there is apt to be more, rather than less, demand for longer and more specialized training, especially in the upper high school and junior college grades. Our point of emphasis here is that a spiral of cause and effect relationships exists between an education that fosters science and a technological society that demands more training. And the corollary is that although power, machines, and trained men increase production, they also require that more income be plowed back into the production of scientific and technical know-how, or, in other words, into education. Thus, in a very practical sense, education is a capital investment. At $400 per year, 13 years of schooling cost about $5,200. The economic yield on this investment is probably higher than for any other use of capital if the increased earning power of the student is considered to be the yield of the capital so invested.

But there is another side to the problem of universal education. Given the enormous variety of occupational pursuits, does it not, by its very nature, demand that schools teach appropriately for the whole range of human ability? Probably no one would think of defending the proposition that every child should take Latin, or, on the other hand, that training for each of the 30,000-odd occupations is the school's business. Instruction in the modern school can be better understood, perhaps, as a search for a middle ground between extreme uniformity (an impossible goal with the existing ranges of human ability) and extreme diversity (which could be neither staffed nor financed).

The compromise is in the direction of teaching what is general,

*School costs increase geometrically as class size becomes smaller while only arithmetically as salary increases. This is the principal reason for high costs in very small schools.

what can be transferred from classrooms to life situations, also of
teaching what must specifically be taught, e.g., typing. We take it for
granted that mathematics is a general discipline, but at the same time
we find we must teach bookkeeping separately, for the correct balancing
of checkbooks is not assured by an "A" in algebra. The fact is that
neither psychologists nor teachers understand how learning is transferred from one situation to another well enough to organize teaching
and learning in the most effective way. The pragmatic theorists support
the view that one learns best by learning the means of solving a problem. But even the most avid formalist would hardly choose a physician
who had learned surgery only out of a book. The point of these comments
is that, as exemplified in driver training, the responsibility for teaching more and more subjects, skills, and applied learning has been left
at the school's doorstep. As our social and economic life has become
more complicated, more specialized, and at the same time "easier" as
the result of more labor-saving and learning-eliminating devices, the
school as an institution has had to absorb scores of functions once
handled elsewhere.

This development, while perhaps inevitable, has increased costs.
But some agreement on the proper functions of the schools and on pri-
orities among these functions is necessary before costs can be said to
be too high, too low, or just right. Publicly agreed-upon educational
policy, wisely conceived, should be the foundation of fiscal policy.
Since we cannot determine the "ought" from the "is," nor from someone else's average, we have the choice of backing into the future by
keeping our eyes on the past and following tradition or of considering
openly the elemental present-day problems that confront education and
society.

At the risk of being trite, another factor in public policy is indicated. In the current struggle between the Communist powers and the
free nations, much has been said about the schools and supremacy in
science. We accept the belief that an uneducated people cannot remain
free and the faith than an educated people can be free if they want to be.
If American democracy means political self-determination, then the
public must be interested in a kind of general education that will enable
people to seek out information and to consider human values in making
decisions. And it is not irrelevant to recall the fine discernment of
Socrates when he observed, "A slave is he who gets his purposes from
someone else."

We have not made the above observations concerning educational policy and some of the factors that determine it because we believe education is either sacrosanct or the legitimate prey of unthinking aggression, but because we believe education is an outgrowth of certain values in American life and that the forces that have shaped education are the same as those found in American culture. In that sense, education is extremely difficult to change by decision. But, paradoxically, it will change as a result of the very processes it engenders in those who become educated. The psychological basis for educational policy rests on the belief of the American people that progress is possible; that vertical mobility is everyman's right; that schooling means more and better opportunities; that parents can provide their children more than they had themselves; that material success is desirable; that science and technology can bring an easier life; that human beings, as such, really matter; that responsible persons are essential to self-government; and that ambition, brains, character, and success are major virtues.

These beliefs lie behind the support of our public school system and indicate what Americans expect of their schools. The school dollar is spent to achieve these ideals and hopes and to assure a vigorous, healthy, productive society. For what other service than public education would California spend a thousand million dollars a year?

POPULATION EXPANSION AND RESULTANT FISCAL PROBLEMS

In the preceding discussion we have dealt with the broad and basic problems that have contributed to the present "crisis" in public school finance in California. The remaining pages of this chapter present statistical analyses of the major contributing factors. The tables and charts are relied upon for much of the meaning, while the text serves to point up the more significant facts.

Population Growth

That the growth of California's population has, during the postwar period, exceeded the critical 5% per year rate cited above tells only a part of the story. The age composition of this growing population and its distribution over the countryside create problems of far greater magnitude than the total growth alone discloses. Table 8.3 presents population data for 1900 through 1970 in terms of totals and for the numbers of persons in each major age group.

Age Composition of the Population. The sheer magnitude of the increase in California's total population from 1.5 million in 1900 to

Table 8.3. Actual and Estimated Civilian Population of California, 1900–70, by Selected Age Groups (thousands)

Year	Total	Under 5 Years Amount	%	5-17 Years Amount	%	18-64 Years Amount	%	65 Years and Over Amount	%
1900 to 1920 see below									
1930	5,677	405	7.1	1,139	20.0	3,766	66.3	366	6.4
1940	6,907	453	6.6	1,228	17.8	4,671	67.6	555	8.0
1950	10,413	1,100	10.6	1,855	17.8	6,653	63.0	895	8.6
51	10,681	1,186	11.1	1,986	18.6	6,574	61.5	937	8.8
52	11,299	1,236	10.9	2,214	19.6	6,868	60.8	931	8.7
53	11,748	1,285	10.9	2,390	20.3	7,059	60.1	1,015	8.6
54	12,254	1,352	11.0	2,569	20.1	7,293	59.5	1,041	8.5
55	12,699	1,406	11.2	2,733	21.5	7,484	58.9	1,079	8.5
56	13,260	1,483	11.2	2,909	21.9	7,753	58.5	1,113	8.4
57	13,830	1,564	11.3	3,102	22.4	8,013	57.9	1,150	8.3
Projected									
58	14,400	1,630	11.3	3,305	23.0	8,281	57.5	1,184	8.2
59	14,955	1,694	11.3	3,508	23.4	8,548	57.1	1,217	8.1
1960	15,530	1,766	11.4	3,694	23.8	8,721	56.8	1,250	8.0
61	16,096	1,825	11.3	3,869	24.0	9,116	56.6	1,285	8.0
62	16,669	1,872	11.2	4,064	24.4	9,417	56.5	1,315	7.9
63	17,252	1,927	11.2	4,260	24.7	9,715	56.3	1,351	7.8
64	17,847	1,981	11.1	4,463	25.0	10,033	56.2	1,370	7.7
65	18,454	2,040	11.1	4,606	25.0	10,385	56.3	1,420	7.7
66	19,074	2,106	11.0	4,757	24.9	10,743	56.3	1,465	7.7
67	19,716	2,180	11.1	4,920	25.0	11,117	56.4	1,497	7.6
68	20,383	2,261	11.1	5,087	25.0	11,503	56.4	1,529	7.5
69	21,074	2,345	11.1	5,267	25.0	11,901	56.5	1,561	7.4
1970	21,790	2,434	11.2	5,441	25.0	12,308	56.5	1,604	7.4

Notes: Totals for earlier census years: 1900=1,460; 1910=2,344; 1920=3,421

Source: 1900-1940—Reference 28; 1950-1970—References 14, 15 and 16.

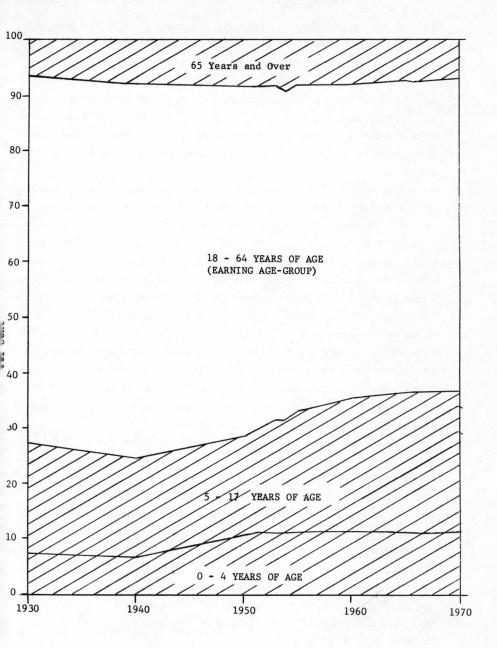

Figure 8.1. Percentage of Total Civilian Population in Selected Age
Groups, 1930-70

Source: Conforms to Table 8.3

14.5 million in 1958 and an estimated 22 million by 1970 has previously
been cited. The changing age composition is perhaps more significant,
however. Had this great population growth occurred mainly among
people in the income-producing ages, no crisis in school finance would
have been created since the ratio of those to be educated to those who
must pay for it would have become more advantageous. Such was the
nature of the first great growth period of California history when few
women and even fewer children accompanied the gold seekers over 100
years ago.

The pendulum is at the other end of the arc during the present
period. Combinations of high birth rates, high in-migration, and increased life expectancy have created a population in which only 57 of
every 100 persons are in the earning age group (18-64). The remaining
43 are largely dependents: 23 are of public school age, 11 plus are of
pre-school age and 8 plus are over 64 years of age. One should add to
these figures the previously cited fact that increasing proportions of the
school-age group (5-17) are actually in school and that the upper limit
of the school-age group is being shifted upward to 19 or 20 by the increased importance of junior college education. Consider also that the
retirement age may be declining from the age 65 used here. These
trends indicate clearly that the significance of the age distribution of
the population, so dramatically apparent in Figure 8.1, is, in reality,
understated as a factor inducing a fiscal crisis.

The School-Age Population. The age composition of the population
within the 5-17 school-age group contributes another highly significant
factor to the crisis climate. During the past decade, school budgets
have enjoyed relative freedom from overpowering growth in the high
schools while they concentrated upon measures to finance rapidly growing elementary education. In the years immediately ahead, high school
growth will be at a rate previously unknown and no significant counterbalancing decrease in the rate of elementary school growth can be anticipated. Costs are higher per child in high schools. An analysis of
how much more and the surprisingly potent impact of this factor on the
total cost of education is presented in later pages.

Enrollment Growth

To this point we have discussed growth in terms of population in
selected age groups. Several measures of actual population in the
public schools are here introduced to describe more accurately the
real increase in school attendance.

Table 8.4. Enrollment in California Public Schools; 1870–1970 (Excluding adults)

Year	Elementary K-8	High 9-12	Total K-12	J. C. 13-14	Total K-14
State Enrollment:					
1870-71			91,332		
1879-80			158,765		
1889-90	Not		221,756	Not	
1899-00	Distributed		269,736	Available	
1909-10			368,391		
1919-20			696,238		
1929-30			1,068,683		
1930-31	847,987	246,635	1,094,622	17,066	1,111,688
1936-37	839,699	313,296	1,152,995	30,255	1,183,250
1939-40	827,560	357,100	1,184,660	43,031	1,227,691
1946-47	1,103,125	364,057	1,467,182	79,429	1,546,611
October Enrollment:					
47	1,091,167	361,957	1,453,124	NA	NA
48	1,168,635	365,269	1,533,904	68,944	1,602,848
49	1,242,194	374,759	1,616,953	78,994	1,695,947
1950	1,306,109	383,316	1,689,425	78,194	1,767,619
51	1,434,736	402,018	1,836,744	80,945	1,917,689
52	1,535,678	429,437	1,965,115	91,541	2,056,656
53	1,668,211	463,048	2,131,259	72,633	2,203,892
54	1,787,679	495,033	2,282,712	86,452	2,369,164
55	1,916,668	531,362	2,448,030	99,410	2,547,440
56	2,046,795	585,744	2,634,539	114,923	2,749,462
57	2,175,568	649,181	2,824,749	132,697	2,957,446
		Projected			
58	2,313,700	706,100	3,019,800		
59	2,460,600	747,800	3,208,400		
1960	2,577,000	805,700	3,382,800		
61	2,700,200	865,600	3,565,800		
62	2,818,400	939,700	3,758,100	Not	
63	2,938,600	1,017,000	3,955,600	Projected	
64	3,064,800	1,064,100	4,128,800		
65	3,186,200	1,112,600	4,298,800		
66	3,295,400	1,165,400	4,460,800		
67	3,402,400	1,223,900	4,626,200		
68	3,513,800	1,283,200	4,797,100		
69	3,633,200	1,332,000	4,965,100		
1970	3,742,900	1,381,800	5,124,700		

Notes: Continuous enrollment series for California Public Schools are subject to inconsistencies arising from varying definitions of terms and methods of counting. A
major change occurred in 1947. Data in the table for years prior to 1947 are
termed "State Enrollment" and represent the total cumulative number of pupils enrolled in schools of the state during the school year. Analysis of the data in
comparison with ADA indicates that state enrollments exceed October enrollments
by about 8%. Prior to 1947 enrollment in special classes was not separated from
adult enrollments. The table includes this special class enrollment after 1947
but excludes them prior to that year. This underestimate is approximately 2%.
The net effect of these two major changes is that data prior to 1947 is about 6%
inflated (8%-2%). The table is presented without adjustment so that data will
conform to published material. The continued rapid growth of enrollments in the
decade after 1947 has rendered these differences of little importance.

Source: 1870-71 to 1929-30, Reference 30. 1930-31 to October 1957, Reference 9. 1958-
1970, Reference 16.

Table 8.5. Graded Enrollment in California Public Schools: By Grades, K-12
October 1947 through October 1957, (thousands of pupils)

Grade	1947	1948	1949	1950	1951	Year 1952	1953	1954	1955	1956	1957
K	110	122	132	137	185	178	213	225	233	251	270
1	162	181	186	185	188	224	222	243	254	261	275
2	137	146	165	171	176	179	215	218	240	252	257
3	131	135	143	162	172	177	181	214	223	244	255
4	119	128	132	141	163	174	179	181	216	228	247
5	112	119	127	131	143	166	177	180	183	219	232
6	104	111	118	127	134	146	168	178	183	187	222
7	104	108	114	121	131	138	151	173	185	190	193
8	100	103	108	114	123	134	141	152	176	189	193
9	99	102	105	109	118	127	137	144	157	182	195
10	95	96	101	102	107	116	126	135	143	156	182
11	84	83	87	88	91	96	104	113	122	129	144
·12	72	72	73	73	75	78	83	91	98	106	114

Notes: Columns would not add precisely to data in Table 8.6 because
"graded" enrollment excludes enrollment in special classes which
is included in Table 8.6. The stepped line indicates the progress of a major increase in enrollment.

Source: Reference 20.

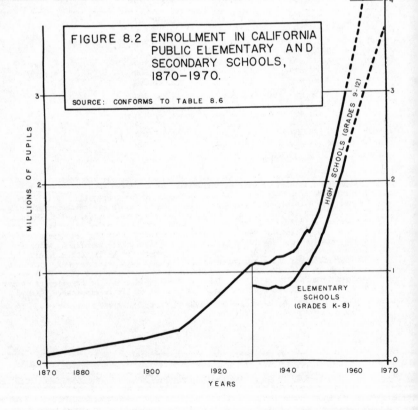

FIGURE 8.2 ENROLLMENT IN CALIFORNIA PUBLIC ELEMENTARY AND SECONDARY SCHOOLS, 1870-1970.

SOURCE: CONFORMS TO TABLE 8.6

MILLIONS OF PUPILS

HIGH SCHOOLS (GRADES 9-12)

ELEMENTARY SCHOOLS (GRADES K-8)

YEARS

The magnitude of the total increase in school enrollment is shown
in Table 8.5 and portrayed graphically in Figure 8.2. The relationship
of enrollment to school-age population is presented in Table 8.7. In
October 1957, school enrollments in grades K-12, both public and parochial, were over 98% of the school-age population interpolated from
July to October of that year. Making allowance for minor errors, the
data show clearly that in today's society virtually everyone of school
age is in school.

Graded Enrollment. Enrollment increases by grade may be
traced by an analysis of Table 8.5 which gives the October enrollment
in each grade, K-12, for the eleven-year period 1947-57. In 1951, a
particularly large class began kindergarten with over 35% more pupils
than had started kindergarten the previous year. The progress of this
wave, which entered grade 7 in the fall of 1958, is shown by the stepped
line.

Parochial School Enrollment. Parochial school enrollment alters
what may be the only counterbalance to the series of crisis-producing
trends outlined above. Table 8.6 presents reported and estimated enrollments in parochial schools from 1950 to 1970. There is a clear
trend that parochial school enrollment is increasing as a percentage of
total enrollment. This changing relationship is presented in Table 8.7.
Parochial schools were educating about 9% of all school children in 1950.
Estimates of the State Department of Finance indicate that they will be
educating about 11% of total enrollment by 1970. In dealing with such a
large total enrollment throughout the state, 2% changes are worthy of
serious note. Further analysis of Tables 8.6 and 8.7 indicates that the
emphasis in the parochial schools is upon the elementary level; in 1957,
parochial school enrollment in the elementary grades was 10.2% of the
total, while in the high school grades it was only 7.7%. It is important
to note that the term "parochial" includes only enrollment in schools
operated by the Roman Catholic Church. Enrollment data for other
denominational schools and for all nonsectarian schools were unavail-
able and therefore not included. The underestimate due to these exclusions is about 8% according to a recent study by the U.S. Department of Health, Education and Welfare.[*]

Differences Among the Counties. On state totals the figures con-
ceal several extremes. In San Francisco County parochial school enrollment comprises over 26% of total enrollment; in many other well-

[*] Reference 3.

populated counties it is less than 4%. In the less populated areas there
is little, if any, parochial school enrollment, possibly due more to non-
availability of schools than to the denominational composition of the
population. Data on this factor are presented in Table 8.8.

While the diversion of a small percentage but a significant number
of students from the public to the parochial schools may serve to some
extent as a counterbalance to fiscal difficulties, it may, on the other
hand, create corollary problems of a social and political nature. As
the proportion of children in parochial schools increases, the potency
of the "double-load" complaint of parochial school parents may also
increase. From this may come a diminishing of their interest in and
support of public schools. We do not suggest that this reduced support
will result from a mere increase in parochial school enrollments from
9 to 11% in twenty years as indicated for the state as a whole. However,
considering the wide variance in such proportions among the counti
of the state, changes of from 15 to 25% in areas of strong denominational interest could well introduce this factor. Our point here is that
a system of good public schools and several other systems of schools
cannot exist side-by-side without introducing several factors that tend
to weaken the excellence of both systems and at the same time increasing the fiscal burdens unnecessarily. The greater the number of separate and independent systems, the fewer students each will have and the
more difficult it will be to meet individual differences without increasing costs.

County Ratios of Elementary to High School Populations. The preceding discussion of the importance of changing ratios of elementary
and high school populations considered only the state as a whole. Just
as the parochial school enrollment factor was shown to vary greatly
from county to county, so also does the ratio of elementary and high
school populations. A county-by-county distribution of these ratios is
presented in Table 8.9. Even the county ratios mask considerable variations among high school districts. For example, within Los Angeles
County, high school students are 32.6% of the total in the South Pasadena area, while in nearby Covina only 18.6% are in high school. Such
variations are often cyclical in nature for the general age of the parent
group determines the preponderance of numbers at the two levels of
education. Pasadena has already felt the impact of the wave in the high
school. Covina awaits its turn.

Table 8.6. Enrollment in Parochial Schools in California: 1950-70

Year	Elementary K-8	High School 9-12	Total K-12
1950	136,228	29,020	165,248
51	152,671	31,818	184,489
52	170,454	35,280	205,734
53	186,194	38,371	224,565
54	200,582	42,120	242,702
55	216,240	45,217	261,457
56	230,724	49,907	280,631
57	247,581	54,444	302,025
Projected			
58	267,400	59,400	326,800
59	289,500	62,900	352,400
1960	308,100	67,800	375,900
61	326,600	72,900	399,500
62	345,400	79,100	424,500
63	365,400	85,600	451,000
64	386,500	89,600	476,100
65	407,500	93,600	501,100
66	427,500	98,100	525,500
67	446,700	103,000	549,700
68	467,100	108,000	575,100
69	488,900	112,100	601,000
1970	510,300	116,300	626,600

Notes: Reliable estimates for years prior to 1950 not available.

Source: Reference 16

Table 8.7. Selected Relationships of School Enrollment Data: 1950-70

Year	Total Enrollment as a % of Population age 5-17	Parochial School Enrollment as a % of Total Enrollment			High School Enrollment as a % of Total (K-12) Enrollment	
		Elementary	High School	Total	Public Schools	Parochial Schools
1950	97.6%	9.4	7.0	8.9	22.7	17.5
51	98.0	9.6	7.3	9.1	21.9	17.2
52	95.5	9.9	7.5	9.5	21.9	17.1
53	96.2	10.0	7.6	9.5	21.7	17.0
54	96.2	10.0	7.8	9.6	21.7	17.3
55	97.0	10.1	7.8	9.6	21.7	17.2
56	98.0	10.1	7.8	9.6	22.2	17.7
57	98.6	10.2	7.7	9.7	23.0	18.0
1960	See Notes	10.6	7.7	10.0	23.8	18.0
1965		11.3	7.7	10.4	25.9	18.6
1970		11.9	7.7	10.9	27.0	18.5

Notes: Entries are omitted for years 1960, 65 and 70 in left column because enrollment projections have been more recently revised than population projections resulting in relationships over 100%

Source: Derived from Tables 8.3, 8.4 and 8.5.

Table 8.8. Enrollment in Parochial Schools as a Per Cent of Total Enrollment; Oct.1957 / Table 8.9. Public Elementary and High School ADA as a Per Cent of Total ADA, 1956-57

Elementary	High School	Total	County	Elementary	High School
10.5%	8.7%	10.1%	1. Alameda	77.4%	22.5%
			2. Alpine		
			3. Amador	59.8	40.1 See Note
6.9	1.1	5.3	4. Butte	73.5	26.5
.8		.6	5. Calaveras	74.8	25.2
11.9		8.5	6. Colusa	72.7	27.3
4.6	.3	3.6	7. Contra Costa	78.6	21.4
8.0		6.0	8. Del Norte	78.6	21.4
2.4	1.7	2.2	9. El Dorado	73.9	26.1
5.5	4.1	5.2	10. Fresno	78.2	21.8
1.2		.9	11. Glenn	74.6	25.4
5.4	3.2	4.9	12. Humboldt	77.4	22.6
9.7	6.5	9.0	13. Imperial	79.2	20.8
			14. Inyo	75.9	24.1
6.7	2.6	5.7	15. Kern	77.0	23.0
4.9	1.7	4.2	16. Kings	76.7	23.3
2.3		1.6	17. Lake	73.2	26.8
			18. Lassen	75.5	24.5
14.1	9.4	13.0	19. Los Angeles	77.0	23.0
5.0	.2	3.9	20. Madera	77.2	22.8
11.2	14.7	12.0	21. Marin	80.8	19.2
			22. Mariposa	74.1	25.9
5.9	.5	4.6	23. Mendocino	77.0	23.0
7.8	1.3	6.3	24. Merced	78.5	21.5
			25. Modoc	76.3	23.7
			26. Mono	83.2	16.8
8.5	9.0	8.7	27. Monterey	80.4	19.6
10.9	5.8	9.6	28. Napa	75.7	24.3
7.8	6.8	7.5	29. Nevada	70.6	29.4
9.2	5.4	8.4	30. Orange	80.9	19.1
3.4		2.5	31. Placer	75.0	25.0
			32. Plumas	74.0	26.0
8.4	4.4	7.5	33. Riverside	77.8	22.2
9.6	7.6	9.1	34. Sacramento	79.6	20.4
15.8		12.2	35. San Benito	75.0	25.0
8.5	3.6	7.3	36. San Bernardino	77.9	22.1
11.2	7.5	10.4	37. San Diego	78.7	21.3
27.6	24.7	26.8	38. San Francisco	72.9	27.1
6.6	6.0	6.5	39. San Joaquin	77.6	22.4
5.6	3.6	5.1	40. San Luis Obispo	75.9	24.1
12.2	10.0	11.7	41. San Mateo	79.8	20.2
11.8	8.0	10.9	42. Santa Barbara	76.6	23.4
8.4	7.6	8.2	43. Santa Clara	79.8	20.2
8.5	14.6	10.3	44. Santa Cruz	76.9	23.1
4.2		3.0	45. Shasta	74.6	25.4
			46. Sierra	71.4	28.6
			47. Siskiyou	75.8	24.2
7.0	8.2	7.4	48. Solano	80.0	20.0
9.2	5.8	7.4	49. Sonoma	76.5	23.5
4.4=	1.1	3.5	50. Stanislaus	75.8	24.2
6.7		5.0	51. Sutter	74.6	25.4
4.9	3.7	4.6	52. Tehama	73.7	26.3
			53. Trinity	79.0	21.0
4.5	.3	3.5	54. Tulare	75.4	24.6
			55. Tuolumne	74.6	25.4
11.0	9.5	10.6	56. Ventura	78.5	21.5
6.2		4.7	57. Yolo	70.1	29.9
8.9	5.2	8.0	59. Yuba	77.3	22.7

For State Totals see Table 8.9

Notes: ADA in grades 1-12 is used as the base versus the K-12 base used in Table 8.7.

Source of both Tables: Reference 8

Notes: Assignment of ADA to Counties based on Community District organization. The unusual high school per cent in Amador County is attributable to population in a state institution.

WEALTH OF CALIFORNIA AS RELATED TO THE PUBLIC SCHOOLS

Throughout this volume income is advanced as the most appropriate measure of ability to support local government. This applies equally to public schools. However, only very indirectly is income brought to bear as a tax base for the support of schools. About half of total school revenues come from state subventions and less than one-sixth of all state funds are now (1958) derived from the income tax. Proposals are made in Chapter 9 for increased recognition of income as a basis for school support with a corresponding decrease in the dependence upon the local property tax. For these reasons income data are related to the school support problem in the analyses that follow.

Income: Personal & Disposable

Basic personal income data for 1929-1956 may be found in Chapter 2, in terms of both actual amounts and per capita figures that are adjusted for the changing value of the dollar by the Bureau of Labor Statistics Consumer Price Index.

The statistic, disposable personal income, which is personal income minus all "personal" taxes levied by all levels of government, is available for California only for certain years. Both income measures are summarized and interrelated in Table 8.10. Although disposable personal income constitutes a more significant measure than personal income, the limited number of years for which such information is available and the fact that county data are available only for personal income force predominant use of the less desirable measure. However, it will be noted from Table 8.10 that trends established for one apply to the other and that approximations of the relationship of the two may be made.

Income Per Capita. Per capita personal income and disposable income have shown consistently increasing trends. Even when adjusted for the declining value of the dollar, income has risen about 40-50% in 1956 over 1939-40, but the sharpest rise occurred during the 1940's.

Income per Wage-Earning Member of the Population. While income per capita has been increasing and income per ADA remaining fairly constant, the proportion of the total population in the wage-earning age group has declined from 68 to 56%. In fact, income per person in the 18-64 age group has increased about 75% in the 1940-56 period. This remarkable fact just about compensates for the sharp rise in the child population.

Table 8.10.   Disposable Personal Income Compared with Personal Income for U.S. and California. Selected Years 1929-53.

Calendar Year	Disposable Personal Income in Current Dollars					Calif. Income Per Capita in 1947-49 Dollars		
	Total		Per Capita					
	United States	Calif.	United States	Calif.	Calif. as a % of U.S.	DPI	Personal Income	DPI As a % of PI
	(millions)							
1929	83,020	5,349	682	967	142	1,341	1,380	97.2
1940	75,924	5,649	575	813	141	1,364	1,409	96.8
1946	157,003	14,153	1,116	1,455	130	1,721	1,957	88.0
1950	204,729	17,615	1,354	1,659	123	1,619	1,803	89.8
1953	204,752	23,046	1,565	1,899	121	1,638	1,895	86.4

Notes: Additional detail on Personal Income is included in Table 8.31.
Source: Reference 27.

Income Per Child. But rising per capita income does not mean
that income per child to be educated has increased at the same rate,
because the ratio of school age to total population has also been rising.
For this purpose the measure of personal income per ADA becomes
important. The reader is referred to Table 8.31 for a 27-year analysis
of this important measure of public ability to support education. In
general, income per ADA has increased only about half as much as income per capita, or 20-25%, using the 1939-40 year as a base. With
the sharp increase in the child population since the war, income per
ADA has hardly held its own.

Measures of Taxable Wealth Compared

The tendency of state figures to mask important county variations,
as noted for other measures, applies also to income. Probably there
are great variations in income per capita and per ADA among districts
within counties too, but the smallest subdivision for which income data
are available is the county. Three measures of wealth per ADA are
shown in Table 8.11. Assessed valuation, personal income, and state
income tax collections per ADA are shown by amounts and by county
rank (No. 1 is high). It is readily seen that a given county may be in a
much different position by one measure than by another. For example,
Contra Costa County ranks lowest in personal income per ADA but 16
counties fall below it when the assessed valuation per ADA measure is
employed. There is a strong probability that the real ability of Contra
Costa County to support its schools is considerably below the level that

Table 8.11. Three Measures of Wealth per ADA in California Counties, 1956-57

| County | Assessed Valuation | | Personal Income | | State Income Tax Paid |
	Amount	Rank	Amount	Rank	Amount
Alameda	$ 8,012	32	$14,601	3	$56
Alpine	(not included)				
Amador	16,598	4	7,770	54	
Butte	7,533	38	9,046	39	27
Calaveras	11,733	11	8,853	43	
Colusa	17,123	3	12,712	6	
Contra Costa	7,410	41	6,882	57	31
Del Norte	6,264	51	9,668	31	
El Dorado	10,132	17	8,293	48	
Fresno	9,097	24	8,532	46	26
Glenn	10,109	18	10,044	26	
Humboldt	5,930	54	10,177	23	37
Imperial	6,045	52	10,268	21	23
Inyo	11,344	13	10,500	19	
Kern	10,385	15	9,088	37	29
Kings	10,272	16	7,485	56	19
Lake	11,574	12	9,332	34	
Lassen	6,024	53	9,351	33	
Los Angeles	8,851	26	14,877	2	67
Madera	6,740	43	8,310	47	17
Marin	7,266	44	12,832	5	74
Mariposa	11,894	10	12,684	7	
Mendocino	6,487	48	9,548	32	35
Merced	7,262	43	7,834	51	18
Modoc	10,527	14	11,972	12	
Mono	60,732	1	12,597	8	
Monterey	9,744	20	13,063	4	39
Napa	5,550	56	9,019	40	31
Nevada	8,559	29	9,056	38	
Orange	8,142	31	7,582	55	39
Placer	9,667	21	7,819	52	20
Plumas	20,550	2	9,763	28	
Riverside	8,821	27	9,277	35	29
Sacramento	5,398	57	11,226	15	36
San Benito	13,184	8	10,562	18	
San Bernardino	6,699	46	8,791	45	22
San Diego	6,484	49	12,529	9	39
San Francisco	15,821	5	31,422	1	166
San Joaquin	7,506	39	10,187	22	31
San Luis Obispo	9,869	19	9,995	27	22
San Mateo	7,700	34	12,269	10	70
Santa Barbara	13,207	7	11,643	13	95
Santa Clara	7,488	40	9,681	30	42
Santa Cruz	9,464	22	8,807	44	33
Shasta	9,008	25	7,803	53	29
Sierra	13,316	6	10,108	24	
Siskiyou	7,843	28	9,173	36	19
Solano	6,508	47	10,823	16	25
Sonoma	7,618	37	8,978	41	31
Stanislaus	5,822	55	8,084	49	24
Sutter	8,254	30	10,707	17	29
Tehama	7,668	36	8,042	50	
Trinity	7,697	35	9,742	29	
Tulare	6,425	50	8,894	42	21
Tuolumne		23	11,259	14	
Ventura	12,451	9	10,077	25	35
Yolo	8,786	28	12,059	11	48
Yuba	7,272	42	10,401	20	23
The State	$ 8,484		$12,643		$54

Notes: ADA (K-12) assigned to counties on Community District basis.
Source: Basic Amounts, AV/ADA - Reference 8; Personal Income - Reference 6; State Income Tax - Reference 25; ADA Divisor - Reference 8.

the state equalization program assigns to it on the basis of assessed
valuation per ADA. Conversely, Sacramento County, lowest in assessed
valuation per ADA, is well above the median on the personal income
measure. The end result of this situation is a somewhat higher state
equalization grant than the personal income of Sacramento County would
appear to justify. This problem is also related to the need for improved
intercounty equalization of property assessed values. Perhaps Contra
Costa is assessing too high and Sacramento County too low. But it would
appear more likely that the real problem lies in the failure of property
assessments to measure taxpaying ability reliably.

In Chapter 9 the proposal is advanced to utilize personal income
data in determining the need for equalization. In this regard the use of
machinery already set up for collection of the state income tax would
be effective. For this reason state income tax collections per unit of
ADA are included in Table 8.11. The report of the Franchise Tax
Board does not list separately the collections for the 20 counties with
the lowest populations, therefore the amount per ADA is given only for
the 38 more populated counties. The progressive nature of the rate structure for the state income tax means that a county with a small number
of very high incomes might well pay more than another county with
an equal total amount of income divided more evenly among its residents.

SOURCES OF REVENUE FOR PUBLIC SCHOOLS

Although schools are generally considered to be the most important single segment of local government, the proportion of total school
revenues in California provided by other than local sources nearly
equals that provided by local taxation. During the period 1950-51
through 1956-57, local revenues averaged 51.5%, state contributions
were 43.3%, funds provided by the federal government (P.L. 874)
amounted to 2.2% and other revenues were 2.5%. The classification
"other revenues" includes principally state and federal vocational
education funds for high school districts, county subventions (intangibles), high school tuition taxes, and income from sale and rental of
school property. The multiple nature of sources of school revenues
emphasizes the intergovernmental nature of the school finance problem.

Proportions of Revenues by Level of Government

The proportion of total school revenues met by local tax sources
has shown an intermittent but continuous decline in the past seven years
and is, for many reasons, destined to decrease even further if existing
(1958) levels of state support prevail. Basic data for this consideration

are provided by type of district — elementary, high school, and unified — and for all districts in Table 8.12. Junior college districts are included in the array for all districts but for reasons of space are not listed separately.

Differences by Level of District. As indicated in Figure 8.3 the state carries relatively more of the revenue burden for elementary schools than for high schools. The heavier dependence upon the state by elementary districts, compared to high school districts, is, first of all, a function of a higher legal tax rate limit and broader tax base for high schools than for elementary schools. The disproportionate ratios of these rates and of other closely related rates are presented in Table 8.13. If either this rate or the amount in any single cell of the table is correctly established, then virtually none of the other rates or amounts is correct.

A second factor related to the larger proportion of state support for elementary than for high school districts is the smallness of elementary districts, which produces greater variability in wealth per ADA and, in turn, requires more state support for the poorer ones. A third factor is the present preponderance of population currently in the elementary schools. As the larger pupil populations now nearing the end of elementary school enter high school (the "wave" line in Table 8.5 will show the year that this will occur), assessed valuations per ADA in high school districts must inevitably fall. As these valuations decline, more and more districts will become eligible for equalization aid and the proportion of state support will increase, unless, of course, the foundation program is reduced. The 33% state contribution to high school districts can then be expected to approach the share now undertaken by the state for elementary districts. Compounding the problem is the fact that estimates of the pre-school population do not indicate that a counterbalancing decrease in elementary ADA may be expected.

There is another side to this coin, however. Major changes in the state foundation program occur mainly when new state funds are added, but during the periods between changes in the foundation program, school costs usually increase. Funds to finance these increased costs must therefore generally come from the districts themselves.

Also involved are differences between the ratio of elementary and high school foundation programs and elementary and high school current expenses of education per ADA. These amounts are included in Table 8.13. It is clear that the ratio of the elementary and high

Table 8.12. General Fund Revenues of California School Districts, By Source 1950-51.
Elementary, High School, Unified and All Districts

Year	Local		State		Federal		Other		Total	
	Amount	%	Amount	%	Amount	%	Amount	%	Amount	%

Elementary Districts

Year	Amount	%	Amount	%	Amount	%	Amount	%	Amount	%
1950-51	$98,640	45.2	$114,762	52.5	$1,672	.8	$3,324	1.5	$218,399	100.0
51-52	110,360	44.2	132,028	52.9	3,626	1.5	3,482	1.4	249,495	100.0
52-53	122,695	43.0	153,260	53.7	4,638	1.6	4,636	1.6	285,229	100.0
53-54	130,316	38.3	200,557	58.9	5,492	1.6	3,934	1.2	340,299	100.0
54-55	142,528	38.7	215,516	58.5	6,987	1.9	3,535	.9	368,565	100.0
55-56	157,361	40.8	217,655	56.4	7,252	1.9	3,586	.9	385,854	100.0
1956-57	192,069	43.9	231,240	52.9	9,626	2.2	4,446	1.0	437,383	100.0

High School Districts

Year	Amount	%	Amount	%	Amount	%	Amount	%	Amount	%
1950-51	91,891	66.6	39,584	28.7	1,845	1.3	4,664	3.4	137,983	100.0
51-52	99,330	66.8	42,748	28.7	2,522	1.7	4,172	2.8	148,742	100.0
52-53	109,271	68.2	44,700	27.9	2,120	1.3	4,168	2.6	160,256	100.0
53-54	112,030	64.5	55,133	31.8	2,022	1.2	4,358	2.5	173,544	100.0
54-55	124,149	65.2	59,360	31.2	2,159	1.1	4,694	2.5	190,361	100.0
55-56	138,037	61.3	79,808	35.5	2,192	1.0	5,018	2.2	225,055	100.0
1956-57	167,240	63.4	87,056	33.0	2,335	1.3	6,182	2.3	263,812	100.0

Unified Districts

Year	Amount	%	Amount	%	Amount	%	Amount	%	Amount	%
1950-51	66,801	54.3	47,137	38.3	3,901	3.2	5,220	4.2	123,060	100.0
51-52	76,808	54.2	53,235	37.6	6,250	4.4	5,356	3.8	141,648	100.0
52-53	93,721	52.2	70,161	39.1	9,644	5.4	5,886	3.3	179,411	100.0
53-54	103,183	48.6	94,487	44.5	8,130	3.8	6,518	3.1	212,315	100.0
54-55	114,419	48.3	105,341	44.5	10,360	4.4	6,650	2.8	236,771	100.0
55-56	128,432	50.2	112,538	44.0	7,730	3.0	7,312	2.8	256,013	100.0
1956-57	159,182	53.5	121,945	41.0	8,400	2.8	7,992	2.7	297,448	100.0

All Districts (including J.C. not included above)

Year	Amount	%	Amount	%	Amount	%	Amount	%	Amount	%
1950-51	273,738	54.0	208,699	41.0	8,786	2.0	16,790	3.0	508,014	100.0
51-52	308,645	53.3	235,006	41.3	13,378	2.5	16,597	2.9	568,616	100.0
52-53	344,953	52.7	275,301	42.0	17,181	2.6	17,384	2.7	654,819	100.0
53-54	362,466	47.9	359,505	47.5	16,179	2.1	18,451	2.5	756,603	100.0
54-55	399,482	48.2	390,595	47.1	19,737	2.4	19,057	2.2	828,870	100.0
55-56	444,413	49.2	421,381	46.6	17,411	1.9	20,908	2.3	904,113	100.0
1956-57	545,077	52.3	451,617	43.3	21,581	2.1	24,383	2.3	1,042,657	100.0

Source: Reference 26.

Table 8.13. Selected School Support Factors, By Level, 1956-57: Tax Rates Expressed Per Grade

Level of District	Principal Foundation Program	District Aid Tax Rate	Legal Tax Rate Limit (without override)	State Mean Equivalent Tax Rate	Current Expense of Educ. per ADA	Mean Tax Revenue per ADA at Legal Tax Rate Limit
Elementary	$220	6.67¢	10.0¢	14.8¢	$290	$ 98
High School	310	12.50	18.75	24.2	444	282
Jr. College	410	16.50	17.50	14.7	474	382

Note: The State Mean Equivalent Tax Rate is listed here for comparative purposes. Its derivation involves many detailed computations.
For the specific method used see Chapter 9.

Source: Reference 7.

school foundation programs ($220/310) is not proportionate to the ratio of current elementary and high school expenses per ADA ($290/444). At present the elementary foundation program comes nearer meeting actual costs per ADA than does the high school foundation program. This disparity, of course, accounts in part for the larger share of high school support borne locally since all expenses greater than the foundation program must be met by local taxation.

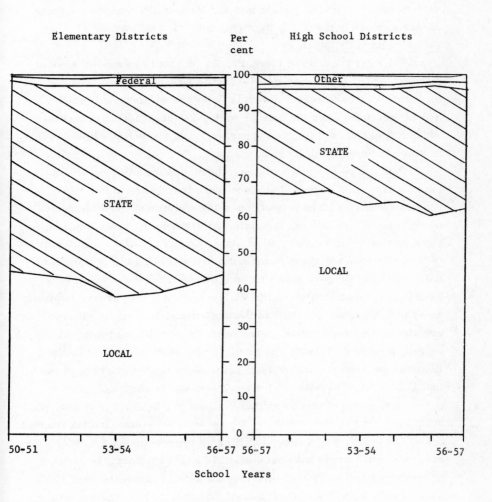

Figure 8.3. Percentage of Income to General Fund By Source, Elementary and High School Districts: 1950-51 to 1956-57

Source: Conforms to Table 8.12

Differences Among the Counties. Each of the more than 1,800 school districts in the state receives differing proportions of its support from local, state, federal, and other sources. An analysis of these differences would be both interesting and enlightening but would call for excessive detail. The differences are great enough at the county level to show the significance of the inquiry. Percentages of income from each of these four sources for selected classes of districts are shown in Table 8.14. Study of these data discloses how wide county variations are masked by state totals. Many of the reasons for these differences are contained in the paragraphs that follow.

Federal and State Revenues

The vast majority of federal funds received by school districts are derived from two sources: (1) Public Law 874, which provides operational funds to school districts in federally "impacted" areas, and (2) revenues from the sale or rental of federal forest reserves, which are earmarked for the support of roads and schools in the county in which the reserve is located.

Public Law 874. School districts in most counties receive no revenue from this source, but since those that do are in the more populous areas, a large proportion of the children of the state derive benefits from this national legislation. California receives more funds from this program than any other state. County benefits range from zero in nonimpacted areas to the noteworthy 10.7% and 7.7% shares in Solano and San Diego counties as compensation for the exempted tax base in naval installations in the Vallejo and San Diego areas. Logically, assessed valuations per ADA in the unified districts serving these areas are among the lowest in the state, reflecting vividly the impact of the exempted federal property and justifying the need for federal funds. However good the legislation is in principle, existing evidence shows that Public Law 874 does not fully compensate the district.

An example of this was cited in Chapter 6 in which payments to school districts in the vicinity of a large military-connected tax-exempt industrial property in Southern California represented only 10% of the revenues which would have been realized had the property been taxed at prevailing rates. Of course, since all federal payments were made under Public Law 874, the schools of that area were relatively better off than other elements of local government.

Revenues from Forest Reserves. The national government has long shared revenues from the sale or rental of forest reserves with

Table 8.14. Income to General Fund of School Districts, By County, 1956-57. Per Cent Distribution by Source of Funds

County	All Districts				Elementary Dists.		H. S. Dists.	
	Local	State	Fed.	Other	Local	State	Local	State
Alameda	50.6	45.7	2.7	1.1	32.1	64.2	62.1	34.2
Alpine	none	17.1	82.9			17.1		
Amador	53.9	45.1		1.0	35.1	64.9	35.7	69.3
Butte	44.6	53.5	.6	1.3	36.4	62.4	52.8	44.9
Calaveras	49.1	48.3	1.8	.8	34.3	63.7	33.3	65.4
Colusa	65.0	32.2	.6	2.2	60.3	36.6	72.8	23.8
Contra Costa	56.2	41.3	1.4	1.1	47.6	49.9	65.6	31.9
Del Norte	41.1	55.3	2.9	.7	28.6	68.1	65.5	30.5
El Dorado	47.1	44.3	7.4	1.1	32.1	.7	64.9	29.4
Fresno	47.6	48.9	.4	3.2	43.6	54.5	64.4	29.3
Glenn	50.1	46.3	1.0	2.5	44.2	53.6	60.4	33.8
Humboldt	44.8	53.0	.9	1.3	39.5	59.8	56.8	40.0
Imperial	40.1	55.7	1.1	3.1	28.6	68.8	61.7	32.4
Inyo	55.7	41.5	2.0	.9	50.2	46.5	69.3	28.9
Kern	58.6	37.3	2.4	1.8	48.4	48.0	75.5	20.6
Kings	58.3	40.7	.2	.9	49.3	49.8	75.2	23.3
Lake	53.2	42.8	2.7	1.2	49.8	46.7	60.4	35.2
Lassen	31.3	49.0	15.9	3.9	20.5	57.4	43.6	32.8
Los Angeles	55.4	41.4	.9	2.3	49.6	48.5	63.0	34.9
Madera	45.5	53.0	1.1	.4	34.1	64.3	66.9	31.9
Marin	53.7	41.6	3.1	1.7	45.6	50.4	69.4	24.6
Mariposa	47.7	45.8	4.9	1.4	entire county unified			
Mendocino	39.8	57.8	1.2	1.4	35.6	61.8	47.5	50.8
Merced	43.3	52.3	2.5	1.9	32.8	62.1	62.7	34.0
Modoc	38.4	42.8	18.3	.4	36.9	46.6	41.0	36.1
Mono	79.3	17.4	2.3	1.0	72.6	22.3	88.5	10.8
Monterey	52.0	40.8	5.1	2.1	43.4	48.2	64.9	29.4
Napa	40.2	51.7	5.1	3.0	32.9	57.4	44.5	47.4
Nevada	49.8	47.4	1.9	.9	45.7	52.0	54.7	42.1
Orange	48.8	44.5	2.1	4.6	37.5	58.9	67.0	26.7
Placer	48.9	46.4	4.1	.6	35.4	59.1	59.5	37.2
Plumas	58.7	26.0	15.1	.1	entire county unified			
Riverside	51.6	43.8	3.0	1.6	42.7	52.1	60.0	36.7
Sacramento	38.1	52.8	4.5	4.5	25.4	66.9	44.6	47.3
San Benito	63.2	36.4	.3	...	50.9	48.9	78.2	20.9
San Bernardino	50.4	43.0	4.0	2.6	41.2	53.1	58.1	36.4
San Diego	43.3	47.2	7.7	1.9	33.1	57.4	52.3	39.9
San Francisco	62.7	31.9	1.2	4.2	entire county unified			
San Joaquin	43.9	50.8	1.5	3.8	42.3	55.2	66.2	28.0
San Luis Obispo	53.9	43.7	.4	2.0	44.3	54.6	67.4	28.3
San Mateo	60.1	37.7	.9	1.3	51.6	47.1	78.1	19.5
Santa Barbara	63.7	34.6	.6	1.1	59.4	39.2	68.8	29.0
Santa Clara	54.3	43.1	.6	2.0	41.6	57.3	70.7	26.4
Santa Cruz	56.8	41.4	...	1.8	47.8	50.2	68.9	29.4
Shasta	46.8	49.5	1.5	2.2	34.6	61.8	58.9	38.1
Sierra	31.6	39.3	29.2	.2	entire county unified			
Siskiyou	38.3	47.7	13.7	.3	24.9	57.4	56.7	34.4
Solano	38.6	49.3	10.7	1.4	31.6	54.4	67.9	20.1
Sonoma	47.6	47.3	.7	4.3	40.6	57.6	59.9	38.1
Stanislaus	37.8	59.9	.6	1.6	28.8	70.0	57.2	40.3
Sutter	45.6	53.6	...	.7	35.9	63.9	62.9	35.5
Tehama	42.1	52.6	3.5	1.8	31.3	63.5	59.0	35.4
Trinity	31.7	45.4	22.0	.8	24.7	59.8	42.8	22.5
Tulare	44.5	51.6	.5	3.4	34.6	63.2	60.5	36.8
Tuolumne	43.4	45.6	7.5	3.5	34.0	54.5	59.3	30.0
Ventura	58.0	36.9	3.0	2.1	50.0	44.4	69.4	26.1
Yolo	48.9	47.3	.7	3.0	40.5	57.8	63.6	28.9
Yuba	39.6	56.6	.9	2.9	32.0	65.9	53.2	38.3
For State Totals see Table 8.16								

Notes: See text for explanation of the unusual data for Alpine County.
Source: Reference 26

the counties of origin for the specific purposes of supporting schools
and building roads. Analysis of Table 8.14 discloses that in many
mountain counties revenues from this source play a major role in supporting education. In fact, diminutive Alpine County receives 83% of its
funds for education from this source and, since the remaining 17% is
derived from state basic aid, no local tax for education is levied.

State Revenues. The complex system of allocation of state subventions to school districts was outlined previously in this chapter and
summarized in Table 8.2. The proportion of total school revenues derived from state funds ranges from 17% in Alpine and Mono counties to
almost 60% in Stanislaus County. These extremes show a gratifying relationship to the assessed valuation per ADA of the counties: Mono and
Alpine counties are very high in assessed valuation per ADA and
Stanislaus County is very low in this measure of wealth for school support. Table 8.15 describes the relationship between county-assessed
valuations per ADA and the proportions of total state revenue. The
general equitable relationship of all counties is clear. But, once again
a general trend obscures important specific inequities. To the extent
that the relationship in Table 8.15 is linear, the equalization program
of the state may be said to be equitable. However, the relationship has
important examples of nonlinearity due principally to the flat grant program, and therefore the model of true equalization remains an un-
achieved goal.

Assessed Valuation

The importance of assessed valuations to both local revenue and
state subventions has been repeatedly emphasized. In succeeding pages
many amounts and relationships of assessed valuation per ADA are presented. Before considering those, however, important methodological
points regarding computation must be clarified.

Equalization of County Assessment Ratios. Details of the variation among counties in the ratio of assessed to true values are presented
in Chapter 6. The need for effective equalization of such ratios increases
in direct proportion to the use by the state of assessed valuation per ADA
in determining equalization aid. Table 8.16 illustrates the nature of the
problem by citing the conflicting treatment of three hypothetical districts with equal amounts of true wealth and equal ADA. The district in
the county with the lowest assessment ratio would receive a 22.3% overpayment of equalization aid. Correspondingly the district located in the
county with the highest assessment ratio would produce so much local

Table 8.15.   Assessed Valuation per ADA and Per Cent of School
District Revenues from State Sources, 1956-57
57 Counties (Alpine Excluded)

Per Cent of School District Revenues from State Sources	Assessed Valuation per ADA (thousands of dollars)												Total
	5	6	7	8	9	10	11	12	13	14	15	16& Over	
60 & Over													
58&59	50												1
56&57		23	58										2
54&55		8	13										2
52&53	12 34	20	4	24 52	51								7
50&51	28	54	39										3
48&49		18 48			10 45		5						5
46&47		37	47 49	29 57	31	11							7
44&45			53	1 30	55	9	22					3	7
42&43		36	43	33	40	25	17						6
40&41			7 21	19	27 44	16	14						7
38&39									46				1
36&37			41			15		56	35				4
34&35									42				1
32&33												6	1
30&31										38			1
Below 30												26 32	2
Total	4	9	12	7	7	5	4	1	3	1		4	57

Figures in cells of this Table refer to County Code numbers. See Table 8.8 for Key.

support on its "overvalued" property that it would receive a 33.3%
underpayment in equalization aid. As pointed out in Chapter 6, the
variation among county assessment ratios is "being improved," and
only the less populated counties are at the extreme ratios. Since funds
for the support of education are in short supply, all artificial barriers
to the equitable sharing of what amounts to a common pool of state
funds must be surmounted.

Computation of Assessed Valuation per ADA.   The gross amounts
of assessed valuation in each school district are firmly established.
However, there are several classes of ADA figures, some based on
level of district, others on type of school, which are available for use
as divisors. The state uses a figure known as Apportionment ADA as
a divisor to determine eligibility for equalization aid. This figure includes all full-time day students but excludes adults. The separation

Table 8.16. Relationship of County Assessment Ratios to the Apportionment of State Equalization Funds

| | Three Elementary School Districts of Equal Size and Equal True Value of Property Subject to Local Taxation | | |
	I	II	III
True Value/ADA	$30,000.00	$30,000.00	$30,000.00
Assessment Ratio of the County	20% State Low	24% State Mean	30% State High
Assessed Value per ADA	$ 6,000.00	$ 7,200.00	$ 9,000.00
Qualifying Tax	1.35	1.35	1.35
Local Contribution per ADA from Qualifying Tax	$ 81.00	$ 97.20	$ 121.50
Basic State Aid	$ 125.00	$ 125.00	$ 125.00
Equalization Aid	$ 89.00	$ 72.80	$ 48.50
Foundation Program	$ 295.00	$ 295.00	$ 295.00
Correct Equalization Payment at state mean assessment ratio	$ 72.80	$ 72.80	$ 72.80
Overpayment to district per ADA	$ 16.20 (22.3%)	0	0
Underpayment to district	0	0	$ 24.30 (33.3%*

*Letter from the State Board of Equalization.

of elementary and high school levels is between grades 8 and 9, regardless of the particular organization of schools in that area.

Elementary district wealth is the assessed valuation of the district divided by the ADA of grades K-8. Similarly, the wealth of high school districts is measured by the assessed valuation divided by the nonadult ADA in grades 9-12. The divisor for junior college district wealth is the ADA in grades 13 and 14. Clearly, the varying size of the divisors means that the resulting wealth measures for the three levels are not mutually comparable. The state computes measures of wealth of unified districts by level and apportions on that basis.

Community District Basis. In this study we have elected to use a measure of wealth not employed in the state aid program. It is assessed valuation divided by the total ADA in grades K-12. This choice has two principal advantages:

1. Changing ratios of elementary and high school ADA do not artificially affect the resulting wealth measure. A district or county with high proportions of elementary ADA would be relatively much poorer on a measure of elementary wealth than high school wealth. The K-12 divisor eliminates such differences.

2. Use of a single divisor is in accord with proposals advanced in Chapter 9 for improved organization of districts under a framework of unification. It is also in accord with proposals for a single foundation program applicable to all grades, K-12.

With the help of punched cards provided by the State Department of Education,[*] all elementary districts of the state were classified according to high school district of attendance and a system of "community" districts was hypothecated for assimilation with existing unified districts. Thus for each of the 232 high school districts, a community district was created. To these were added the 95 existing unified districts for a total of 327. Of course, no such simple method will serve to reorganize properly the 1,800-odd districts in the state. Many of the high school districts that serve as the areas of community districts are woefully inadequate in terms of size and proximity to other schools. However, this study cannot purport to solve each local problem of district organization, and therefore elected to treat high school districts as offering the best single objective basis for forming a state system of unified and community districts. About 35 small rural elementary districts are either in no high school district or are divided between adjacent high school districts. The assignment of these to community districts was done on the basis of proximity of the elementary schools to nearby high schools. The total assessed valuation and likewise the ADA of the districts involved in these transfers comprises less than one-half of 1% of the state total, so that the potential margin of error is negligible.

The community districts were then listed according to the county which now has jurisdiction over the high school district. A few elemen-

[*] This study could not have been completed without statistical data from the State Department of Education. Dr. Henry Magnuson and Mr. Peter Tashnovian of the Bureau of Education Research provided fiscal data and cost information by supplying copies of punched cards. These cards were processed at the Western Data Processing Center on the UCLA campus on machines placed at the disposal of colleges and universities by International Business Machines (Reference 8).

In addition to the above, essential information for the community district pattern was provided by Dr. Drayton Nuttall, chief of the Bureau of School District Organization (Reference 13).

tary districts are components of a high school district in another county.
In these cases, the community district ADA and the assessed valuation
of the counties affected are increased or decreased by the amounts relating to the transferred elementary district. Two elementary districts
which send graduates to high schools in Nevada and Arizona were excluded entirely. All financial data for districts are based on the latest
completed apportionment, based on 1956-57 data and made during 1957-
58. Several district reorganizations which became effective on July 1,
1957 or 1958 are not reflected in the data.

Variation in Assessed Valuation per ADA. Much space could be
devoted to the information contained in Table 8.17. It shows the ranges
in wealth per ADA between the wealthiest and poorest districts and
likewise between other areas of actual, or possible, school district
organization.

It may be clearly noted that district organization alone can reduce the variations in wealth from 7,000:1 to 22:1. A major discussion
of these variations in presented in Chapter 9; we merely point out here
that the equalization program is but one of several ways to achieve
more equality of educational opportunity.

Assessed Valuation per ADA and the District Tax Rate. If each
district aspired to the same educational standards and if each were
operated with equal efficiency, its tax rate would bear a direct inverse
relation to its wealth. Of course there is variation among districts in
the desire of citizens to raise or lower the educational program through
changes in the tax rate. Also, some districts make their dollars provide greater returns than other districts. In the main, however, the
wealth level of the district determines the tax rate which will be required to support the educational program. This relationship is portrayed graphically in Tables 8.18 and 8.19 for elementary and high
school districts. Although the state equalization program may be expected to have attenuated the need for the poorer districts to levy excessively high tax rates, it is clear that these districts have found it
necessary to increase tax rates sharply to meet the pressing demands
of educating their children.

The large concentration of districts in the .81-.90 interval of
Table 8.18 is caused by the fact that the legal maximum tax rate for
these districts is $.90. This is clearly an artificial barrier to rational
levels of taxation since it is apparent from the small number of districts in the .91-1.00 and 1.01-1.10 intervals, that once the electorate

Table 8.17. Ranges of Assessed Valuation per ADA under Selected Organizational Structures: 1956-57

Organizational Structure	No. of Units	ADA in Divisor	State Mean	Poorest Name (County)	Amount	Wealthiest Name (County)	Amount	Wealthiest Divided by Poorest
Elementary and Existing Unified	1,589	K-8	$ 10,943	William Booth* (Sonoma)	$ 172	Bush Bar (Shasta)	$1,227,335	7,136:1
High School and Existing Unified	327	9-12	37,566	Ione (Amador)	5,984	Sierra (Fresno)	341,785	57:1
Junior College & Existing Unified	40	13&14	109,310	Modesto (Stanislaus)	40,698	Contra Costa (Contra Costa)	245,477	60:1
Community	327	K-12	8,484	Grant** (Sacramento)	3,262	Emery (Alameda)	71,457	22:1
Counties (Excluding Alpine)	57	K-12	8,484	Sacramento	5,398	Mono	60,732	11:1
Regions	9	K-12	8,484	San Diego	6,484	Central and South Coast	11,242	1.7:1

Notes: *William Booth is the poorest elementary district with an AV/ADA other than zero. Technically the poorest district is Reservation, also in Sonoma County, with 19 ADA and no assessed valuation. There are several districts with some assessed valuation but no ADA which creates a misleading AV/ADA quotient of infinity.

**Calexico in Imperial County is actually the poorest Community district ($2,842) for technical but invalid reasons. See Figure 9.1 for definitions of regions.

Source: Reference 8.

Table 8.18. Assessed Valuation per ADA and the General Purpose Tax Rate in Elementary Districts Supporting Grades K-8, 1956-57. (N = 725)

General Purpose Tax Rate per $100 of Assessed Valuation

Assessed Valuation per ADA (thousands of dollars)	$.41-.60	.61-.70	.71-.80	.81-.90	.91-1.00	1.01-1.10	1.11-1.20	1.21-1.40	1.41-1.60	1.61-1.80	1.81-1.99	2.00 & Over	Total
40 & Over	5	3	4	13		1	1	1					28
20-39		2	3	26	1	1	2	6	4	1			46
15-19			2	15	1	5	6	14	9	2	1	2	57
10-14	1	1	2	59	1	7	19	29	23	13	1	2	158
5-9		1	6	121	2	7	23	80	44	16	11	6	317
0-4		2	4	55		1	1	20	23	8	3	2	119
Total	6	9	21	289	5	22	52	150	103	40	16	12	725

Notes: Districts levying no tax are not included

Source: Reference 8

Table 8.19. Assessed Valuation per ADA and General Purpose Tax Rate in High School Districts Operating Grades 9-12, 1956-57, (N=214).

Assessed Valuation per ADA (thousands of dollars)	Tax Rate per $100 AV in Dollars							Total
	0-.25¢	.26-.50	.51-.75	.76-1.00	1.01-1.25	1.26-1.50	1.51& Over	
60 & Over			18	2	2	1		23
50-59			10	2	5			17
40-49			12	4	12	2		30
35-39			6	7	9	6		28
30-34			9	7	20	3		39
25-29			5	4	10	11	4	34
20-24			1	6	13	6	3	29
0-19			3		7	4		14
Total	0	0	64	32	78	33	7	214

Source: Reference 8.

decides to go above the .90 limit, rates of 1.20 and over become typical. This phenomena is not as apparent in Table 8.19 for high school
districts. The high school legal maximum (without an override) is $.75,
but the concentration is not heavier at that point than at higher rates.
This fact tends to support these points made previously: (1) the range
of wealth among high school districts is far less than among elementary districts, (2) local taxation plays a much greater role in financing
high school districts and (3) the average tax rate per grade is far higher
for high school districts.

Assessed Valuation per ADA and Size of District. It is popularly
accepted that the small district exists partly because of unwillingness
to share a favorable tax base with its neighbors. Tables 8.20 and 8.21
present graphically the relationship between the number of pupils in
ADA and the wealth of the district as measured by assessed valuation
per ADA. The negative relationship in the chart is clearer if the number of cases in the two upper quadrants are compared. Thus, as the
size of the district grows the wealth per child tends to decrease. The
trend is more apparent in elementary districts than in high school districts. This is to be expected since the high school districts being fewer
in number must of necessity be based on the wealth of a larger area.

Assessed Valuation per ADA of Elementary Districts within High
School Districts. The marked difference between the range in wealth of
elementary and of high school districts, shown in Table 8.17, suggests
great differences in wealth among the elementary districts that comprise a high school district. While the broader wealth of a high school
district constitutes an effective estimate of the mean wealth of the
larger area, it by no means precludes the possibility of gross inequality
among the component elementary districts. A distribution of the 232
high school districts by the range of wealth of their component elementary districts is presented in Table 8.22. To point up the fact that these
ranges describe more than exceptional extremes, several specific situations are described below. Two main types are immediately apparent:
(1) areas in which the central town or city elementary district is relatively poor and the surrounding small, usually rural, elementary districts are wealthy, and (2) the reverse, in which the central area is
wealthy and is surrounded by relatively poor districts. This type is
especially prevalent in suburban areas in which a large and rapid ADA
growth has reduced the wealth per pupil while the assessed valuation of
the central city area remains untapped.

Table 8.20. Assessed Valuation per ADA and Size, 1956-57, Elementary and Unified Districts (N = 1,589)

Assessed Valuation per ADA (thousands of dollars)	Average Daily Attendance												Total
	0-25	26-50	51-75	76-100	101-400	401-900	901-2000	2001-4000	4001-6000	6001-8000	8001-16000	16000 & over	
100 & Over	29	6	4	3	8	1							51
50-99	51	20	11	3	5	3	2	1			1		97
45-49	15	7	2	2	2								28
40-44	9	15	4	299	6	1	1			8			36
35-39	11	13	3	2	2	3	1						35
30-34	18	15	8	9	5	3	1		1				60
25-29	22	21	9	3	13	4	2	2					76
20-24	19	20	17	14	25	7	1	3		1		1	108
15-19	21	21	25	16	56	12	6	5		1	2	1	166
10-14	30	34	19	25	126	52	25	17	3	4	5	5	345
5-9	15	21	8	12	102	84	73	60	21	12	16	6	430
0-4	22	4	4	3	23	36	32	20	7	3	3		157
Total	262	197	114	92	373	206	144	108	32	21	27	13	1,589

Source: Reference 5.

Table 8.21. Assessed Valuation per ADA and Size, 1956-57, High School and Unified Districts (N = 327)

Assessed Valuation per ADA (thousands of dollars)	Average Daily Attendance										Total
	0-99	100-199	200-399	400-599	600-799	800-999	1000-1999	2000-3999	4000-7999	8000 & Over	
100 & Over	3	2	3	1	1	1		1			12
90-99	2	1	1	1		1	1				7
80-89	1		1	60			2		13		4
70-79	1	3	5	2	1	1					13
60-69	2	2	2	2			1				9
55-59	2	5	1	2	1		1	1	1	1	15
50-54	1	3	7	1			1				13
45-49	2	2	7		1		7				19
40-44	1	2	11	2		1	4	3	4	3	31
35-39	3	8	8	2	3	2	7	7		2	42
30-34	1	4	11	10	7	2	10	8	4		57
25-29		1	4	6	7	5	9	7	7	1	47
20-24		1	3	5	5	4	8	7	7		40
0-19		1	4	2	2	1	2	3	3		18
Total	19	35	68	36	28	18	52	38	26	7	327

Source: Reference 8.

High school districts with larger numbers of component elementary districts tend to have greater ranges in assessed valuation per ADA. Some of the more striking cases from the chart are identified in the following table by the letters which refer to cells in Table 8.22.

Not all the striking situations inherent in Table 8.22 are found in the fringes of the distribution. The asterisk in the lower left quadrant identifies a district which is an excellent and relatively typical example of differences in elementary district wealth within the same high school district.

Table 8.22.   Relationship of the Number and Ratio of Wealthiest to Poorest of Component Elementary Districts in High School Districts, 1956-57

Ratio of Wealthiest to Poorest

Number of Component Elementary Districts	0–4:1	5–9:1	10–14:1	15–19:1	20–29:1	30–39:1	40–49:1	50–99:1	100:1 &Over	Total
20 & Over						2 c		1 b	2 a	5
18&19		1 e							1 d	2
16&17	1 f		1		3		1			6
14&15				1	2	1		1		5
12&13	2	1	2	1				2		8
10&11	1	8	3		1					13
8&9	6	8	2	2	2	1	2	1	2 g	26
6&7	17	6	6	4	1					34
4&5	43	10	7 *	1	1	1		1 h		64
2&3	49	10	1	1		2		1 i		64
0&1	6									6
Total	125	44	22	10	10	7	3	7	5	233*

Note: *Although there are only 232 high school districts the total in this distribution is 233 because 1 unified district would receive a presently independent elementary district under a community district organization.

The Mean number of Component Elementary Districts is 6.4.

The Modal number of Component Elementary Districts is 4.

The letters in selected cells refer to the next table.

Source: References 8 and 13.

If the Huntington Beach Districts described in Table 8.23 were all consolidated, the new district's wealth of $21,272 per ADA would require no equalization aid and the amounts paid to Westminster and Fountain Valley (a total of $309,336) would be saved for the general use of education. This would amount to about 15 cents per elementary ADA in the state and over $49,000 for Los Angeles schools. These districts express sufficient community affinity to attend the same high school but adamantly continue to claim independence at the elementary level, to the detriment not only of their poorer neighbors but to all taxpayers and children in the state.

Table 8.23. Selected Examples of Ranges of Assessed Valuation per ADA Among Component Elementary Districts of High School Districts: 1956-57.

Code Letter	High School District	No. of Elem. Dists.	Ratio of Wealthiest to Poorest	AV/ADA High	AV/ADA Low
	High Number of Districts, High Ratio				
a	Kern County Union	33	2,164:1	$ 584,362	$ 275
a	Shasta Union	32	613:1	1,227,335	2,263
b	Siskiyou Union	32	65:1	326,168	5,481
c	El Dorado County Union	27	32:1	161,069	5,221
c	San Benito County Union	22	30:1	200,695	6,050
d	Oroville (Yuba)	18	145:1	437,898	3,526
	High Number of Districts, Low Ratio				
e	Lodi (San Joaquin)	18	6:1	62,920	9,368
f	Analy (Sonoma)	16	3:1	25,942	7,727
	Low Number of Districts, High Ratio				
g	Healdsburg (Sonoma)	8	174:1	30,021	172
g	Oakdale (Stanislaus)	8	120:1	286,765	7,455
h	Atascadero (S.L.O.)	4	64:1	322,015	5,087
i	Jackson (Amador)	3	97:1	684,696	7,234

Source: References 8 and 13.

Huntington Beach Union High School District--Orange County

Component Elementary Districts	ADA	AV	AV/ADA
Westminster	3,038	$13,421,730	$ 4,418
Fountain Valley	216	2,267,240	10,496
Seal Beach	616	16,395,000	26,615
Ocean View	636	17,430,600	27,407
Huntington Beach	1,111	69,984,950	62,993
Total Elementary	5,617	119,499,525	21,272

EXPENDITURES BY SCHOOL DISTRICT

The real purpose of all school support is to provide funds to assure, in the best possible way, as good an education as people want and are willing to pay for. It is therefore the expenditure aspect of the picture which represents the culmination of this detailed analysis of the school finance problem. Expenditures fall into two main categories, current expenses and capital outlays. These terms mean exactly what they say: current expenses are the costs of operating the educational program; capital outlays are the more periodic costs of buildings and equipment. In order to avoid repetition here of a point already well stated, the reader is referred to Chapter 4 for further discussion of the distinctions between these two types of expenditure.

Current Expense of Education by Level of District. It is clear that greater costs per ADA are incurred by districts operating on higher levels of education even though no detailed continuum is available. Separate costs for grade 1, grade 2, and so on, have never been calculated, much as such information is needed for the rational establishment of foundation programs and budget policies. However, data are available for all districts. Table 8.24 presents such data for selected years and shows the contrasting costs at these various levels of public education. High school costs per student are markedly above those for elementary pupils although the margin between the two is gradually shrinking. This trend is, we believe, largely attributable to more widespread use of the "single" salary schedule which provides equal pay for equal training, irrespective of the level of the school.

Table 8.24. Current Expense of Education per ADA by Level: Selected Years 1929-30 to 1956-57.

Year	Elementary	High School	Junior College	Unified	Total	H.S. as a % of Elem.
1929-30	$101	$192	$262	Included	$132	189%
1936-37	94	152	171	in 1st 3	118	164%
1946-47	135	232	197	columns	170	171%
1949-50	194	313	307	$252	239	161%
1956-57	290	444	474	357	346	153%

Source: 1929-30 to 1949-50 — Reference 18; 1956-57 — Reference 4.

Analysis of Current Expense of Education (CEE) by Object. As shown in Figure 8.4, the proportion of total CEE which is directed to each of the major account classifications has remained relatively con-

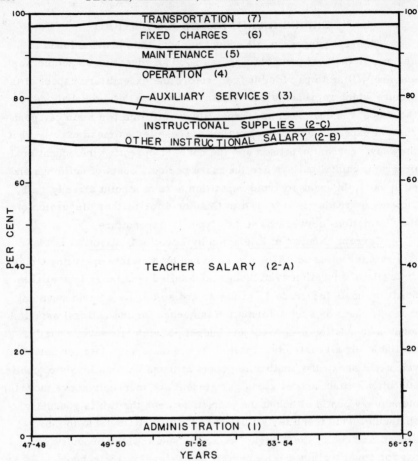

Figure 8.4. Per cent of Current Expense of Education by Account
          Classification, All Districts: 1947-48 — 1956-57

Source: Reference 4.

stant over the past eleven years. For the school year 1956-57, Table
8.25 presents a series of frequency distributions by level of district
showing the percentage of total CEE directed to the principal account
classifications. This table is specifically designed to show how district
variations are obscured by state averages. Another source of variation
within certain account classifications lies in the differences among districts in classifying expenditures. For example, since a high percentage
of cost for "administration" is often criticized, some districts charge,
or pro-rate, as many costs as possible to "instruction," while others
adhere more rigorously to the California School Accounting Manual.

Table 8.25. Number and Level of Districts by Percent of Total Current Expense of Education for Selected Account Classifications: 1956-57

Administration

	Below 2%	2	3	4	5	6	7	8	9	10	11	12 & Over	Total	Mean
Elementary	577	168	189	148	151	81	55	35	25	16	11	16	1472	4.22
High School	13	16	75	45	43	19	9	8	2	1		1	232	3.88
Unified	1	10	32	27	16	4	2	1			1	1	95	3.43
All	591	194	296	220	210	104	66	44	27	17	12	18	1799	3.94

Teacher Salaries

	Below 50%	50 51	52 53	54 55	56 57	58 59	60 61	62 63	64 65	66 67	68 69	70 71	72 73	74 & Over	Total	Mean
Elementary	72	35	35	74	68	95	104	156	190	158	138	118	66	158	1467	65.86
High School	19	10	24	16	27	35	40	31	18	8	3			1	232	60.96
Unified		2	4	1	3	7	17	16	19	15	11				95	65.14
All	91	47	63	91	98	137	161	203	227	181	152	118	66	159	1794	64.06

Other Instructional Expense

	Below 1%	1	2	3	4	5	6	7	8	9	10	11	12 & Over	Total	Mean
Elementary	13	11	77	253	315	301	241	118	90	36	14	5	17	1491	6.23
High School				1	2	4	21	42	52	45	33	15	17	232	8.74
Unified				1	3	5	22	32	15	9	7		1	95	7.72
All	13	11	77	255	320	310	284	192	157	90	54	20	37	1818	7.61

Operation

	Below 6%	6	7	8	9	10	11	12	13	14	15	16	17	18 & Over	Total	Mean
Elementary	57	45	86	155	235	211	200	151	102	63	44	44	31	48	1472	9.72
High School		2	5	16	35	46	37	42	20	17	7	3	1	1	232	10.22
Unified	1	2	1	6	21	28	17	9	6	2		1	1		95	9.97
All	58	49	92	177	291	285	254	202	128	82	51	48	33	49	1799	9.96

Maintenance

	Below 1%	1	2	3	4	5	6	7	8	9	10 11	12 13	14 & Over	Total	Mean
Elementary	185	309	273	229	133	84	56	55	35	16	32	20	45	1472	3.34
High School	2	13	31	53	49	32	20	13	7	5	5	2		232	4.65
Unified	2	7	16	25	26	10	4	2	2		1			95	4.23
All	189	329	320	307	208	126	80	70	44	21	38	22	45	1799	4.00

Transportation

	Below 2%	2 3	4 5	6 7	8 9	10 11	12 13	14 15	16 17	18 19	20 & Over	Total	Mean
Elementary	385	214	181	140	164	128	79	62	34	23	78	1488	3.44
High School	15	60	51	59	19	9	11	4		2	2	232	3.22
Unified	35	18	19	5	7	9		1		1		95	1.53
All	435	292	251	204	190	146	90	67	34	26	80	1815	2.71

Notes: The means shown in the "all" district row of each section include 23 separate junior college districts which are not included in "All" line of the frequency distributions.

The total number of districts in each section varies slightly because certain very small, and usually inoperative, elementary districts record no expenditure for that purpose.

Source: Distributions--Reference 8; Means--Reference 4.

Current Expense of Education per ADA by Size of District. The number of pupils being educated by a district bears an important relationship to the amount of expenditure required. An elementary district with less than twenty pupils, of which there are 212 in the state, must of necessity have a high cost per ADA since one teacher's salary will be divided among nineteen or fewer pupils. Most districts of this size are also wealthy, as shown in Tables 8.20 and 8.21.

For elementary districts the relationship depicted in Table 8.26 indicates that the size of the district is not important above the point at which one good-sized elementary school becomes possible. The large and overly large districts do not operate at a lower per pupil expense. A similar relationship exists for high schools, as shown in Table 8.27. The "L" shaped curve, similar to the elementary distribution, tends to straighten out at about the point at which the district is of sufficient size to operate a high school program without resorting to overly small classes.

Current Expense of Education per ADA by Wealth of District. Districts with varying amounts of wealth face a basic policy decision — shall the tax rate or the educational program be considered first? In poor districts little can be done to keep the tax rate low since even the most minimum of school programs requires a heavier than average tax burden. In wealthy districts there is an opportunity to keep the educational program below normal and thereby keep the tax rate even further below normal. The array of districts presented in Tables 8.26-30 indicates that the wealthy districts have not, in the main, elected this course but have chosen rather to support a higher level of current expense per ADA despite the accompanying higher tax rate effort. Among the more wealthy of these districts — those above $35,000 AV per ADA in which the qualifying tax rate will raise the amount of the foundation program without either basic or equalization aid from the state — current expense of education per ADA ranges from under $200 to over $1,000. These charts express graphically a story that would require many words: The wealth of a district is clearly reflected in its educational program. This fact emphasizes most dramatically the need for virtually perfect equalization if the children of the state are to have comparable educational opportunities.

The terms needed for a rigorous analysis of educational finance have now been defined and the impact of related factors has been presented in table, chart and text. The stage is set for detailed examination of current expenses of education.

Table 8.26. Current Expense of Education per ADA and Size of District: 1956-57. Elementary Districts.

Current Expense of Education per ADA (dollars)	Average Daily Attendance												Total
	0-25	26-50	51-75	76-100	101-400	401-900	901-2000	2001-4000	4001-6000	6001-8000	8001-16000	Over 16000	
1000 & Over	8	1	5	1									15
900-999	9	2	1		2								14
800-899	18		1	1	1								21
740-799	4				1								5
680-739	10	5	1		4								20
620-679	19	6	2	1									28
560-619	31	2	2	2	3								40
500-559	33	15	8	2	7		1						66
470-499	19	12	3	3		1	1						39
440-469	15	8	3	2	5	1	1	1					36
410-439	12	25	6	2	7		1						53
380-409	19	20	10	9	10	2	3	1					74
350-379	18	19	11	9	19	8	4	3					91
320-349	10	29	20	14	44	7	7	4	3	1	2		141
290-319	17	14	16	23	60	25	22	20	5	3	4	2	211
260-289	8	19	13	14	111	54	42	40	13	5	5	1	324
230-259	5	9	7	10	65	65	43	19	6	1	4		234
200-229	1	3	3	2	25	14	1	4					53
Under 200		1			2								3
Total	256	190	112	95	366	177	126	92	27	10	15	3	1469

Table 8.27. Current Expense of Education per ADA and Size of District: 1956-57. High School Districts

Current Expense of Education per ADA ($)	Average Daily Attendance												Total
	0-25	26-50	51-75	76-100	101-400	401-900	901-2000	2001-4000	4001-6000	6001-8000	8001-16000	Over 16000	
1000 & Over	1	1	2	1	2								7
900-999			1		1								2
800-899				1	2		1						4
740-799			2	1	1		1						5
680-739				2	7	2							11
620-679					9	3	1						13
560-619					7	2	3						12
500-559					15	8	5	2	2				32
470-499					3	8	4	1		1	4		21
440-469					5	12	7	7	5	2			38
410-439					4	10	13	6	1		1	1	36
380-409					3	7	9	5	5	1	2		32
350-379					1	3	6	3	1	2	1		17
Under 350						1		1					2
Total	1	1	5	5	60	56	50	25	14	6	8	1	232

Source of both tables--Reference 8.

Table 8.28. Assessed Valuation per ADA and Current Expense of Education per ADA: 1956-57. All Reporting Elementary Districts (N = 1,464)

Current Expense of Education per ADA ($)	Assessed Valuation per ADA (thousands of dollars)												Total
	0-4	5-9	10-14	15-19	20-24	25-29	30-34	35-39	40-44	45-49	50-99	100& Over	
1,000 & Over		1		1							2	8	12
900-999		1			1	1	1				2	8	14
800-899			2		1	1	1		1	2	4	9	21
700-799				1	1	1	1	1		1	7	5	18
600-699			2	3	2	4	2	2	2	1	19	7	44
550-599	1	1	2	4	3	3	4	2	2		12	4	38
500-549		2	6	3	6	3	8	2	4	6	13	5	58
450-499		4	15	6	5	4	4	4	4	3	11	2	62
400-449		5	14	10	12	19	11	9	5	7	10		102
350-399	2	14	23	21	12	14	16	6	9	4	12		133
300-349	7	60	74	55	36	17	6	4	5	2	1		267
250-299	72	220	139	45	17	3	4		4	1	3		508
200-249	50	91	35	7		1							184
Under 200	1			1				1					3
Total	133	399	312	157	96	71	58	31	36	27	96	48	1464

Table 8.29. Assessed Valuation per ADA and Current Expense of Education per ADA, 1956-57. Elementary Districts 0-100 ADA (N=638)

	Assessed Valuation per ADA (thousands of dollars)												Total
	0-4	5-9	10-14	15-19	20-24	25-29	30-34	35-39	40-44	45-49	50-99	100 & Over	
1,000 & Over													0
900-999												2	2
800-899												1	1
700-799											1	3	4
600-699						1						1	2
550-599											1		2
500-549			1				2	1	1		2	1	8
450-499			1	1		2			2		2		8
400-449		1	1	5	1	1	2	1		1	2		15
350-399		3	10	8	4	4	2		2		1		34
300-349	3	25	33	25	14	3			1				104
250-299	29	114	96	22	6	2			1				270
200-249	27	49	24	3									103
Under 200	1			1									2
Total	60	192	166	65	25	13	7	2	7	1	9	8	555

Source of both tables: Reference 8.

Table 8.28 shows all elementary districts and the absence of a clear relationship is evident. On the other hand, Table 8.29 for over 500 medium-sized districts exhibits a striking relationship.

Table 8.30. Assessed Valuation per ADA and Current Expenses of Education per ADA, 1956-57: High School Districts (N=232)

Current Expense of Educ. per ADA ($)	Assessed Valuation per ADA (thousands of dollars)												Total
	0-19	20-24	25-29	30-34	35-39	40-44	45-49	50-54	55-59	60-79	80-99	100 & Over	
900 & Over										2	1	4	7
800-899					2		1		1			2	6
700-799					2	1	1			3	2	1	10
650-699					2	2	2	2	1	4			13
600-649			1		1	1	1	2		1	1		8
550-599		1		2	1	2		1		2	1		10
500-549	2		4	6	3	5	2	3	5		1	1	32
450-499	2	6	8	13	12	3	3	1					48
400-449	3	11	14	15	4	3	4	2					56
350-399	7	12	10	5	4	2							40
Under 350		1	1										2
Total	14	31	38	41	31	19	14	11	7	12	6	8	232

Source: Reference 8

Economic, Demographic and Fiscal Factors Related to CEE

The following analysis covers all school districts of all types and all ADA K-14 credited to them. It does not, however, include the costs of the offices of county superintendents or of special state schools, or those of the University of California and the state colleges. The basic data presented in Table 8.31a are from officially published reports of CEE and the ADA benefiting from these costs. Some of these data are available in published form only for calendar years rather than school years. All such material has been interpolated on a straight line basis to yield half-year figures to conform with school year data. The more significant interrelationships among these basic data are included in b of the summary table. The tabular presentation is completed with c which converts the previous material to an index using 1939-40 as the base year. The index is graphically presented in Figure 8.5. The resulting 27 year time series is, within the limits of space, interpreted below.

Total CEE in Current Dollars and in Dollars of Constant Value (Columns a and i). The gross amount of CEE increased from $125 million in 1929-30 to over $950 million in 1956-57. This increase, in

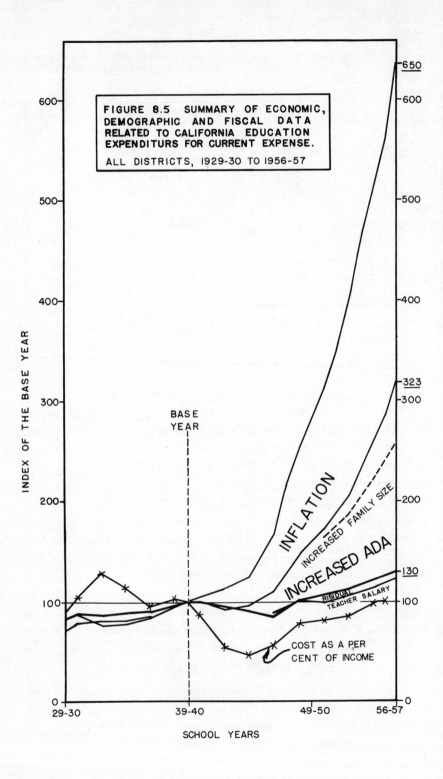

FIGURE 8.5 SUMMARY OF ECONOMIC, DEMOGRAPHIC AND FISCAL DATA RELATED TO CALIFORNIA EDUCATION EXPENDITURS FOR CURRENT EXPENSE.

ALL DISTRICTS, 1929-30 TO 1956-57

current dollars, represents an index of 650 starting with 100 for the
base year, 1939-40. However, in 1956-57 it took $2.01 to buy what
$1.00 bought in 1939-40 according to the Consumer Price Index. Thus
much of the increase is attributable to inflation. To correct for this
decreased value of the dollar, the total amounts of CEE have been deflated using the above price index and are shown as Column g in Table
8.31a. This adjustment accounts for more than half of the increase since
the base year. The index for CEE in standard dollars is 323 compared
to 650 prior to adjustment for inflation. (See Table 8.31c.) The above
adjustment does not, however, consider the great increases in the
number of children receiving the benefits of these expenditures.

Effect of Increased Family Size on Increased ADA. The population growth which has brought increased numbers of children into California's schools has involved marked changes in age composition during
the 27-year period under study. In the base year 1939-40 there were
236 units of ADA for every 1,000 persons age 18-64; by 1956-57 this
ratio had climbed to 348. Although various minor factors affect this relationship (e.g., parochial school enrollments and changes in methods
of counting ADA) the change is so striking that specific analysis was
considered worthwhile. In Column t an estimate of "normal" ADA computed on the proportion prevailing the base year (.236) is presented for
each year for which estimates of the 18-64 population are available.
This computation permits a graphic indication of the effect of family
size as shown in Figure 8.5. Although a unit of ADA may seem to be
just that, one that is created by increased family size brings with it no
additional wage earner and no increase in assessed valuation. On the
other hand, increases in ADA attributed to in-migration of population
probably are accompanied by increased income and assessed valuation.

Current Expense of Education per ADA in Constant Dollars. This
more meaningful figure is presented for the 27 years under study in
Column j. Expressed as an index of the base year it was 130 in 1956-57
(see Column x). The original 650 index for total CEE has been reduced
to 130 by adjustment for these two basic factors: inflation and increasing ADA. Inspection of columns j and x will show that this increase has
not been constant since 1929-30. On the contrary, the depression and
the immediate postwar years were periods of declining CEE per ADA.

Increases in Median Teacher Salaries. The 30% increase in CEE
after adjustment for inflation and increased ADA is due to several factors.
The dominant role of teacher salaries in CEE is clearly shown in Table
8.25 and Figure 8.4; it was over 64% in 1956-57. Increases in CEE per
ADA are likely to be attributable to increases in teacher salaries more

Table 8.31a. Summary of Economic, Demographic, and Fiscal Data Related to Educational Expenditures, 1929-30 — 1956-57. Part I. Basic Data

Year	CEE	ADA	Population Total	Population 18-64	Population 5-17	Personal Income	BLS Index	Median Teacher Salary
Column	a	b	c	d	e	f	g	h
Units			Thousands			Millions	47-49= 100	Dollars
1929-30	$123,867	942	5,677	3,766	1,139	$5,290	71.0	
30-31	129,147	978				4,713	66.7	
31-32	127,265	1,008				3,864	60.7	
32-33	112,513	1,026				3,304	56.6	
33-34	110,403	1,034				3,408	55.7	
34-35	113,606	1,011				3,805	57.0	
35-36	118,582	1,020				4,418	57.8	
36-37	123,709	1,045				4,974	59.3	
37-38	132,995	1,075				5,110	60.4	
38-39	140,065	1,101				5,172	59.8	
1939-40	146,073	1,105	6,907	4,671	1,228	5,548	59.6	
40-41	151,814	1,121	6,979			6,585	61.2	
41-42	161,328	1,131	7,173			8,670	66.7	
42-43	164,936	1,083	7,433			11,645	72.6	
43-44	172,451	1,127	7,826			13,967	75.4	
44-45	183,118	1,175	8,303			14,923	77.2	
45-46	202,488	1,243	8,910			15,639	81.4	
46-47	243,889	1,433	9,485			16,360	90.0	$2,793
47-48	315,212	1,519	9,783			17,123	99.0	3,321
48-49	369,005	1,615	10,028			17,722	102.2	3,583
1949-50	410,263	1,716	10,299	6,568	1,920	18,731	102.3	3,638
50-51	452,119	1,781	10,559	6,721	2,100	21,176	106.8	3,667
51-52	507,311	1,902	10,990	6,963	2,302	23,907	112.8	3,990
52-53	580,249	2,033	11,523	7,176	2,479	25,865	115.2	4,266
53-54	674,597	2,203	12,001			26,895	116.0	4,587
54-55	742,158	2,376	12,476	7,388	2,651	28,293	115.8	4,707
55-56	823,046	2,546	12,979	7,618	2,821	30,969	116.8	4,887
56-57	950,214	2,744	13,545	7,883	3,005		120.0	5,163

Sources for Table 8.31:

Column	Reference
a & b	18, 4
c, d & e	Table 8.3
f	27
g	Table 2.6
h	10

Other Columns derived as shown.

Table 8.31b. Summary of Economic, Demographic, and Fiscal Data Related to Educational Expenditures, 1929-30 — 1956-57. Part II. Relationships of Basic Data

Year	CEE BLS	CEE BLS ADA	CEE BLS 18-64	PI BLS	PI BLS ADA	PI BLS Capita	PI BLS 18-64	PI BLS 5-17	ADA 18-64	Median Teacher Salary BLS
Column	i	j	k	l	m	n	o	p	q	r
Derivation	a/g	i/b	i/d	f/g	l/b	l/c	l/d	l/e	b/d	h/g
Units	thousands	dollars	dollars	millions	dollars	dollars	dollars			dollars
1929-30	$174,460	$185.20	$46.32	$7,451	$7,909	$1,313	$1,978	$6,452	.250	
30-31	193,623	197.98		7,066	7,225					
31-32	209,662	207.99		6,366	6,315					
32-33	198,786	193.75		5,837	5,689					
33-34	198,210	191.69		6,118	6,917					
34-35	199,309	197.14		6,675	6,603					
35-36	205,159	201.14		7,643	7,493					
36-37	208,615	199.63		8,388	8,027					
37-38	220,190	240.83		8,460	7,869					
38-39	234,222	212.74		8,649	7,856					
1939-40	245,089	221.79	52.47	9,309	8,424	1,347	1,993	7,581	.236	
40-41	240,062	221.29		10,760	9,598	1,542				
41-42	241,871	213.85		12,998	11,493	1,812				
42-43	227,184	209.77		16,040	14,810	2,158				
43-44	228,715	202.94		18,524	16,436	2,367				
44-45	237,199	201.88		19,330	16,451	2,328				
45-46	248,757	200.12		19,212	15,457	2,156				
46-47	270,988	189.10		18,178	12,686	1,916				$3,103
47-48	318,396	209.61		17,296	11,387	1,768				3,355
48-49	361,062	223.57		17,340	10,737	1,729				3,505
1949-50	401,044	233.70	64.45	18,310	10,671	1,778	3,019	10,327	.271	3,556
50-51	423,332	237.70	66.92	19,828	11,133	1,878	3,153	10,092	.283	3,434
51-52	449,744	236.46	72.34	21,194	11,143	1,928	3,224	9,753	.291	3,537
52-53	503,688	247.76	81.04	22,452	11,044	1,948	3,231	9,353	.307	3,703
53-54	531,549	263.98		23,185	10,524	1,932				3,954
54-55	640,896	269.74	86.75	24,433	10,283	1,958	3,307	9,217	.322	4,065
55-56	704,663	276.77	92.50	26,514	10,414	2,043	3,480	9,399	.334	4,184
56-57	791,845	288.57	100.45						.348	4,303

Table 8.31c. Summary of Economic, Demographic, and Fiscal Data Related to Educational
Expenditures, 1929-30 — 1956-57

Part II cont.   Part III. Key Factors Expressed in Index Form, 1939-40=100

Year	CEE/PI	"Normal" ADA	"Normal" ADA/ADA	Total CEE	CEE/BLS	CEE BLS/ADA	Teacher Salary BLS	Residual	CEE/PI
Column	s	t	u	v	w	x	y	z	aa
Derivation	a/f	.236d	t/b	a	i	j	r	x-y	s
Units	%	thousands	%			1939-40 data used as divisors as an index with 1939-40=100				
1929-30	2.34%	889	94.4%	85	71	83			89
30-31	2.74			88	79	89			104
31-32	3.29			87	86	94			125
32-33	3.41			77	81	87			130
33-34	3.24			76	81	86			123
34-35	2.99			78	81	89			114
35-36	2.68			81	84	91			102
36-37	2.49			85	85	90			95
37-38	2.60			91	90	92			99
38-39	2.71			96	96	96			103
1939-40	2.63	1,102	99.7	100	100	100			100
40-41	2.31			104	101	100			88
41-42	1.86			110	99	96			71
42-43	1.42			113	93	95			54
43-44	1.23			118	93	91			47
44-45	1.23			125	97	91			47
45-46	1.29			139	101	90			49
46-47	1.49			167	111	85	89	-4	57
47-48	1.84			216	130	94	97	-3	70
48-49	2.08			253	147	101	101	0	79
1949-50	2.19	1,550	87.0	281	164	105	102	3	83
50-51	2.13	1,586	83.4	310	173	107	99	8	81
51-52	2.12	1,643	80.8	347	183	107	102	5	81
52-53	2.24	1,694	76.9	397	206	112	107	5	85
53-54	2.51			462	237	119	114	5	95
54-55	2.62	1,744	73.4	508	261	122	114	8	100
55-56	2.66	1,798	70.6	563	288	125	121	4	101
56-57	-	1,860	67.8	650	323	130	124	6	-

than to any other factor. Median teacher salary data, available only for
the years 1946-47 to the present, are presented in current dollars in
Column h, in dollars of constant value in Column r and as an index of the
the base year in Column y. These estimates — and they must be designated estimates both because they are medians and because 1948-49
was employed to establish a base comparable to 1939-40 — produce an
index of 124 for 1956-57 accounting for four-fifths of the increase in
CEE per ADA (24/30).

Other Factors Influencing Current Expense of Education per ADA.
The residual increase due to other factors becomes then the difference
between 130 and 124 or 6 points of the 650 total. (See Figure 8.5.) This
difference is presented in Column z for the years for which teacher
salary data are available. The indeterminant status of these remaining
factors is an excellent example of the need for basic research in education so that all factors may be thoroughly examined. The increase due
to these factors has been negligible and has remained relatively constant for the past seven years. Some possible components of this
residual are listed below:

      1. Changes in class size. In 1946-47 and 1947-48 costs
decreased per ADA while teachers' salaries increased. It is
highly probable that increases in class size occurred during
these years to enable salaries to go up. During other years
changes in class size may well have occurred which would compound the problem of analysis. Suffice it to say that the two most
important factors contributing to school costs — mean salary
per position and the mean number of positions per child — are
not known. Both are essential to exact analysis.

      2. Changes in the cost of supplies and equipment which are
not in accord with changes in the general cost of living.

      3. Inclusion of new and more costly services in the normal
educational program, for example, driver-training.

Relationship of Personal Income to Current Expense of Education. Finally, the most significant statistical measure of all is the relationship between income and school costs. This factor is shown as
an index in Column aa in Part III of Table 8.31c and in Figure 8.5.
Since 1929 the index has ranged from 130 to 46 with the high in 1932-33
and the low in 1943-44 and 1944-45. As of 1956-57 it was 101. This index was 100 in 1939-40, when 2.63% of personal income was spent on
the current expenses of public schools. In 1955-56 we were spending
2.66% (101 x 2.63% = 2.66%). Thus, huge as school costs are, the
percentage of California's income so spent is relatively small. In a
very real sense, education pays for itself and more, for ability to
produce income depends upon education and vice versa. The dollar
that goes for education is, however, a dollar that should yield a maxi-

mum return. Greater fiscal efficiency and equity are therefore the
chief concerns of the next chapter.

Capital Outlay Costs

The preceding pages have been devoted to examining the current
expenses of education. They comprise the major, but not by any means
the total, costs of education. The construction and equipment of buildings is a continuing problem of great magnitude.

Types and Purposes of Capital Outlay. All capital outlays may
be divided into two major classes: (1) housing for growth in enrollment,
which on the state level includes not only net in-migration but also
intrastate migration necessitating additional school construction, and
(2) replacement of existing facilities. There has been a minimum of
the latter during the last decade but this will become a major problem
in the years to come. An estimate of the magnitude of the replacement
problem is included in Chapter 9.

Districts do not report these two types of expenditures separately.
They are simply required to classify capital outlay into four divisions
on the basis of purpose: (1) land, (2) improvement of grounds, (3)
building construction, and (4) equipment. The proportions of expenditures made for each of these classifications in 1956-57 is presented in
Part II of Table 8.32.

Sources of Funds for Capital Outlay. The state does not play as
large a role in assisting districts on capital outlays as it does in providing funds for current expense. About 70% of all capital improvements
made in 1956-57 were district-financed; state aid covered only the remaining 30%. Prior to the postwar period capital outlay was almost exclusively a local function. It must also be remembered that most state
aid for capital outlay, unlike state aid for current expense, is in the
nature of a loan and must be repaid if it is within the ability of the district to do so.

As enrollment growth and increased construction costs per square
foot have created more and more severe capital outlay problems in districts, the state has aided local districts by floating several major state
bond issues. Expenditures from these state funds as well as expenditures
by districts from their general and building funds are presented for the
period 1945-46 to date in Part I of Table 8.32 and in Figure 8.6. The
two larger state funds are in the Public School Building Fund and the
State School Building Fund.

District capital outlays may be made from the general fund de-

Table 8.32 Expenditures for Capital Outlay by School Districts, by Funds: 1945-46 to 1956-57
Part I. Amounts by Fund, 1945-46 to 1956-57 (thousands of dollars)

Year	District Funds		State Funds				Total All Funds	Local as % of Total
	General Fund	Building Fund	Special Accumulative Bldg. Fund	Emergency School Bldg. Fund	Public School Bldg. Fund	State School Bldg. Fund		
Column	a	b	c	d	e	f	g	h $(a+b)/g$
1945-46	13,153	2,626	968				16,747	94.2
46-47	15,531	14,826	5,289				35,646	85.2
47-48	28,586	52,922	4,564	795			86,866	93.8
48-49	38,034	98,035	3,109	19,472			158,649	85.8
1949-50	43,140	113,520	3,069	25,025			184,754	84.8
50-51	47,781	116,992	3,327	13,279	17,962		199,340	82.6
51-52	43,596	104,540	1,484	3,831	86,155		239,605	61.8
52-53	48,146	138,667	247	1,614	101,292	25	291,990	64.0
53-54	55,192	169,029	670	215	41,139	13,327	282,572	79.4
54-55	61,140	189,582	3,650	77	7,341	57,065	318,855	78.6
55-56	57,004	195,978	2,946		1,180	86,404	343,512	73.6
56-57	59,788	215,133	2,738		283	116,442	394,384	69.7

Part II. Percent by Sub-Class, by Fund, 1956-57

Class	a	b	c	e	f	g
Land	6.4	9.2			11.0	9.3
Improvement of Grounds	12.9	5.0	.5		.8	4.9
Buildings	41.9	80.0	95.3	99.3	85.5	75.9
equipment	33.7	5.9	4.2	.5	2.7	9.9

Source: Part I, 1945-46 to 1954-55--Reference 5; 1955-56 and 1956-57--Reference 26.
Part II--Reference 11.

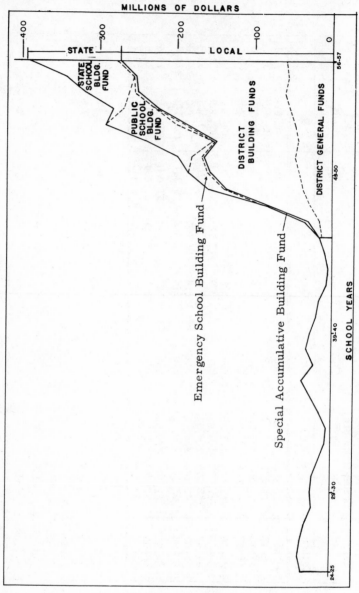

Figure 8.6. Expenditures for Capital Outlay by Fund, 1924-25 to 1956-57

Source: Conforms to Tables 8.32 and 8.33

Table 8.33. Total Expenditures for Capital Outlay by California School Districts, 1924-25--1956-57, with Expenditures Adjusted for Changing Construction Costs

| Year | In Current Dollars | | Construction Cost Index (1947-49=100) | Annual Total in Constant Dollars |
	Annual	Cumulative		
Column	a	b	c	d (a/c)
Units	All amounts in thousands of dollars			
1924-25	$36,874	$36,874	51.5	$71,600
25-26	41,662		51.0	81,690
26-27	39,065		51.0	76,598
27-28	33,897		51.0	66,465
28-29	24,897		51.5	48,344
1929-30	26,054	202,449	51.0	51,086
30-31	24,176		48.0	50,367
31-32	16,115		43.0	37,477
32-33	7,940		41.5	19,133
33-34	6,877		45.5	15,114
34-35	16,202	273,759	47.5	34,109
35-36	28,472		47.5	59,941
36-37	38,605		49.5	77,990
37-38	23,699		51.5	46,017
38-39	32,944		50.5	65,236
1939-40	27,858	425,337	49.5	56,279
40-41	20,288		52.0	39,015
41-42	16,990		57.5	29,548
42-43	7,022		63.0	11,146
43-44	5,081		64.5	7,878
44-45	8,674	483,392	65.5	13,243
45-46	16,747		72.0	23,360
46-47	35,646		85.0	41,936
47-48	86,866		97.5	89,093
48-49	158,649		103.5	153,284
1949-50	184,754	966,054	105.0	175,956
50-51	199,340		111.5	178,780
51-52	239,605		117.5	203,919
52-53	291,990		120.5	242,315
53-54	282,572		122.0	231,616
54-55	318,855	2,298,416	123.5	258,182
55-56	343,512		128.5	$267,324
56-57	$394,384	$3,036,312	NA	

Sources: Cols. a & b--1924-25 to 1954-55, Reference 5; 1955-56 & 1956-57, Reference 26.

Col. c--Reference 29 (Department of Commerce Composite interpolated to school years).

rived from the sale of bonds and federal grants. In the more distant
past much capital outlay was made from the general fund but increasingly the sale of bonds has been necessary to meet local building needs
(compare columns a and b of Table 8.32). The general fund is traditionally used for the purchase of equipment while the building fund and state
aid are used mainly for the actual construction of buildings (compare
Column a with columns b and f of Part II of Table 8.32).

The federal government provides assistance to districts in impacted areas through Public Law 815 which serves a purpose in the
field of capital outlay similar to that of Public Law 874 with regard to
current expenses. Expenditures of these federal funds are not separately accounted for since they are included in the building fund of districts. An estimate of the importance of this source may be made from
the fact that of total revenue to the building funds of all California's
school districts in 1956-57, 5.1% was derived from federal subventions.

Amounts Expended for Capital Outlay. Complete data for the
past 32 years are included in Table 8.33 and in Figure 8.6. Very large
sums of money are represented by the curve in this latter diagram.
During the 32-year period shown, more than $3 billion have been ex-
pended. As was seen previously, decreased enrollment growth is not
anticipated so that the upward slope of the curve is destined to continue.

Much of the increase in capital expenditures may be attributed to
rising construction costs. In recent years increases in construction
costs have been more marked than increases in the Consumer Price
Index used to deflate increases in current expenses. In 1955-56 the
construction cost index was 128.5 compared to 116.8 for the Consumer
Price Index. (Both indices use the same base year; compare Column g,
Table 8.31 with Column c, Table 8.33.) The effect on total capital outlay of rising construction costs is reflected in Column d of Table 8.33.

In the preceding pages we have presented many facts essential to
an understanding of the current status of local and state support for
public education in California. Relationships of population, enrollment
and income to revenues and expenditures for education have been described. The next chapter will propose several ways of achieving
greater efficiency in the use of both state and district funds. The fore-
seeably necessary expenditures for education are truly tremendous.
When viewed in the light of recent increases in costs they provide
compelling reasons for demanding a fiscal system of maximum efficiency.

*   *   *

Bibliography and references for Chapter 8 are consolidated with
those for Chapter 9 at the end of Chapter 9.

The great doctrine, which it is desirable to maintain, and to carry out in reference to this subject is equality of school privileges for all children of the town, whether they belong to a poor district or a rich one, a small district or a large one.

The highest talents and attainments must be culled for superintending the mind of the race, during the period when it is most susceptible to influence. — Horace Mann, 1849

NEED OF A BLUEPRINT

Qualitative analysis of the data contained in the preceding chapter would require a comprehensive statement of standards, for only with a model could actual practice be compared with the best practice possible. Such a model should represent the best thinking of professionals and citizens alike but at present we do not have one. Therefore, we do not have adequate answers to such questions as: What is the best organizational pattern for education? What class size is best for each age and subject matter? How should teachers' salaries be established? What is the optimal range of district sizes? What are the proper functions of state law and state regulation? To what extent should these be restrictive or permissive? What is the ideal pattern of support for each grade level? To what extent should local districts depend upon the state for support? For which functions should the public schools be primarily and for which only partially responsible? What things should schools not attempt to do? To what extent should diversity of practice be encouraged — with the inevitable result of excellence in some districts and inferiority in others? How much leeway should be allowed in compliance with state standards?

Research as a Tool

Educational policy should be formulated with the full benefit of statistical data and research findings, not only from within education in the strict sense of the term, but also from related academic fields and other branches of government. More uniform and complete reporting of statistical data would be of great aid in policy formulation. We do not know, for example, either the number of positions or the mean salary per position throughout the state, or how costs vary by level in unified districts where there is freedom of choice in expenditures among grade levels. An annual or biennial report on education should be published by the Superintendent of Public Instruction. The analyses and forecasts by the State Department of Finance, some of which have been utilized in this study, would be of interest to many. Studies by private organizations often duplicate each other and sometimes, while similar, are not comparable for technical reasons. There is not now any one published comprehensive statement of information on the California public school system.

Modern Techniques. Methods of data collection and analysis have changed profoundly and dramatically within the last few years. By using punched cards and high-speed computing machines, information could be made available a few days after it was collected, whereas many of the methods now in use involve delays of months between data collection and publication. With modern equipment there is no longer any technical reason for a delay of one year in the apportionment of state funds to districts. In fact, quarterly or even monthly apportionments would be possible.

Lack of Research. Some of the most elemental educational policy problems have not been attacked except in very small-scale studies, and usually the results have been inconclusive. Three major reasons account for the limited nature and value of this research. The first is the lack of adequate statistical methods, and the second is the forbidding amount of labor involved in calculations when many factors are to be measured. Both of these problems have been partially or wholly solved. Some of the big problems can now be brought under the scrutiny of research. The third reason is still with us, namely, the failure to initiate, finance, and maintain adequate research. The expenditure of a billion dollars a year for schools would appear to justify more research than is now undertaken. If industry employed as little research as does education, we might still be using the spinning wheels, horse collars, and kerosene lamps of our grandfathers' day. One of the reasons for passing fads in educational practice is that new ideas are not given a thorough experimental trial before being put into widespread use. In the paragraphs that follow we have stated briefly some of the major problems and cost factors having important implicati ns for fiscal policy.

Persistent Policy Problems

Class Size. About $20 to $25 million dollars per year would be required to reduce average class size in the state by one child (excluding the additional cost of new buildings needed). Class size is generally largest in the elementary school and diminishes at the higher levels. This may, however, be due to increasing specialization of subject matter more than to the learning-teaching factor. From some points of view it would seem more reasonable that the younger and less mature

child would require smaller classes. Much of the research on the problem of class size is conflicting and controversial. One idea is that
small classes permit a teacher to use a variety of methods and that as
classes become larger the teacher is more and more restricted to
methods of mass instruction. Certainly the amount of individual attention decreases as class size increases. It may be that the classroom
with one teacher may be less effective than a team of six or eight
teachers and a group of, say, 200 children. Such a plan may afford
more flexibility and effectiveness. A small-scale try-out of this plan
is now being made through the Claremont Graduate School under a
grant from the Fund for the Advancement of Education.

Class size is one of the problems that has been "solved" by assuming that tradition approximates best practice. Hundreds of millions
of dollars worth of buildings have been built to house the traditional
thirty-five children per room. Obviously a better orientation to this
problem would be relevant to fiscal policy.

Teachers' Salaries. The fact that many teachers make a lifetime
career of teaching results in a lag of from ten to twenty years between
the effect of salary inducements as a selective factor in recruiting
teachers and the average competency of the teaching force as a whole.
The law of supply and demand has doubtless had a major effect on the
salaries of teachers, for during the depression teachers were actually paying for jobs and bidding against each other for positions. Now,
however, districts are bidding against each other in what might be
called a "bull" market. But the supply and demand process has serious
defects. Under this system, discriminating selection occurs when jobs
are scarce and salaries are low; conversely, when teachers are scarce
and prices are high there is less selectivity, and persons of marginal
competence are employed. In short, quality and price are inversely
related whereas the opposite relationship would result in better schools.

The proposition that instructional salaries should be a matter of
public policy rather than a consequence either of the pressure of
teacher organizations or of supply and demand deserves earnest consideration. It is neither likely nor desirable that group pressures or
supply and demand will ever cease to influence salary schedules and
thus, to some degree, both selection and competency. But from the
point of view of the public interest there remains the problem of
attracting the quality and quantity of persons whom we desire as teachers in the public schools. We have no basic policy concerning this
problem at the present time.

Population and Teacher Recruitment. Population changes inevitably involve public school policy. With each increase in enrollment, teacher recruitment is made from an adult age group that is relatively smaller than the school age group. Should the public schools accept all the children and hire additional instructors thus lowering standards of teacher competency? Should they increase class size? Or should they enroll only as many children as they are adequately staffed to teach? In medicine, for example, the last course would probably be chosen. Public education, however, is following the first course since we have apparently assumed that every child has a right to attend school and that a poor teacher is better than no teacher. The fact is, however, that no specific policy on this problem was ever made.

Elementary-Secondary Enrollment Ratio. Another fiscal problem related to population growth is that as a wave of children enters school initial costs are not as great as they will be later, since elementary costs are lower than those at the high school level. Within about six years (see the "wave" line in Table 8.5) the current expenses of the public schools in this state will have increased about $114 million due to this factor alone. The formula for calculating the effect of this factor on total cost is as follows:

$$\text{Predicted Cost} = \text{Total Cost (Reference Year)} \times \frac{R_o}{R_1}$$

R_o = Proportion elementary cost is of total cost for reference year;

R_1 = Proportion elementary cost is for year to be predicted;

and

$$R_o = \frac{p_o K_o}{q_o + p_o K_o}, \qquad R_1 = \frac{p_1 K_o}{q_1 + p_1 K_o},$$

where:

p = Proportion elementary ADA is of total ADA;

q = 1.00 - p;

K_o = Ratio of elementary costs per ADA to high school costs per ADA in base period;

K_1 = Ratio of elementary costs per ADA to high school costs per ADA for predicted period (use in formula for R_1 if this factor is a variable).

In California the following apply:

	p	q	K_o	R_o	R_1	R_o/R_1
1946-47	.645	.355	.584	(.544)		
1956-57	.703	.297	.657	.6086		
1965	.645	.355			.544	1.119

The last column indicates that an 11.9% increase in school costs may be anticipated when the crest of the student wave reaches high school in the middle 1960's. Thus an increase in current expenses of about $114 million ($950 million x .12) may be ascribed to this <u>one cause alone.</u>

ADMINISTRATIVE CONTROLS

While the value of the educational dollar depends upon many intangibles, it is nonetheless true that to a considerable extent economy and efficiency can be assessed. Several means of evaluation and control are indicated below.

1. <u>Educational Cost Index.</u> In most studies, as in this one, the Consumer Price Index is used to estimate changes in dollar value. Yet there is evidence to indicate that this index may introduce a considerable amount of error. Certainly this is true of supplies, transportation, and equipment. And there is no assurance that the cost of living of school employees necessarily follows the Consumer Price Index pattern. Moreover, differences in urban and rural living costs may mask the equivalence of presumably competitive salary schedules. An index of educational costs would be costly to establish and maintain but its benefits might well outweigh its price. An exploratory study of this problem should be made.

2. <u>School Construction Cost Index.</u> It is also quite likely that the cost of school construction does not follow the pattern of general construction costs. An index of such costs would be far simpler to compose and maintain than the index proposed above, and its feasibility should be investigated.

3. <u>Business Practices Clearing House.</u> Some superintendents and business managers have discovered superior methods in business and management. The State Department of Education could well be responsible for communicating better practices to school districts generally.

4. <u>Local Standards and Budgetary Policy.</u> A budget may be regarded as a monetary plan for obtaining the objectives of the school system. These objectives should be stated in terms of policies, operating procedures, and a specific program of services and <u>instruction</u> in the schools. These policies will be the standards of the system stated in terms of salary, class size, and numbers of counsellors and librarians as well as of specific types of instruction in mathematics, reading, science, and so on. Thus, the budget can and should be, in

part, a statement of what it would cost to carry out the publicly agreed-upon objectives, policies and program of the school district. Provision should be made in the budget for indicating costs based on policy standards.

Changes in the budget imply corresponding changes in objectives and policies or in the number of children served and proposed changes should therefore indicate how the school program will be affected. This information should be made public. At this point public policy in education and fiscal policy are joined. The people and their representatives, the board of education, should weigh the value of a given policy or practice against its cost in dollars. When the budget is obscure or when there are few or no written policies, when a cut or an increase is not explained in terms of instruction and services, it is nearly impossible for anyone to know whether it makes sense or not.

Perhaps nothing would aid in evaluating educational expenditures so much as to have: (1) a rational model issued at the state level representing the best policies and practices; (2) written local policies indicating the operating standards of the district; (3) budgets so structured that they indicate their relationship to policy standards and to the teaching realities in individual schools; and (4) public budgetary confirmation as an act of purchase by the public of a program of education.

FISCAL EFFICIENCY VERSUS LOCAL INITIATIVE

The complexities of the fiscal and organizational problems of education in California arise from several conditions. First, both wealth and population are unequally distributed with respect to area. There are high and low densities of each. Second, there is a low correspondence between the concentrations of wealth and of population. Third, the greater the number of local governmental units, the greater is the likelihood of accentuatung differences between areas of density of population and areas of concentrated wealth. These relationships account for greatly differing ratios of population to wealth among the state's approximately 1,800 school districts — over 7,000 to 1, for example, among elementary districts (see Table 8.19).

Variability in Wealth and Possible Compensations

Given these conditions, the variability in assessed wealth per child largely depends upon the number of local school districts, as Table 8.17 illustrates very clearly. As the number of such subdivisions decreases, the range of differences decreases and the wealth of each approaches the state mean. Obviously the state itself would provide the most stable unit from the standpoint of the taxpayer. The next least variable subdivisions would be, in order, regions, (see Figure 9.1 for the nine-region map of the state used by the Department of Finance for statistical purposes), counties, community or unified districts, and elementary districts. Local fiscal variability in wealth per child may be compensated for by any one or several combinations of the five methods outlined below.

High Percentage of Central Support. The formula for measuring fiscal inequality among school districts under various proportions of central and local support is given below (central support is presumed to be on a flat-grant basis):

$$ \underline{I} = \frac{(\underline{R} - \underline{P}) \times \underline{L}}{(\underline{R} \times \underline{L}) \quad (\underline{S} \times \underline{C})} \times 100, $$

where:

$\underline{I}$	=	Percentage of inequality in support;
$\underline{R}$	=	Wealth per ADA of richest area;
$\underline{P}$	=	Wealth per ADA of poorest area;
$\underline{L}$	=	Proportions of local support;
$\underline{S}$	=	State mean wealth per ADA;
$\underline{C}$	=	Proportion of central support on a flat grant basis.

Applied to California the formula gives the following results:

Organizational Unit	Percentage of inequality based on 50% of state support
Elementary Districts	11,041%
Community or Unified Districts	580
Counties (all)	399
Counties (all except the five very wealthiest counties, all of which are also very small) *	75
Regions	32

* The counties excluded are Alpine, Mono, Plumas, Colusa and Amador which have a combined ADA of 8,106, less than 1/2 of 1% of the state total.

It is instructive to note that if, among elementary districts, a toleration of no more than 10% inequality were to be allowed, state support would have to be increased to over 99.9%. Central support on a flat grant basis amounts, in effect, to equalization by collection of taxes rather than by the variable disbursement of tax funds.

Equalizing Central Support. State funds allocated to subdivisions in inverse proportion to wealth have the effect of increasing the resources of the poorer districts and decreasing those of the wealthier ones. Flat grants, on the other hand, except for the differential in

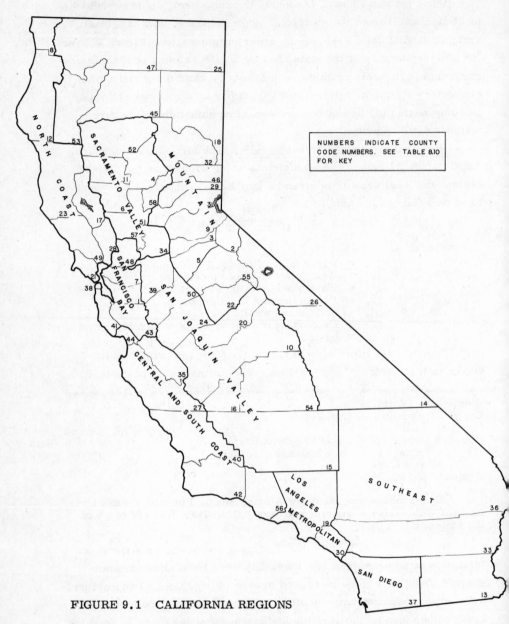

NUMBERS INDICATE COUNTY
CODE NUMBERS. SEE TABLE 8.10
FOR KEY

FIGURE 9.1 CALIFORNIA REGIONS

(utilized for statistical purposes by the
State Department of Finance)

collecting more from the wealthy than from the poor, raise the effective fiscal level of both those of high and of low wealth. But the inequitable differences in wealth remain. The greater the proportion of state funds equalized, the less will be the amount of state funds required to reduce inequality among its subdivisions. The higher the local district tax rate in an equalization formula, the larger will be the proportion of state funds allocated to poor districts. Conversely, the lower the district tax rate, the broader will be the distribution of funds, and the nearer to a flat-grant basis it becomes.

Fewer Districts. Increasing the size and decreasing the number of subdivisions would also reduce the need for a high proportion of state funds. In other words it is possible to organize in such a way as to minimize variability in wealth.

Variable Tax Rates. Higher tax rates in poorer districts and lower tax rates in wealthier districts afford another means of obtaining comparable levels of support.

Combining Methods. In the apportionment proposal developed later in this chapter, all methods outlined above are employed for operating costs up to the state average but only the last is employed for costs above the state mean.

The State-Local District Dilemma

Although the state would be the most efficient and equitable unit for financing public education, several considerations make a single state educational system undesirable. Local school districts have the advantage of providing for adaptability to local needs, encouraging diversity that often leads to better practice, and heightening the interest of the local community.

Optimum Size of District. According to the evidence, the advantages of local districts are not directly proportional to size, for there is an optimum range in the sizes of districts. Specifically, a district too small to conduct at least one good-sized elementary school and high school will either have inadequate offerings or be unduly expensive. Such a district would be unified, i.e., it should have a single board and superintendent. A district should be large enough to afford good management, but not so large that it engulfs a natural community in a massive population sprawl that lessens or destroys civic interest. It seems safe to say that rarely should a district have fewer than 1,000 ADA. On the other hand, a district with 10,000 ADA is large enough to provide, without undue cost, a wide range in instructional offerings.

Responsibility for Equity. There is a strong tendency for local interest, particularly in fiscal matters, to supersede interest in larger governmental units or in neighboring communities. Those responsible for larger units of school government at the county and state levels must, therefore, lend their influence to promote the general welfare. Through its fiscal system, the state should eliminate insofar as possible the islands of poverty and wealth that operate to its detriment by lowering the equality of opportunity for children and overburdening some taxpayers at the expense of others.

ANALYSES OF THE APPORTIONMENT OF STATE AID FOR 1957-58

Present Inequities in Support

An estimate of the difference in treatment accorded poorer and moderately wealthy districts under current formulas is shown by the relationship between local wealth and the percentage of state support. The calculations summarized in Table 9.1 are all based on districts of over 100 ADA and all receive equalization aid. Group 1 is composed of districts with from 0 to $10,000 assessed valuation per ADA; Group 2 of districts over $10,000 but under $15,833 AV per ADA which is the cut-off point for equalization aid.

It is especially noteworthy that in the poorer districts having over 100 ADA, 32.1% of the assessed valuation ($7 billion) supports 53.3% of the ADA. It is also of particular interest that the poorer group must raise $89.02 per ADA in local support to obtain the amount of the foundation program, whereas those with nearly twice the wealth (and probably even more income per capita) need to raise only $77.43 or $11.59 less. For the poorer group the tax rate for calculating local responsibility is $1.35, whereas for the wealthier districts it is 60 cents. True, the foundation program is $295 for the poorer districts compared to $220 for the wealthier, but 66% of this $75 increase is borne by the district itself while only 34% is derived from state funds.

Other inequities, the effect of which is not calculated here, are inherent in the two foundation programs and tax levels for high school districts. Furthermore, small high school districts, which are usually wealthy (see Table 8.21), qualify for equalization aid by levying only a 45 cent tax rate while larger districts must levy a rate of at least 50 cents. In the above discussion of inequitable bases for allocating state aid we have not considered fully the problem of differences among the foundation program levels for elementary schools, high schools, and junior colleges. Suffice it to say that the several inconsistencies are

Table 9.1. Differences in State and Local Support of Two Classes of Districts Receiving Equalization Aid

Characteristics	Group (1)	Group (2)
	Elementary Level	
Size	Over 100 ADA	Over 100 ADA
Range of AV per ADA	0-$10,000	$10,001-$15,833
Total ADA	1,063,132	734,569
Per cent of Total ADA	53.3	36.7
Total AV	$7,010,354,133	$9,479,304,012
Per cent of Total AV	32.1	43.5
Mean AV/ADA	$6,594	$12,904
Foundation Program per ADA	$295	$220
Total Foundation Program	$313,623,940	$161,605,180
District Aid Tax Rate	$1.35	$.60
Total District Aid	$94,639,781	$56,875,824
District Aid per ADA	$89.02	$77.43
Total State Aid (Basic Equal.)	$218,984,159	$104,729,356
State Aid per ADA	$206	$142.57
State Aid per ADA as a % of F.P.	69.9%	64.8%

Source: Computations conform to existing systems outlined in Reference 7.

quite unsupportable, for if any one of the bases is right, the others are wrong (see also Table 8.13 and its accompanying text).

Inefficiencies in the Allocation of State Funds

One measure of the efficiency of a fiscal system is the extent to which tax funds are disbursed in terms of need. Elsewhere we have called attention to the inefficiency of "flat grants" which are made irrespective of need, or without regard to the ability of a locality to raise funds with less effort than is required of the state itself. Under the above conditions, waste or "loss" results from the amount of basic aid that is not required to meet the foundation program in wealthier districts; loss also results from some wealthy districts having an assessed valuation greater than is needed to support the foundation program at the minimal tax rate required of other districts. To cite an example:

Coalinga in Fresno County, an oil field area, has wealth assessed at $124,477,120. The K-8 ADA is 1,894 and the AV per ADA is $65,722 (about six times the state average). The Foundation Program is $416,680 (1,894 x $220) which could be raised by a tax rate of only 33-1/2 cents per $100 of assessed valuation, with no state aid of any kind. Yet, the district receives $192,625 in state funds for elementary school support. These state monies are collected, for the most part, from districts which are far poorer and less able to pay.

In Coalinga, $64.9 million or about 56% of the total assessed valuation would support the Foundation Program at a $ .60 tax rate which is the minimum that other less fortunate districts must levy. There is thus a loss of the remaining 44% of the assessed valuation, which at a $.60 tax rate would yield $331,295. The sum of the "lost" state aid ($192,625) plus the "lost" District Aid ($331,295) amounts to $523,920, which would be available to other districts in the state, were this district subject to the same tax rates as districts of average wealth. The case becomes even stronger when the $1.35 tax rate required of poorer districts is considered.

The large number of districts now in existence is in itself another source of waste. The offices of county superintendents become over-burdened with the responsibility of nursemaiding small, inadequately administered districts. In Riverside County the county office was re-quired to spend 53% of its time on the affairs of small districts with less than 6% of the county's ADA.* The intended purpose of this office — to coordinate county educational programs — is not served by such re-quirements. At the state level, also, the added clerical work involved in servicing over 1,800 districts is important. Dividing the state into approximately 327 areas would provide the same proximity of repre-sentation now afforded for high school purposes.

Methods of Calculation

Master Tables. The following analyses have been made to obtain estimates of the amounts of state funds that are now allocated to districts whose needs for state aid are either marginal, minimal, or nonexistent. The analyses were made from master tables prepared on IBM equipment. They permit the calculation of the effect of a given factor in apportion-ment, and also enable relatively rapid estimates to be made in design-ing a more efficient plan of apportioning state funds. The essential basis for constructing master tables is first to divide the districts into as many formula categories as necessary; second, to arrange the districts in each category in the order of wealth; and third, to list the districts in the above order showing ADA, assessed valuation, and assessed valuation per ADA, and cumulative sums for the first two.**

* Reference 1.

** A master table for the nine California regions is shown below:

Region	Assessed Valuation per ADA	Average Daily Attendance			Assessed Valuation	
		Amount (K-12)	Cumulative Amount	Cum. %	Amount in Thousands	Cumulative Amount
San Diego	$ 6,484	150,855	150,855	5.9	$ 978,082	$ 978,082
Sacramento Valley	6,567	134,792	285,647	11.2	885,121	1,863,203
North Coast	6,721	74,656	360,303	14.1	501,677	2,364,880
Southeast	7,316	152,974	513,277	20.0	1,119,137	3,484,017
San Joaquin Valley	8,284	296,042	809,319	31.5	2,452,489	5,936,506
Los Angeles Metro.	8,783	1,047,836	1,857,155	72.3	9,203,458	15,139,964
San Francisco Bay	8,862	543,044	2,400,199	93.4	4,812,562	19,952,527
Mountain	10,250	59,122	2,459,321	95.7	606,018	20,558,545
South Coast	11,243	111,257	2,570,578	100.0	1,250,812	21,809,357

Classification of Districts. The elementary school districts were classified by size and by assessed valuation per ADA as follows:

ADA	A	B	C
1-25			
26-50			
51-75			
76-100			
100 & Over			

Class A districts receive equalization aid, hence no excess payments are made. Class B districts receive just basic aid but only a part of it is needed to support the foundation program. Class C districts receive basic aid but need none of it to support the foundation program, and, in addition, possess assessed wealth in excess of the amount required to support the foundation program.

Basic Aid Excess Payments. The amount of basic aid paid to the wealthier districts in excess of need is determined by the sum of the amounts paid to: (a) Class B districts that receive no equalization aid but whose district aid is less than the foundation program, plus (b) all of the basic aid apportioned to Class C districts in which the district aid alone equals or exceeds the foundation program.

Loss of Tax Base. In Class C districts, district aid equals or exceeds the foundation program. These districts not only require no state aid, but also can maintain the foundation program with a lower tax rate than the qualifying rate. The assessed valuation multiplied by the district aid tax rate, less the amount of the foundation program, indicates the excess in district aid. (In reading the tables note that the 1956-57 ADA is used, and the apportionment bases for the year 1957-58 are observed. This is correct since the apportionment is based on the previous year's ADA.)

Potential "savings" in districts that have no need of part or all of their state aid and that have untapped local wealth are indicated in Table 9.2. Districts in Class A receive equalization aid and are therefore excluded. The Class B districts need only a part of the flat grant of $125, and the Class C districts need none of the flat grant and have, in addition, considerable surplus local wealth. In the calculations of possible savings the current apportionment formula was followed except that state aid was credited only to the extent of supplementing the local tax base up to the amount of the foundation program. It will be seen that a total of $8,549,870 in basic aid is apportioned to districts not needing

it to meet the amount of the foundation program.* An additional
$4,355,614 of district aid is lost in districts of high wealth, making a
total of $12.9 million.

The amount of excess grants and local wealth is more difficult to
estimate for high school districts since small high schools are
apportioned funds under an excessively complex formula. The estimated

Table 9.2. Summary of Excess Grants and Loss of Tax Base for
Elementary Schools

Class of District (ADA)		No. of Dists.	ADA	Basic Aid	District Aid Excess	Total
1-25	B	65	983	$ 85,159	$ 364,524	$
	C	61	918	146,400	364,524	510,924
Total		126	1,901	231,559	364,524	596,083
26-50	B	48	1,922	104,624		
	C	32	1,275	159,375	405,806	565,118
Total		80	3,197	264,017	405,806	669,823
51-75	B	30	1,909	66,805		
	C	19	1,241	155,125	442,936	598,061
Total		49	3,150	221,930	442,936	655,356
76-100	B	29	2,633	115,774		
	C	8	719	89,875	264,544	354,419
Total		37	3,382	205,649	264,544	470,193
Total 1-100	B	172	7,477	453,380		
	C	120	4,153	550,380	1,477,810	
Total		292	11,630	913,645	1,477,810	2,391,455
Over 100	B	135	151,364	5,462,600		
	C	35	17,389	2,173,625	2,877,804	5,051,429
Total		170	168,754	7,626,715	2,877,804	10,504,519
Total All Classes	B	307	158,842	5,825,470		
	C	155	21,542	2,724,400	4,355,614	7,080,014
Total		462	180,384	$8,549,870	$4,355,614	$12,905,284

*The amount of $120 per ADA is fixed by the Constitution, but a
part of the potential savings could be made now. An amendment to the
Constitution would be required to eliminate or reduce the flat-grant
amount. These estimates of savings are conservative for we have not
questioned the more expensive unnecessarily small school or the higher
district aid tax rate in poorer districts.

savings in apportionments to high schools are, therefore, based only on districts having more than $37,000 assessed valuation per ADA, the wealthier half. These estimates of potential savings are conservative since the foundation program for all small high schools was calculated as if they had no fewer than 267 ADA, which is the basis for the ADA foundation program of $310 per ADA.

Table 9.3. Potential Savings at the High School Level for Districts with over $37,000 Assessed Valuation per ADA

1.	Foundation Program at $310 per ADA	$84,052,780
2.	Adding ADA to make every school no smaller than 267	2,136,520
3.	Total Foundation Program	$86,189,300
4.	District Aid at a tax rate of $.50	66,345,554
5.	State Aid needed (Line 3 minus Line 4)	19,843,746
6.	Basic Aid received	33,892,250
7.	Excess Apportionment (Line 6 minus Line 5)	$14,048,504

The total amount of "loss" in elementary and high school districts is the sum of $12,905,248 and $14,048,504 or $26,953,752. Not all of this could be saved under present constitutional provisions. If, however, basic aid were reduced to the constitutional minimum of $120, there would still be a possible saving of $5,257,534 at the elementary level alone. The above calculations do not take into account any changes in the foundation program or district aid tax rate changes, or any possible savings in apportionments to junior colleges. As will be seen in the following section, a broader fiscal base would permit much more of the loss to be recovered.

IMPROVING FISCAL SYSTEM FOR CURRENT EXPENSES

In this section proposed applications of concepts and methods discussed previously are offered. These proposals stress the following:

A district and intermediate unit organizational pattern that will minimize variation in wealth but not do violence to the identity of communities.

A revenue system that will maximize efficiency of the tax base at state, county, and district levels.

A foundation level of support so designed to recognize realistically actual cost rates and also mean tax rates as far as possible.

A disbursement system that will minimize waste and reduce the need for a high percentage of state aid.

A degree of flexibility that will permit adjustments from time to time within the same general framework and leave to localities the many adjustments that properly belong at the district level.

Methodological Proposals

In accordance with the objectives indicated above, the following proposals are made. These proposals are not necessarily interdependent but several of them have been combined in a new apportionment formula. (The application of this formula to grades K-12 is reported in some detail later in this chapter.) The proposals are that:

1. The nine regions mentioned earlier (see Figure 9.1) be employed as intermediate units in lieu of counties. (The regions used in this study are the statistical regions used by the State Department of Finance. Some modification of this plan may be preferable for school purposes.)

2. For apportionment purposes, the community districts and unified districts be the minimal units.(Community districts should be established by the Legislature. See Chapter 8 for an explanation of how they would be set up.)

3. Regions, or counties, and unified or community districts be employed as areas of taxation to reduce the deleterious effect of islands of wealth which do not fully contribute to the support of schools.

4. State funds be equalized to counties.

5. County funds, together with state funds, be equalized to unified or community districts.

6. A county- or region-levied but state-collected income tax, with the return of the full amount to regions or counties, be the source of at least one-half of county, or regional, revenues for school purposes.

7. A county- or region-wide property tax be levied in the amount of approximately one-third (or, in combination with an income tax, one sixth) of the state mean equivalent tax rate for current expenses.

8. A summary budget within the community district be employed to determine the tax rate within the districtfor costs up to the state mean cost per ADA and that the qualifying tax rate for equalization aid be about 7/8 of the state mean equivalent tax rate for counties and districts combined (see Table 9.5).

9. Within the community district there be no tax rate maximum for costs up to the state mean cost per ADA.

10. The foundation program for elementary and secondary (K-12) ADA be combined. (Such a program will return to local areas the decision of what proportions of their funds shall be expended for each level of education. It will also tend to ease the burden on rapidly growing districts.)

11. The State School Fund be apportioned during the same

year as costs are incurred. (Machine accounting procedures make this possible and will permit the present apportionment for growth to be returned to the general apportionment.)

12. The maximum tax rate be set at approximately one standard deviation above the state mean cost per ADA among districts of average wealth.

13. As a general policy, if state funds are wholly equalized, the state and local units share support on a 50-50 basis, but that if state funds are not completely equalized, state support be not less than 3/4 of mean costs.

14. Legal and constitutional changes be initiated which will permit the apportionment of state funds with efficiency, equity, and economy.

Regional Apportionments

As fiscal bases, the nine regions shown in Figure 9.1 would, in many ways, be preferable to counties. They have the advantage of removing artificial boundary lines within natural socio-economic areas. The mean assessed wealth per ADA in these regions varies from $6,484 in San Diego to $11,243 in the South Coast Region, a far smaller variation than among counties.

A somewhat more efficient fiscal system would be possible under a regional plan. If a foundation program of $300 per ADA is presumed as for other bases, and the same rate of state aid is maintained, a regional tax of $1.00 and a unified or community district qualifying rate of about 56 cents would be possible. Under such a plan all districts of $53,571 or less assessed valuation per ADA in grades K-12 would receive state aid.[*] Such an arrangement would in no way affect school district organization, but county offices would become regional offices instead.

Relationship of State to Local Revenues

State funds apportioned to districts must be allocated either on some systematic basis or by administrative decision based on the budgetary problems of each district. The latter would entail not only excessive administrative costs but also the possibility of differential treatment. An alternative is a statutory formula. Such a formula might include an indefinite number of variables. The complexity of the formula is largely a result of the number of variables and exceptions, which must be taken into account. The present formula is very complex for both reasons.

If state and local funds are to be related inversely as in an equalizing

[*]Only four districts would be excluded under the formula.

program, a reference base has great advantages. The foundation program provides just that. It may be arbitrary as it is at present, or it may be governed by the somewhat more realistic factors of actual costs and average tax rates. We propose: (1) that a more realistic level is preferable; (2) that for districts of adequate size a simpler method is possible since variable factors tend to strike an average; and (3) that administrative controls belong properly at the district rather than at the state or county levels.

An analysis of the apportionment of state funds by school level and purpose was made to determine the amount of the principal apportionment available for grades K-12. This analysis is shown in Table 9.4. The amounts shown in the column headed "Apportionment," but listed under "Special Purposes," are the approximations listed in Part I of Reference 7. Line 9 indicates the amount per ADA ($167.71) which has been employed in the proposed formula for the principal apportionment of the State School Fund.

The analyses of the apportionment (Table 9.4), of costs (Table 9.5), and of estimated district costs (Table 9.6), have been necessitated by the fact that the most recent cost data are for 1956-57, the year prior to the increase in the State School Fund from $180 to $194 per ADA. This adjustment, while necessary, adds complexity to what would otherwise be a simple reconciliation of the state and district shares of current operating expenses.

The Relationship of the Foundation Program to Current Expense. To establish a cost rate per ADA for grades K-12, an analysis was made of the current expense of education for the year 1956-57, as shown in Table 9.5. The data are those reported by the State Controller for that year in Reference 26. The costs and ADA of junior college students in unified and high school districts were deducted from unified and community district totals. Costs for junior college students were prorated using junior college district costs per ADA. The K-12 rate of $339.55 per ADA (Col. j, Table 9.5) includes adults, but a correction for the cost of adults cannot be made from the available data. The rate shown is probably lower than that for grades K-12, but the error is not greater than, perhaps, $1 per ADA. The figure $339.55 is employed as the base for calculating the foundation program rate in Table 9.6.

The foundation program, as conceived in this study, is a minimum level of combined state and local support of the cost of educating children in regular classes in grades K-12 (junior college costs are not included).

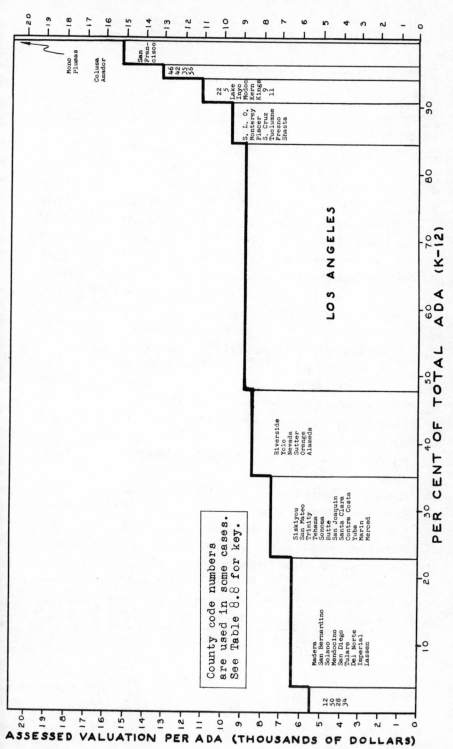

FIGURE 9.2 DISTRIBUTION OF ADA AND ASSESSED VALUATION AMONG CALIFORNIA COUNTIES, 1956-57

Table 9.4 Analysis of State Apportionment for 1957-58 by Level and Purpose

	Level or Purpose	ADA	Apportionment	Apportionment per ADA
1.	Districts, K-8	1,993,080	$343,061,141	$172.13
2.	J.H., 7 & 8	(205,367	32,092,802	(156.27)
3.	Elementary, K-8	1,787,713	310,968,339	173.95
4.	Districts, 9-12 (+JC)	577,776	88,108,467	152.50
5.	J.H. and 7 & 8	(205,367)	(32,092,802)	(156.27)
6.	Secondary, 7-12	783,143	120,201,269	153.49
7.	Districts, 13 & 14	106,863	16,186,217	151.47
8.	District Total Formula	2,677,719	447,355,825	167.07
9.	District Total, K-12	2,570,856	431,169,608	167.71
	Special Purpose Apportionment			
10.	Handicapped	38,284	14,166,429	370.04
11.	Transportation	(2,639,435)	11,003,052	(4.01)
12.	Driver Training		1,830,621	--
13.	Project Connected		25,000	--
14.	Total Special Apportionment		27,025,102	--
	Other Apportionments			
15.	Adults	66,636	9,588,801	143.90
16.	Growth		34,439,553	--
17.	District Reorganization		80,735	--
18.	Adjustment for Previous Years		114,275	--
19.	County Funds + County Schools 6,408		14,697,014	--
20.	Balance (witheld)		133,499	--
21.	County Sch. Serv. Fund Surplus		335,858	--
22.	Sub-Total, Spec. App. and Reserves		86,414,837	--
23.	Grand Total	2,750,763	$533,770,662	$194.04

Source: Reference 7

Table 9.5. Current Expenses of Education by Level of School Showing State and District Proportions of Support Based on 1956-57 Cost Data

Type of District	Grade Span	ADA	Assessed Valuation	Total Current Expense	State Apportionment	Dist. Taxes for CEE	Total Dist. & City Taxes
Column		a	b	c	d	e	f
Derivation			Columns a through d are basic data			c-d	basic data
Elementary	K-6or8	1,317,288	14,636,191,037	382,570,509	229,765,292	152,805,217	192,069,425
High School	7 or 9– 12 or 14	559,325	14,527,890,702	248,479,174	85,646,789	162,832,385	167,239,643
Junior College	13&14	77,909	8,996,617,638	36,961,762	11,355,624	25,606,138	26,585,600
Unified	K-12or14	789,833	7,176,581,652	282,203,015	120,520,691	161,682,324	159,182,107
Community and Unified	K-12	2,608,065	21,812,772,690	885,556,058	426,491,905	459,064,153	497,538,320
Total	K-14	2,744,355	21,812,772,690	950,214,460	447,288,396	502,926,064	545,076,776

	AV per ADA	State Aid per ADA	Dist. Taxes per ADA	CEE per ADA	Mean Equivalent Tax Rate for CEE	Total Mean Equivalent Tax Rate
	g	h	i	j	k	L
	b/a	d/a	e/a	c/a	e/b	f/b
Elementary	11,111	174.42	116.00	290.42	1.0440	1.3123
High School	25,974	153.13	29.12	444.25	1.1208	1.1512
Junior College	115,476	145.75	328.67	474.42	.2846	.2955
Unified	9,086	152.59	204.70	357.29	2.2529*	2.2181
Community and Unified	8,364	163.53	176.02	339.55	2.1046	2.2809
Total	7,948	162.98	183.26	346.24	2.3051	2.4989

Table 9.6. Estimates of District Costs per ADA, 1956-57, in Schools
           Maintaining Grades K-12, Corrected for Increases in State
           Aid Effective in 1957-58

Bases for the Foundation Program in Unified and Community Districts

1. Actual Current Expense per ADA in 1956-57,
    Grades K-12 plus adults in high school
    (Table 9.5, Col. j) $339.55*

2. Estimated Special Apportionments per ADA:

        Transportation $4.28
        Handicapped   4.98
        Driver Training   .71
                            $9.97   9.97

3. Current Expense less Special Aids (1 minus 2)   329.58

4. Total State Funds per ADA ($436, 523, 983/2,608,065)   167.37

        Principal Apportionment, K-12 $431,169,608
        State Aid for Adults in H.S.   5,354,375

            Total State Aid $436,523,983

        ADA, K-12   2,570,856
        Adults in High School   37,204

            Total ADA $ 2,608,065

5. Amount from District Taxes per ADA ($329.58 - $167.37) 162.21

6. State Mean Equivalent Tax Rate for Current Expense   1.9118*
    Mean Assessed Valuation per ADA = $8,484.63

*Costs of adults in high schools cannot be separated from total
costs. The effect on tax rates is negligible.

---

*Note on Table 9.5: This rate is higher than that in Col. L since
only district and state funds were employed in the calculations for a
general formula. The differences are due to the receipt of federal revenues which were omitted here because they are not apportioned to districts and because an adjustment for federal revenues is made in the
apportionment of state funds.

    Sources: Cols. a and d - Reference 7; Cols. b, c, and f - Refer-
ence 26; all other columns derived as shown.

If the foundation program is established in this manner, the cost of educating adults must also be omitted. In addition, districts now receive separate reimbursements for the excess costs of educating handicapped children, a portion of transportation costs, and, in high schools, the excess costs of driver training. Accordingly, these amounts of state aid are excluded from the current expense of education in arriving at a mean rate per ADA for foundation program purposes. These adjustments are shown in Table 9.6. The foundation program is thus based on the current costs of regular classes in the common schools and it excludes the additional costs which are reimbursed by special forms of state aid.

Other Costs Excluded from Foundation Program Support. Costs which the foundation program is not presumed to support are those for community services, the costs of food services, and capital outlay costs for equipment, furniture, and the like. These costs must be borne by the district. The difference between the state mean equivalent tax rate for the support of the foundation program, shown in Table 9.5, and the total tax rate, reflects the additional costs pointed out above.

Local Revenues. The proposed apportionment plan has been developed by assuming, as constants, for the purposes of a working model: (1) Mean costs per ADA in 1956-57; (2) the present statutory total amount of state aid; (3) the same proportions of state aid as now obtain for special purposes, e.g., handicapped children; and (4) a state mean equivalent tax rate necessary to produce local revenue, which, with state aid, provides a sufficient amount to meet average costs per ADA. The actual state mean equivalent tax rate of $1.9118 was changed to $1.92, a more convenient divisible number.

The question of how this rate should be divided to provide a county rate, a qualifying rate for equalization aid under the foundation program, and a rate that is optional with each district, cannot be answered by mathematical calculations alone. Again, the dilemma of local autonomy and the theoretical advantages of a broad tax base call for a compromise, unless, of course, school districts were to be abolished and a county system of schools substituted for them.

A relatively low tax rate for counties is necessary if all or nearly all counties are to receive state aid. Were a regional unit to be be employed, a higher tax rate could be used since the range of differences among regions is lower than that among counties. With these considerations in mind, together with the information gained from trial calculations, it was found that one-third of the $1.92 rate, or $ .64, appeared to be an acceptable rate, inasmuch as all but two counties are included and 99.99% of the ADA comes within the equalization formula.[*] It is presumed that if all or a part of county revenues are obtained through a county income tax, the property tax rate would be reduced proportionately.

The remaining amount of the state mean equivalent tax rate is $1.28 ($1.92 less $ .64). A suitable division of this amount between a qualifying rate and a residual rate is necessary since both a high foundation program and a reasonable degree of local option are desirable. Once more, these two criteria are antithetical, for there is no means by which both local autonomy and the lowest possible tax rate may be achieved. Hence the choice is between the degree of local freedom and the level of educational support. The task is to achieve a degree of both. But what degree?

A full $1.28 tax rate would either disqualify a large portion of the districts or make the mean tax the minimum tax. Either of these alternatives would force increased costs or abolish local choice. There is obviously no one answer to this problem. Considering, however, the efficiency of the use of both state and local tax monies, and the level of support as two major criteria, it was found that a $ .96 district aid tax rate would bring 99.6% of the ADA of the state under both state and county support and would also enable each district to exercise a choice in establishing a tax rate necessary to attain average costs as defined earlier.

The proportions of total support thus provided are, in general terms: state, one-half; county, one-sixth; district qualifying tax, one-fourth; and district residual tax, one-twelfth. These proportions would permit the district of average wealth to support average costs. The factors from which the plan was developed are shown in Table 9.7. The equalization of state funds would enable even the poorest community district in the state to support its schools for grades K-12 at an average cost level with a tax rate of $2.66 or only $ .74 more than the state mean.

The Community District as a Fiscal Unit. The community district embraces the high school and the elementary districts within its boundaries. It is here used as a fiscal base in two ways. First, it is a dis-

---

[*] A low flat-grant adjustment to the very small per cent of ADA excluded would appear to be preferable, if necessary, to a major change in the county tax rate.

Table 9.7. Factors Employed in Developing a State Aid Formula for the
Apportionment of State Funds for Current Expenses (less
special aid) in Grades K-12 in School Districts

Fixed Factors

1. Total ADA, K-12 (no adults). 2,570,856

2. Total Assessed Valuation $21,812,772,690

3. Total Assessed Valuation per ADA (2/1) $8,484.63

4. State Aid on Formula (from Table 9.4, line 9). . . . $431,169,608

5. State Aid on Formula per ADA, 1957-58 (4/1). $167.71*

Empirical Factors

6. State Mean Current Expense of Education per ADA, K-12. . . . $329.58

7. State Mean District Aid per ADA. $161.87

8. State Mean Equivalent Tax Rate for CEE ($161.87/8,484.63). 1.9078

Formula Factors

9. Criterion of Support (state average with average local effort)330.00

10. State Aid, excluding special aid for transportation,
handicapped students and driver training $167.71

11. District Tax Rate Division for All Local Aid:
County . . . . $ .64
Community District 96
Total. $1.60

12. County and Community District Aid per ADA at $1.60 tax
rate (3 x 11). $135.75

13. Total Theoretical Level of Foundation Program (10 + 12). . . $303.46

14. Foundation Program (with allowance for variability). $300.00**

15. County Cut-off Point (AV per ADA at which the $.64 tax
rate will raise an amount equal to the F.P. of $300) . 46,875

16. Community District Cut-off Point (.0096 x AV/ADA ÷ $300) .$31,250

17. County Cut-off Point (no equalization aid if Constitutional
minimum of $120 per ADA is retained) 28,125

18. Community District Cut-off Point (no state aid above $120
per ADA if Constitutional minimum is retained) 18,750

Notes: *Variation from Table 9.6, line 5, is due to the omission of Adult
ADA.

**This Foundation Program of $300 is equivalent to elementary and
secondary programs, as presently proportioned, of $283 and $355 respectively. The Community District tax (see Table 9.7) will permit an average
level of support for both elementary and high schools without undue tax
burdens. The poorest Community District in the state would require a
current expense of education tax rate of $2.66 to attain average support
of instruction in grades K-12.

trict to which state funds are apportioned on the equalization formula;
and   second, it is the tax base for the support of all districts within it,
up to average costs. The community district resembles the unified
district, but its subdistricts retain a margin of independent taxing
power. The fiscal board of a community district would not, however,
exercise administrative powers under the plan here proposed. The
component elementary district remains an operating district. Its tax
base for the total budget less average current expense (and for costs
in excess of the state mean for current expenses for the prior year)
would be its own assessed wealth.

Operation of the Proposed Plan

State Level. The proposed plan for the principal apportionment
of the state school fund in conjunction with county and district funds is
outlined below. The foundation program for grades K-12 is $300 per
ADA. This foundation program is equivalent to elementary and high
school foundation programs of $283 and $355, respectively. It would
be supported by a county tax of $ .64 and a unified or community dis-
trict tax of $ .96, or a total of $1.60. A comparison between the
present and proposed apportionment plans shows the following differences (data for the present plan are averages):

	Foundation Program K-12	Local Tax Rate
Present Plan	$271	$1.34
Proposed Plan	$300	$1.64
Difference	$ 29	$ .26

About $17 per ADA would be added to the present foundation pro-
gram by a tax of $ .26 making a comparable foundation program of
$288 under the present method. The difference in support under the
two methods of apportionment is estimated to be about $12 per ADA,
or approximately $31 million for the state. The operation of the plan
at the state level may be summarized in this way:

Foundation Program ($300 x $2,570,578)		$771,173,400
State Aid	$431,169,608	
County Aid		
(21,809,354,686 x $ .64)	139,579,870	
District Aid (AV x $ .96)	209,369,805	
Total Local Aid		
(AV x $1.60)	$348,949,675	
Total Support		$780,119,283
Surplus		$ 8,945,883
Total per ADA		$303.48

County Level. State funds would be equalized to counties. Each county would be charged with providing an amount equal to $ .64 on each $100 of the assessed wealth of the county. This amount could also be established as one-sixth of the mean current expense per ADA. It is presumed that a county-wide tax equal to this amount would be levied and placed in a county school fund. To this fund would be added all state apportionments to community districts in the county and the total of state and county funds would equal the apportionments to districts as calculated by the State Department of Education. The following calculations indicate total amounts as they would apply to the equalization of state funds to counties. Under the formula two counties, Alpine and Mono,[*] would not receive equalization aid.

Foundation Program		$771,173,400
State Aid	$431,169,608	
County Aid	139,579,870	
Total		$570,749,478
Amount per ADA		$222
Remainder charged to District Aid		$200,423,922

District Level. All funds, state and county, would be apportioned to unified or community districts. The amount of the foundation program would be the total ADA in grades K-12 multiplied by $300. Each community or unified district would be charged with providing an amount of district aid equal to .0096 times the assessed valuation of the property within the community or unified district. For example:

Foundation Program (1000 ADA x $300)	$300,000
District Aid ($8,000,000 AV x .0096)	76,800
State and County Aid (FP - DA)	$223,200
State and County Aid per ADA	$223.20

1. Foundation program for grades K-12. — The proposed foundation program ($300 per ADA) applies to grades kindergarten through twelve, whereas the present method provides for two levels, namely, kindergarten through grade eight and grades nine through twelve. Elsewhere, attention has been called to the facts that the existing foundation programs are not consistent with actual costs, that they discriminate against the poorer districts, and that they are supported by an inconsistent pattern of tax rates and of state aid. Moreover, the junior

---

[*] Funds available to Mono County are subject to legal review of a protest made by Los Angeles City regarding taxation of its extensive holdings there. An adjustment of actual funds available to Mono County should therefore be made.

high school is not recognized in the present design, except that funds
are automatically transferred from the elementary to the high school
district in apportioning state funds for junior high school ADA. In
unified districts and in districts having a single board common to the
elementary and high school districts, the allocation of funds for any
type of school is properly left to the local administrative board.

2. Budgetary control. — A community district budget is prepared as a summary of the budgets of its component districts. In
Table 9.8 all calculations necessary to the allocation of funds within
a community district are shown. Revenues needed for budget items in
account classifications 1-7, less any special state reimbursements
are indicated for each district. The amount of the budget of each subdistrict supported by state, county and community district funds may
not exceed the state mean cost for that level as published by the State
Comptroller for the most recent prior year.

The division of all monies within the community district would be
based upon either the amount of the budget of each subdistrict for the
current expense of education, or the mean cost per ADA by type of
school, whichever is lower (see Table 9.8). Obviously a subdistrict
should not be allocated monies beyond its own budgetary needs. On the
other hand, a subdistrict desiring to support its schools at a level
equal to that of the state average, may do so through support on a
community district basis. Just as state and county funds were combined to support the community districts within a county, so are state,
county, and community district funds combined within the community
district to support the several districts within its boundaries. This
plan is designed to provide relief for the taxpayer in the poorer districts and, at the same time, to assure his children a moderate level
of school support if average tax rates are levied.

While the foundation program assures support of schools in a
community district to within about 90% of average costs, it need not
carry with it the rigidity of requiring uniform expenditures in the
subdistricts within each community district. An additional tax beyond
$ .96 is necessary to attain average costs, but while such a tax per-
mits average costs to be attained, it in no sense forces, or even assures, "average cost" unless the community district levies the tax.
"Average cost" refers to the current expenses of education, budget
classifications one through seven. Other costs, which are not included
in these account classifications, are: food services, community ser-

Table 9.8. Example of Calculations Related to an Hypothetical Community District and Sub-Districts under PROPOSED STATE AID PLAN

Line		ADA	Assessed Valuation	AV per ADA	Budget Items 1-7		Special St. Aid	Net Budget
					Amount	per ADA		
	Column	a	b	c	d	e	f	g
	Derivation	hypothetical		b/a	hypoth'tl	d/a	hyp.	d/f
	Sub-Dist.							
1.	1 Elem	750	6,000,000	8,000	262,500	350	2,000	260,500
2.	2 Elem	2,500	25,000,000	10,000	687,500	275	10,000	677,500
3.	3 Elem	250	5,000,000	20,000	100,000	400	none	100,000
4.	4 H.S.	1,000	36,000,000	36,000	425,000	425	5,000	420,000
5.	Total	4,500	36,000,000	8,000	1,475,000	328	17,000	1,458,000

Line		Net Budget per ADA	Published State Mean Cost per ADA	Lesser of Col. h or i	Community District Budget	Sub-Dist Total Budget	Sub-Dist Optional Increment	Sub-Dist Tax Rate
		h	i	j	k	l	m	n
		g/a	basic data	–	a x j	hyp.	l-k	m/b
6.	1 Elem	$347	$290	$290	$217,500	$259,500	$42,000	$.70
7.	2 Elem	271	290	271	677,500	730,000	52,500	.21
8.	3 Elem	400	290	290	72,500	110,000	37,500	.75
9.	4 H.S.	420	444	420	420,000	474,000	54,000	.21
10.	Total	324	–		1,387,500	–	–	–

State and County Aid Calculations

11. Total Foundation Program (4,500 ADA x $300) $1,350,000

12. Community District Aid ($36,000,000 AV x .0096) $ 345,600

13. State and County Aid (FP – DA) $1,004,400

14. Total CEE Budget based on state average costs per ADA (line 10, column k) $1,387,500

15. Total Support through Foundation Program $1,350,000

16. Balance to be obtained by additional Community District Tax (line 14 minus line 15) $ 37,500

17. Community District Tax Rate for Costs above State Mean Costs (line 16 / Total in Col. b) $ .104

18. Total Community District Tax Rate (.96 + Line 17) $ 1.064

Note: The assessed valuation per ADA, K-12, of this hypothetical district is $8,000. This is below the state mean of $8,485.

vices, and capital outlay expenditures for instructional equipment as well as for other types of capital outlay. Revenues to pay for these costs would be obtained by a tax levied by each of the subdistricts. The subdistrict tax would also be levied for costs in excess of average costs for budget classes 1-7 (see Table 9.9).

If, on the other hand, it is considered better policy to provide for lower costs in some community districts than is assured by the proposed foundation program, this may be accomplished by merely fixing a qualifying tax rate which is below the $ .96 district aid rate employed in calculating the allocation of state and county funds.

Table 9.9. Tax Rates for the Hypothetical Subdistricts in a Community District as shown in Table 9.8

Sub-dist.	County	Community District			H.S. District	Subdist. for total Budget	Total Tax Rate
		Qualifying	Optional	Total			
1	.64	.96	.104	1.064	.15	.75	2.60*
2	.64	.96	.104	1.064	.15	.21	2.06*
3	.64	.96	.104	1.064	.15	.70	2.55*
4	See H.S. district column.						

Total of All Property Taxes: as levied by:

_____

*These rates are comparable to the total state mean equivalent tax rate of $2.15 (see Table 9.7, line 7).

3. Eligibility. — Any unified or community district having an assessed wealth of $31,250 per ADA or less for grades K-12 will receive state and county aid. Only six districts would not have qualified in 1956-57. The total ADA in these districts was 10,273, or 4% of the state total. The total assessed wealth of these six districts was $520,525,765, or $50,669 per ADA K-12.* This average is 5.97 times greater than the state mean of $8,484. Average support at the state mean rate of $330 per ADA could have been obtained from a tax rate of $ .65. But these districts would also have been $1.29 or $ .53 below the state mean rate of $1.92, even though no state aid were received.

_____

*The six districts whose assessed wealth per ADA in grades K-12 is over $31,250 are in three counties. The total assessed wealth untapped by even the present proposal is $199.5 million. This would result in either an adjustment in the foundation program at the state level of about $ .75 per ADA, or a slightly higher county tax in the three counties affected. The technical calculations are omitted here, but the adjustments necessary would be relatively minor.

4. Alternative Method for Special Services. — An alternative to
the method employed above for the local allocation of special state aid
funds would be preferable in many districts. Such community-wide
services as transportation and special classes for the handicapped can
be operated more effectively and financed more efficiently if done by
the community district.

FINANCING CAPITAL OUTLAY COSTS FOR CONSTRUCTION

Most of the expenditures for school construction in California,
ever since the days of the Gold Rush, have been made for new construction that has been occasioned by increases in the state's population.
Inevitably, however, the cost for the replacement of these buildings
will become a larger percentage of building costs. While these two
problems are similar in some ways, they differ in others. Replacement
can be anticipated more easily and for longer periods of time. The
replacement of capital in private business is usually financed by amor-
tizing future replacement costs and by paying for the reconstruction on
a cash basis. The advantages of this method are obvious since interest
costs are avoided.

Replacement Capital Outlay, Past and Future

Although separate amounts of expenditure for growth and replacement are not available we have developed estimates of the amount of
floor space needed to house enrollment increases during each of the
past five decades. Multiplying these enrollment increases by the present state-prescribed number of square feet per pupil produces an
estimate of the number of square feet built during the decade. An approximate overall cost of $15 per square foot, the rate which prevails
at the present time, is used to complete the transformation of enrollment increases to amounts of capital outlay. The material presented
in Table 9.10 is based on a mean useful life for buildings of fifty years.

From an estimated $143 million needed for building replacement
during the half-century now ending, we can foresee that from 15 to 36
times that amount will be needed during the half-century now beginning
($2,205 million if building costs were to remain constant at today's
levels and $5,177 million if they should rise at a rate comparable to
increases during the past 15 years). It is preferable to state these
amounts by decades since the burden will not be felt evenly throughout
the half-century. Fifty years after the depression years, there will be
few high schools to rebuild since high school enrollment actually decreased during that period. Conversely, fifty years after the postwar

decade now ending rebuilding costs will be exceptionally heavy. Expressed as an average yearly amount for the next half century, cash replacement costs range from $44 to $104 million per year depending upon the level of construction costs.

Also included in Table 9.10 are illustrations of the added cost to taxpayers when funds are borrowed rather than expended as cash. For example, the $44 million per year cash amount, when borrowed for a 20-year term becomes $59 million at the desirable interest rate of 3% and $71 million at the more realistic rate of 5%.

The smallest estimated difference between total cash costs and total bonding costs for financing the replacement of existing structures within the coming half-century is $765 million (see Part II of Table 9.10). Considering the probability of increases in construction costs, and of interest rates averaging above 3%, an amount of from two to four times $765 million — possibly $2 billion in interest alone — is a realistic possibility. Most of this debt servicing will occur late in this century and during the early part of the next, but some of it is already beginning. Offsetting these interest costs, but to an unknown degree, are the probability of inflation and the increases in economic productivity. Interest costs, however, are virtually certain whereas the other factors are subject to the many contingencies of the future. Hence, it is doubtless less expensive to finance reconstruction on a cash basis.

How might this be done? Certainly the small district could not easily raise sufficient funds within a year or so to build a new school. On the other hand, without great difficulty the state could rebuild one-fiftieth of the schools each year on a continuing basis. The fiscal base might be the state, the region, or the county, or these jointly. Given one of these alternatives as an acceptable base, the cash plan of financing replacement costs would save taxpayers hundreds of millions of dollars.

Financing New Construction

New construction costs fall largely on districts near the periphery of metropolitan areas and near new industrial or governmental installations. The magnitude of state loans to districts since 1949 points out the seriousness of the problem in some localities.

The total cost of this construction is not only the price of the buildings themselves but, in addition, the debt servicing charges which may increase the total cost as much as fifty per cent or more. The two

Table 9.10. Estimated Capital Outlay Expenditures for Replacement by Decade: 1907-08 through 2007-08; Based on Decennial Enrollment Increases

Part I: ENROLLMENT INCREASE, SQUARE FOOT REQUIREMENTS AND ESTIMATED TOTAL COSTS

Construction Decade Ending	Enrollment Increase Elem.	High School	Total	Sq. Ft. Required Elem @55 H.S. @80	Replacement Decade Ending Fifty years after Construction	Cost per Sq.Ft.	Total Costs
Column No.	a	b	c	d		e	f
Derivation	basic data		a+b	55a 80b	Decade	see note dxe	
Units	thousands of pupils					dollars millions	
1867-68			46	2,530*	1917-18	3.98	7
77-78			87	4,785*	27-28	5.93	29
87-88	44	–	44	2,420	37-38	5.42	14
97-98	67	8	75	4,325	47-48	6.95	30
1907-08	45	30	75	4,875	1957-58	13.00	63
At No Increase in Construction Costs							
1917-18	171	85	256	16,215	1967-68	15.00	243
27-28	342	350	692	46,810	77-78	15.00	702
37-38	30	-146	30	1,650**	87-88	15.00	25
47-48	244	30	244	13,420**	97-98	15.00	201
1957-58	1,084	287	1,371	68,980**	2007-08	15.00	1,034
At 2% per Year Increase in Construction Costs							
					1967-68	15.00	253
					77-78	18.72	876
Columns a through d are					87-88	22.46	37
same as above					97-98	26.95	362
					2007-08	32.34	2,231
At 3% per Year Increase in Construction Costs							
					1967-68	16.90	274
					77-78	21.97	1,028
Columns a through d are					87-88	28.56	47
same as above					97-98	37.13	498
					2007-08	48.27	3,330

Notes: *Assumed to be at the elementary level.
**Adjusted for the resumption of use of high school facilities left unused by the enrollment decrease during the decade ending 1937-38.
#During the forty-year period 1916 to 1956 the Construction Cost Index rose at a rate of 2.4% per year, with markedly higher rate of increase during the more recent years. This rate provides the rationale for selection of 2% and 3% per year increases for use in the table. The 3% rate is probably the more accurate.
Materials supplied by the State Allocations Board for costs of construction under the State Building Aid Program indicate that $15 per square foot is an acceptable approximation of a mean cost in recent years. Construction costs in past years were adjusted by decennial means of the published construction cost index. Future costs were adjusted according to the rates of increase cited above.

Part II: SUMMARY OF HALF-CENTURY COSTS BASED ON SELECTED METHODS OF
FINANCING

Half-Century Ending	Total Costs			Yearly Average Costs		
	Cash	20 Yr. Bonds at:		Cash	20 Yr. Bonds at:	
		3% Int.	5% Int.		3% Int.	5% Int.
Units	all figures in millions of dollars					
Column	g	h	i	j	k	l
Derivation	Sum f	1.346g*	1.604g*	.02f	.02h	.02i
1957–58	143	192	229	2.86	3.84	4.58
2007–08						
Rate of increase in Construction costs per decade — None	2,205	2,970	3,538	44	59	71
20%	3,759	5,063	6,031	75	101	121
30%	5,177	6,973	8,306	104	139	166

Notes: *$1.346 and $1.604 are the present values of $1 at 2% and 3% for
20 years compounded annually.

Source: Cols. a, b & c, 1867–68 to 1927–28 -- Reference 30.
1937–38 to 1957–58 -- Reference 6.

   Col. d -- The rates of 55 and 80 sq. ft. per pupil at elementary
and high school levels from Education Code Section 5049.

   Col. e -- Construction Cost Index -- Reference 21.

   Cols. h & i -- $1.346 and $1.604 are the present values of $1 at
2% and 3% for 20 years compounded annually.

principal variables are the interest rate and the term of the bonds. In
general, interest rates are lower when the governmental unit is economically productive, the indebtedness low, and the wealth base broad.
It is mainly for these reasons that state bonds usually bear lower interest rates than district bonds bear. (Expertness in the intricacies of
marketing bonds is also an important element in obtaining a higher
value.) It is inefficient and costly for many small school districts to
prepare and market bond issues for relatively small amounts. Hence,
the unified district or community district is a much better bond base
than a subdistrict. The employment of a system of broader tax bases
will reduce the need for state building aid to school districts and at
the same time provide more stability and flexibility at the local level.
The community district would therefore offer relief both to the state
and to subdistricts as well by providing first a broader tax base and
second a ten instead of a five percent debt limitation.

   A problem sometimes encountered is the unwillingness of the
electorate in one part of an area to vote for bonds to construct buildings

in another part of the area. This problem might be accentuated in some
community districts especially in the first few years after their establishment. The difficulty could be lessened, however, if the approval
of bond issues required but a majority vote rather than the present two-
thirds majority. Districts whose building needs exceed the ten per
cent limit of assessed wealth should be able to obtain state funds for
that purpose.

SUMMARY

The costs of operating the public schools have increased 650%
since 1939-40. For the period 1946-47 to 1956-57 a total of $6.07
billion has been expended for current expenses. In addition, approximately $2.54 billion has been expended for new sites, buildings, and
equipment during the past decade — 42% of the amount required for
current operations. The amount for capital outlay, however, was
expended largely from money borrowed via districts and state bonds.
The estimated interest costs on these bonds will be an added one
billion dollars.

Analysis of Present Cost Level. The increase in current expense, stated for simplicity in terms of 100%, has been due to: (1)
inflation (34.7%); (2) increased population (42.8%), of which about one-
third is attributable to increased family size; and (3) increases in cost
per child (22%), of which about four-fifths has been due to increases in
teachers' salaries. The average cost per child (current expense of
education per ADA) in grades K-14 was $346 in 1956-57. In constant
dollars this was 31% above the figure for the base year of 1939-40.

Future Costs. Average costs per ADA will increase approximately 12% as the present wave of population growth reaches high
school, where costs are higher, due to that reason alone. Total costs
will rise rapidly as a predicted 80% increase in school population (K-12)
takes place by 1970; as increased high school costs are felt; and as
teachers' salaries advance. The present one billion dollars in current
expenditures may well increase to $2 or $2.5 billion by 1970 and to
proportionately higher amounts if more inflation occurs.

Percentage of Income Devoted to Education. In spite of the increase in current expenses, only 2.7% of personal income was devoted
to public education in 1956-57, which is well below the depression high
of 3.4% and about the same as that for the base year of 1939-40. This
relatively constant percentage of personal income reflects the fact that,
although dependents have increased, income per adult from 18 to 64
has increased 75% between 1939-40 and 1956-57.

If real income continues to increase as it has in the past, there may be only a small increase in the percentage of income required for the public schools; if not, it will probably increase sharply.

Revenues

State aid ($583 million in 1957-58) is disbursed under a formula that resulted in a "loss" of about $31 million in the level of school support for that year. In effect, this "loss" is due to: (1) heavy flat-grant apportionments to wealthy districts whose rates of taxation are significantly below the state average; (2) a pattern of district organization that encourages the continuance of an inefficient fiscal system, which in turn encourages the status quo in organization; (3) the isolation of hundreds of millions of dollars of assessed industrial wealth by school district boundaries which prevent that wealth from supporting, in many instances, even the nearby schools where the employees of these industries reside; and (4) the virtual impossibility of attaining high fiscal efficiency under present constitutional provisions.

Effect of Growth on State Aid. The constitutional guarantee of $180 per ADA is reduced to about $167 by the present one-year lag in apportionment. A part of the State School Fund is apportioned on a prior year basis. The apportionment for "growth" is now a necessity, but attention should be called to the fact that a change to a current year basis would increase state aid by about $12 to $13 per child.

Other Fiscal Problems

Differences exist among counties in the ratio of assessed to "true" wealth. Although the relative standing of a given county is officially known, it has not been available to the public, nor has it been used in adjusting the apportionments of state funds to school districts, although a provision to that effect is included in Chapter 1466 of the Statutes of 1949. (Thanks to action by the Legislature in 1959, however, these ratios will be published from now on.)

Revision in Method of Apportionment. A change in the method of apportionment is indicated and a proposed plan is given in some detail under Recommendations (see also the last section of this chapter). This method, or another embodying similar principles, will provide relief for the taxpayer in poor districts and raise the efficiency of state aid. An increase in school support of about $12 per ADA is possible with the same average tax rate, and the same amount of state funds per child. This amount, together with advantages to be gained by apportioning funds on a current year basis, would provide an additional $25.00 per K-12 ADA or about $65 million dollars.

Community Districts. A type of district resembling the unified district for fiscal purposes, but permitting the component elementary districts a degree of autonomy is recommended. The community district would have a number of major advantages and no apparent disadvantages.

RECOMMENDATIONS

The foregoing sections of this chapter have offered a number of suggestions for changes in fiscal procedures. Here, for the sake of space and brevity, these recommendations are presented in summary form. It is hoped that the following proposals might be considered by the California Legislature and by professional and civic groups as suggesting means by which the effectiveness of both state and local tax bases may be increased, the efficiency of all tax revenues improved, and higher educational standards achieved for all children in the state. In brief, we recommend:

General Considerations:

1. A joint policy standards board be established as an unofficial, nonpolitical advisory body on a permanent basis.

2. A state educational research board be established. This should bring together public and private agencies and colleges and universities not only to coordinate routine statistical procedures but more particularly to promote significant research in the several disciplines related to education.

3. Research funds be obtained for the educational research board by invitation to professional organizations, by requests for foundation grants, and by legislative appropriation.

4. An amendment to the state Constitution to be made which would remove the restraints to a more efficient apportionment formula and permit apportionments to be made on a current-year basis.

5. As greater state funds are needed in the immediate years ahead, a gradual change to an apportionment for each current year be made. From this method and that suggested by 4 above, an approximate increase of $25 per ADA is possible under the present provision of $180 per ADA.

6. All district school boards be requested to prepare written statements of local policies and operating standards.

Organization:

7. Studies be made of the feasibility of creating from eight to ten regional school districts which would function for both fiscal and administrative purposes in lieu of counties.

8. A system of community districts be established and that the community district or the unified district be the minimum units to which state school funds are apportioned.

Informational Studies:

9. Statistical standards for recording, reporting, analyzing, and publishing be developed by the State Department of Education, State Research Board, and the several other agencies concerned.

10. An annual or biennial report on education, comprehensive in nature, be made by the State Department of Education.

11. Preliminary studies be made toward establishing an index of the educational operating costs and school construction costs.

12. The ratio of assessed to "true" wealth be published by counties, and that this factor be employed in adjusting assessed valuation for state apportionment purposes.

Administrative and Management Studies:

13. Studies of best practice in specialized fields such as site acquisition, transportation, bonding, and others be prepared jointly by business officials and specialized personnel and published by the State Department of Education.

Fiscal Policy:

14. The Legislature adopt, as a general policy, a level of state support of the public school system which approximates 50% of current operating expenses if all state funds are equalized, or 75% if the principal apportionment is largely on a flat grant basis.

15. All state funds apportioned to school districts be equalized to counties.

16. County taxes (to the extent of one-sixth of state average costs) be levied, one-half of this amount being a county-levied but state-collected income tax and the other a property tax.

17. State and county funds be combined and equalized to districts.

18. A plan of apportionment embodying the principles herein employed be adopted.

19. There be no legal tax limit in any district for current expenses short of the level required to cover average state expenditures per ADA for the most recent year for which data are available.

20. The tax limit for amounts above the state average be set at a point at which about two-thirds of the medium-sized or larger districts of average wealth normally deviate.

Capital Outlay:

21. All costs of building replacement be financed by the state or by a regional district on a cash basis for 1/50 of the construction each year, presuming mean building life to be 50 years.

22. Hereafter all bonds be issued only by unified or community districts and that the latter be given the right to assume all bonds of their component districts.

23. State building aid be continued for districts whose building needs for grades K-12 exceed 10% of their assessed wealth, but that the repayment rate not exceed the rate required for 10% bonding.

24. A majority vote be sufficient in a community district to authorize the sale of bonds up to 10% of its assessed wealth.

25. Site acquisition be so regulated by law that the public interest is protected against inflated prices and that suitable sites for schools are included in plans for subdivision development.

NOTES TO CHAPTERS 8 AND 9

1. Hollis P. Allen and Frank Farner, The Facts About Your School Districts in Riverside County, a publication of the Riverside County Committee on School District Organization, 1957.

2. Assembly Interim Committee on Public Education, Fifty-seventh Legislative Session, Second Report, 1949.

3. Fred F. Beach and Robert F. Will, The State and Non-Public Schools. U.S. Department of Health, Education and Welfare, Misc. Circular No. 28, 1958.

4. Ralph Boyden (earlier years) or Ray H. Johnson and Dorothy Kirshman (later years), "General Fund Expenditures of California School Districts for the Fiscal Year . . .", California Schools, annually, usually March or April.

5. _____, "Three Decades of Capital Investment," California Schools, XXVI (June 1955), 297-310.

6. California State Chamber of Commerce, Economic Survey Series, 1957, "Personal Income in California Counties."

7. California State Department of Education, Apportionment of the State School Fund for the Fiscal Year Ending . . . , Part I.

8. _____, Bureau of Education Research. Punched cards containing wealth and cost data for all districts for the school year 1956-57. The set consists of 5 decks, each containing a card for each district in the state. Columns on the cards contain the following: identification and name of district, grade span, assessed valuation, tax rate, ADA, CEE as a total and per ADA, and total expenditures for each account classification, per ADA and as a per cent of total expenditures.

9. _____, Bureau of Education Research. Unpublished (mimeographed) enrollment and attendance summaries supplied by Henry W. Magnuson, Bureau Chief.

10. _____, Bureau of Education Research. Salaries of Certificated Employees in California Public Schools, 1957-58.

11. _____, Bureau of School Apportionments and Reports. Unpublished (photostated) data regarding purposes of expenditures for capital outlay, by fund, 1956-57, supplied by Ray H. Johnson and Dorothy Kirshman.

12. _____, Bureau of School District Organization. Financing Small Elementary Schools and Small High Schools in California, 1955.

13. _____, Bureau of School District Organization. Unpublished list of High School Districts with Component Elementary Districts, 1957-58, supplied by Drayton B. Nuttall, Bureau Chief.

14. California State Department of Finance, Budget Division, "California's Population in 1957." Unpublished material prepared by Carl M. Frisén, senior research technician for population studies, 1958.

15. California State Department of Finance, Budget Division, "Projections of California's Civilian Population by Single Year of Age and for Selected Age-Groups." Unpublished (mimeographed) material prepared by Carl M. Frisén, senior research technician for population studies, 1958.

16. _____, Unpublished (photostated) Enrollment Projections for Public and Parochial Schools prepared by Carl M. Frisén, senior research technician for population studies, 1958.

17. California State Superintendent of Public Instruction, Biennial Report, 1929-30.

18. California Taxpayers' Association, "Expenditures of California School Districts from General Funds, 1929-30 to 1950-51," Association Report No. 13, 1952.

19. Clayton D. Hutchins, Albert R. Munse and Edna D. Booher, Trends in Significant Facts on School Finance, 1929-30 to 1953-54. U. S. Department of Health, Education and Welfare Circular No. 498, 1957.

20. Henry W. Magnuson and Peter Tashnovian, "Teacher Load in California Public Schools, October 31 . . .," California Schools, annually, usually February or March.

21. Henry W. Magnuson, Thomas A. Shellhammer and Peter Tashnovian, "Teacher Load in California Public Schools," California Schools, April 1953, August 1954, and July 1955.

22. National Education Association, Committee on Tax Education and School Finance, "Equalization of Property Assessments," January 1958.

23. Drayton B. Nuttall, "School District Organization Changes in California, 1956-57," California Schools, XXIX, No. 1 (January 1958), pp. 24-32.

24. Senate Interim Committee on State and Local Taxation, California Legislature, 1953 Regular Session. Property Assessments and Equalization in California, March 1953.

25. State of California Franchise Tax Board. Annual Report, 1957.

26. State Controller, Annual Report of Financial Transactions Concerning School Districts of California, Fiscal Year, 1956-57.

27. U. S. Department of Commerce, Office of Business Statistics. Personal Income by States since 1929, 1956.

28. _____, Census Bureau. Current Population Reports, Series P-25.

29. _____, Construction Volume and Costs, 1915-1956, 1958.

30. U. S. Department of Health, Education and Welfare, Biennial Survey of Education in the United States, 1953-54, Chapter II, "Statistics of State School Systems."

PART VI

TRENDS AND CONCLUSIONS

JOHN A. VIEG

The problem of local finance is inseparable from that of local government itself: How can citizens provide themselves with the public services they need, manage them with reasonable efficiency, and devise an equitable system of revenue for their support? Considering the size and mobility of California's population, the profusion and complexity of its machinery of local government, the varieties and conflicts of interest within its body politic, and the not always nicely articulated aids and controls through which the state is involved in the life of its local subdivisions, the solution to this question is not easy to find.

The time is long since past when it would be possible in such a study to keep the focus of inquiry limited to the local level itself. Counties, cities, special districts, and, above all, school districts have become so dependent in recent years upon state aid and shared revenues that no one can understand the problems involved without looking at the California system of state and local finance as a whole.

PATTERNS AND TRADITIONS

By any ordinary test California local government serves the 15 million people of the state honestly and well. Yet in many places it suffers from a number of chronic ailments that impair its efficiency, hinder its adjustment to changing economic and social conditions, and could, ultimately, undermine local freedom and initiative. Complaints about taxation come mainly from four types of people: (1) those whose need for the services of government tends to be less than that of the community in general, (2) those who either do not appreciate the amount of work being done or do not understand the conditions under which local governments are required to operate, (3) those who believe the revenue system is in some way unjust or inequitable, and (4) those who want service without having to pay for it. Something can perhaps be done to meet the criticisms of the first three groups. The fourth is hopeless. Meanwhile, the California version of the good life has come to include a fantastic number of gadgets and conveniences bought in most cases on the miscalled "easy payment plan." Added to mortgage and insurance payments these installment bills entail a heavy drain on the average man's take-home pay and seriously affect his ability to pay for the costs of local government.

The federal division of labor between the nation and the states resembles a marble cake rather than a layer cake and this is also true of the functional division of labor among California's local units. In all the more populous sections of the state every parcel of property

is included in from two to seven or eight different units, each of which
possesses autonomous power to spend money and levy taxes. Yet no
agency, other than the voter himself, is clothed with the responsibility
of weighing the relative benefits derived from these several units; and
the voter finds his responsibility difficult to carry because few units
ever have identical boundaries.

THE GOVERNMENTS AND THE ECONOMY

With 159,000 square miles, California ranks as the third largest
state in the union, immediately behind Alaska and Texas and just ahead
of Montana. Its size and population make it a good deal bigger than
many important countries of the world. The joint product of historical
development and ad hoc improvement, California's machinery of local
government consists of 57 counties, 351 cities, the consolidated City-
County of San Francisco, 1,818 school districts, and around 3,000
special districts. Except for the counties, whose boundaries have remained stable for nearly half a century, these numbers are constantly
changing. New cities and special districts are being incorporated in
the suburban hinterlands of many large cities though, as a welcome
departure from the general pattern, the number of school districts is
slowly declining.

With a few outstanding exceptions the counties are currently the
weakest link in the chain of local government. Yet their potential value
has greatly increased. Given the emerging pattern of "rurban" development made possible by California's climate, roads, and automobiles, the county, properly modernized, could play a much larger role
than it does today — one that could both help simplify the governmental
map and make the whole process of local politics and administration
more clearly understandable and controllable. The position of the
cities, thanks to what they have done to reduce the number of elective
officials and improve internal management, is much more encouraging.
With respect to school districts, the causes of inefficiency lie not so
much in their internal organization as in the irrationality of their boundaries and, in the case of special districts, in their multiplicity, their
overlapping of other units, and the difficulty of making their governing
officials general responsible to their constituents.

Problems of finance among all these units are further complicated
and intensified by wide differences in mean levels of wealth and income.
Were the burden of taxation spread more equitably it would pose few
difficulties, for the people of California own private tangible wealth

valued at more than $100 billion and received in 1957 personal income
amounting to $34.5 billion (just about 10% of the national total) — this
against state and local expenditures totaling just under $4.5 billion for
that same year. As an index of the role of local government in the
California economy, nearly one out of every 13 persons in the labor
force is now employed by some local unit.

NATURE, VOLUME, AND DISTRIBUTION OF LOCAL EXPENDITURES

The core of the average citizen's analysis of local finance is
simply this: "Government expenditures must be higher than ever today
because my taxes are higher than ever before." Pressed by other
demands upon his pocketbook, he jumps, not unnaturally, to the conclusion that public expenditures must be too high and that they should
therefore be cut. Yet the question "Are expenditures too high?" is
quite different from the question "Can expenditures be cut?" The
answer to the second will nearly always be "Yes" but this has almost
no bearing upon the first. Government expenditures are too high when,
for the last dollar in the local budget, social costs exceed social benefits; when the situation is reversed, they are too low. The trouble
arises in measuring them. Voting appears to offer the only practical
method whereby the people of a community can weigh social costs
against benefits. Yet it does not really compare them. The truth of
the matter is that no formula can do this because the satisfactions and
sacrifices of different individuals per dollar of expenditure are never
precisely equal.

Accurate comparisons of public expenditures for different years
are possible only if current costs are separated from capital outlays.
Even so, due allowance must be made for three potential sources of
error: the defects or inconsistencies in governmental accounting; the
shortcomings of partial analysis, such as examining fire protection
without reference to insurance rates; and the fallacy of comparing
differences in expenditure without regard to differences in levels of
service. It goes without saying that allowance must also be made for
the effects of inflation and increase in population.

Three striking facts are revealed by a systematic analysis of
local expenditures. There is a very wide range, alike among cities,
counties, and school districts, in their per capita expenditures, from
the standpoint of both totals and amounts devoted to separate functions.
When current expenditures are adjusted for inflation and population
growth, they show only a slight increase over the past twenty years

and this has occurred chiefly among counties and school districts.
Capital outlays have been much higher in relation to operating costs in
recent years than they were in the late 1930's: they were twice as great
for counties in 1957 as in 1937, and three times as great for cities.

CALIFORNIA'S EXISTING REVENUE SYSTEM

California's local governments are confronted today by a combination of revenue problems that are rapidly developing into a crisis.
City councils, county boards, and school trustees share with the members of the Legislature the responsibility for meeting this threat in a
way that will insure adequate funds for all essential services, preserve
the fiscal solvency of the state, and neither constrict nor impede private enterprise.

Taken in the aggregate, California's local governments derived
their revenues from these sources in 1956-57, the latest fiscal year
for which figures were available at the time of writing: property taxes,
46.2%; other taxes, 6%; service charges, 13.2%; and grants-in-aid and
shared revenues, 34.6%. Their fiscal difficulties stem from several
factors peculiarly related to community needs and resources as well
as to the organizational factors already cited. On the expenditure side,
probably the most important have been the backlog of public works
projects deferred during the depression and World War II; the general
burgeoning of population, especially among children of school age; the
vast movement of people into new subdivisions and suburbs; and the
widespread demands for improved as well as expanded service. On the
revenue side, those of chief significance have been excessive reliance
on the general property tax, the failure of state and local legislative
bodies to formulate a more diversified revenue system and the ease
and effectiveness with which the ordinary citizen can protest against
local levies as compared with state and national taxes. While the pattern of local taxation is generally agreed to be regressive in character,
that of the state is progressive, the slight regressivity of its excises
being more than offset, according to a 1958 report of the State Board
of Equalization, by the progressivity of its other taxes. It has now
(December 1958) been a full quarter century since there has been a
comprehensive examination of California's revenue program as a
whole.

VARIATION IN LOCAL INDEBTEDNESS

Though the state has set a fine example in financing most of its
own capital improvements on a pay-as-you-go basis, local governments

have not followed suit nearly as well as they might have done. Handicapped in some ways by the limitations of their revenue sources, though
certainly more by their neglect of long-range planning and effective
management, many of them have borrowed both more and earlier than
was necessary. As of June 30, 1957, the grand total of state and local
bonded debt amounted to approximately $4.3 billion, the proportions
being as follows: state, 26.7%; counties, 7.3%; cities, 23.6%; school
districts, 29.6%; and special districts (the latest figures available were
for 1956) 12.8%.

Figures on county indebtedness indicate that the ratio of bonded
debt to assessed valuation changed for the median county from 2.6% in
1937 to 1.4% in 1947, and 4.7% in 1957. Meanwhile, the ratio of debt
service to the total cost of government in the median county shifted
from 7.7% in 1937 to 2.5% in 1947, and 3.2% in 1957. Statistics on the
bonded indebtedness of California's cities varied in 1957, as follows:
in terms of per capita debt the range between the first and third quartiles ran from 41 cents to $46.89, with the median at $20.22; bonded
indebtedness as a percentage of assessed valuation ranged from .06%
at the first quartile to 4.68% at the third, with the median at 1.70%;
debt service as a percentage of the total cost of government varied
from .4% at the first quartile to 6.3% at the third, with 3.2% at the
median.

Among school districts the variation in taxable wealth per ADA
(per child in average daily attendance) is so great and the operation of
the state loan plan so illogical that, as of 1955-56, among the 377
elementary districts, or 21%, levying taxes for debt service per se
(79% had none at all), at one extreme 27 had rates of less than 40 cents
per $100 of assessed valuation, at the other 14 had rates of more than
$2.00, and the rest were scattered rather evenly in between. Subven-
tions and grants made by the state to its local governments should presumably be in inverse relation to their ability to support themselves,
yet a ranking of the counties of California from the standpoint of subventions and grants per capita, personal income per capita and composite local debt per capita reveals numerous anomalies.

From the standpoint of having to incur additional indebtedness
during the next two or three decades California's school districts,
more than her other local units, undoubtedly face a tougher prospect.
Their need for new buildings and grounds is so great, and in many

cases so desperate, that despite substantial state assistance in the
period since the war the Assembly Subcommittee on School Construction
Funds found itself obliged to report in March 1959 that the people of
California will soon have to find "another method" of financing school
construction. The subcommittee found that: (1) under the present
system of borrowing, yearly interest charges are getting to be astronomical; (2) a pay-as-you-go plan would yield many advantages; (3)
construction costs must somehow be equalized from county to county;
and (4) the state should discontinue the practice of issuing school bonds
which cannot be paid off until their expiration date.

PRESENT PATTERN OF SCHOOL FINANCE

Many school districts in California are healthy, wealthy, and
perhaps even a bit complacent but many others are wracked by the
kind of problems that plagued Mother Hubbard and the Old Woman Who
Lived in a Shoe. Their troubles stem, as suggested earlier, from the
explosive expansion of school population but also from certain inequities latent in the state program of school finance. Approximately half
of the current expense of education is covered by the local property
tax; except for federal grants covering an additional 2 or 3%, all the
other revenues come from the state. The need for state aid, even for
current operations, is perhaps best shown by the fact that the poorest
district has but $272 of assessed valuation per ADA while the wealthiest
has $1,227,335 or over 7,000 times as much.

Despite the vast need for state aid to hundreds of poor districts,
great waste and inefficiency are involved in distributing state funds to
wealthy districts. Irrespective of its resources, every local district
receives a flat grant of either $125 per ADA or $2,400, whichever
amount is greater. This basic aid goes to districts rolling in wealth
as well as to those in distress. It is only equalization aid which is apportioned on the basis of need. Allocations are made on the basis of
foundation program formulas which, depending upon the size, level,
and wealth of the district, vary from $218 per ADA for elementary
districts of average or above average wealth to $410 for junior college
districts. To qualify for such aid a district must first tax itself at or
above the minimum rate prescribed for districts of its class; the amount
of aid it receives is then the difference between the yield of its own legal
rate and the total guaranteed by the foundation program applicable to
its situation.

As indicated above, equalization aid is given on the basis of need. Yet it should be remembered that in most cases this need is largely the result of a kind of gerrymandering — of drawing district boundary lines in such a way as to form both islands of wealth and islands of poverty. The range in taxable wealth per ADA between the richest and poorest districts could be reduced tremendously if the people of California wanted to do so. By consolidating all districts into 327 potential community districts (each formed around some sizable, central urban community and based as much as possible on the 327 existing high school and unified districts), the ratio would drop from 7,136 to 1 down to 22 to 1. Were each county, except Alpine, to serve as a district for all its public schools, as San Francisco does today, the ratio would fall even further and become 11 to 1. Finally, were the state to use for purposes of school finance the nine regional areas used for statistical purposes by the State Department of Finance, the ratio would drop to an almost utopian 1.7 to 1.

One important reason why many of California's school districts have fallen on hard times financially is that, despite the secular trend toward increasing state support, the legislature has failed during the past few years to appropriate enough money to enable the state to "keep up its share." Thus for all districts, local support, which accounted for only 47.9% of general fund revenues in 1953-54, was obliged to carry 52.3% of the load in 1956-57. (By its action in June 1959, however, the legislature took a long step toward easing the burden on local taxpayers beginning with fiscal 1960. State aid was increased by $26.5 million annually primarily for the purpose of aiding distressed districts by enlarging their ADA payments from $193.37 to $210 per child.)

When it comes to expenditures there is a wide range among local districts in the proportions of their current budgets allocated to such functions as administration, instruction, maintenance, and transportation. Costs of administration vary from less than 2 to more than 12%. Allocations for teachers' salaries vary from under 50 to something over 74%, maintenance from 1 to 14% and transportation from 2 to 20%. The range of current expenditures per ADA among districts is, if anything, more striking. Among 555 districts in the middle range of 101-600 ADA, 105 spent less than $250 per child while 2 spent over $900. Among the 271 largest districts, all with more than 600 ADA, 56 spent less than $250 per child while the one most favorable situated spent over $500.

TOUCHSTONES OF POLICY

Americans are frequently described by others and criticized by themselves as being materialistic, and so, to a degree, they are — just like people everywhere. But no proposal for public policy has any chance of adoption in free and open discussion if it cannot be squared with at least one of the major moral-political principles embodied in their civic scriptures. The American ethos is libertarian, egalitarian, individualistic, and localistic and any change made in California's system of state and local finance must square with one or more of those standards. The best reforms would square with all of them.

There are, however, some other considerations that should also be borne in mind in dealing with anything as fundamental as the reconstruction of a state-local revenue system. They have to do with the necessity of conscientiously trying to reconcile the rational with the traditional. The people of California are accustomed to their present revenue system, and it has many good features. They want it improved in the way that makes the greatest possible use of the sciences of economics, government, sociology, and administration but they will not accept recommendations that do not also respect their history, which is to say their traditional way of meeting these problems. The proposals in this report are based on those several considerations as touchstones of policy.

MODERNIZING THE ORGANIZATION OF LOCAL GOVERNMENT

Modern technology commits men to increasing mutual dependence upon each other. If their political system is to bear some rational relation to the economic system underlying it, the various units and levels of government within a state like California must exhibit a similar interdependence. The Legislature at Sacramento decided in the crisis of the depression that it was no longer feasible to think in terms of separate sources of revenue for the state and its localities. The experience of the past generation has confirmed the wisdom of that decision and calls for its extension today. This does not mean that it is not important to secure for each local unit every bit of financial independence its circumstances will allow. Without a substantial measure of self-support, nothing like genuine self-government could long endure. To achieve this end, some of the weaker units will need to combine with others and some of the stronger ones will need to be enlarged in area or function.

Probably the best way to get started on such a modernization program would be for the Legislature to establish a commission on local government and metropolitan areas having indefinite tenure and charge it with proposing and, upon adoption, cultivating a plan of reorganization which, while conserving the basic values of the existing pattern, would make the local revenue sources of each city, county, school district, and special district more nearly equal to its needs. (Governor Brown appointed a 19-member Commission on Metropolitan Government on March 29, 1959.) With respect to problems of educational finance it should consult closely with the Bureau of School District Organization in the State Department of Education. Meanwhile the state should re-examine the effects of its own subventions and grants to see whether they might not inadvertently be prolonging and aggravating the problem rather than helping to solve it.

As for the malaise of "metropolitanitis" which is in many ways the heart of the problem, Californians have always lived with bigness. Yet they are destined to have to wrestle with the problem of scale more intensively than ever in the future. How can they manage to do this successfully and still conserve the values of the small town or middling city? The answer lies in accepting the metropolis as a basic feature of modern life and balancing appreciation of its assets with recognition of its liabilities. Maintaining their historic cities and counties in full vigor, Californians might profitably explore these three alternatives: (1) to encourage the counties to urbanize themselves wherever the situation is appropriate, and to accept responsibility for such broader-than-municipal functions; (2) to cultivate more extensive intergovernmental cooperation on the local level, both by contract and otherwise; (3) to create, wherever they would be of substantial service, politically viable, multipurpose districts co-extensive with the metropolitan area (including some allowance for growth) and vest them with governmental authority and revenue capacity commensurate with the functions they would be expected to perform.

IMPROVING CONTROL OVER LOCAL EXPENDITURES

Something can be done about the cost of government. It is useless to search for a magic formula insuring high standards of service with low taxes and service charges but there are at least five dependable keys to effective expenditure control. First, both citizens and officials should practice greater self-restraint in proposing new functions and, when they do, they should face simultaneously the question

of how the new service is to be paid for. This may sound like a counsel
of perfection but there is simply no escape from the proposition that
free government means personal responsibility with respect to the demand for public services. To be cavalier at this point is to open up a
whole box of troubles later on. Second, the state legislature and local
electorates alike should insist that every city, county, school district,
and special district operate under a clear and tight system of political
control and administrative management, and that accounts and records
be kept in accordance with these purposes.

Third, the state should encourage, perhaps even require, every
local subdivision to plan each year's budget, current as well as capital,
in the light of projections extending at least six years ahead, except
that site acquisitions should be planned 12 years in advance wherever
possible. It would be a kindness toward them rather than a hardship
if the state, giving, say, two years' notice, were thereafter to make
all local assistance conditional upon the completion and adoption of
appropriate master plans. Fourth, since the bulk of every budget
usually goes for personal services, every local government should
adopt the strategy of using fewer but abler employees to man the public
services, openly accepting all that this implies in terms of higher
salaries and adherence to the test of merit. Fifth, local governments
should follow the practice of progressive business everywhere in utilizing only the most efficient procedures, equipment, and facilities.
Few if any of California's local jurisdictions have gone as far as they
could on this score.

FACING THE REVENUE PROBLEM IN CALIFORNIA

Probably the best way to approach the problem of improving the
local revenue system would be openly to recognize the necessity to
develop a unified state-local revenue plan for California. This recognized, serious consideration should be given to a number of specific
changes, some pertaining primarily to the local and others to the
state level: (1) With respect to the ad valorem or general property
tax, we recommend a critical review of present exemptions, greater
flexibility in rate limitations, improvement in assessment methods
(including elimination of duplicate assessment by cities and counties
wherever now practiced), increased emphasis on intercounty equalization, introduction of quarterly installment payments, use of an averaging technique in the valuation of business inventories, revision of the
"in lieu" formula with respect to federally owned property, and adop-

tion of a county-wide property tax as a basic local source for school district revenue.

(2) With respect to the 1% local retail sales tax, we believe it should be retained at the present level as long as food for home use remains exempt. (3) We suggest that every municipality in the state review its business license ordinance with a view to making it produce greater revenue in line with the practice of California's more progressive cities, and that counties be empowered to enact such ordinances for unincorporated areas. (4) Charges for service have become an important source of revenue for local governments during the past decade or two and they are entirely appropriate wherever the benefit principle can be fairly applied, as in the case of fees for certain regulatory services and charges for sewage connections and refuse disposal. There may be other functions beyond these which could reasonably be supported in this way but in general we recommend a hold-the-line policy in this area. (5) Given the mobility of wealth and the fluidity of income in modern society — and these are features that seem to be especially pronounced in contemporary California — we are convinced that the crisis gathering in local finance cannot be dispelled without increasing reliance on the formula of shared revenues. The Legislature has already gone far in recognizing this principle but we believe it could wisely go farther yet, provided local elective officials prove willing to share the onus of what must, pro forma, wear the appearance of state levies.

(6) Turning to the state government and exploring its capacity to contribute to the solution of problems of local finance, we may begin by urging that the state continue to apply the benefit principle to its own operations wherever appropriate. The gasoline and diesel fuel "taxes" and the various other motor vehicle fees doubtless provide the clearest examples: they are of tremendous significance in the total scheme of state finance and are thoroughly accepted as the proper way of paying for California's magnificent though costly highways. (7) The key to increasing revenues in the state's General Fund, however, lies in expanding the taxes based on the principle of ability-to-pay; without advances here the state would not be in a position to share additional revenues with its local units. We believe there should be substantial increases in the rates at which both the personal and corporate income taxes are levied. Retaining the exemptions presently in force, we recommend eight (instead of six) brackets for the individual income tax.

These should begin at $0, 2, 4, 6, 8, 10, 15 and 20 thousand and the
rates should start at 1% and increase by 1% for each succeeding bracket
up to 8 at the top. As for the bank, franchise, and corporate income
taxes, we recommend that the rates for all three be increased from 4
to at least 6%.

(8) Insurance premiums comprise another source of revenue of
which the state could justifiably make further use. We recommend
that the tax on gross premiums, currently set at 2.35%, be increased
to 3.35%. (9) In place of its present wholly nominal tax on the privilege of severing or extracting natural resources from the soil or water
of the state, we recommend that California adopt a severance tax comparable with that employed by other states similarly endowed with
natural resources, particularly Louisiana, Oklahoma, and Texas. Their
severance taxes amounted, respectively, to 22.2%, 14.4% and 30.1%
of total state tax collections in 1957, while California's amounted to a
mere .078 of 1%.

(10) Inasmuch as considerable time may be required for making
some of the basic changes recommended above, it may be that the 3%
sales and use tax will have to be retained indefinitely. (With respect
to liquor and tobacco taxes, we make no recommendation. They contribute relatively far less revenue in California than in other leading
states, but there are serious differences of opinion among public finance authorities on both whether and how such commodities should be
taxed, and it is impossible to formulate a recommendation based upon
a generally accepted principle.) Apart from those few services which
it would be fair and proper to finance by user charges proportioned to
benefits, the people of California should aim, for the long run, at a
truly equitable revenue system based squarely on the principle of
ability-to-pay. In the light of present knowledge, such a system would
have something like these dimensions: the personal and corporate
income taxes would be expected through roughly equal amounts to
yield approximately 50% of the state's total tax income; the sales and
use tax, 30%; the severance tax, 10%; the insurance premiums tax, 5%;
gift and inheritance taxes, 4%; and miscellaneous ad valorem taxes, 1%.

MINIMIZING THE COST OF DEBT SERVICE

Other things equal, the simplest and best way to minimize the
cost of debt service is to obviate the need for borrowing through careful planning and spending and through the accumulation of capital outlay reserves. Beyond this, the essentials are to borrow at the lowest

possible rate of interest and to redeem bonds in the shortest possible time. As a means of insuring these objectives, each local unit should be required to report annually to the State Controller and the Director of Finance the amount of its Cumulative Capital Outlay Fund and likewise the requirements of its capital improvement program over the next five years.

In return the state should do three things. First, it should establish a local credit reserve fund in which local governments, if they wished, could deposit their own reserves until they were actually needed. The state would manage this fund as productively as possible and, after deducting expenses, pay each city, county, school district and special district its pro rata share of interest earned. Second, assuming the tighter and longer-range local planning recommended above, the state should accept the proposal made in April 1959 by the Assembly Subcommittee on Public Indebtedness and lower from 66 2/3 to at least 60% the size of the popular majority required for local bond issues, making the rule apply to special districts as well as to counties, cities, and school districts and to so-called lease-purchase arrangements as well as to general obligation bonds. Otherwise, local units might be unable to borrow at the most opportune times. Third, after establishing appropriate safeguards, the state should make its own superior credit resources available to all local units as it is already doing on a limited scale for school districts. The principal reason for the relatively high interest rates most small and middle-sized jurisdictions have to pay on bonded indebtedness is not any danger of default but simply the fact that they are obliged to sell their bonds within a narrow market. It goes almost without saying that communities should redeem their debts serially rather than through the accumulation of sinking funds.

MAXIMIZING THE VALUE OF THE SCHOOL TAX DOLLAR

Further inflation aside, California faces the prospect of seeing current expenditures for education increase from their present level of $1 billion to at least $2 billion and perhaps as much as $2.5 billion by 1970. The reasons for this huge increase lie in three factors: an 80% increase in school population, the certainty of a greater ratio of high school to elementary pupils, and the need for increases in teachers' salaries. The demands upon the taxpayers implicit in this situation will obviously be heavy but they can be met and mastered without hardship if steps are taken now to place school finance on a basis of genuine equity and efficiency.

As a first step, a state educational research board should be established and every local school district should be required to prepare and maintain on a current basis, both for its own use and for the board's, formal statements of its major policies, its operating standards, and its vital problems. Studies should be made of the feasibility of using the State Finance Department's nine statistical regions for certain fiscal purposes in connection with school finance and meanwhile the various county committees on school district organization should be authorized and required to devise within two years a pattern of unified and community districts to serve as minimal units for the apportionment of all state funds.

Equity calls for both equal educational opportunity and equity in taxation, but the disparities in wealth per child among California's elementary school districts are now so great that only by having the state provide 99.9% of their revenues could the inequity be reduced to a 10% difference in tax rates. Efficient use of school monies means combining state and local funds to maximize the value of both and at the same minimize the tax rates necessary to raise them. No state money should be allocated to districts wholly able to support themselves yet, in 1957-58, over $31 million was "lost" or "wasted" through the inefficient coordination of state and local resources. In other words, had these resources been used efficiently, state aid (for needy districts) could have been $31 million greater. To deal with these gross improprieties, we believe (assuming favorable action on the recommendations offered above) that the state should adopt one or the other of these two policies: (a) use its own funds exclusively for equalization purposes and limit its support to approximately 50 per cent of current operating expenses, or (b) continue the present plan of basic aid plus equalization aid but accept responsibility for supporting approximately 75% of current expenditures.

In either case, we recommend that the county also levy a school tax (ideally an income tax) and that the funds so derived be combined with state funds for equalizing district revenues. No district should be eligible for equalization aid without levying a property tax at a rate equal to the computation tax, and no tax limit should be imposed on a district short of the effort required to support its schools at the level of state mean costs per ADA for the preceding year. The legal maximum (without an override) should be set at the point at which approximately two-thirds of the medium-sized and larger districts of average wealth normally deviate.

With respect to capital outlays, costs for new school sites and buildings and for the replacement of existing structures will rise tremendously during the next few decades. Assuming favorable action on the recommendations previously made for minimizing the cost of debt service, we urge that new construction be made the exclusive responsibility of unified and community districts but that the state defray all building costs exceeding 10% of assessed valuation and that the costs of replacement be put on an actually determined current-cash basis depending upon the mean life of the structures involved.

NEEDS AND PROSPECTS

In presenting its report on Local Government Finance in California: 1940-53, the Senate Interim Committee on State and Local Taxation called for an end to hand-to-mouth operations and urged the adoption of long-range policies that would insure the solvency of both the state and its local units. They suggested that, at the state level, the objectives of fiscal policy should be to meet the need for growing expenditures and preserve the "commendable balance" in the revenue system as a whole and that, at the local level, the objectives should be to develop "fiscal self-sufficiency and autonomy" and eliminate "the inequities which by and large characterize local tax structures."

While there are some elements of balance in the state revenue system, many things can be done — and should be done — to make it both more productive and more equitable. On the local level, considerable "autonomy" certainly deserves to remain as a long-range goal but "fiscal self-sufficiency" has ceased to be a practical or even an appropriate objective. The sounder approach would look to the development of a broadly unified state-and-local revenue system within which cities, counties, school districts, and special districts could achieve substantial autonomy on the twin foundations of shared revenues and local taxes and service charges

California taxes are high in some ways, yet the state and its localities generally have considerable room for adjustment and maneuver. Differences in tax burdens throughout the country are commonly expressed in per capita amounts or percentages of income. Of these two measures clearly the second is the more significant; but there is a third that is even more illuminating, namely, degree of sacrifice, which one writer has computed by dividing taxes as a percentage of personal income by per capita personal income itself. It is particularly instructive in this concluding chapter to note the relative degree of sacrifice required,

on the average, from the taxpayers of California for supporting their
state and local services in 1957, the year on which so much of the
statistical analysis in this volume rests. In terms of taxes per capita,
California's were the highest in the union. On a per capita basis California's taxes, at $237.14, were the highest in the union. Taking them as
a percentage of income, California, at 9.4, ranked 17th in the nation
or almost exactly on a par with Colorado, which, however, stood 10th
in per capita exactions. But from the standpoint of the degree of sacrifice required of its taxpayers, California ranked 38th — with Mississippi
1st, Colorado 27th and Delaware 48th.*

In the months that have elapsed since the completion of this study
in preliminary form, the voters have elected a new governor and a new
Legislature. Under Governor Edmund G. Brown's motto of "fiscal responsibility" these new leaders have not only looked hard and long at
the problem of state and local finance but have put through a major revision of the California revenue system, the first since the dark days
of the depression more than 25 years ago. The time available during the
1959 session did not enable them to give adequate consideration to the
plight of local units but the changes they made in state levies will go
far to insure its solvency in years to come and save it from the danger
of unbalanced budgets. It is estimated that the net result of the new
taxes will be to produce approximately $180 million in additional revenue
toward the 1959-60 budget and nearly $223 million when fully effective,
this against a target of $256 million sought by the governor.

Most of these new funds will come from the following sources:
increased personal income taxes, $62.8 million; a new three-cent per
package cigarette tax, $61.8 million; increased bank (8 to 9-1/2%) and
corporation (4 to 5-1/2%) income taxes, $35.3 million; increased horse-
racing taxes, $10.4 million; a slightly increased beer tax (from two to
four cents per gallon instead of the seven cents recommended by the
governor), $3.6 million; an increased insurance premiums tax, $5 million; and moderately increased inheritance and gift taxes, $2 million.
The one conspicuous omission from the list of taxes recommended by
the administration (and by this study) is a severance tax on the petroleum
industry which, at the rate proposed by Governor Brown, would have
yielded an additional $60 million and put the state treasury clearly in
the black.

*Henry J. Frank, "Measuring State Tax Burdens," National Tax
Journal (June 1959) pp. 179-85.

Having put its own house in reasonably good financial order, it is to be hoped that the state will proceed at the earliest opportunity to help its various subdivisions to do likewise. Despite the $26.5 million of additional aid for needy school districts included in the budget for 1959-60, much remains to be done before the fiscal future of our cities, counties, schools, and special districts is assured. Speaking as citizens and taxpayers as well as professional analysts, the authors of this study would say that the problem of local finance lies less in our pocketbooks than in our perspectives and procedures. This generation of Californians need only match the ingenuity and civic spirit of those who founded the Golden State and there will be no need to worry about adequate financial support for our local public services.

APPENDIX TABLES

Table 2.a Geographic, Demographic & Political Characteristics
of California Cities and Counties. As of June 1958

2.a	1940 Federal Census	1957 Population	Percentage Change	Land Area (Sq. Miles)	Date Incorporated	Charter	General Law	Council Mgr.	Mayor Council
Alameda County	513,011	873,900	70.3%	733.0	1853	X			
Alameda	36,256	70,642	94.8	21.6	1854	X		X	
Albany	11,493	17,590	53.0	3.3	1908	X		X	
Berkeley	85,547	113,805	33.0	18.8	1878	X		X	
Emeryville	2,521	2,889	14.6	2.9	1896		X		X
Fremont	-----	26,788	----	N.A.	1956		X	X	
Hayward	6,739	55,230	719.5	13.8	1876	X		X	
Livermore	2,885	12,595	336.6	2.3	1876		X	X	X
Newark	------	6,948	----	N.A.	1955		X	X	
Oakland	302,163	384,575	15.4	55.3	1852	X		X	
Piedmont	9,866	10,639	7.8	1.8	1907	X			X
Pleasanton	1,278	3,112	143.5	1.0	1894		X		X
San Leandro	14,601	64,571	342.2	8.2	1872	X		X	
Unincorporated Urban Area	------	24,860	----						
Urban Pop.-Total	472,071	749,244	68.0						
-Percentage	92.0	90.8							
Alpine County	323	400	23.0	700.0	1864		X		
Markerville					1864		inactive		
Urban Pop.-Total									
-Percentage	------	----							
Amador County	8,973	9,000	.3	598.0	1854		X		
Amador	249	151	-60.6	0.3	1915		X		X
Ione	------	1,605	----	N.A.	1953		X		X
Jackson	2,024	1,879	-7.7	1.1	1905		X		X
Plymouth	460	382	-20.4	0.6	1915		X		X
Sutter Creek	1,134	1,151	1.5	0.7	1913		X		X
Other Urban Population	-- ---	-----	----						
Urban Pop.-Total	------	-----	----						
-Percentage	------	-----							
Butte County	42,840	72,500	69.2	1,677.0	1850	X			
Biggs	574	784	43.3	0.3	1903		X		X
Chico	9,787	14,696	58.2	5.6	1872	X		X	
Gridley	2,338	3,088	32.1	0.8	1905		X		X
Oroville	4,421	7,019	58.8	1.2	1905	X			X
Other Urban Population	------	6,412	----						
Urban Pop.-Total	13,708	31,215	12.8						
-Percentage	32	42.9							
Calaveras County	8,221	9,400	14.3	1,028.0	1850		X		
Angels	1,163	1,147	-1.4	1.0	1912		X		X
Other Urban Population	-----	-----	----						
Urban Pop.-Total	-----	-----	----						
-Percentage	-----	-----							
Colusa County	9,788	11,900	21.6	1,153.0	1850		X		
Colusa	2,285	3,422	49.8	1.0	1870		X		X
Williams	814	1,243	52.7	0.5	1920		X		X
Other Urban Population	-- --	-----	----						
Urban Pop.-Total	--.---	3,422	----						
-Percentage	-----	28.8							
Contra Costa County	100,450	356,700	255.1	734.0	1850		X		
Antioch	5,106	15,507	203.7	2.6	1872		X	X	
Brentwood	-----	1,854	----	N.A.	1948		X	X	
Concord	1,373	28,537	1,978.4	6.0	1905		X	X	
El Cerrito	6,137	23,633	285.1	3.3	1917		X	X	
Hercules	343	343	No Change	3.1	1900		X		X
Martinez	7,381	8,769	18.8	3.0	1864		X	X	
Pinole	934	3,000	221.2	0.8	1903		X		X
Pittsburg	9,520	16,574	74.1	1.8	1903		X	X	
Richmond	23,642	102,944	335.4	42.0	1905	X		X	
San Pablo	-----	18,270	----	2.5	1948		X	X	
Walnut Creek	1,578	7,928	402.4	1.1	1914		X		X
Other Urban Population	-----	30,651	----						
Urban Pop.-Total	51,786	255,753	394.0						
-Percentage	51.6	71.7							

373

Table 2. a Geographic, Demographic & Political Characteristics
of California Cities and Counties. As of June 1958

2. a	1940 Federal Census	1957 Population	Percentage Change	Land Area (Sq. Miles)	Date Incorporated	Charter	General Law	Council Mgr.	Mayor Council
Del Norte County	4,745	19,200	304.6	1,003.0	1857		X		
Crescent City	1,363	2,709	98.8	1.2	1854		X		X
Other Urban Population	-----	-------	----						
Urban Pop. -Total	-----	2,709	----						
-Percentage	-----	14.1							
El Dorado County	13,229	20,100	51.9	1,725.0	1850		X		
Placerville	3,064	3,833	25.1	2.1	1854		X		X
Other Urban Population	-----	-----							
Urban Pop. -Total	3,064	3,833	25.0						
-Percentage	23.2	19.1							
Fresno County	178,565	336,800	88.6	5,985.0	1856	X			
Clovis	1,626	4,462	174.4	0.9	1912		X		X
Coalinga	5,026	6,021	19.8	2.7	1906		X		X
Firebaugh	704	1,261	79.1	0.3	1914		X		X
Fowler	1,531	1,917	25.2	0.9	1908		X		X
Fresno	60,685	123,238	103.1	26.3	1885	X		X	
Huron	-----	1,373	----	N. A.	1951		X		X
Kerman	-----	1,784	----	N. A.	1946		X		X
Kingsburg	1,504	2,859	90.1	0.6	1908		X		X
Mendota	-----	2,549	----	N. A.	1942		X		X
Orange Cove	-----	2,522	----	N. A.	1948		X		X
Parlier	776	1,419	82.9	0.4	1921		X		X
Reedley	3,170	5,280	66.9	1.7	1913		X		X
Sanger	4,017	8,212	104.4	3.0	1911		X	X	
San Joaquin	240	632	163.3	0.8	1920		X		X
Selma	3,667	6,806	85.6	2.1	1893		X		X
Other Urban Areas	----	27,332	----						
Urban Pop. -Total	76,565	189,281	14.7						
-Percentage	42.9	56.2	----						
Glenn County	12,195	17,200	41.0	1,312.0	1891		X		
Orland	1,366	2,392	75.1	0.9	1909		X		X
Willows	2,215	3,765	70.0	1.0	1886		X		X
Other Urban Areas	-----	-------	----						
Urban Pop. -Total	-----	3,765	----						
-Population	-----	21.9	----						
Humboldt County	45,812	99,200	116.5	3,573.0	1853		X		
Arcata	1,855	4,720	154.4	2.1	1858		X		X
Blue Lake	503	1,069	112.5	0.6	1910		X		X
Eureka	17,055	27,951	63.8	10.0	1856	X			X
Ferndale	901	1,032	14.5	1.0	1893		X		X
Fortuna	1,413	3,217	127.7	1.0	1906		X		X
Trinidad	94	267	184.0	0.6	1870		X		X
Other Urban Areas	-----	6,407	----						
Urban Pop. -Total	17,055	42,358	148.0						
-Percentage	37.2	42.7							
Imperial County	59,740	69,900	17.0%	4,284.0	1907		X		
Brawley	11,718	13,209	12.7	2.1	1908		X	X	
Calexico	5,415	7,486	38.2	1.7	1908		X	X	
Calepatrica	1,799	2,463	36.9	1.4	1919		X		X
El Centro	10,017	17,791	77.6	3.6	1908		X	X	
Holtville	1,772	3,297	86.1	0.8	1908		X		X
Imperial	1,493	1,759	17.8	1.5	1904		X		X
Westmoreland	1,010	1,213	20.0	0.4	1934		X		X
Other Urban Areas	-----	-----	----						
Urban Pop. -Total	27,150	41,783	54.0						
-Percentage	45.4	59.7	----						
Inyo County	7,625	12,000	57.4	10,091.0	1866		X		
Bishop	1,490	3,270	119.5	N. A.	1903		X		X
Other Urban Areas	-----	-----	----						
Urban Pop. -Total	-----	3,270	----						
-Percentage	-----	27.3	----						
Kern County	135,124	273,400	102.3	8,170.0	1866		X		
Bakersfield	29,252	54,093	84.9	15.6	1898	X		X	
Delano	4,573	11,092	142.6	4.5	1915		X	X	
Maricopa	670	800	19.4	0.7	1911		X		X
McFarland	-----	2,922	----	N. A.	1957		X		X
Shafter	1,258	3,266	159.6	1.3	1938		X		X

374

Table 2.a Georgraphic, Demographic & Political Characteristics
of California Cities and Counties. As of June 1958

2.a	1940 Federal Census	1957 Population	Percentage Change	Land Area (Sq. Miles)	Date Incorporated	Charter	General Law	Council Mgr.	Council	Mayor Council
Kern County (Continued)										
Taft	3,205	3,967	23.8	1.7	1910		X			X
Tehachapi	1,264	3,033	140.0	1.5	1909		X	X		
Wasco	-----	6,291	----	1.3	1945		X			X
Other Urban Areas	-----	95,884	----							
Urban Pop. -Total	27,030	180,548	568.0							
-Percentage	27.4	66.0	----							
Kings County	35,168	47,200	34.2	1,395.0	1893		X			
Corcoran	2,092	4,824	130.6	1.0	1914		X			X
Hanford	8,234	10,274	24.8	2.7	1891		X	X		
Lemoore	1,711	2,333	36.4	1.0	1900		X			X
Other Urban Areas	-----	-----	----							
Urban Pop. -Total	8,235	15,098	83.0							
-Percentage	23.4	32.0	----							
Lake County	8,069	11,300	40.0	1,256.0	1861		X			
Lakeport	1,490	1,983		2.2	1888		X			X
Other Urban Areas	-----	-----								
Urban Pop. -Total	-----	-----								
-Percentage	-----	------								
Lassen County	14,479	14,700	1.5	4,548.0	1864		X			
Susanville	1,575	5,338	33.9	1.2	1900		X			X
Other Urban Areas	-----	2,725	----							
Urban Pop. -Total	-----	8,063	----							
-Percentage	-----	54.9	----							
Los Angeles County	2,785,643	5,598,300	101.0	4,071.0	1850	X				
Alhambra	38,935	53,558	37.6	7.5	1903	X		X		
Arcadia	9,122	37,271	308.6	10.9	1903	X		X		
Avalon	1,637	1,506	-8.7	1.2	1913		X	X		
Azusa	5,209	18,579	256.7	4.5	1898		X			X
Baldwin Park	-----	32,334	----	6.1	1956		X	X		
Bell	11,264	18,415	63.5	1.6	1927		X	X		
Bellflower	-----	53,073	----	6.1	1957		X	X		
Beverly Hills	26,823	30,443	13.5	5.7	1914		X	X		
Bradbary	-----	828	----	2.0	1957		X			X
Burbank	34,337	90,966	164.9	16.9	1911	X		X		
Claremont	3,057	10,651	248.4	3.4	1907		X	X		
Compton	16,198	63,739	293.0	8.2	1888	X		X		
Covina	3,049	16,890	454.0	3.9	1901		X	X		
Culver City	8,976	31,367	249.0	4.0	1917	X		X		
Dairy Valley	-----	3,454	----	8.7	1956		X			X
Downey	-----	97,656	----	11.8	1956		X	X		
Duarte	-----	15,870	----	6.5	1957		X		X	
El Monte	4,746	11,507	142.0	2.3	1912		X			X
El Segundo	3,738	13,778	269.0	5.5	1917		X	X		
Gardena	5,909	30,576	417.0	4.2	1930		X			X
Glendale	82,582	114,460	39.0	29.2	1906	X		X		
Glendora	2,822	15,033	433.0	4.8	1911		X	X		
Hawthorne	8,263	31,504	281.0	3.7	1922		X	X		
Hermosa Beach	7,197	15,274	112.0	1.3	1907		X	X		
Huntington Park	28,646	29,459	3.0	3.0	1906		X	X		
Industry	-----	504	----	5.4	1953		X	X		
Inglewood	30,114	61,001	103.0	7.8	1908	X		X		
Inwindale	-----	729	----	9.5	1957		X	X		
Lakewood	-----	74,733	----	7.4	1954		X	X		
La Puente	-----	20,066	----	3.2	1956		X	X		
La Verne	3,092	5,907	91.0	2.5	1906		X	X		
Long Beach	164,271	324,822	98.0	45.1	1897	X		X		
Los Angeles	1,504,277	2,243,901	49.0	454.8	1850	X				X
Lynwood	10,982	28,754	162.0	4.2	1921		X	X		
Manhattan Beach	6,398	32,535	409.0	4.0	1912		X	X		
Maywood	10,731	13,483	26.0	1.2	1924		X			X
Monrovia	12,807	25,286	97.0	9.0	1887		X	X		
Montebello	8,016	30,019	274.0	7.5	1920		X			X
Monterey Park	8,531	33,045	287.0	7.5	1916		X	X		
Norwalk	-----	83,010	----	9.1	1957		X	X		
Palos Verdes Estates	987	8,416	753.0	N.A.	1939		X			X
Paramount	-----	25,128	----	4.3	1957		X			X
Pasadena	81,864	110,475	35.0	22.6	1886	X		X		
Rico Rivera	-----	52,113	----	8.5	1957		X	X		
Pomona	23,539	62,138	164.0	16.1	1888	X		X		
Redondo Beach	13,092	41,723	219.0	9.4	1892	X		X		

Table 2.a Geographic, Demographic & Political Characteristics of California Cities and Counties, As of June 1958

2.a	1940 Federal Census	1957 Population	Percentage Change	Land Area (Sq. Miles)	Date Incorporated	Charter	General Law	Council Mgr.	Council	Mayor Council
Los Angeles County (Continued)										
Rolling Hills	-----	2,136	----	3.0	1957		X	X		
Rolling Hills Estates	-----	3,768	----	1.4	1957		X	X		
San Fernando	9,094	15,668	72.0	2.3	1911		X	X		
San Gabriel	11,867	21,755	83.0	3.7	1913		X	X		
San Marino	8,175	12,945	58.0	3.7	1913		X	X		
Santa Fe Springs	-----	12,009	----	6.0	1957		X	X		
Santa Monica	53,500	75,132	40.0	8.1	1886	X		X		
Sierra Madre	4,581	8,732	91.0	3.5	1907		X	X		
Signal Hill	3,184	4,592	44.0	2.1	1924		X			X
South El Monte	-----	N.A.	----	5.0	1958		X			X
South Gate	26,945	51,449	91.0	7.0	1923		X			X
South Pasadena	14,356	18,881	32.0	3.4	1888		X	X		
Torrance	9,950	93,372	838.0	20.8	1921	X		X		
Vernon	850	432	51.0	2.4	1905		X			X
West Covina	1,072	45,006	4,098.0	10.5	1923		X	X		
Whittier	16,115	32,217	100.0	5.6	1898	X		X		
Other Urban Areas	53,370	950,402	1,681.0							
Urban Pop. -Total	2,373,368	5,458,343	130.0							
-Percentage	85.2	97.2	----							
Madera County	23,314	38,400	65.0	2,148.0	1893		X			
Chowchilla	1,967	4,254	117.0	1.1	1923		X			X
Madera	6,457	13,872	115.0	4.0	1907		X	X		
Other Urban Areas	-----	-----	----							
Urban Pop. -Total	6,457	18,126	180.0							
-Percentage	27.7	47.2	----							
Marin County	52,907	128,800	143.0	521.0	1850		X			
Belvedere	457	1,767	287.0	1.4	1896		X	X		
Corte Madera	1,098	4,164	279.0	0.7	1916		X	X		
Fairfax	2,198	4,661	112.0	5.0	1931		X			X
Larkspur	1,558	3,805	144.0	3.0	1908		X	X		
Mill Valley	4,847	9,436	95.0	2.8	1900		X	X		
Ross	1,751	2,402	37.0	1.5	1908		X			X
San Anselmo	5,790	10,446	80.0	2.6	1907		X			X
San Rafael	8,573	16,527	93.0	8.2	1874	X		X		
Sausalito	3,540	4,945	40.0	1.5	1893		X	X		
Other Urban Areas	-----	48,500	----							
Urban Pop. -Total	22,750	102,782	352.0							
-Percentage	43.0	79.8	----							
Mariposa County	5,605	4,500	-24.0	1,455.0	1850		X			
Hornitos	-----	-----	----		1870		inactive			
Urban Pop. -Total	-----	-----	----							
-Percentage	-----	-----	----							
Mendocino County	27,864	55,500	99.0	3,510.0	1850		X			
Fort Bragg	3,235	4,861	50.0	1.4	1889		X			X
Point Arena	374	481	29.0	5.8	1908		X			X
Ukiah	3,731	10,350	177.0	4.0	1876		X	X		
Willits	1,625	3,716	129.0	2.0	1888		X			X
Other Urban Areas	-----	-----	----							
Urban Pop. -Total	6,966	18,957	172.0							
-Percentage	25.9	34.2	----							
Merced County	46,988	86,900	85.0	1,983.0	1855		X			
Atwater	1,235	5,668	395.0	2.0	1922		X			X
Dos Palos	978	1,911	95.0	0.6	1935		X			X
Gustine	1,355	2,065	52.0	0.6	1915		X			X
Livingston	895	1,944	117.0	1.0	1922		X			X
Los Banos	2,214	5,418	145.0	0.7	1907		X			X
Merced	10,135	20,394	101.0	5.2	1889		X	X		
Other Urban Areas	-----	-----	----							
Urban Pop. -Total	10,135	31,480	211.0							
-Percentage	21.6	36.2	----							
Modoc County	8,713	9,100	4.0	4,094	1874		X			
Alturas	2,090	2,816			1901		X			X
Other Urban Areas	-----	------	----							
Urban·Pop. -Total	-----	2,816	----							
-Percentage	-----	30.9	----							
Mona County	2,299	2,600	22.0	3,028.0	1861		X			
Urban Pop. -Total	-----	-----	----							
-Percentage	-----	-----	----							

Table 2. a Geographic, Demographic & Political Characteristics
of California Cities and Counties. As of June 1958

2. a	1940 Federal Census	1957 Population	Percentage Change	Land Area (Sq. Miles)	Date Incorporated	Charter	General Law	Council Mgr.	Mayor Council
Monterey County	73,032	182,900	150.0	3,324.0	1850		X		
Carmel	2,837	4,398	55.0	2.0	1916		X		X
Del Rey Oaks	-----	1,708	----	N. A.	1953		X		X
Gonzales	-----	1,904	----	N. A.	1947		X		X
Greenfield	-----	1,482	----	N. A.	1947		X		X
King City	1,768	2,605	47.0	1.0	1911		X		X
Monterey	10,084	21,840	116.0	6.6	1889	X		X	
Pacific Grove	6,249	10,741	72.0	2.1	1889	X		X	
Salinas	11,586	21,748	88.0	8.2	1874	X		X	
Seaside	-----	15,381	----	N. A.	1954		X	X	
Soledad	861	2,738	218.0	1.2	1921		X		X
Other Urban Areas	-----	20,961	----						
Urban Pop. -Total	30,756	100,412	266.0						
-Percentage	42.1	54.9	----						
Napa County	28,503	60,700	113.0	790.0	1850		X		
Calistoga	1,124	1,418	26.0	2.4	1886		X		X
Napa	7,740	19,214	148.0	4.3	1882	X		X	
Saint Helena	1,758	2,297	30.0	4.6	1876		X		X
Other Urban Areas	------	-----	----						
Urban Pop. -Total	7,740	19,214	148.0						
-Percentage	27.2	31.7	----						
Nevada County	19,283	18,200	-6.0%	979.0	1851		X		
Grass Valley	5,701	5,523	-3.0	1.0	1816	X			X
Nevada City	2,445	2,562	5.0	1.0	1856		X	X	
Meadowlake					1866		inactive		
Other Urban Areas	-----	-----	----						
Urban Pop. -Total	5,701	8,085	42.0						
-Percentage	27.2	44.4	----						
Orange County	130,760	511,400	291.0	782.0	1889		X		
Anaheim	11,031	78,397	611.0	21.6	1878		X	X	
Brea	2,567	7,258	183.0	3.5	1917		X	X	
Buena Park	-----	31,805	----	N. A.	1953		X	X	
Costa Mesa	-----	26,651	----	N. A.	1953		X	X	
Cypress	-----	1,616	----	N. A.	1957		X		X
Dairyland	-----	550	----	N. A.	1955		X	X	
Fountain Valley	-----	594	----	N. A.	1957		X		X
Fullerton	10,442	49,272	372.0	20.0	1904		X		X
Garden Grove	-----	58,380	----	N. A.	1956		X	X	
Huntington Beach	3,738	10,067	169.0	18.0	1909	X			X
Laguna Beach	4,460	8,218	84.0	3.0	1927		X	X	
La Habra	2,499	17,827	613.0	4.8	1925		X		X
Newport Beach	4,438	21,258	379.0	6.9	1906	X		X	
Orange	7,901	21,334	170.0	7.1	1888		X		X
Placertia	1,472	4,821	228.0	0.5	1926		X	X	
San Clemente	479	1,108	1,384.0	5.8	1928		X	X	
Santa Ana	31,921	69,345	117.0	15.4	1886	X		X	
Seal Beach	1,553	3,553	129.0	1.4	1915		X		X
Stanton	-----	6,794	----	N. A.	1956		X		X
Tustin	953	1,805	89.0	1.1	1927		X		X
Westminster	-----	16,221	----	N. A.	1957		X	X	
Other Urban Areas	-----	-----	----						
Urban Pop. -Total	76,548	438,309	473.0						
-Percentage	58.5	85.7	----						
Placer County	28,108	49,600	76.0	1,431.0	1851		X		
Auburn	4,013	4,874	21.0	2.7	1888		X	X	
Colfax	794	820	3.0	0.3	1910		X		X
Lincoln	2,044	2,410	18.0	1.3	1890		X		X
Rocklin	795	1,334	68.0	1.5	1893		X		X
Roseville	6,673	11,079	66.0	2.5	1909		X	X	
Other Urban Areas	-----	-----	----						
Urban Pop. -Total	10,686	15,953	49.0						
-Percentage	38.0	32.0	----						
Plumas County	11,548	11,700	1.0%	2,570.0	1854		X		
Portola	-----	2,261	----	N. A.	1946		X		X
Urban Pop. -Total	-----	-----	----						
-Percentage	-----	-----	----						
Riverside County	105,524	241,300	129.0	7,179.0	1893		X		
Banning	3,874	8,358	115.0	7.2	1913		X	X	
Beaumont	2,208	3,513	59.0	4.5	1912		X		X

Table 2.a Geographic, Demographic & Political Characteristics
of California Cities and Counties. As of June 1958

2.a	1940 Federal Census	1957 Population	Percentage Change	Land Area (Sq. Miles)	Date Incorporated	Charter	General Law	Council Mgr.	Mayor Council
Riverside County (Continued)									
Blythe	2,355	5,065	115.0	1.6	1916		X		X
Cabazon	-----	855	----	N.A.	1955		X		X
Coachella	-----	4,287	----	N.A.	1946		X		X
Corona	8,764	12,707	45.0	16.0	1896		X	X	
Elsinore	1,552	2,304	48.0	2.7	1888		X		X
Hemit	2,595	4,235	63.0	2.6	1910		X	X	
Indio	2,296	7,830	241.0	6.3	1930		X	X	
Palm Springs	3,434	12,671	269.0	36.1	1938		X	X	
Perris	1,011	2,710	168.0	1.5	1911		X		X
Riverside	34,696	75,673	118.0	40.3	1883	X		X	
San Jacinto	1,356	2,207	63.0	2.1	1888		X		X
Other Urban Areas	-----	10,626	----						
Urban Pop.-Total	53,363	147,675	177.0						
-Percentage	50.6	61.2	----						
Sacramento County	170,333	427,100	151.0	985.0	1850	X			
Folsom	-----	2,206	----	N.A.	1946		X		X
Galt	-----	1,549	----	N.A.	1946		X		X
Isleton	1,837	1,586	15.0	0.3	1923		X		X
North Sacramento	3,053	9,235	202.0	3.0	1924		X	X	
Sacramento	105,958	163,611	54.0	23.1	1850	X		X	
Other Urban Areas	-----	17,582							
Urban Pop.-Total	109,011	190,428	75.0						
-Percentage	64.0	44.6	----						
San Benito County	11,392	15,500	36.0	1,396.0	1874		X		
Hollister	3,881	6,017	55.0	0.8	1874		X		X
San Juan Bautista	678	1,031	52.0	1.0	1896		X		X
Other Urban Areas	-----	-----	----						
Urban Pop.-Total	3,881	6,017	55.0						
-Percentage	34.1	38.8	----						
San Bernardino County	161,108	435,700	170.0	20,131.0	1853	X			
Barstow	-----	10,017	----	2.9	1947		X		X
Chino	4,204	9,146	118.0	5.0	1910		X		X
Colton	9,686	18,878	95.0	7.0	1887		X	X	
Fontana	-----	13,695	----	N.A.	1952		X		X
Monte Vista(Montclair)	-----	11,280	----	N.A.	1956		X	X	
Needles	3,624	4,776	32.0	1.8	1913		X	X	
Ontario	14,197	41,656	193.0	15.5	1891		X	X	
Redlands	14,324	25,719	80.0	17.2	1888		X	X	
Rialto	1,770	15,359	8,577.0	7.6	1911		X	X	
San Bernardino	43,646	84,648	94.0	23.6	1869	X			X
Upland	6,316	12,650	100.0	13.0	1906		X	X	
Other Urban Areas	-----	33,264	----						
Urban Pop.-Total	96,000	281,088	192.0						
-Percentage	59.6	64.5	----						
San Diego County	289,348	900,400	211.0	4,258.0	1850	X			
Carlsbad	-----	6,963	----	7.6	1952		X	X	
Chula Vista	5,138	35,557	592.0	11.5	1911		X	X	
Coronado	6,932	18,764	171.0	6.0	1890		X	X	
El Cajon	1,471	27,776	1,789.0	9.5	1912		X	X	
Escondido	4,560	10,262	125.0	3.0	1888		X	X	
Imperial Beach	-----	14,287	----	N.A.	1956		X	X	
La Mesa	3,925	23,797	506.0	6.2	1912		X	X	
National City	10,344	31,785	207.0	7.3	1887		X	X	
Oceanside	4,651	20,489	341.0	12.7	1888		X	X	
San Diego	203,341	500,744	146.0	131.0	1850	X		X	
Other Urban Areas	-----	8,427	----						
Urban Pop.-Total	238,890	698,881	193.0						
-Percentage	82.5	76.6	----						
San Francisco City & County	634,536	776,000	22.0	45.0	1850	X			
San Joaquin County	134,207	238,400	78.0	1,410.0	1850		X		
Escalon	-----	2,106	----	N.A.	1957		X		X
Lodi	11,079	20,100	81.0	4.1	1906		X	X	
Manteca	1,981	6,995	253.0	7.1	1918		X		X
Repon	-----	1,769	----	N.A.	1945		X		X
Stockton	54,714	82,309	50.0	21.2	1850	X		X	

378

Table 2.a Geographic, Demographic & Political Characteristics
of California Cities and Counties, As of June 1958

2.a	1940 Federal Census	1957 Population	Percentage Change	Land Area (Sq. Miles)	Date Incorporated	Charter	General Law	Council Mgr.	Council	Mayor Council
San Joaquin County (Continued)										
Tracy	4,056	10,602	161.0	2.3	1910		X	X		
Other Urban Areas	-----	22,795	----							
Urban Pop. -Total	69,849	142,801	104.0							
-Percentage	52.0	59.9	----							
San Luis Obispo County	33,246	61,300	84.0	3,326.0	1850		X			
Arroyo Grande	1,090	2,061	89.0	3.9	1911		X			X
Paso Robles	3,045	6,598	117.0	2.7	1889		X	X		
Pismo Beach	-----	1,930	----	N. A.	1946		X			X
San Luis Obispo	8,881	17,691	99.0	5.2	1856	X		X		
Other Urban Areas	-----	6,788	----							
Urban Pop. -Total	11,926	31,077	171.0							
-Percentage	35.9	50.7	----							
San Mateo County	111,782	378,100	238.0	454.0	1856	X				
Atherton	1,908	7,269	281.0	4.9	1923		X			X
Belmont	1,229	11,800	860.0	3.5	1926		X			X
Burlingame	15,940	21,985	38.0	4.3	1908		X			X
Colma	354	297	-19.0	3.0	1924		X			X
Daly City	9,624	30,506	217.0	3.6	1911		X	X		
Hillsbough	2,747	6,685	143.0	6.2	1910		X	X		
Menlo Park	3,258	25,669	688.0	3.6	1927		X	X		
Millbrae	-----	14,508	----	6.0	1948		X			X
Pacifica	-----	20,763	----	N. A.	1957		X	X		
Redwood City	12,453	39,002	213.0	8.0	1868	X		X		
San Bruno	6,516	20,037	208.0	9.9	1914		X	X		
San Carlos	3,520	19,505	454.0	3.1	1925		X			X
San Mateo	19,403	65,999	240.0	13.1	1894	X		X		
South San Francisco	6,629	35,690	438.0	27.7	1908		X	X		
Woodside	-----	5,157	----	N. A.	1956		X			X
Other Urban Areas	-----	12,500	----							
Urban Pop. -Total	80,090	337,075	321.0							
-Percentage	71.7	89.2	----							
Santa Barbara County	70,555	116,000	64.0	2,745.0	1850		X			
Guadalupe	----	2,489	----	N. A.	1946		X			X
Lompoc	3,379	6,665	97.0	3.0	1888		X			X
Santa Barbara	34,958	55,675	59.0	19.5	1850	X		X		
Santa Maria	8,522	14,216	67.0	4.0	1905		X	X		
Other Urban Areas	-----	6,400	----							
Urban Pop. -Total	46,859	82,956	77.0							
-Percentage	66.4	71.5	----							
Santa Clara County	174,949	527,500	202.0	1,305.0	1850	X				
Alviso	677	1,054	56.0	10.3	1852	•		X		
Campbell	-----	8,286	----	N. A.	1952		X			X
Cupertino	-----	1,752	----	N. A.	1955		X			X
Gilroy	3,616	6,019	66.0	1.5	1870		X			X
Los Altos	-----	19,572	----	N. A.	1952		X			X
Los Altos Hills	-----	3,138	----	N. A.	1956		X			X
Los Gatos	3,597	5,797	61.0	1.6	1887		X	X		
Milpitos	-----	1,924	----	N. A.	1954		X			X
Monte Sereno	-----	2,343	----	N. A.	1957		X			X
Morgan Hill	1,014	2,416	138.0	2.6	1906		X			X
Mountain View	3,946	26,143	562.0	6.3	1902	X		X		
Palo Alto	16,774	48,003	186.0	10.4	1894	X		X		
San Jose	68,457	130,576	91.0	27.7	1850	X		X		
Santa Clara	6,650	43,281	551.0	8.7	1857	X		X		
Saratoga	-----	15,276	----		1956		X			X
Sunnyvale	4,373	41,867	857.0	13.5	1912		X	X		
Other Urban Areas	-----	31,000	----							
Urban Popl. -Total	107,413	368,948	243.0							
-Percentage	61.4	69.9								
Santa Cruz County	45,057	70,700	57.0	439.0	1850		X			
Capitola	-----	1,848	----	N. A.	1949		X			X
Santa Cruz	16,896	22,794	35.0	12.0	1866	X		X		
Watsonville	8,937	11,911	35.0	1.9	1868	X				X
Other Urban Areas	-----	9,485	----							
Urban Pop. -Total	27,833	44,190	59.0							
-Percentage	57.3	62.5	----							

* Special

Table 2.a Geographic, Demographic & Political Characteristics
of California Cities and Counties, As of June 1958

2.a	1940 Federal Census	1957 Population	Percentage Change	Land Area (Sq. Miles)	Date Incorporated	Charter	General Law	Council Mgr.	Mayor Council
Shasta County	28,800	49,000	70.0	3,800	1850		X		
Anderson	-----	4,246	----	N.A.	1956		X		X
Redding	8,109	12,216	51.0	8.6	1887		X	X	
Other Urban Areas	-----	-----	-----						
Urban Pop.-Total	8,109	16,462	103.0						
-Percentage	28.2	33.6	----						
Sierra County	3,025	2,400	26.0	958.0	1852		X		
Loyalton	925	956	3.0	N.A.	1901		X		X
Urban Pop.-Total	-----	-----	----						
-Percentage	-----	-----	----						
Siskiyou County	28,598	31,400	10.0	6,313.0	1852		X		
Dorris	893	892	----	.7	1908		X		X
Dunsmuir	2,359	3,932	67.0	.4	1909		X		X
Etna	456	769	69.0	.7	1878		X		X
Fort Jones	360	525	46.0	.4	1872		X		X
Montague	493	718	46.0	1.2	1909		X		X
Mount Shasta	1,618	1,909	18.0	.8	1905		X		X
Tulelake	785	1,028	31.0	1.2	1937		X		X
Ureka	2,485	4,373	76.0	3.1	1857		X		X
Other Urban Areas	-----	5,244	----						
Urban Pop.-Total	-----	13,549	----						
-Percentage	-----	43.2	----						
Solano County	49,118	117,200	139.0	827.0	1850		X		
Benicia	2,419	7,284	201.0	3.1	1850		X		X
Dixon	1,108	2,683	142.0	.6	1878		X	X	
Fairfield	1,312	11,787	963.0	2.0	1903		X	X	
Rio Vista	1,666	2,533	52.0	3.2	1894		X		X
Suisun City	706	1,960	178.0	1.3	1868		X		X
Vacaville	1,614	9,018	750.0	3.3	1892		X	X	
Vallejo	20,072	48,176	140.0	22.5	1866	X			X
Other Urban Areas	-----	2,924	----						
Urban Pop.-Total	20,072	84,405	321.0						
-Percentage	40.9	72.1	----						
Sonoma County	69,052	140,800	104.0	1,579.0	1850		X		
Cloverdale	809	2,823	249.0	1.6	1872		X		X
Healdsburg	2,507	3,987	59.0	1.7	1867		X		X
Petaluma	8,034	12,595	57.0	3.4	1858	X		X	
Santa Rosa	12,605	29,644	135.0	8.1	1868	X		X	
Sebastopol	1,856	2,731	47.0	1.9	1902		X	X	
Sonoma	1,158	2,928	153.0	1.2	1900		X		X
Other Urban Areas	-----	-----	----						
Urban Pop.-Total	23,146	54,708	136.0						
-Percentage	33.5	38.9	----						
Stanislaus County	74,866	147,900	98.0	1,506.0	1854		X		
Ceres	1,332	3,671	175.0	1.8	1918		X		X
Modesto	16,379	34,375	110.0	7.6	1884	X		X	
Newman	1,214	1,988	64.0	.8	1908		X		X
Oakdale	2,592	4,678	80.0	1.0	1906		X		X
Patterson	1,109	2,901	162.0	1.2	1919		X		X
Riverbank	1,130	2,719	241.0	1.4	1922		X		X
Turlock	4,839	8,605	78.0	1.9	1908		X		X
Other Urban Areas	-----	13,272	----						
Urban Pop.-Total	23,810	70,221	195.0						
-Percentage	31.8	47.5	----						
Sutter County	18,680	30,000	61.0	607.0	1850		X		
Live Oak	-----	2,067	----	N.A.	1947		X		X
Yuba City	4,968	10,312	108.0	2.4	1908		X	X	
Other Urban Areas	-----	-----	----						
Urban Pop.-Total	4,968	10,312	108.0						
-Percentage	26.6	34.4	----						
Tehama County	14,316	22,000	54.0	2,976.0	1856	X			
Corning	1,472	2,543	72.0	1.7	1907		X		X
Red Bluff	3,824	5,553	45.0	2.0	1876		X		X
Tehama	175	314	79.0	1.0	1906		X		X
Other Urban Areas	-----	-----	----						
Urban Pop.-Total	3,824	8,096	112.0						
-Percentage	26.7	36.8	----						

Table 2. a Geographic, Demographic & Political Characteristics
of California Cities and Counties. As of June 1958

2. a	1940 Federal Census	1957 Population	Percentage Change	Land Area (Sq. Miles)	Date Incorporated	MCharter	General Law	Council Mgr.	Mayor Council
Trinity County	3,970	7. 900	99. 0	3,191. 0	1850		X		
Urban Pop. -Total	-----	-----	----						
-Percentage	-----	-----	----						
Tulare County	107,152	148,300	38. 0	4,845. 0	1852		X		
Denuba	3,790	5,458	44. 0	1. 0	1906		X		X
Exeter	3,883	4,165	7. 0	1. 0	1911		X		X
Lindsay	4,397	5,492	25. 0	1. 6	1910		X		X
Porterville	6,270	7,835	25. 0	6. 5	1902		X	X	
Tulare	8,259	13.274	61. 0	3. 4	1888	X		X	
Visalia	8,904	14,521	63. 0	3. 7	1874	X		X	
Woodlake	1,146	2,525	120. 0	1. 5	1941		X		X
Other Urban Areas	-----	-------							
Urban Pop. -Total	35,503	53.270	50. 0						
-Percentage	33. 1	35. 9	----						
Tuolumne County	10,887	15,100	39. 0	2,275	1850		X		
Sonora	2,257	2, 448	8. 0	N. A.	1851		X		X
Other Urban Areas	-----	-----	----						
Urban Pop. -Total	-----	-----	----						
-Percentage	-----	-----	----						
Ventura County	69,685	163,200	134. 0	1,857	1872		X		
Fillmore	3,252	4,725	45. 0	1. 2	1914		X	X	
Ojai	1,622	3,930	142. 0	1. 8	1921		X		X
Oxnard	8,519	34,326	303. 0	4. 9	1902		X	X	
Port Hueneme	-----	8,750	----	3. 5	1948		X		X
Santa Paula	8,986	12,186	36. 0	4. 7	1902		X	X	
Ventura	13,264	25,880	95. 0	6. 6	1866	X		X	
Other Urban Areas	-----	-----	----						
Urban Pop. -Total	34,021	89,797	164. 0						
-Percentage	48. 8	55. 0	----						
Yolo County	27,243	56,400	107. 0	1,034	1850		X		
Davis	1,672	7,216	332. 0	3. 1	1917		X	X	
Winters	1,133	1,670	47. 0	2. 6	1898		X		X
Woodland	6,637	11,682	86. 0	2. 6	1874		X	X	
Other Urban Areas	-----	-----	----						
Urban Pop. -Total	6,637	18,888	185. 0						
-Percentage	24. 4	33. 4	----						
Yuba County	17,034	27,000	59. 0	638. 0	1850		X		
Marysville	6,646	7,826	18. 0	2. 5	1851	X			X
Wheatland	496	587	18. 0	. 2	1874		X		X
Other Urban Areas	----	8,170	----						
Urban Pop. -Total	6,646	15,996	141. 0						
-Percentage	39. 0	59. 2	----						

Totals
State Urban Pop. -

	1940 Federal Census	1957 Population	Percentage Change
Total	4,902,265	10,556,669	115. 0
-Percentage	71. 0	75. 0	

Table 2. b Economic Characteristics of California Cities: 1950

County City	Economic Base	Economic Type	Employment Resident Labor Force Ratio	Per Cent Labor Force Total Pop.	Employed as Per Cent of Labor Force	Per Family And Other Unrelated Individual Income
	a	b	c	d	e	f
Alameda						
Alameda	Mm	E	124	43.2	89.8	$ 3,361
Albany	Rr	D	23	41.1	93.6	3,852
Berkeley	Ed	B	94	44.8	93.4	2,769
Emeryville	Rm	E		48.4	90.7	2,925
Hayward	Mm	E	168	39.1	91.7	3,449
Livermore	Rr			40.9	94.5	3,104
Oakland	Rm	E	116	50.2	90.4	3,182
Piedmont	Rr	D	4	39.5	97.7	5,340
San Leandro	Mm	B	103	40.3	93.3	3,998
Butte						
Chico	Mr	E	145	38.3	94.3	
Gredley	Ry			38.2	85.8	2,653
Oroville	Ry			42.5	85.4	2,708
Colusa						
Colusa	Rr			35.5	97.4	2,886
Contra Costa						
Antioch	Mm	B	101	41.9	94.2	3,765
Concord	Rr	D		37.5	94.6	3,941
El Cerrito	Mr	D	49	39.5	93.9	4,051
Martinez	Mr			43.4	94.2	3,720
Pittsburg	Mm	E	152	46.0	90.5	3,357
Richmond	Mm	B	85	38.6	86.6	3,416
San Pablo	Mr	B	76	36.8	84.1	3,307
El Dorado						
Placerville	Rr			42.1	91.1	2,234
Fresno						
Clovis	Mr			34.0	82.8	2,234
Coalinga	Mg			43.5	94.6	3,877
Fresno	Rr	E	141	42.1	91.7	3,177
Reedley	Rr(a)			33.7	84.0	2,284
Sanger	Rr(a)			36.8	76.1	2,558
Selma	Rr			35.2	78.7	2,523
Glenn						
Willows	Rr			43.7	94.9	3,286
Humboldt						
Arcata				43.1	97.7	3,199
Eureka	Rm	B	99	44.2	93.9	3,347
Imperial						
Brawley	Rr(a)	B	101	38.4	83.4	2,216
Calexico	Rr(a)			37.1	93.0	2,286
El Centro	W (a)	E	204	42.1	91.9	3,161
Inyo						
Bishop	Rr			46.5	94.9	3,578
Kern						
Bakersfield	Rr	E	191	45.4	91.8	3,705
Delano	W (a)			37.6	79.5	2,255
Taft	Rr			45.1	94.6	3,703
Wasco	W (a)			38.7	79.6	2,477
Kings						
Corcoran	W (a)			39.9	89.0	3,575
Lassen						
Susanville	T			40.4	71.0	3,337

County City	a	b	c	d	e	f
Los Angeles						
Alhambra	Mr	B	97	43.1	95.3	$ 3,632
Arcadia	Mr	B	101	38.2	96.0	4,134
Avalon	X					
Azusa	Mr	D	65	34.7	94.2	3,362
Bell	Rr	D	28	44.0	94.8	3,528
Beverly Hills	Rr	E	181	49.9	94.6	3,991
Burbank	Mm	E	156	41.6	94.5	3,779
Claremont	Ed			31.4	96.5	1,168
Compton	Rr	D	64	39.9	93.5	3,550
Covina	Rr			41.1	96.0	2,926
Culver City	Rr	B	95	42.3	94.4	3,692
El Monte	Mr			39.1	92.4	3,063
El Segundo	Mm			38.3	96.1	3,774
Gardena	Mr	B	111	39.5	93.1	3,422
Glendale	Rm	D	83	44.0	95.2	3,438
Glendora	Rr			38.5	94.3	2,500
Hawthorne	Mr	D	73	40.6	93.0	3,367
Hermosa Beach	Mr	B	90	41.6	94.5	3,245
Huntington Park	Rm	B	96	50.4	94.7	3,728
Inglewood	Rm	D	67	42.6	95.3	3,728
La Verne	Ed			38.3	96.7	2,205
Long Beach	Rr	D	75	42.5	92.0	2,995
Los Angeles	Mr	B	113	44.5	91.5	2,875
Lynwood	M	D	54	40.7	95.4	3,800
Manhatten Beach	Mr	D	48	40.6	95.7	3,780
Maywood	Rm	D	29	49.8	94.3	3,487
Monrovia	Rm	B	87	39.5	93.8	3,021
Montebello	Rm	D	44	41.5	94.7	3,938
Monterey Park	Rm	D	42	40.7	95.2	3,738
Pasadena	Rr	E	134	42.8	94.5	2,740
Pomona	Rm	B	111	39.9	93.1	2,946
Redondo Beach	Rr	D	35	37.3	92.4	3,218
San Fernando	Rr	E	160	38.9	91.9	2,905
San Gabriel	Rr	D	50	39.0	95.3	4,017
San Marino	Rr	D	60	37.7	98.7	8,326
Santa Monica	Mm	E	178	44.9	92.7	3,024
Sierra Madre	Rr			37.3	96.2	3,181
Signal Hill	Mm			41.2	90.9	3,093
South Gate	Mr	D	81	43.1	95.0	3,798
South Pasadena	M	D	57	47.3	96.3	3,671
Torrance	Mr	B	99	40.0	93.4	3,641
Vernon	Mm	E				
West Covina	Rr			35.5	98.3	3,632
Whittier	Ar	D	65	41.6	95.8	3,525
Madera						
Madera	Rr(a)	E	156	36.4	84.1	2,587
Marin						
Fairfax	Rr			40.8	97.4	3,658
Larkspur	Rr			38.8	97.3	3,875
Mill Valley	Rr			41.6	97.1	4,391
San Anselmo	Rr			38.6	96.9	3,915
San Rafael	Rr	E	163	43.3	97.3	3,652
Sausalito	Rr			45.8	96.4	3,529
Mendocino						
Fort Bragg	Mr			42.9	94.8	3,079
Ukiah	Rr			41.5	94.7	2,981
Willits	Mr			40.6	96.1	3,521
Merced						
Atwater	Rr			34.3	91.5	3,163
Los Banos	Rr			45.7	90.2	3,371
Merced	Rr	E	148	40.4	87.9	3,000
Modoc						
Alturas	Rr			43.6	95.9	3,795

County City	a	b	c	d	e	f
Monterey						
Carmel	X			45.8	96.8	$ 3,121
Monterey	Rr	E	212	46.9	88.6	2,971
Pacific Grove	X			38.9	94.6	3,191
Salinas	W	E	224	49.5	90.3	3,177
Seaside	Rr			38.4	94.4	2,750
Napa						
Napa	Rm	E	156	41.5	93.4	3,407
Nevada						
Grass Valley	Rr			40.3	87.4	2,383
Nevada City	Rr			43.2	86.3	2,474
Orange						
Anaheim	Rr	B	89	41.5	92.2	2,859
Brea	Mr			38.2	94.7	3,232
Buena Park	Rm			37.2	95.1	3,211
Costa Mesa	Mr			34.9	92.6	2,833
Fullerton	Mr	B	96	42.2	93.4	3,215
Garden Grove	Rr			33.8	94.6	2,625
Huntington Beach	Rr			45.7	93.1	3,222
Laguna Beach	Rr			36.8	95.7	2,478
La Habra	Mr			39.2	94.1	3,054
Newport Beach	Rr	E	120	37.6	95.3	3,183
Orange	Mr(a)	E	123	39.9	90.1	2,730
Santa Ana	Rr	B	111	39.8	92.2	2,976
Seal Beach	Rm			38.4	93.0	3,125
Stanton	Rm			38.7	91.9	2,534
Westminster	Rm					
Placer						
Auburn	W			43.2	95.2	3,265
Roseville				42.8	94.3	3,521
Riverside						
Banning	X			34.1	88.2	1.972
Beaumont	X			30.6	88.0	1,425
Blythe	W (a)			44.9	89.2	2,679
Coachella	Rr(a)			34.8	78.0	2,225
Corona	Mr(a)	B	85	37.4	89.7	2,273
Hemet	Rr(a)			38.5	91.7	2,302
Indio	Wr(a)			43.7	91.8	2,990
Palm Springs	X			45.9	93.7	2,412
Riverside	Rm	E	129	38.3	93.4	2,857
Sacramento						
North Sacramento	G			44.2	93.2	3,845
Sacramento	G	E	130	47.0	92.9	3,310
San Benito						
Hollister	W(a)			42.1	93.6	2,545
San Bernardino						
Barstow	T			40.9	96.3	3,701
Chino	Rm(a)			34.1	92.7	2,355
Colton	Mr	D	78	34.3	90.6	3,076
Needles	T			36.9	94.7	3,829
Ontario	Mr	B	98	37.2	94.1	2,959
Redlands	Rr	D	83	37.6	95.3	2,113
Rialto	Rm			37.0	93.8	3,155
San Bernardino	Rr	E	130	36.9	93.1	2,952
Upland	Rm(a)			38.5	96.6	2,774
San Diego						
Carlsbad	W(a)			34.8	94.4	2,444
Chula Vista	Mr	D	72	38.3	94.3	3,494
Coronado	G	D	67	38.4	96.1	3,229
El Cajon	Rr			37.0	90.1	3,179
Escondido	W(a)			37.7	94.2	2,250
La Mesa	Rm	B	91	37.1	94.9	3,411
National City	Rr	D	51	35.9	92.4	3,049
Oceanside	Rr	B	114	38.8	92.6	2,952
San Diego	Rm	B	112	43.6	92.1	2,783

Table 2.b Economic Characteristics of California Cities: 1950 (Continued)

County City	a	b	c	d	e	f
San Joaquin						
Lodi	Rm	B	111	39.6	91.0	$ 2,597
Mantica	Rr			38.7	88.3	2,672
Stockton	Rm	E	153	42.6	89.1	2,940
Tracey	T			41.4	90.1	3,427
San Luis Obispo						
San Luis Obispo	Ed	E	129	42.5	94.9	3,235
San Mateo						
Atherton	X			39.0	98.8	3,857
Belmont	Rm			40.9	97.0	4,212
Burlingame	Rr	D	54	45.7	96.8	4,420
Daly City	Mr	D	48	43.0	93.7	3,843
Hillsbough	X			43.8	98.8	5,917
Menlo Park	Rr	D	71	32.6	97.9	3,244
Millbrae	Rm			40.8	96.4	5,113
Redwood City	Rm	B	98	40.6	96.0	3,762
San Bruno	Rm	D	48	41.9	96.8	4,066
San Carlos	Rr	D	56	37.8	97.8	4,869
San Mateo	Rr	D	47	40.4	97.3	4,420
South San Francisco	Mm	D	70	41.4	95.7	3,903
Santa Barbara						
Lompoc	W(a)			42.5	94.4	3,078
Santa Barbara	X	E	117	42.1	93.7	2,544
Santa Maria	Rm(a)	E	168	45.5	92.3	3,231
Santa Clara						
Gilroy	W(a)			39.4	93.6	3,210
Los Gatos	Rr			36.4	94.8	2,500
Mountain View	Rm			40.9	93.7	3,505
Palo Alto	Ed	E	120	40.6	96.6	3,729
San Jose	Rm	E	134	41.1	90.2	2,946
Santa Clara	Rm	D	67	40.6	88.7	2,782
Sunnyvale	Mr			40.4	85.7	3,632
Santa Cruz						
Santa Cruz	X	B	94	37.6	92.7	2,252
Watsonville	Rm(a)	E	152	46.6	86.5	3,000
Shasta						
Redding	Rm	E	147	45.4	91.4	3,478
Siskihou						
Yreka	Rr			42.9	94.4	3,170
Solano						
Beneca	G			38.8	92.4	3,477
Fairfield	G			41.4	95.6	3,698
Vacaville	Rr			38.3	89.7	3,013
Vallejo	G	D	81	49.7	92.4	2,739
Sonoma						
Healdsburg	Rr			38.8	93.8	2,630
Petaluma	Rm	E	120	42.9	94.2	3,302
Santa Rosa	Rr	E	129	40.9	94.1	2,727
Sebastopol	Rr			36.1	93.3	2,114
Stanislaus						
Modesto	Rr	E	235	44.5	90.1	2,873
Oakdale	Rr(a)			35.2	91.1	3,033
Riverbank	Rm			32.3	74.0	2,056
Turlock	W			39.4	92.6	2,720
Sutter						
Yuba City	Rr(a)			41.6	88.8	3,316
Tehama						
Corning	W			39.0	92.1	2,969
Red Bluff	Rr			41.2	93.5	2,957

Table 2.b Economic Characteristics of California Cities: 1950 (Continued)

County City	a	b	c	d	e	f
Tulare						
Dinuba	W(a)			38.6	83.8	$ 2,266
Exeter	W(a)			39.0	79.5	2,708
Lindsay	Rm(a)			42.9	73.5	2,717
Porterville	W(a)			39.4	84.8	2,598
Tulare	Rr(a)	E	128	38.1	84.7	2,886
Visalia	Rm	E	139	41.5	92.9	3,591
Woodlake	Rm(a)			37.0	78.3	2,000
Ventura						
Fillmore	W(a)			44.5	91.2	3,239
Ojai	Rr			38.6	94.7	3,303
Oxnard	G(a)	E	132	42.5	88.5	2,922
Port Huenume	G			47.7	89.9	3,315
Santa Paula	W(a)	E	138	41.9	89.3	2,763
Ventura	Rr	E	119	47.6	95.6	3,758
Yolo						
Davis	Ed			37.1	98.1	2,789
Woodland	Rm(a)			41.1	96.3	3,397
Yuba						
Marysville	W			46.1	90.3	2,806

Sources: Column a : California Blue Book, 1950, pp. 806-1064.

Column b : County Data - Ibid (California Blue Book, 1950).
City Data - Census of Population: 1950 Pt. 5 California: U.S. Department
of Commerce Bureau of Census. 17th Census, pp. 51-189.
= Municipal Year Book: 1955 (Chicago: International City
Managers' Association), pp. 65-100.

Column c : Municipal Year Book.

Column d, e, f: Census of Population.

Table 3.a. Per Capita Operating Costs for All Counties (except San Francisco) by Functions and Total: 1957

Counties	General Govern- ment	Prot. to Per. & Prop.	Health & Sanita- tion	Highways and Bridges	Recrea- tion	Charities & Correc- tions	Miscel- laneous	Educa- tion	Total
Alameda	$ 7.02	$ 3.78	$ 3.13	$ 4.48	$ .12	$41.11	$ 3.76	$ .56	$ 63.96
Alpine	92.50	32.50	2.50	220.00	....	72.50	5.00	7.50	432.50
Amador	15.47	12.16	2.76	15.24	.44	78.01	2.54	4.31	130.94
Butte	9.92	8.75	1.78	13.47	.80	75.47	1.98	1.49	113.65
Calaveras	15.85	8.62	1.81	20.85	....	69.79	3.83	3.09	123.83
Colusa	15.76	15.34	10.85	29.66	.12	86.61	3.47	3.22	165.34
Contra Costa	9.56	5.87	3.87	5.68	.27	37.11	3.50	1.66	68.14
Del Norte	13.06	8.59	1.54	17.21	.94	31.02	2.04	.77	72.18
El Dorado	15.34	8.38	2.36	9.48	1.57	54.40	6.18	3.72	101.42
Fresno	7.57	7.36	3.71	5.41	.07	51.98	.16	.28	79.65
Glenn	16.15	14.85	7.69	20.71	.52	66.80	5.27	2.13	127.22
Humboldt	10.01	7.67	1.96	7.10	.43	44.33	3.82	1.41	76.73
Imperial	9.71	9.76	1.81	8.28	.57	35.19	4.89	1.05	71.38
Inyo	19.26	13.39	4.55	18.51	.91	48.43	7.44	3.97	116.45
Kern	20.43	16.72	5.10	9.12	4.17	47.39	2.92	2.55	108.41
Kings	10.97	11.69	8.07	7.35	1.02	52.88	4.39	2.25	98.62
Lake	16.46	13.63	.80	21.59	.71	109.74	5.04	.47	168.94
Lassen	12.38	9.67	.66	17.15	1.26	35.76	4.44	2.38	83.71
Los Angeles	9.57	4.98	.94	3.93	1.32	38.41	3.69	.17	63.09
Madera	12.06	9.44	3.49	9.39	.61	69.62	2.11	1.78	108.50
Marin	12.84	7.69	1.78	4.33	.04	18.86	1.56	1.94	49.04
Mariposa	30.22	6.67	1.11	41.56	....	89.33	2.67	3.11	174.66
Mendocino	10.67	8.18	3.37	12.93	.16	37.70	3.23	.36	76.73
Merced	8.40	10.61	2.46	2.84	1.12	48.39	3.13	1.31	78.26
Modoc	19.46	13.04	3.80	25.00	.76	83.59	2.61	4.13	152.40
Mono	39.17	17.50	1.25	75.00	2.50	54.17	8.33	5.83	203.75
Monterey	6.73	6.18	2.10	5.38	.11	24.09	2.31	.88	47.79
Napa	8.38	6.39	2.34	4.33	....	32.43	3.44	1.11	58.42
Nevada	10.08	6.38	4.58	17.06	.76	72.21	1.25	.76	113.08
Orange	7.17	6.78	1.35	2.37	.33	24.36	1.26	.98	44.61
Placer	12.48	8.01	3.02	11.33	.47	42.17	1.43	1.32	80.23
Plumas	17.12	12.80	2.37	38.39	1.53	41.70	8.39	3.73	126.02
Riverside	8.36	10.03	1.55	4.43	.15	48.41	3.69	.63	77.32
Sacramento	6.44	4.63	3.68	2.47	.05	44.35	2.37	.56	64.67
San Benito	9.35	10.84	1.62	10.26	.52	40.00	2.99	1.69	77.27
San Bernardino	8.46	3.62	1.89	3.86	....	39.73	1.56	1.03	60.15
San Diego	9.76	3.35	1.64	2.25	.45	27.96	3.98	.58	50.21
San Joaquin	6.62	6.57	3.24	4.06	.48	52.48	3.08	.94	77.47
San Luis Obispo	11.57	7.98	4.16	9.85	4.11	65.88	1.54	2.61	107.72
San Mateo	6.22	4.49	3.39	2.83	1.04	25.20	1.61	1.01	45.94
Santa Barbara	11.80	8.18	2.04	4.04	2.52	45.97	3.98	1.30	79.82
Santa Clara	10.89	4.55	2.00	2.72	.16	34.63	2.16	1.19	58.57
Santa Cruz	10.01	7.00	2.50	3.67	.11	66.72	2.03	1.16	93.20
Shasta	15.26	10.10	1.89	15.60	.36	48.71	2.74	1.94	96.61
Sierra	33.75	12.50	1.67	114.17	....	45.83	11.25	3.75	222.92
Siskiyou	13.77	8.84	1.24	31.96	.16	55.39	3.88	2.48	117.71
Solano	7.78	5.63	2.11	4.18	.34	28.00	1.15	1.18	50.38
Sonoma	8.00	5.53	1.65	8.02	.40	49.49	3.07	1.27	77.43
Stanislaus	8.40	8.10	1.19	3.50	.53	61.26	1.69	1.70	86.36
Sutter	7.38	7.28	3.45	15.40	.14	50.56	1.08	2.34	87.61
Tehama	12.37	17.89	.75	23.18	1.41	55.36	1.12	2.30	114.38
Trinity	17.30	11.89	3.24	71.35	.41	74.87	4.59	3.78	187.44
Tulare	8.34	10.51	7.38	9.58	.64	59.76	1.91	1.42	99.53
Tuolumne	16.56	11.85	2.12	8.15	1.39	56.82	6.29	2.52	105.70
Ventura	9.92	7.04	1.18	6.24	1.26	37.83	4.61	1.49	69.63
Yolo	9.70	9.45	3.66	9.08	.13	48.67	.36	1.50	82.65
Yuba	8.17	7.33	4.14	11.32	.29	59.42	2.76	.76	94.19

Table 3.b Per Capita Operating Costs for All Cities (except San Francisco) by Functions and Total: 1957

Cities	General Govern- ment	Prot. to Per. & Prop.	Sani- tation	Conserv. of Health	Streets	Educa- tion	Recrea- tion	Miscel- laneous	Total
Alameda Co.									
Alameda	$ 3.94	$17.36	$ .58	$ 1.64	$ 6.79	$ 4.46	$ 6.33	$ .57	$ 42.33
Albany	3.61	16.61	.61	.89	2.28	3.85	3.72	1.39	33.11
Berkeley	6.50	21.41	4.36	2.59	9.32	2.21	5.45	7.88	59.80
Emeryville	13.85	119.76	1.04	.35	16.61	....	....	14.88	166.49
Fremont	4.14	10.54	....	....	2.86	.71	.18	.39	18.82
Hayward	4.36	13.25	1.34	16.07	8.18	1.30	1.96	3.14	52.32
Livermore	6.99	11.71	2.07	....	9.94	1.97	....	1.28	35.42
Newark	5.71	6.71	....	....	3.57	.86	3.43	.29	20.57
Oakland	4.60	25.93	2.99	2.33	5.02	2.69	6.34	8.36	59.52
Piedmont	4.18	24.18	1.18	....	13.27	.27	10.09	4.91	58.09
Pleasanton	10.00	15.45	8.18	....	10.00	.91	.30	3.94	50.61
San Leandro	3.69	11.68	3.25	.02	5.79	1.67	2.47	2.19	31.03
Amador Co.									
Amador	6.62	....	....	....	6.62	....	....	....	13.25
Ione	3.74	4.98	7.48	....	6.85	....	....	....	26.17
Jackson	3.81	9.52	1.43	....	8.57	....	3.33	.95	28.10
Plymouth	2.62	5.24	....	2.62	10.47	....	....	....	20.94
Sutter Creek	2.61	3.48	1.74	....	9.56	....	.87	....	19.11
Butte Co.									
Biggs	5.13	11.54	6.41	....	8.97	2.56	....	1.28	35.90
Chico	5.20	21.02	.89	....	9.59	2.33	5.55	.62	45.46
Gridley	5.31	14.06	5.31	.63	10.31	1.56	3.75	4.06	46.25
Oroville	8.15	19.69	11.85	....	11.85	3.85	4.46	.92	60.77
Calaveras Co.									
Angels	1.33	8.00	.67	....	4.67	....	.67	....	18.67
Colusa Co.									
Colusa	3.48	15.65	5.80	.29	5.80	2.03	4.06	.87	37.97
Williams	7.50	16.67	5.00	....	9.17	....	.83	1.67	41.67
Contra Costa Co.									
Antioch	5.92	17.00	4.46	.13	4.71	.06	3.50	1.72	38.52
Brentwood	8.00	17.00	....	....	11.50	....	....	.50	37.00
Concord	3.58	9.31	1.54	....	9.15	.08	2.15	.31	26.42
El Cerrito	6.90	15.70	.80	....	5.88	.17	1.95	1.18	32.58
Hercules	2.91	5.81	5.81	....	5.81	....	2.91	....	23.26
Martinez	12.77	28.28	3.31	....	6.96	.34	3.31	5.02	63.06
Pinole	4.33	9.67	3.00	....	11.33	....	1.67	.33	30.33
Pittsburg	5.07	18.22	4.34	....	8.45	.18	4.04	.48	42.78
Richmond	8.33	31.41	.81	.43	10.07	3.57	8.44	5.97	69.65
San Pablo	4.16	9.03	....	....	5.80	....	2.52	.88	22.55
Walnut Creek	15.88	17.65	....	....	12.71	.12	8.24	1.29	59.53
Del Norte Co.									
Crescent City	5.71	32.86	1.07	....	16.43	1.79	1.43	1.07	60.71
El Dorado Co.									
Placerville	5.42	10.84	2.58	....	10.84	....	.77	2.58	37.16
Fresno Co.									
Clovis	8.29	14.34	14.57	.22	4.93	....	.45	1.12	44.82
Coalinga	5.98	15.78	8.47	....	5.98	....	2.66	1.83	40.70
Firebaugh	9.52	19.03	1.59	.79	14.27	....	2.38	.79	53.13
Fowler	5.00	13.50	1.00	....	6.50	....	1.50	1.00	28.50
Fresno	5.87	32.42	7.24	.63	4.64	.08	7.33	2.81	61.94
Huron	8.01	19.66	2.18	....	3.64	....	....	.73	37.87
Kerman	3.36	10.09	5.61	....	17.38	....	2.80	1.68	42.60
Kingsburg	5.64	17.29	12.03	....	10.90	....	3.38	.75	50.73
Mendota	4.99	19.34	4.99	....	9.98	....	.62	.62	41.80
Orange Cove	4.44	9.63	10.74	.37	5.56	....	....	.37	37.41
Parlier	2.50	13.13	4.38	....	3.75	....	.63	1.25	26.25
Reedley	3.85	12.31	.58	.19	6.35	....	4.23	1.73	29.23
Sanger	4.51	11.71	5.85	.24	4.88	....	4.27	4.27	37.07
San Joaquin	2.50	10.00	7.50	....	7.50	....	....	....	27.50
Selma	3.28	16.41	1.25	.31	6.41	....	3.28	.63	32.19

Table 3. b Per Capita Operating Costs for All Cities (except San Francisco) by Functions and Total: 1957

Cities	General Govern- ment	Prot. to Per. & Prop.	Sani- tation	Conserv. of Health	Streets	Educa- tion	Recrea- tion	Miscel- laneous	Total
Glenn Co.									
Orland	$ 4.55	$14.05	$ 4.96	$	$ 8.26	$ 1.24	$ 5.37	$	$ 38.43
Willows	3.25	14.00	3.00	....	8.50	3.25	4.00	.75	37.50
Humboldt Co.									
Arcata	5.51	18.43	2.54	.21	17.37	1.06	3.18	1.27	51.48
Blue Lake	5.45	9.09	2.73	....	10.00	....	.91	....	40.91
Eureka	7.05	17.67	4.47	.54	11.77	2.00	2.79	5.51	54.34
Ferndale	4.55	19.09	2.73	....	5.45	2.73	....	1.82	40.00
Fortuna	4.04	11.19	3.42	....	9.64	.31	2.80	.62	32.95
Trinidad	6.67	3.33	....	....	3.33	....	....	....	13.33
Imperial Co.									
Brawley	5.76	20.68	7.58	....	5.83	1.44	3.64	.83	46.89
Calexico	4.38	20.75	4.50	.50	5.50	2.38	6.75	5.13	51.50
Calipatria	4.40	12.00	2.40	....	4.40	....	.40	1.60	25.20
El Centro	6.30	20.52	6.58	.84	8.54	2.19	4.05	5.11	57.73
Holtville	5.14	17.03	5.14	....	9.19	....	4.59	6.49	48.38
Imperial	5.65	20.87	4.78	....	9.13	2.17	.43	2.61	50.00
Westmoreland	3.53	16.47	....	....	14.12	....	1.76	....	35.88
Inyo Co.									
Bishop	3.67	17.74	2.45	....	8.26	....	1.22	.61	33.94
Kern Co.									
Bakersfield	6.72	34.34	8.80	.04	15.02	....	5.71	5.75	77.82
Delano	4.78	16.32	4.33	....	6.13	....	1.35	1.44	34.44
Maricopa	3.75	13.75	....	....	3.75	....	1.25	1.25	23.75
Shafter	5.67	15.52	5.67	....	10.45	....	1.49	.90	39.70
Taft	6.68	21.27	8.65	....	11.62	....	.49	3.21	51.93
Tehachapi	7.91	10.55	3.96	....	2.64	....	....	....	25.72
Wasco	1.97	9.24	3.79	....	6.06	....	....	.61	21.67
Kings Co.									
Corcoran	5.18	12.23	7.67	....	4.77	....	2.90	.83	34.20
Hanford	8.41	20.91	3.03	....	10.36	3.13	4.89	5.38	56.59
Lemoore	5.83	13.75	1.25	....	9.17	....	2.08	.42	32.50
Lake Co.									
Lakeport	2.73	8.18	4.09	....	11.36	1.82	3.18	.45	32.73
Lassen Co.									
Susanville	4.28	14.13	.37	....	13.01	.19	1.86	.74	34.76
Los Angeles Co.									
Alhambra	5.07	20.47	4.61	.02	4.63	2.81	4.93	6.18	49.32
Arcadia	6.01	17.41	.21	1.07	5.04	2.84	1.56	2.52	36.89
Avalon	4.33	9.00	7.33	....	3.00	....	5.50	2.33	31.83
Azusa	5.83	16.79	3.32	.21	8.93	2.46	5.72	4.55	47.91
Baldwin Park	3.06	5.42	....	....	1.39	.65	....	.03	10.55
Bell	3.42	14.88	2.44	....	5.05	4.24	.98	2.72	33.72
Beverly Hills	9.52	37.55	13.68	.94	9.42	6.71	12.68	19.29	114.26
Burbank	6.60	22.62	7.21	.36	7.41	....	6.11	8.66	59.45
Claremont	6.25	13.01	3.28	....	6.15	.10	4.61	1.43	35.36
Compton	2.77	13.32	.47	....	7.19	.39	1.43	2.20	28.06
Covina	10.70	19.93	....	....	12.18	....	3.40	17.94	64.66
Culver City	7.19	22.63	4.67	.03	7.84	....	5.21	12.72	61.45
Dairy Valley	6.46	.31	....	....	1.23	....	....	....	8.00
Downey	.88	.44	....	....	.08	....	....	....	1.39
El Monte	10.48	22.24	2.56	....	4.64	....	6.48	2.80	51.20
El Segundo	11.46	31.77	6.45	....	18.79	2.15	26.04	19.75	120.06
Gardena	4.53	14.53	2.50	....	4.33	....	3.67	5.00	34.57
Glendale	3.98	20.13	5.95	.01	7.10	2.94	4.43	2.86	48.20
Glendora	5.48	10.96	3.72	....	5.28	2.35	2.28	1.76	31.89
Hawthorne	5.50	14.22	3.22	....	5.56	....	2.19	5.84	37.13
Hermosa Beach	5.22	15.35	6.94	.45	7.96	.13	2.74	5.29	44.20
Huntington Park	6.97	23.59	3.03	....	2.32	....	5.12	7.97	49.06
Inglewood	4.88	17.77	2.26	.02	7.44	.02	4.97	8.13	45.55
Lakewood	2.67	3.65	.21	....	4.31	....	1.96	.39	13.19
La Puente	2.39	.15	....	....	....	....	....	....	2.54

Table 3.b Per Capita Operating Costs for All Cities (except San Francisco) by Functions and Total: 1957

Cities	General Govern- ment	Prot. to Per. & Prop.	Sani- tation	Conserv. of Health	Streets	Educa- tion	Recrea- tion	Miscel- laneous	Total
La Verne	7.00	12.40	3.00	....	7.00	....	3.20	2.20	35.00
Long Beach	5.83	21.33	5.50	1.56	8.06	3.39	8.75	23.05	78.83
Los Angeles	9.97	26.58	3.07	1.89	5.16	1.89	4.28	1.20	59.55
Lynwood	2.76	13.45	1.98	....	4.84	....	4.22	2.27	29.82
Manhattan Beach	.65	12.23	3.60	....	4.33	1.63	1.87	2.58	29.23
Maywood	3.29	14.30	2.01	....	2.82	....	2.01	.74	25.17
Monrovia	5.54	19.18	2.77	....	4.79	10.40	4.11	6.05	53.15
Montebello	6.43	18.27	3.43	....	6.73	.03	6.97	2.60	44.60
Monterey Park	5.69	11.97	2.91	....	6.66	1.56	2.63	3.31	35.16
Palo Verdes Estates	3.68	15.40	....	....	6.19	....	6.58	.92	32.77
Paramount	.48	....	....	....	....	....	....	....	.48
Pasadena	7.21	24.28	2.87	1.77	4.55	4.92	11.76	6.46	69.45
Pomona	4.54	18.81	6.05	.14	9.14	2.83	4.14	3.58	50.08
Redondo Beach	4.07	16.78	4.99	.14	4.33	1.62	3.23	5.38	40.68
Rolling Hills	....	....	....	....	....	....	....	....	....
San Fernando	5.70	19.82	5.94	....	7.15	....	6.00	3.27	48.61
San Gabriel	4.49	19.24	.80	....	4.84	....	6.13	3.02	38.80
San Marino	5.28	24.46	.07	....	4.05	7.16	6.51	4.05	51.95
Santa Monica	6.22	22.44	8.24	.05	5.10	3.62	9.09	4.81	62.20
Sierra Madre	4.33	10.70	4.97	....	5.73	2.80	2.80	1.53	33.37
Signal Hill	8.30	44.68	10.64	....	26.81	.64	2.13	9.57	102.77
South Gate	3.05	15.69	2.82	.02	4.62	....	6.11	4.35	36.67
South Pasadena	5.50	19.26	2.77	.10	4.84	3.68	6.25	4.23	47.09
Torrance	3.26	13.41	1.68	.14	5.38	.53	3.96	3.98	33.74
Vernon	411.92	2253.89	85.49	56.99	352.33	2.59	....	233.16	3,650.26
West Covina	3.37	9.37	.99	....	5.45	....	1.13	.63	20.96
Whittier	4.95	20.48	5.77	....	6.14	2.98	6.26	5.89	55.75
Madera Co.									
Chowchilla	2.08	10.00	6.04	....	2.71	....	....	2.08	23.54
Madera	3.27	11.67	8.53	....	4.40	....	3.00	3.00	34.20
Marin Co.									
Belvedere	9.19	8.11	5.41	....	12.43	....	2.16	7.57	46.49
Corte Madera	5.11	10.89	.22	.22	5.78	....	2.44	.89	26.22
Fairfax	3.71	14.23	....	....	5.57	....	3.51	1.03	28.04
Larkspur	4.44	9.11	4.67	....	6.00	1.11	.44	.22	26.67
Mill Valley	6.70	14.40	2.90	....	5.90	3.30	4.50	1.50	39.70
Ross	4.00	12.40	....	....	6.40	....	2.40	1.20	26.80
San Anselmo	3.14	20.38	....	....	5.81	2.10	1.62	.48	33.90
San Rafael	8.17	18.34	.97	.34	9.60	2.00	2.86	1.20	43.54
Sausalito	5.65	16.29	....	....	5.81	1.94	2.26	1.13	33.06
Mendocino Co.									
Fort Bragg	2.67	11.80	4.19	....	4.19	.95	4.38	.95	29.13
Point Arena	4.00	8.00	2.00	....	4.00	....	....	....	18.00
Ukiah	7.15	16.43	1.93	....	8.60	2.80	4.06	5.02	46.76
Willits	3.75	14.00	4.50	....	17.75	2.25	3.75	1.00	48.00
Merced Co.									
Atwater	7.00	9.67	6.67	....	9.00	....	3.00	1.17	38.67
Dos Palos	6.28	13.61	5.23	....	13.61	....	....	1.05	39.77
Gustine	6.22	12.89	6.22	....	9.33	....	2.67	1.33	40.44
Livingston	6.19	13.33	5.71	....	11.43	....	.95	.95	39.05
Los Banos	5.54	11.63	5.72	....	9.78	....	2.21	2.21	37.10
Merced	5.27	18.93	5.27	....	8.00	....	4.20	1.02	43.02
Modoc Co.									
Alturas	6.00	13.33	1.33	....	9.67	....	.33	2.33	34.00
Monterey Co.									
Carmel	6.14	24.56	.45	....	8.64	8.64	.68	3.64	52.75
Del Rey Oaks	3.51	5.85	.59	....	8.19	....	1.17	....	19.31
Gonzales	4.10	15.90	1.54	....	6.67	....	1.03	....	34.36
Greenfield	4.72	17.54	.67	....	6.07	....	....	1.35	36.44
King City	6.67	16.00	3.00	....	5.33	1.00	9.00	1.67	42.67
Monterey	10.67	23.67	6.14	....	6.14	3.11	2.38	6.82	59.89
Pacific Grove	4.09	12.64	7.45	....	6.18	3.00	10.55	2.27	46.91
Salinas	14.99	21.69	3.19	....	8.97	6.71	6.75	.74	64.53
Seaside	2.86	8.33	....	....	3.15	....	1.55	.42	16.31
Soledad	3.67	13.33	1.33	....	3.67	....	1.67	1.33	26.67

Table 3. b Per Capita Operating Costs for All Cities (except San Francisco) by Functions and Total: 1957

Cities	General Govern- ment	Prot. to Per. & Prop.	Sani- tation	Conserv. of Health	Streets	Educa- tion	Recrea- tion	Miscel- laneous	Total
Napa Co.									
Calistoga	$ 3.75	$17.50	$ 1.25	$ .63	$ 6.88	$ 1.25	$ 1.25	$ .63	$35.00
Napa	6.33	21.67	....	.78	9.94	2.11	2.44	2.56	49.33
St. Helena	5.42	14.17	2.08	.42	6.67	2.08	.83	.42	32.08
Nevada Co.									
Grass Valley	3.67	9.83	1.50	.17	8.33	2.50	1.17	1.50	30.17
Nevada City	5.85	13.27	2.34	....	5.46	3.12	3.51	.78	35.52
Orange Co.									
Anaheim	5.25	12.32	2.82	....	4.06	1.45	3.45	3.98	35.43
Brea	5.23	14.15	3.08	....	6.15	....	3.08	2.62	36.46
Buena Park	3.56	11.31	2.07	....	2.98	....	5.96	.55	26.44
Costa Mesa	5.61	12.78	3.43	....	2.35	....	....	.57	24.74
Cypress	3.09	....	....	....	.62	....	....	....	3.71
Dairyland	5.45	3.64	....	....	7.27	....	....	....	16.36
Fullerton	5.44	14.87	4.50	....	4.35	2.04	4.12	2.98	38.75
Garden Grove	2.21	.67	....	....	.69	....	....	.02	3.58
Huntington Beach	10.92	43.54	9.23	....	26.31	6.77	20.92	40.62	65.23
Laguna Beach	9.62	26.43	15.30	....	11.82	....	8.46	6.26	78.25
La Habra	2.93	11.27	2.07	....	5.00	....	1.20	2.33	26.33
Newport Beach	8.04	26.48	9.64	....	8.89	2.21	10.68	4.75	71.03
Orange	4.60	16.28	3.44	....	5.16	2.79	3.07	1.02	36.47
Placentia	6.88	15.31	3.44	....	2.50	....	3.13	....	31.25
San Clemente	8.61	20.83	7.08	....	13.19	....	13.89	6.25	71.94
Santa Ana	4.21	18.81	3.86	....	5.93	2.14	4.91	7.39	47.49
Seal Beach	8.81	18.57	7.86	....	6.90	....	6.90	1.90	52.14
Stanton	3.96	.22	....	....	....	....	....	.22	4.39
Tustin	9.60	16.38	4.52	....	14.69	....	1.13	1.13	47.46
Placer Co.									
Auburn	7.00	17.80	3.20	....	10.40	2.60	....	.60	41.60
Colfax	3.81	11.43	3.81	....	4.76	....	....	....	24.76
Lincoln	7.00	13.33	4.33	....	7.33	1.67	4.33	1.33	40.67
Rocklin	5.25	16.49	5.25	....	7.50	....	.75	.75	35.98
Roseville	6.00	15.48	6.00	....	5.39	2.26	3.39	2.61	43.22
Plumas Co.									
Portola	2.65	10.17	2.65	....	9.73	....	.44	.44	33.17
Riverside Co.									
Banning	5.63	15.58	2.21	.11	5.30	....	2.54	.99	32.37
Beaumont	5.00	15.00	3.06	.28	6.39	....	4.44	1.67	36.11
Blythe	3.76	20.98	10.29	.20	9.50	1.19	2.57	1.78	50.47
Cabazon	9.36	24.56	....	....	2.34	....	....	....	36.26
Coachella	2.89	7.11	.26	....	1.58	1.58	.26	.26	15.26
Corona	7.24	18.02	1.89	.16	8.34	1.50	7.16	.55	45.41
Elsinore	2.77	17.31	5.88	....	6.23	1.73	4.15	....	38.77
Hemet	5.52	16.78	6.67	....	9.43	4.60	1.61	1.15	49.89
Indio	6.22	19.44	4.67	....	6.78	2.11	3.67	3.22	46.22
Palm Springs	11.93	29.63	10.15	.07	6.89	2.81	5.41	8.30	76.37
Perris	4.43	11.07	5.54	....	8.12	1.11	1.48	.37	32.47
Riverside	3.83	16.29	5.54	.17	11.65	3.42	5.41	1.86	48.49
San Jacinto	3.62	14.95	5.89	....	5.89	1.81	4.98	1.36	39.87
Sacramento Co.									
Folsom	2.50	8.21	5.36	....	3.21	....	1.07	....	21.43
Galt	4.52	9.04	....	....	4.52	....	....	.65	18.72
Isleton	6.06	14.55	5.45	....	8.48	....	2.42	.61	41.21
North Sacramento	9.68	15.37	5.26	....	8.42	....	3.47	.53	43.68
Sacramento	5.64	22.11	7.19	1.96	7.72	1.96	8.37	11.25	67.60
San Benito Co.									
Hollister	3.45	12.69	6.53	.91	7.07	.91	1.45	1.27	34.81
San Juan Bautista	3.88	7.76	8.73	.97	3.88	.97	.97	....	27.16
San Bernardino Co.									
Barstow	2.90	13.38	1.60	.20	7.69	....	....	.90	27.15
Chino	2.44	11.56	5.22	.11	6.22	.11	2.56	.44	30.00
Colton	4.59	16.49	5.41	.16	6.97	1.78	4.16	3.41	43.19

Table 3.b Per Capita Operating Costs for All Cities (except San Francisco) by Functions and Total: 1957

Cities	General Govern- ment	Prot. to Per. & Prop.	Sani- tation	Conserv. of Health	Streets	Educa- tion	Recrea- tion	Miscel- laneous	Total
Fontana	$ 4.45	$ 9.03	$	$ .19	$ 5.03	$	$ 2.45	$ .97	$22.13
Monte Vista	4.10	2.80	....	.10	1.40	....	....	.20	8.60
Needles	7.71	11.87	6.04	.21	2.29	....	3.54	2.71	35.62
Ontario	4.42	16.73	5.21	.96	4.18	1.61	3.26	3.65	40.33
Redlands	7.79	15.19	3.74	.13	6.55	3.06	3.87	2.00	42.64
Rialto	5.92	10.03	2.08	.07	3.78	....	.78	.98	25.26
San Bernardino	3.37	22.34	4.94	.99	7.41	1.82	3.53	3.59	46.91
Upland	4.77	14.31	3.92	.15	5.31	2.46	4.31	7.38	43.00
San Diego Co.									
Carlsbad	7.27	9.80	.30	....	6.67	1.21	1.01	.20	26.67
Chula Vista	3.31	12.80	1.91	.06	7.86	1.91	4.06	1.86	34.09
Coronado	4.16	14.50	4.10	....	4.96	7.62	21.21	6.18	62.78
El Cajon	6.80	11.12	1.72	.08	5.08	....	1.44	.80	27.64
Escondido	6.70	17.24	1.87	.10	11.72	9.75	1.87	2.17	51.53
Imperial Beach	1.45	.91	....	....	.45	....	....	....	2.82
La Mesa	3.21	13.28	2.71	....	6.79	....	2.92	13.78	43.55
National City	5.65	12.86	4.68	....	5.88	1.77	3.06	6.57	40.59
Oceanside	6.14	17.14	7.45	....	4.41	1.77	4.55	5.27	47.55
San Diego	4.97	15.16	5.75	.17	5.81	1.83	4.84	6.62	47.30
San Joaquin Co.									
Lodi	6.45	19.65	5.15	....	6.80	2.40	7.25	3.40	51.15
Manteca	4.00	11.08	5.23	....	9.08	.31	1.38	.77	33.54
Ripon	10.00	14.74	1.05	....	5.26	.53	....	.53	33.16
Stockton	6.09	25.83	3.02	....	8.10	3.84	7.07	5.74	60.58
Tracy	11.07	16.43	5.45	....	5.71	....	7.32	6.87	53.84
San Luis Obispo Co.									
Arroyo Grande	4.40	14.40	.80	....	7.60	....	....	.80	28.40
El Paso Robles	5.69	17.54	4.00	....	10.92	2.92	6.77	.92	50.92
Pismo Beach	5.00	12.86	4.29	....	4.64	....	1.43	2.50	33.21
San Luis Obispo	4.17	15.11	1.78	.06	8.11	1.78	1.89	3.67	36.61
San Mateo Co.									
Atherton	3.14	13.43	.14	....	8.29	....	....	1.29	26.29
Belmont	3.98	10.25	3.31	....	3.31	.17	1.86	1.86	25.00
Burlingame	5.96	19.06	4.55	....	5.64	3.32	5.23	4.05	48.08
Colma	26.94	30.30	3.37	....	3.37	....	....	3.37	67.34
Daly City	3.86	11.06	2.60	.26	3.97	1.91	1.14	2.00	27.37
Hillsborough	4.34	32.01	2.84	....	4.19	....	1.05	4.49	50.11
Menlo Park	3.36	8.60	....	....	4.28	.20	4.00	.68	21.32
Millbrae	2.76	11.10	2.34	....	4.76	....	1.31	1.59	26.61
Redwood City	3.63	18.35	3.50	....	6.18	3.10	4.20	5.80	47.00
San Bruno	3.64	11.77	6.82	....	4.23	1.73	3.05	3.32	36.50
San Carlos	4.05	17.30	3.55	....	6.45	.05	2.65	2.80	37.15
San Mateo	4.03	15.97	2.14	....	7.75	2.00	3.65	4.20	40.23
So. San Francisco	4.04	16.72	2.54	....	6.00	1.81	3.56	3.17	38.44
Woodside	.78	.19	....	....	....	....	....	....	.97
Santa Barbara Co.									
Guadalupe	2.14	13.57	1.79	....	3.93	....	....	1.79	23.57
Lompoc	5.43	16.14	6.29	.14	8.14	2.14	6.43	.86	45.86
Santa Barbara	8.37	16.60	1.43	1.32	7.45	2.46	7.05	3.92	49.19
Santa Maria	3.47	15.67	5.73	....	6.00	1.93	3.47	1.53	37.80
Santa Clara Co.									
Alviso	7.69	10.77	....	....	3.08	....	....	1.54	23.08
Campbell	4.12	8.47	.47	....	6.00	....	....	.24	19.29
Cupertino	5.88	3.21	....	....	1.60	....	....	....	10.70
Gilroy	5.42	12.92	3.99	....	12.60	3.03	1.44	4.47	44.03
Los Altos	3.68	4.59	....	....	6.55	....	.45	1.09	16.36
Los Altos Hills	4.74	1.84	....	....	2.37	....	....	....	6.32
Los Gatos	10.17	19.83	2.00	....	10.50	4.17	2.67	1.67	51.00
Milpitas	11.43	17.67	....	....	6.76	....	....	....	35.86
Morgan Hill	5.22	18.26	8.70	....	14.78	....	.87	1.74	50.43
Mountain View	9.07	10.49	5.23	....	4.96	.88	2.23	3.04	36.51
Palo Alto	8.54	18.85	8.33	....	9.74	3.07	9.00	17.20	76.59
San Jose	4.87	18.34	1.44	4.48	6.60	1.41	3.33	9.11	50.78
Santa Clara	2.35	11.08	2.58	....	2.93	3.40	1.88	18.45	43.58
Saratoga	.86	....	....	....	.07	....	....	....	.93
Sunnyvale	4.46	11.19	5.30	....	12.38	.57	3.73	1.59	42.43

Table 3.b Per Capita Operating Costs for All Cities (except San Francisco) by Functions and Total: 1957

Cities	General Govern- ment	Prot. to Per. & Prop.	Sani- tation	Conserv. of Health	Streets	Educa- tion	Recrea- tion	Miscel- laneous	Total
Santa Cruz Co.									
Capitola	$ 4.00	$ 2.50	$ .50	$	$ 8.00	$	$ 2.00	$ .50	$17.50
Santa Cruz	5.83	26.54	7.79	....	9.50	4.37	4.04	3.37	61.96
Watsonville	4.60	16.13	9.20	1.27	4.40	2.00	1.40	2.07	44.07
Shasta Co.									
Anderson	3.57	5.95	1.19	....	.24	....	.24	.24	11.43
Redding	13.50	19.93	8.71	....	10.43	....	5.21	5.50	63.86
Sierra Co.									
Loyalton	2.04	8.16	....	....	9.18	....	....	....	19.39
Siskiyou Co.									
Dorris	5.00	8.33	....	....	1.67	....	....	.83	17.50
Dunsmuir	4.83	11.19	6.10	....	9.16	....	.51	1.27	33.06
Etna	3.33	4.44	2.22	....	5.56	....	....	1.11	17.78
Fort Jones	3.33	6.67	5.00	....	6.67	....	....	3.33	25.00
Montague	5.57	8.36	2.79	....	6.96	....	....	....	26.46
Mt. Shasta	5.64	16.92	7.69	....	10.77	....	.51	2.56	44.10
Tulelake	4.67	14.00	4.00	....	8.67	.67	.67	.67	36.67
Yreka	4.76	12.62	2.14	....	9.29	.71	2.14	1.19	34.05
Solano Co.									
Benicia	5.00	14.29	.71	.14	5.14	1.43	2.57	.86	30.29
Dixon	4.80	15.20	3.20	....	14.40	....	6.80	.40	41.60
Fairfield	2.58	8.42	....	....	8.25	....	3.58	.67	25.67
Rio Vista	21.60	13.20	6.40	....	6.80	....	5.20	....	56.80
Suisan	2.73	11.36	....	....	6.36	....	.45	.91	21.82
Vacaville	4.00	9.38	1.25	....	8.00	....	.75	.88	24.75
Vallejo	6.70	21.55	....	.30	5.13	1.88	1.38	3.38	43.93
Sonoma Co.									
Cloverdale	8.57	9.43	.57	....	8.57	1.14	5.14	3.71	38.00
Healdsburg	6.50	20.50	3.75	....	4.50	2.00	8.00	2.00	48.00
Petaluma	6.92	18.31	2.92	....	7.54	1.92	3.62	4.46	47.46
Santa Rosa	7.15	18.07	3.02	....	8.95	1.70	5.34	4.89	49.54
Sebastopol	6.33	16.00	4.00	....	7.00	2.67	6.33	1.00	44.00
Sonoma	5.82	15.27	6.91	....	8.73	2.55	2.55	1.82	45.09
Stanislaus Co.									
Ceres	2.82	10.98	1.69	....	5.91	....	3.10	.56	25.34
Modesto	8.91	22.14	3.64	2.22	10.49	1.02	7.77	4.29	62.70
Newman	4.76	14.76	1.90	....	11.43	.48	5.24	.95	39.52
Oakdale	9.33	12.44	3.78	....	7.78	....	2.89	1.78	38.67
Patterson	7.14	11.90	1.90	....	9.52	....	2.38	1.43	35.24
Riverbank	4.95	9.57	3.63	....	6.93	....	.33	.66	27.39
Turlock	5.77	21.28	7.56	.51	7.05	1.03	6.15	.38	52.05
Sutter Co.									
Live Oak	1.93	8.70	3.87	....	3.38	....	.97	....	24.66
Yuba City	5.38	11.23	2.31	....	3.15	....	1.00	10.31	34.23
Tehama Co.									
Corning	6.34	11.88	5.15	....	12.67	1.58	.79	.79	41.19
Red Bluff	4.48	18.08	2.88	....	8.16	1.76	1.76	1.12	38.88
Tehama	3.02	3.02	....	....	12.08	....	....	....	18.13
Tulare Co.									
Dinuba	2.50	13.50	7.67	....	4.00	.17	3.83	1.00	32.67
Exeter	4.65	13.49	7.44	....	4.88	.23	5.35	1.16	37.21
Lindsay	5.00	13.52	5.37	....	6.48	.37	2.96	4.26	38.15
Porterville	10.00	20.25	8.63	....	11.13	2.75	9.63	.88	64.63
Tulare	4.62	14.54	6.54	....	6.85	1.08	3.77	1.31	39.00
Visalia	5.62	17.05	7.95	....	13.84	2.40	4.18	2.26	53.42
Woodlake	3.43	10.29	6.86	....	10.29	....	4.00	....	36.00
Tuolumne Co.									
Sonora	4.25	13.00	2.00	.25	8.50	1.00	.25	.50	29.75

Table 3.b Per Capita Operating Costs for All Cities (except San Francisco) by Functions and Total: 1957

Cities	General Govern- ment	Prot. to Per. & Prop.	Sani- tation	Conserv. of Health	Streets	Educa- tion	Recrea- tion	Miscel- laneous	Total
Ventura Co.									
Fillmore	5.62	9.79	2.50	....	3.33	....	1.46	.42	24.37
Ojai	9.16	12.98	4.58	....	4.58	....	4.07	.51	35.88
Oxnard	4.81	15.84	4.71	.16	6.19	1.52	2.35	2.77	39.77
Port Hueneme	3.20	10.97	....	....	2.40	....	.69	.11	17.94
San Buenaventura	5.06	18.38	2.30	....	3.25	.60	5.55	3.28	39.74
Santa Paula	4.00	12.46	4.46	....	3.62	2.31	1.62	2.31	31.69
Yolo Co.									
Davis	4.43	9.98	7.21	....	6.24	....	.97	.69	30.49
Winters	1.98	9.90	7.52	....	5.54	....	.79	1.98	27.72
Woodland	4.59	18.35	8.31	.26	8.91	1.56	7.88	5.45	55.65
Yuba Co.									
Marysville	6.84	31.79	9.05	1.05	3.89	3.05	7.16	1.47	64.74
Wheatland	5.00	21.67	6.67	....	5.00	....	....	....	38.33

Table 7.a Variation in Bonded Indebtedness Among All Counties (except San Francisco)
by Medians, Quartiles and Range: 1937, 1947, 1957

Total County Bonded Debt on June 30 of Base Year [1]

	$ Per Capita [2]			Percentage of Assessed Valuation [3]			Debt Service as % of Total Cost of Government		
	1937 (a)	1947 (b)	1957 (c)	1937 (d)	1947 (e)	1957 (f)	1937 (g)	1947 (h)	1957 (i)
State Aggregate[5]	$ 72.09	$40.92	$125.62	6.7%	3.7%	7.3%	13.2%	5.2%	5.9%
Adjusted[6]	187.43	61.79	125.62						
Counties:									
High	380.94	52.04	212.48	18.2	5.2	12.2	17.1	5.9	9.4
Q[3]	43.99	26.61	129.32	3.6	2.4	7.6	10.7	3.4	4.2
Median	30.14	17.17	87.48	2.6	1.4	4.7	7.7	2.5	3.2
Q[1]	16.00	10.08	54.92	1.1	.7	2.2	4.3	1.3	2.4
Low	00.00	00.00	00.00	0.0	0.0	0.0	0.0	0.0	0.0
Median: Adjusted [6]	78.36	25.93	87.48						
Alameda	45.34	40.62	90.68	4.8	4.7	6.4	9.9	5.9	3.3
Alpine	8.86	00.00	00.00	.3	0.0	0.0	5.1	0.0	0.0
Amador	.23	.75	53.52	0.0	0.0	1.3	.3	.2	3.2
Butte	43.76	20.78	66.85	3.9	1.9	3.7	11.4	.8	2.7
Calaveras	16.24	5.38	155.10	1.1	.3	6.0	3.6	1.5	4.7
Colusa	380.94	31.12	35.42	18.2	1.2	1.0	8.2	4.7	1.0
Contra Costa	47.49	18.29	180.87	3.8	2.3	9.2	13.5	3.0	6.0
Del Norte	31.18	00.00	86.69	1.5	0.0	7.1	4.4	0.0	9.4
El Dorado	16.95	11.54	75.52	1.3	.7	3.3	3.7	2.0	4.4
Fresno	52.03	24.79	103.83	3.4	1.5	5.0	10.8	4.3	4.3
Glenn	33.94	18.01	127.91	1.9	.9	4.7	8.1	2.2	2.7
Humboldt	9.12	17.72	71.66	.9	1.8	4.7	3.0	1.3	3.3
Imperial	43.48	31.73	61.76	7.1	3.9	4.2	17.1	2.2	3.7
Inyo	32.14	26.72	172.54	1.6	1.2	6.5	6.0	2.8	3.0
Kern	13.54	9.35	94.48	.6	.6	3.8	5.7	1.5	6.3
Kings	33.10	10.62	57.50	1.3	.5	2.3	7.3	.9	2.8
Lake	29.68	8.87	40.08	2.7	.7	1.6	5.8	1.2	1.6
Lassen	21.87	10.71	20.23	1.9	1.0	1.3	5.1	3.2	1.2
Los Angeles	62.86	39.11	123.53	6.7	3.5	7.0	12.0	5.0	5.2
Madera	12.24	10.24	30.58	.9	.9	1.5	4.3	.1	1.2
Marin	33.97	27.84	133.28	3.6	3.3	9.7	12.2	4.2	3.8
Mariposa	19.91	13.43	33.22	2.0	.9	1.5	2.8	1.4	1.9
Mendocino	13.71	10.91	120.43	1.5	1.2	8.4	3.4	1.7	3.6
Merced	42.65	8.76	56.33	3.4	.8	3.6	10.5	3.2	3.1
Modoc	29.07	25.60	80.44	1.7	1.6	3.0	8.1	1.4	2.9
Mono	00.00	00.00	11.54	0.0	0.0	.2	0.0	0.0	2.9
Monterey	44.22	26.28	130.95	3.3	2.0	7.6	11.5	4.3	5.6
Napa	24.87	25.62	137.12	2.8	3.0	12.2	10.7	2.9	2.5
Nevada	23.08	17.17	13.39	2.4	1.6	.7	4.3	3.2	1.1
Orange	50.75	29.07	153.62	3.4	1.7	8.4	10.7	5.0	4.3
Placer	17.43	17.43	7.14	1.3	1.5	.4	5.8	1.5	3.1
Plumas	2.14	26.59	110.14	.1	1.2	2.1	.5	2.7	4.8
Riverside	79.41	46.11	151.11	.1	5.2	7.5	10.0	3.7	4.0
Sacramento	68.95	36.88	106.25	7.8	4.0	9.1	11.8	4.6	3.9
San Benito	13.03	1.44	5.81	1.0	4.1	.2	6.8	.4	1.0
San Bernardino	33.32	25.78	130.72	3.8	2.8	9.0	8.6	3.1	3.6
San Diego	62.51	27.54	77.85	7.9	3.6	6.4	10.7	4.5	3.8
San Joaquin	23.24	26.62	107.28	2.4	2.0	6.7	6.4	3.9	3.0
San Luis Obispo	85.80	25.20	115.91	6.7	2.5	5.6	14.6	1.5	5.8
San Mateo	30.14	24.86	150.21	2.6	2.7	9.0	13.8	3.4	5.9
Santa Barbara	46.95	9.93	87.30	3.0	.6	3.4	10.7	2.7	3.1
Santa Clara	38.44	14.83	143.97	4.2	1.4	8.9	9.4	2.9	4.3
Santa Cruz	25.18	12.52	98.23	3.0	1.7	5.2	9.4	2.0	3.7
Shasta	15.75	14.73	145.61	.9	.9	6.0	5.5	.9	4.0
Sierra	5.02	8.00	8.75	.6	.5	.4	.6	1.3	.2
Siskiyou	7.27	16.69	123.52	.7	1.4	6.9	3.2	.7	1.3
Solano	21.62	16.00	102.16	2.4	2.2	7.9	8.5	2.5	4.0
Sonoma	37.21	17.05	149.26	3.9	1.7	9.9	8.9	3.4	2.8
Stanislaus	25.78	31.70	107.42	2.9	3.5	7.7	7.4	2.6	3.4
Sutter	38.84	12.13	69.70	2.8	.8	3.2	7.7	2.5	2.4
Tehama	40.29	13.69	56.32	2.9	.9	2.9	7.5	3.1	2.9
Trinity	1.79	1.40	39.00	.2	.2	2.5	.2	1.3	1.3
Tulare	28.65	18.36	72.19	3.2	2.0	4.1	10.8	2.6	2.4
Tuolumne	6.74	8.98	41.59	.5	.6	2.0	1.2	1.2	1.7
Ventura	34.49	52.04	212.48	2.9	3.4	8.5	9.8	5.9	7.2
Yolo	51.18	32.82	80.03	3.8	2.6	4.3	9.3	3.9	3.5
Yuba	48.77	1.65	87.48	3.5	.2	5.0	4.0	1.6	2.4

1. All basic data were derived from the State Controller's Annual Reports for Counties. See Table 7.2
2. Population estimates used for 1937 were those developed by the California Taxpayers' Association (interpolated for January 1 of that year) and for 1947 and 1957 those of the State Department of Finance.
3. All indebtedness noted in this table consists of general obligation bonds. Because of changes in reporting practices that for 1957 (under all three headings)* consists of all bonded debt of California 57 counties plus San Francisco's debt as given in the State Controller's report on Cities plus all school district debt. But for these additions figures for 11957 would not correspond to those for 1937 and 1947. *for State aggregate only.
4. Debt service includes both interest payments and redemptions of principal.
5. It cannot be claimed that these figures on state aggregates are very significant because responsibility for different segments of local indebtedness rests with the taxpayers of the unit which incurred the particular debt, not on the taxpayers of the state as a whole.
6. These figures have been adjusted through use of the U. S. Department of Commerce Cost-of-Construction Index (1956).

Table 7. b Basic Data Relating to Bonded Indebtedness of All Cities (except San Francisco): 1937, 1947, 1957

Cities	Total Bonded Debt (In Thousands)			Total Debt Service (In Thousands)			Total Cost of Government (In Millions)		
	1937	1947	1957	1937	1947	1957	1937	1947	1957
Alameda Co.	$12,173.2	23,672.9	32,726.5	$1,246.1	1,707.1	2,360.4	$12.1	23.3	60.6
Alameda	582.5	226.0	2,385.0	67.2	49.5	81.9	1.5	3.0	6.6
Albany	27.0	....	57.0	5.5	....	3.0	.1	.3	.7
Berkeley	906.5	1,214.0	34.0	98.3	174.1	18.9	1.9	3.2	7.3
Emeryville	....	....	....	....	....	....	.1	.2	.5
Fremont	*	*	....	*	*	....	*	*	.6
Hayward	302.0	144.0	4,931.0	30.2	122.9	320.5	.2	.5	3.6
Livermore	58.0	48.5	577.5	8.2	9.4	47.7	∞	.1	.5
Newark	*	*	....	*	*	....	*	*	.2
Oakland	10,118.2	20,430.4	23,554.0	1,008.3	1,292.0	1,789.8	7.6	15.0	36.9
Piedmont	137.0	....	....	28.4	12.6	....	.3	.3	.8
Pleasanton	42.0	20.0	193.0	....	3.1	15.2	∞	.1	.2
San Leandro	....	1,590.0	995.0	....	43.6	83.4	.2	.6	2.7
Amador Co.		30.0	236.0	.7	2.9	21.3	.3	.6	.2
Amador	....	....	....	....	....	....	*	∞	∞
Ione	*	*	150.0	*	*	10.4	*	*	.1
Jackson	50.0	30.0	41.0	.7	2.9	4.6	∞	∞	.1
Plymouth	....	....	....	....	....	∞	∞	∞	∞
Sutter Creek	....	....	45.0	....	....	6.2	∞	∞	∞
Butte Co.	147.1	30.0	140.0	20.2	14.8	14.0	.4	.6	1.7
Biggs	....	....	....	....	....	....	∞	∞	.6
Chico	58.1	15.0	....	7.9	4.6	....	.2	.3	.9
Gridley	5.0	....	140.0	....	∞	14.0	.1	.2	.3
Oroville	84.0	18.0	....	12.3	10.1	....	.1	.2	.4
Calaveras Co.	....	....	120.0	....	....	9.6	∞	∞	∞
Angels	....	....	120.0	....	....	9.6	∞	∞	∞
Colusa Co.	33.3	41.5	40.7	7.1	9.8	6.0	.1	.	.3
Colusa	33.3	3.8	....	7.1	1.6	....	.1	.1	.2
Williams	....	38.1	40.7	....	8.2	6.0	∞	∞	.1
Contra Costa Co.	2,182.5	5,404.3	32,482.9	215.4	405.9	735.4	1.3	4.8	12.2
Antioch	174.5	464.0	2,100.0	19.5	38.9	188.0	.1	.3	1.0
Brentwood	*	*	....	*	*	....	*	*	.1
Concord	3.0	....	350.0	....	....	133.4	∞	.1	1.0
El Cerrito	29.0	....	....	4.8	....	....	.1	.3	.9
Hercules	....	....	....	....	....	....	∞	∞	∞
Martinez	195.3	358.5	911.1	17.9	31.6	91.8	.2	.5	.9
Pinole	....	....	....	....	....	....	∞	∞	.1
Pittsburg	268.0	148.0	1,422.0	26.0	20.0	81.8	.2	.8	1.1
Richmond	1,459.8	4,407.0	6,629.8	147.1	311.7	207.2	.7	2.7	5.9
San Pablo	....	....	90.0	....	....	8.4	....	....	.5
Walnut Creek	53.0	27.0	2,000.0	....	3.7	24.9	∞	.1	.7
Del Norte Co.	....	116.0	36.0	....	13.7	9.5	.1	.1	.2
Crescent City	....	116.0	36.0	....	13.7	9.5	.1	.1	.2
El Dorado Co.	89.0	65.5	492.5	10.3	11.6	31.8	.1	.1	.3
Placerville	89.0	65.5	492.5	10.3	11.6	31.8	.1	.1	.3
Fresno Co.	3,192.3	2,836.0	4,457.5	227.0	355.7	431.3	2.5	4.4	14.8
Clovis	20.7	8.1	117.0	....	1.6	10.7	∞	.1	.3
Coalinga	16.1	....	....	6.1	....	....	.2	.3	.5
Firebaugh	....	28.0	90.0	....	2.9	23.5	∞	∞	.1
Fowler	4.5	21.5	8.0	....	1.7	2.2	∞	.1	.2
Fresno	2,898.5	2,614.0	2,957.0	191.1	314.4	278.6	2.1	3.3	11.8
Huron	....	....	131.0	....	....	10.8	....	....	.1
Kerman	....	....	133.2	....	....	8.6	....	∞	.1
Kingsburg	38.8	37.6	106.7	....	5.4	12.8	∞	.1	.2
Mendota	....	....	62.0	....	....	6.7	....	∞	.1
Orange Cove	*	*	369.0	*	*	24.7	*	*	.1
Parlier	....	34.0	14.0	....	3.2	2.6	∞	∞	.1
Reedley	126.6	50.1	6.6	14.7	10.7	2.1	.1	.2	.3
Sanger	39.0	16.7	297.0	6.6	8.5	32.9	.1	.1	.5
San Joaquin	*	....	....	*	....	....	*	∞	∞
Selma	48.3	26.0	166.0	8.6	7.2	15.1	∞	.1	.3
Glenn Co.	52.0	36.0	123.0	5.8	3.1	13.7	.1	.1	.3
Orland	13.0	....	....	....	....	....	∞	.1	.2
Willows	39.0	36.0	123.0	5.8	3.1	13.7	.1	.1	.2

Table 7.b Basic Data Relating to Bonded Indebtedness of All Cities (except San Francisco): 1937, 1947, 1957

Cities	Total Bonded Debt (In Thousands)			Total Debt Service (In Thousands)			Total Cost of Gov't (In Millions)		
	1937	1947	1957	1937	1947	1957	1937	1947	1957
Humboldt Co.	$ 1,400.4	$1,572.0	$ 3,262.0	$ 115.2	$ 131.5	$ 297.8	$ .7	$1.0	$ 3.4
Arcata	96.0	104.0	384.0	....	6.6	21.2	.1	.1	.5
Blue Lake	....	2.0	284.0	....	.6	17.5	∞	∞	.1
Eureka	1,296.4	1,436.0	2,372.0	115.2	124.2	236.2	.6	.8	2.6
Ferndale	....	....	119.0	....	....	11.1	∞	.1	.2
Fortuna	8.0	30.0	103.0	....	.1	11.8	∞	.1	.2
Trinidad	....	....	....	....	....	....	∞	∞	∞
Imperial Co.	1,209.2	848.6	2,617.6	113.9	132.1	260.2	.9	1.5	4.7
Brawley	407.3	221.0	472.0	40.0	33.8	51.9	.2	.4	.8
Calexico	111.0	1.0	408.0	13.0	17.1	48.2	.1	.2	1.1
Calipatria	47.5	20.3	4.5	....	3.6	2.0	∞	∞	.1
El Centro	490.8	507.8	1,380.5	61.0	66.1	124.6	.4	.6	2.1
Holtville	73.2	31.6	86.6	....	5.3	10.8	∞	.1	.3
Imperial	79.5	67.0	266.0	....	6.2	22.8	∞	∞	.1
Westmorland	....	....	....	....	....	....	∞	∞	.1
Inyo Co.	29.8	62.0	13.0	....	7.2	4.5	∞	.1	.2
Bishop	29.8	62.0	13.0	....	7.2	4.5	∞	.1	.2
Kern Co.	1,089.2	163.6	3,217.7	34.8	27.9	220.2	.8	1.8	6.4
Bakersfield	1,007.2	67.1	2,955.0	24.9	18.0	198.7	.6	1.3	5.1
Delano	75.5	40.5	7.5	8.2	7.6	3.6	.1	.2	.6
Maricopa	*	....	....	*	....	....	∞	∞	∞
Shafter	*	....	....	*	....	....	*	.1	.2
Taft	6.5	....	23.8	1.7	....	6.5	.1	.1	.2
Tehachapi	....	56.0	97.0	....	2.4	11.5	∞	∞	.1
Wasco	*	....	134.4	*	....	....	*	.1	.2
Kings Co.	238.2	110.3	293.3	20.1	18.6	55.0	.2	.5	1.2
Corcoran	21.0	....	85.0	....	4.6	22.9	.1	.2	.3
Hanford	181.0	93.8	208.3	20.1	12.5	29.9	.1	.3	.8
Lemoore	36.3	16.5	....	....	1.4	2.1	∞	.2	.2
Lake Co.	48.0	42.8	80.3	....	5.4	15.7	∞	.1	.1
Lakeport	48.0	42.8	80.3	....	5.4	15.7	∞	.1	.1
Lassen Co.	30.6	6.1	....	....	2.7	.8	∞	.1	.3
Susanville	30.6	6.1	....	....	2.7	.8	∞	.1	.3
Los Angeles Co.	271,291.1	237,495.5	614,353.0	17,023.8	38,667.9	44,720.0	106.3	202.2	511.5
Alhambra	....	520.0	1,104.0	100.5	72.0	153.6	.8	1.6	3.8
Arcadia	537.8	632.8	311.5	72.5	44.4	28.8	.3	.6	2.7
Avalon	221.0	128.3	27.6	....	18.1	12.5	.2	.4	.6
Azusa	181.0	95.6	33.8	19.9	13.9	5.0	.2	.5	2.2
Baldwin Park	*	*	....	*	*	....	*	*	.4
Bell	....	....	....	....	....	....	.1	.3	.8
Beverly Hills	2,773.0	2,338.0	4,188.0	229.8	186.9	361.6	1.2	1.8	5.9
Burbank	563.1	454.1	1,816.8	54.2	80.8	216.9	1.1	5.4	14.7
Claremont	139.0	208.5	265.0	20.3	23.0	19.9	.1	.1	.6
Compton	175.7	66.8	776.3	21.3	10.9	89.5	.3	.8	3.0
Covina	121.9	76.0	263.0	15.6	13.2	25.7	.1	.1	1.4
Culver City	247.0	121.0	1,540.0	31.1	19.2	111.0	.5	.9	3.0
Dairy Valley	*	*	....	*	*	....	*	*	∞
Downey	*	*	....	*	*	....	*	*	.1
El Monte	69.1	31.9	1,054.1	7.2	4.9	71.3	.1	1.0	1.0
El Segundo	221.0	128.0	1,465.0	32.7	16.4	126.1	.2	.3	2.3
Gardena	....	....	....	....	....	299.1	∞	.4	1.5
Glendale	1,694.6	929.9	9,625.0	164.2	126.4	4.1	5.0	5.5	13.0
Glendora	117.5	48.8	664.0	13.7	7.2	59.3	.1	.1	1.5
Hawthorne	128.0	63.0	700.0	15.5	18.0	10.2	.2	.4	2.5
Hermosa Beach	176.5	97.5	43.0	18.5	11.6	12.2	.1	.2	.9
Huntington Park	362.0	150.3	10.0	42.1	30.1	10.7	.5	1.4	2.3
Inglewood	373.5	195.5	48.5	39.6	26.4	....	.6	1.3	4.1
Lakewood	*	*	....	*	*	....	*	*	1.6
La Puente	*	*	....	*	*	....	*	*	.1
La Verne	93.0	39.0	38.0	11.9	8.7	7.7	∞	.1	.3
Long Beach	15,258.7	13,740.1	29,359.5	1,337.7	1,477.4	1,369.8	7.2	16.3	56.2
Los Angeles	226,286.3	201,846.2	516,101.0	13,270.2	34,928.9	38,503.3	74.0	141.5	315.4
Lynwood	37.0	17.0	340.0	3.2	8.1	28.8	.3	.6	1.3
Manhattan Beach	129.6	130.4	1,720.0	....	21.3	118.4	.2	.4	2.1
Maywood	....	....	....	....	....	....	.1	.2	.5
Monrovia	529.2	273.0	244.4	56.6	40.4	32.9	.3	.6	2.0

397

Table 7.b Basic Data Relating to Bonded Indebtedness of All Cities (except San Francisco): 1937,1947,1957

Cities	Total Bonded Debt (In Thousands)			Total Debt Service (In Thousands)			Total Cost of Gov't (In Millions)		
	1937	1947	1957	1937	1947	1957	1937	1947	1957
Montebello	$ 98.0	$ 56.0	$115.0	$ 8.5	$ 7.4	$ 21.1	$ .2	$ .7	$ 1.9
Monterey Park	513.0	406.5	837.0	44.8	38.0	58.2	.3	.3	2.0
Palos Verdes Est.	*	....	....	*	....	....	*	.1	.4
Paramount	*	*	....	*	*	....	*	*	∞
Pasadena	9,808.4	6,645.6	21,786.5	762.1	653.4	1,162.1	5.6	8.5	22.6
Pomona	1,113.7	644.0	3,614.0	105.6	80.9	142.0	.6	1.2	4.4
Redondo Beach	245.7	331.2	138.8	30.2	35.9	19.3	.2	.4	2.1
Rolling Hills	*	*	....	*	*	....	*	*	∞
San Fernando	131.0	76.0	465.0	15.5	16.7	37.1	.2	.5	1.1
San Gabriel	85.5	329.0	186.0	12.6	26.1	19.9	.1	.4	1.0
San Marino	87.0	45.0	321.0	10.0	5.9	27.5	.2	.4	1.0
Santa Monica	2,848.0	2,603.5	5,937.0	253.2	198.4	667.1	1.7	3.8	9.2
Sierra Madre	201.0	175.0	68.1	29.6	22.5	12.0	.1	.2	.5
Signal Hill	107.0	....	....	25.3	....	....	.2	.3	.7
South Gate	116.3	73.8	8.8	10.8	8.4	8.0	.7	1.2	2.9
South Pasadena	546.3	292.8	369.0	53.1	39.6	31.0	.4	.6	1.6
Torrance	93.0	20.0	3,430.0	13.8	6.9	253.7	.3	.8	4.9
Vernon	4,019.9	2,703.2	2,254.0	....	271.4	289.3	1.0	.8	2.4
West Covina	....	....	80.0	....	....	6.5	∞	.1	1.0
Whittier	742.0	764.5	3,360.5	70.4	48.3	286.9	.1	1.4	3.9
Madera Co.	128.5	562.3	325.5	14.4	24.3	40.7	.1	.3	1.0
Chowchilla	....	51.5	86.5	....	5.4	9.8	∞	.1	.2
Madera	128.5	510.8	239.0	14.4	18.9	30.8	.1	.2	.9
Marin Co.	371.0	551.1	755.0	40.0	40.7	92.6	.7	1.0	2.9
Belvedere	....	....	140.0	....	2.0	8.2	∞	∞	.1
Corte Madera	4.5	....	90.0	....	....	12.9	∞	∞	.2
Fairfax	....	....	....	....	....	....	∞	.1	.2
Larkspur	18.0	6.8	100.0	....	1.8	12.6	∞	∞	.2
Mill Valley	50.3	380.5	316.0	5.6	13.2	38.2	.1	.2	.5
Ross	97.0	53.0	25.0	....	6.6	3.7	∞	∞	.1
San Anselmo	73.7	12.0	....	18.8	3.8	3.6	.1	.2	.4
San Rafael	82.6	81.4	84.0	10.8	6.7	13.4	.2	.4	1.0
Sausalito	45.0	17.5	....	4.8	6.7	....	.1	.1	.3
Mendocino Co.	136.6	194.5	431.0	13.6	20.9	49.3	.2	.5	2.0
Fort Bragg	28.0	46.0	13.0	2.7	5.0	5.3	∞	.1	.2
Point Arena	....	....	....	....	....	....	∞	∞	∞
Ukiah	84.9	51.0	280.0	10.9	11.4	25.4	.2	.3	1.4
Willits	23.8	97.5	138.0	....	4.5	18.5	∞	.1	.3
Merced Co.	172.2	177.2	1,900.8	8.5	29.4	94.7	.4	.7	2.6
Atwater	....	54.4	377.0	....	7.5	32.9	.1	.1	.4
Dos Palos	....	24.0	34.5	....	3.4	2.4	∞	∞	.1
Gustine	54.5	119.0	128.0	....	3.1	24.7	∞	.1	.1
Livingston	....	48.0	26.7	....	5.3	2.8	∞	∞	.1
Los Banos	58.8	17.0	....	....	6.1	....	.1	.1	.4
Merced	58.9	14.8	1,300.0	8.5	4.0	31.9	.1	.4	1.5
Modoc Co.	54.0	56.5	106.0	.1	11.8	12.2	∞	.1	.2
Alturas	54.0	56.5	106.0	.1	11.8	12.2	∞	.1	.2
Monterey Co.	1,065.3	858.2	4,853.5	101.1	109.7	257.7	.1	.2	5.9
Carmel	19.0	11.0	18.0	3.8	1.1	4.3	.1	.1	.3
Del Rey Oaks	*	*	....	*	*	....	*	*	∞
Gonzales	*	*	240.0	*	*	12.8	*	*	.1
Greenfield	*	*	277.0	*	*	14.4	*	*	.1
King City	29.5	66.5	6.0	....	9.6	7.3	∞	.1	.2
Monterey	451.5	....	1,445.6	44.0	33.1	75.0	.3	.6	1.8
Pacific Grove	126.5	171.5	427.5	13.6	10.3	40.7	.1	.2	.7
Salinas	438.8	575.0	2,280.0	39.8	52.1	87.4	.3	.6	2.2
Seaside	*	*	....	*	*	....	*	*	.4
Soledad	....	33.2	159.4	....	3.5	15.9	∞	∞	.1
Napa Co.	439.5	1,319.0	3,886.0	42.0	76.9	249.0	.2	.8	2.0
Calistoga	....	108.0	139.0	....	7.9	14.1	∞	.1	.1
Napa	407.0	1,205.0	3,747.0	42.0	62.2	234.9	.2	.7	1.8
St. Helena	32.5	6.0	....	....	6.7	....	∞	.1	.1
Nevada Co.	83.1	8.0	441.0	7.2	7.7	27.6	.1	.2	.4
Grass Valley	50.0	8.0	326.0	7.2	4.5	19.9	.1	.1	.3
Nevada City	33.1	....	115.0	....	3.2	7.7	.1	.1	.1
Orange Co.	3,635.7	3,346.7	10,441.6	271.0	444.3	974.9	3.5	5.7	25.4
Anaheim	500.0	254.6	4,826.0	52.2	37.4	416.6	.4	.8	5.7

398

Table 7.b Basic Data Relating to Bonded Indebtedness of All Cities (except San Francisco): 1937,1947,1957

Cities	Total Bonded Debt (In Thousands)			Total Debt Service (In Thousands)			Total Cost of Gov't (In Millions)		
	1937	1947	1957	1937	1947	1957	1937	1947	1957
Brea	$ 182.0	$114.1	$ 378.9	$ 17.2	$ 12.9	$ 44.7	$ .1	$ .1	$ .5
Buena Park	*	*	....	*	*	....	*	*	1.3
Costa Mesa	*	*	....	*	*	....	**	**	.8
Cypress	*	*	....	*	*	5.1	*	*	**
Dairyland	*	*	....	*	*	5.7	*	*	**
Fullerton	456.0	159.9	1,221.0	57.9	33.5	108.3	.3	.6	3.4
Garden Grove	*	*	....	*	*	....	*	*	.3
Huntington Beach	254.5	30.8	830.0	18.1	16.7	74.6	.3	.5	1.3
Laguna Beach	14.0	4.0	154.0	1.8	1.2	13.5	.2	.3	.9
La Habra	106.0	82.0	589.0	8.2	10.0	47.3	**	.1	.7
Newport Beach	1,086.2	591.5	121.0	10.7	103.8	49.3	.7	.8	2.4
Orange	200.8	4.3	102.0	29.6	124.7	6.8	.2	.3	1.3
Placentia	....	3.0	....	....	....	....	**	**	.11
San Clemente	....	88.0	968.0	....	11.7	48.8	.1	.2	.9
Santa Ana	618.3	1,700.9	1,106.0	77.4	53.6	120.9	.9	1.6	5.5
Seal Beach	218.0	313.7	146.7	....	38.8	33.4	.1	.2	.3
Stanton	*	*	....	*	*	....	*	*	**
Tustin	....	....	....	....	....	....	**	**	.1
Placer Co.	368.8	210.5	1,132.5	47.3	31.3	66.5	.4	.6	1.6
Auburn	48.0	49.0	....	7.6	6.7	3.1	.1	.1	.3
Colfax	....	2.0	53.0	....	1.2	5.2	**	**	**
Lincoln	39.3	18.0	117.5	4.3	3.1	9.5	**	.1	.2
Rocklin	....	....	....	....	....	....	**	**	.1
Roseville	281.5	141.5	962.0	34.8	20.4	48.8	.3	.4	1.0
Plumas Co.	*	....	342.3	*	....	28.8	*	**	.1
Portola	*	....	342.3	*	....	28.8	*	**	.1
Riverside Co.	1,286.2	806.7	3,698.0	135.9	114.1	247.8	2.0	4.8	14.4
Banning	30.0	....	....	8.6	....	....	.1	.3	.6
Beaumont	24.5	4.0	25.0	....	1.1	5.9	**	.1	.2
Blythe	44.0	....	20.0	....	....	5.6	**	.1	.4
Cabazon	*	*	....	*	*	....	*	*	**
Coachella	*	....	135.0	*	....	20.4	*	**	.1
Corona	214.6	81.4	222.0	24.4	17.8	26.7	.1	.2	.7
Elsinore	46.0	20.0	60.0	....	5.4	7.0	**	.1	.2
Hemet	17.6	131.6	570.0	5.3	3.3	43.4	**	.1	.4
Indio	....	115.0	1,108.0	....	9.4	8.3	**	.1	.7
Palm Springs	*	....	755.0	*	....	66.1	*	.2	1.6
Perris	....	84.6	30.0	....	2.5	4.9	**	**	.2
Riverside	845.0	337.2	640.0	97.6	70.7	49.3	1.5	3.5	9.3
San Jacinto	64.5	33.0	133.0	....	3.8	10.3	**	.1	.2
Sacramento Co.	7,557.4	7,742.6	12,511.9	578.4	532.9	1,788.3	1.2	5.9	18.4
Folsom	*	....	122.0	*	....	6.8	*	**	.1
Galt	*	....	....	*	....	....	*	**	**
Isleton	62.6	26.6	205.0	6.7	6.4	16.3	**	**	.1
No. Sacramento	9.0	25.0	310.0	2.0	6.2	19.1	**	.1	.6
Sacramento	7,485.8	7,691.0	11,874.9	569.6	520.2	1,746.1	1.2	5.7	17.6
San Benito Co.	27.0	385.5	235.0	....	25.4	18.3	.1	.2	.3
Hollister	....	385.5	235.0	....	25.4	18.3	**	.1	**
San Juan Bautista	27.0	....	....	....	....	....	**	**	**
San Bernardino Co.	2,723.8	1,513.9	8,648.0	262.1	205.1	295.5	2.1	5.0	16.1
Barstow	*	*	246.0	*	*	17.1	*	*	.4
Chino	91.0	65.0	443.0	9.8	9.1	41.3	.1	.1	.4
Colton	106.4	60.0	1,863.0	11.8	5.5	12.8	.3	.7	1.5
Fontana	*	*	2,655.0	*	*	....	*	*	.5
Monte Vista	*	*	....	*	*	....	*	*	.1
Needles	72.0	52.0	239.0	7.9	8.7	13.6	.1	.1	.3
Ontario	361.9	268.7	1,448.2	35.6	40.6	69.0	.3	.9	3.0
Redlands	860.5	428.0	135.0	87.1	54.8	23.4	.4	.8	1.9
Rialto	163.0	83.0	603.0	....	12.5	57.2	**	.1	.8
San Bernardino	846.3	430.7	89.8	87.2	57.6	39.4	.8	2.1	6.4
Upland	222.8	126.5	926.0	22.7	16.4	21.7	.1	.3	.8
San Diego Co.	15,190.3	22,746.6	48,804.8	1,504.1	2,074.6	3,724.6	6.7	6.9	51.4
Carlsbad	*	*	55.0	*	*	7.1	*	*	.4
Chula Vista	101.0	30.0	419.0	11.6	10.5	41.5	.1	.2	1.6
Coronado	154.0	53.4	15.0	18.6	10.0	2.7	.2	.4	1.6
El Cajon	36.7	22.0	537.0	....	2.1	31.2	**	.1	1.1
Escondido	121.6	172.3	50.0	12.9	13.4	8.8	.2	.2	.9
Imperial Beach	*	*	....	*	*	.1	*	*	**
La Mesa	9.5	31.0	601.0	2.0	2.7	47.9	.1	.3	1.3
National City	190.0	160.0	116.0	20.5	35.3	28.0	.1	.4	1.8
Oceanside	259.5	357.8	642.0	22.1	37.5	82.3	.2	.5	1.9
San Diego	14,318.1	21,920.2	41,900.8	1,416.4	1,963.2	3,475.0	5.9	14.8	41.7

399

Table 7.b Basic Data Relating to Bonded Indebtedness of All Cities (except San Francisco):1937,1947,1957

Cities	Total Bonded Debt (In Thousands)			Total Debt Service (In Thousands)			Total Cost of Gov't (In Millions)		
	1937	1947	1957	1937	1947	1957	1937	1947	1957
San Joaquin Co.	$5,819.0	$5,788.4	$2,369.0	$521.0	$613.4	$337.9	$ 2.2	$ 4.2	$ 10.6
Lodi	83.3	24.0	13.0	14.3	1.3	.7	.3	1.0	2.2
Manteca	69.0	83.0	397.0	....	8.9	42.7	**	.1	.4
Ripon	*	....	44.0	*	....	3.7	*	*	.1
Stockton	5,522.9	4,975.4	1,442.0	478.4	574.6	254.9	1.7	2.9	7.0
Tracy	143.8	706.0	473.0	28.3	28.7	35.9	.1	.3	.9
San Luis Obispo Co.	325.1	234.4	738.5	35.2	33.0	39.4	.3	.7	2.3
Arroyo Grande	....	51.0	22.0	....	5.0	3.3	**	**	.2
El Paso Robles	116.0	66.0	332.0	10.9	8.5	26.6	.1	.2	.6
Pismo Beach	*	....	118.2	*	....	7.1	*	*	.1
San Luis Obispo	209.1	117.4	266.4	24.3	19.5	2.4	.2	.7	1.5
San Mateo Co.	1,459.4	1,566.9	8,474.1	143.6	245.9	745.4	1.9[1]	4.3	18.0
Atherton	12.0	2.0	....	....	1.1	....	**	.1	.2
Belmont	....	50.0	128.0	....	.5	12.0	**	**	.4
Burlingame	415.0	166.0	234.0	44.2	39.6	29.3	.4	.7	2.1
Colma	*	....	....	*	....	....	*	**	**
Daly City	23.0	20.0	832.5	9.5	8.6	41.0	.1	.3	1.3
Hillsborough	108.0	331.0	334.0	....	25.8	26.9	.1	.3	.6
Menlo Park	....	....	285.0	....	....	9.8	**	.1	.8
Millbrae	*	*	1,165.0	*	*	135.4	*	*	.9
Redwood City	747.5	468.3	2,694.0	25.6	81.2	220.2	.3	1.0	3.3
San Bruno	158.0	12.0	215.0	20.0	3.6	61.8	.1	.3	1.3
San Carlos	23.9	71.4	286.0	....	5.4	30.5	.1	.2	1.0
San Mateo	280.0	238.1	1,306.1	29.9	30.6	95.4	.4	.8	4.0
So. San Francisco	65.6	208.1	994.5	14.4	19.6	83.0	.1	.4	1.9
Woodside	*	*	....	*	*	....	*	*	**
Santa Barbara Co.	2,114.5	1,087.3	3,581.8	246.9	190.0	255.1	1.5	2.5	6.1
Guadalupe	*	....	50.0	*	....	6.4	*	**	.1
Lompoc	20.0	....	110.0	6.2	....	12.3	.1	.3	.6
Santa Barbara	1,998.5	1,047.3	3,421.8	229.3	177.7	236.4	1.2	1.9	4.3
Santa Maria	96.0	40.0	....	11.3	12.3	....	.2	.4	1.1
Santa Clara Co.	2,471.6	3,226.1	28,617.5	295.6	297.4	1,266.4	3.0	6.3	30.6
Alviso	....	....	....	....	....	....	**	**	**
Campbell	*	*	....	*	*	....	*	*	.3
Cupertino	*	*	....	*	*	....	*	*	**
Gilroy	161.5	91.0	14.0	23.4	15.2	1.6	.1	.1	.4
Los Altos	*	*	700.0	*	*	....	*	*	.6
Los Altos Hills	*	*	....	*	*	....	*	*	.1
Los Gatos	....	....	112.3	3.1	....	10.1	.1	.1	.4
Milpitas	*	*	....	*	*	....	*	*	.1
Morgan Hill	....	21.8	182.0	....	1.9	5.6	**	**	.2
Mountain View	32.6	2.5	977.0	5.7	1.4	39.3	.1	.2	1.4
Palo Alto	972.3	641.7	6,377.5	111.2	65.5	263.0	1.2	2.2	10.2
San Jose	1,087.7	2,300.0	10,326.7	120.8	192.3	674.1	1.2	2.8	9.6
Santa Clara	110.5	23.1	3,086.0	15.5	8.2	114.8	.3	.6	4.1
Saratoga	*	*	....	*	*	....	*	*	**
Sunnyvale	107.0	146.0	6,842.0	16.0	12.8	157.9	.1	.3	3.1
Santa Cruz Co.	1,181.2	847.2	2,450.5	132.4	129.5	236.0	.7	1.5	3.8
Capitola	*	*	....	*	*	....	*	*	**
Santa Cruz	802.9	499.4	818.5	88.4	67.7	89.9	.4	1.0	2.5
Watsonville	378.4	347.9	1,632.0	43.9	61.8	146.1	.3	.5	1.2
Shasta Co.	83.1	385.5	310.0	10.9	42.7	38.9	.3	.7	2.4
Anderson	*	*	....	**	*	....	*	*	**
Redding	83.1	385.5	310.0	10.9	42.7	38.9	.3	.7	2.3
Sierra Co.	....	21.0	10.0	....	1.9	2.5	**	**	**
Loyalton	....	21.0	10.0	....	1.9	2.5	**	**	**
Siskiyou Co.	203.5	117.5	573.6	11.6	27.7	49.6	.2	.3	.8
Dorris	....	3.8	52.0	....	1.4	5.1	**	**	.1
Dunsmuir	128.3	9.2	....	3.7	8.6	....	.1	.1	.2
Etna	....	13.0	35.0	....	2.7	4.2	**	**	**
Fort Jones	....	4.3	16.5	....	.7	.7	**	**	**
Montague	....	....	59.0	....	....	3.5	**	**	**
Mt. Shasta	....	32.0	8.0	....	5.8	1.4	**	.1	.1
Tulelake	*	20.0	170.0	*	3.0	19.2	*	.1	.1
Yreka	75.2	35.2	233.1	7.9	5.4	15.6	.1	.1	.2
Solano Co.	1,008.9	154.5	7,708.0	144.1	27.0	577.7	.1	3.1	4.6
Benicia	103.0	43.0	3.0	14.2	8.1	3.3	**	.1	.3
Dixon	....	31.0	114.0	....	6.3	13.5	**	**	.2
Fairfield	72.0	27.5	1,027.0	....	2.2	63.3	**	.1	.7

400

Table 7. b Basic Data Relating to Bonded Indebtedness of All Cities (except San Francisco):1937,1947,1957

Cities	Total Bonded Debt (In Thousands)			Total Debt Service (In Thousands)			Total Cost of Gov't (In Millions)		
	1937	1947	1957	1937	1947	1957	1937	1947	1957
Rio Vista	$ 32.5	$ 10.0	$ 320.0	$	$ 2.6	$ 19.5	$ **	$ .1	$ .3
Suisun	....	27.0	4.0	....	5.9	2.2	**	.1	.1
Vacaville	31.4	16.0	168.0	....	1.9	26.1	**	.1	.4
Vallejo	770.0	....	6,036.0	129.9	....	449.9	.6	2.6	2.7
Sonoma Co.	374.9	1,408.5	2,403.5	34.2	117.6	146.2	.7	1.3	6.9
Cloverdale	....	13.0	364.0	....	1.7	8.2	**	**	.2
Healdsburg	10.0	18.0	125.0	3.7	22.8	17.6	.1	.2	.5
Petaluma	113.6	632.5	847.0	11.8	42.0	77.3	.2	.3	.9
Santa Rosa	174.0	661.5	806.5	18.7	58.5	122.0	.3	.6	4.8
Sebastopol	77.3	28.5	112.0	....	4.5	14.5	.1	.1	.2
Sonoma	....	55.0	149.0	....	8.1	15.6	**	.1	.2
Stanislaus Co.	411.1	792.8	3,770.0	91.4	44.1	265.7	.7	1.6	4.6
Ceres	....	31.0	57.0	....	4.8	6.5	**	**	.1
Modesto	289.0	655.5	2,746.0	35.7	21.0	166.9	.5	1.0	3.1
Newman	3.0	24.0	....	....	3.6	3.1	**	**	.1
Oakdale	53.2	63.9	107.0	6.6	7.6	9.8	**	.2	.3
Patterson	....	6.0	60.0	....	2.3	12.0	**	**	.1
Riverbank	....	....	105.0	....	....	9.1	**	**	.2
Turlock	65.9	12.5	695.0	14.9	4.8	58.3	.1	.3	.6
Sutter Co.	121.0	38.0	740.0	9.3	9.7	51.8	.1	.2	.7
Live Oak	*	*	295.0	*	*	13.8	*	*	.1
Yuba City	121.0	38.0	445.0	9.3	9.7	38.0	.1	.2	.6
Tehama Co.	119.5	24.2	375.0	9.8	9.3	33.8	.1	.2	.6
Corning	64.9	19.2	180.0	....	4.3	20.0	**	.1	.2
Red Bluff	54.6	5.0	195.0	9.8	5.0	13.8	.1	.1	.4
Tehama	....	....	....	....	....	....	**	**	**
Tulare Co.	670.2	802.4	661.9	83.9	64.7	88.7	.9	1.9	4.7
Dinuba	157.8	31.8	....	7.9	6.5	5.0	.1	.2	.3
Exeter	52.9	21.1	....	6.1	4.5	....	.1	.1	.2
Lindsay	50.3	99.9	25.6	11.2	12.9	6.6	.1	.3	.5
Porterville	93.6	50.9	302.0	10.2	11.7	36.6	.1	.3	.9
Tulare	171.8	537.8	250.0	22.8	18.1	28.9	.2	.4	1.0
Visalia	143.9	45.5	4.8	25.6	10.4	2.7	.2	.5	1.7
Woodlake	*	15.5	79.5	*	.4	8.9	*	**	.1
Tuolumne Co.	42.0	32.0	5.0	3.5	4.2	4.2	.1	.1	.2
Sonora	42.0	32.0	5.0	3.5	4.2	4.2	.1	.1	.2
Ventura Co.	1,123.9	1,020.5	4,140.0	122.5	122.6	365.7	.7	1.9	5.1
Fillmore	51.5	48.0	241.5	6.1	8.0	21.5	**	.1	.2
Ojai	18.2	43.5	9.5	....	4.4	2.8	**	**	.2
Oxnard	180.5	279.0	2,130.0	20.9	32.5	164.0	.1	.6	2.0
Port Hueneme	*	*	124.0	*	*	13.6	*	*	.2
San Buenaventura	768.8	512.0	1,262.0	80.5	62.9	123.6	.4	.9	2.0
Santa Paula	105.0	138.0	368.0	14.1	14.5	40.2	.1	.2	.5
Yolo Co.	79.4	650.5	1,345.0	3.1	22.0	66.1	.2	.5	1.4
Davis	68.5	240.5	1,145.0	....	20.8	42.3	.1	.1	.4
Winters	....	10.0	....	....	1.3	....	**	**	.1
Woodland	10.9	400.0	200.0	3.1	....	23.8	.2	.3	1.0
Yuba Co.	10.0	30.0	154.0	17.0	5.8	18.1	.2	.4	.9
Marysville	10.0	30.0	143.0	17.0	5.8	16.8	.2	.4	.9
Wheatland	....	....	11.0	....	....	1.3	**	**	**

Source: State Controller's Reports Concerning Financial Transactions of Cities and Counties for the fiscal years indicated.

* Municipality was incorporated after this date.

** Less than $50,000.

[1] Including $41,018 for Bayshore and Lawndale which have since been annexed to adjacent cities.

Table 7.c Variation in Bonded Indebtedness Among All Cities (except San Francisco)
by Medians, Quartiles, and Range: 1957
Total Municipal Bonded Debt June 30, 1957 [1]

Total for All	$ Per Capita [2]	Percentage of Assessed Valuation %	Debt Service as % of Total Cost of Gov't %		$ Per Capita	Percentage of Assessed Valuation	Debt Service as % of Total Cost of Gov't
Total for All Cities:				**Glenn Co.**			
High	5,839.49	35.90	35.8	Orland	....	....	....
Q[3]	56.89	4.68	6.3	Willows	30.75	2.33	7.4
Median	20.22	1.70	3.2	**Humboldt Co.**			
Q[1]	.41	.06	.4	Arcata	81.36	7.84	4.2
Low	....	....	....	Blue Lake	258.18	35.90	21.0
Alameda Co.				Eureka	84.86	6.63	9.0
Alameda	33.76	4.46	1.2	Ferndale	108.18	8.23	20.3
Albany	3.17	.36	.4	Fortuna	32.02	2.41	6.7
Berkeley	.30	.04	.3	Trinidad	....	....	....
Emeryville	....	....	....	**Imperial Co.**			
Fremont	....	....	....	Brawley	35.76	3.27	6.1
Hayward	88.05	8.29	8.9	Calexico	51.00	3.94	4.5
Livermore	56.82	4.58	9.8	Calipatria	1.80	.16	2.4
Newark	....	....	....	El Centro	77.60	3.64	5.8
Oakland	58.01	4.16	4.9	Holtville	23.41	1.71	3.5
Piedmont	....	....	....	Imperial	115.65	5.72	12.5
Pleasanton	58.48	6.35	6.4	Westmorland	....	....	....
San Leandro	15.54	1.16	3.1	**Inyo Co.**			
Amador Co.				Bishop	3.98	.28	2.1
Amador	....	....	....	**Kern Co.**			
Ione	93.46	11.35	14.9	Bakersfield	62.67	2.50	3.9
Jackson	19.52	1.91	6.2	Delano	.68	.08	.6
Plymouth	....	....	.1	Maricopa	....	....	....
Sutter Creek	39.10	5.50	16.8	Shafter	....	....	....
Butte Co.				Taft	5.88	.37	2.6
Biggs	....	....	....	Tehachapi	31.98	4.02	8.5
Chico	....	....	....	Wasco	....	3.81	....
Gridley	43.75	4.98	4.4	**Kings Co.**			
Oroville	....	....	....	Corcoran	17.62	1.15	8.6
Calaveras Co.				Hanford	20.35	.86	3.8
Angels	80.00	10.60	24.2	Lemoore	....	....	1.4
Colusa Co.				**Lake Co.**			
Colusa	....	....	....	Lakeport	36.47	3.16	11.3
Williams	33.92	2.32	8.2	**Lassen Co.**			
Contra Costa Co.				Susanville	....	....	.2
Antioch	133.70	11.54	18.2	**Los Angeles Co.**			
Brentwood	....	....	....	Alhambra	19.79	1.25	4.0
Concord	13.46	1.27	13.3	Arcadia	8.36	.49	1.1
El Cerrito	....	....	....	Avalon	4.60	8.54	2.2
Hercules	....	....	....	Azusa	1.80	.15	.2
Martinez	113.03	4.62	10.8	Baldwin Park	....	....	....
Pinole	....	....	....	Bell	....	....	....
Pittsburg	85.80	7.09	7.5	Beverly Hills	135.10	2.80	6.1
Richmond	88.40	4.75	3.5	Burbank	19.97	.94	1.5
San Pablo	4.93	.89	1.6	Claremont	27.16	2.35	3.3
Walnut Creek	235.30	14.82	3.8	Compton	11.67	1.19	3.0
Del Norte Co.				Covina	19.41	1.34	1.8
Crescent City	12.86	.37	4.6	Culver City	45.56	2.46	3.7
El Dorado Co.				Dairy Valley	....	....	....
Placerville	127.10	8.63	12.3	Downey	....	....	....
Fresno Co.				El Monte	84.33	5.82	7.3
Clovis	26.22	4.36	4.2	El Segundo	116.64	1.41	5.4
Coalinga	....	....	....	Gardena	....	....	19.6
Firebaugh	71.37	6.11	17.7	Glendale	81.58	5.63	....
Fowler	4.00	.52	1.3	Glendora	43.31	4.49	3.9
Fresno	24.46	2.04	2.4	Hawthorne	21.88	1.78	.4
Huron	95.41	10.99	16.4	Hermosa Beach	2.74	.28	1.4
Kerman	74.66	10.24	7.8	Huntington Park	.29	.02	.5
Kingsburg	40.09	3.18	6.0	Inglewood	.86	.06	....
Mendota	38.68	5.81	4.9	Lakewood	....	....	....
Orange Cove	136.67	27.80	17.9	La Puente	....	....	....
Parlier	8.75	1.98	4.0	La Verne	7.60	.80	2.9
Reedley	1.27	.15	.7	Long Beach	90.39	5.71	2.4
Sanger	36.22	4.73	7.3	Los Angeles	230.00	14.75	12.2
San Joaquin	....	....	....				
Selma	25.94	3.42	4.4				

Table 7.c	$ Per Capita	Percentage of Assessed Valuation	Debt Serv. as % of Total Cost of Gov't		$ Per Capita	Percentage of Assessed Valuation	Debt Serv. as % of Total Cost of Gov't
Los Angeles Co. (cont'd)				**Orange Co. (cont'd**			
Lynwood	11.05	1.34	2.2	Brea	58.29	4.89	9.4
Manhattan Beach	52.87	6.79	5.7	Buena Park	....	....	....
Maywood	....	....	....	Costa Mesa	....	....	....
Monrovia	9.66	.71	1.6	Cypress	....	....	35.8
Montebello	3.83	.25	1.1	Dairyland	....	....	31.3
Monterey Park	26.16	2.59	3.0	Fullerton	25.44	1.76	3.2
Palos Verdes Estates....		....	....	Garden Grove	....	....	....
Paramount	....	....	....	Huntington Beach	127.69	1.85	5.8
Pasadena	197.21	7.27	5.1	Laguna Beach	17.85	.76	1.6
Pomona	61.25	4.81	3.2	La Habra	39.27	4.44	6.6
Redondo Beach	3.25	.22	.9	Newport Beach	5.69	.20	2.1
Rolling Hills	....	....	....	Orange	4.74	.31	.5
San Fernando	28.18	2.51	3.3	Placentia	....	....	....
San Gabriel	8.27	.56	1.9	San Clemente	134.45	7.84	5.6
San Marino	23.23	.87	2.7	Santa Ana	15.79	1.23	2.2
Santa Monica	72.26	3.49	7.3	Seal Beach	34.93	1.19	10.8
Sierra Madre	8.67	.62	2.3	Stanton	....	....	....
Signal Hill	....	....	....	Tustin	....	....	....
South Gate	.16	.01	.3				
So. Pasadena	18.60	1.45	1.9	**Placer Co.**			
Torrance	38.07	2.76	5.2	Auburn	....	....	1.1
Vernon	5,839.49	1.11	11.9	Colfax	50.48	4.56	13.4
West Covina	1.93	.20	.6	Lincoln	39.17	3.18	28.1
Whittier	102.09	6.70	7.4	Rocklin	....	....	....
				Roseville	83.65	8.63	4.7
Madera Co.							
Chowchilla	18.02	2.44	5.5	**Plumas Co.**			
Madera	15.93	2.20	3.6	Portola	151.37	18.84	21.9
Marin Co.				**Riverside Co.**			
Belvedere	75.68	3.63	7.5	Banning	....	....	....
Corte Madera	20.00	1.32	8.0	Beaumont	6.94	.55	3.4
Fairfax	....	....	....	Blythe	3.96	.36	1.4
Larkspur	22.22	2.26	6.9	Cabazon	....	....	....
Mill Valley	31.60	7.36	7.2	Coachella	35.53	6.60	19.9
Ross	10.00	.58	4.5	Corona	17.47	1.00	3.9
San Anselmo	....	....	.9	Elsinore	26.04	1.82	4.2
San Rafael	4.80	.24	1.4	Hemet	131.03	8.66	12.3
Sausalito	....	....	....	Indio	123.11	9.85	1.1
				Palm Springs	55.93	1.57	4.2
Mendocino Co.				Perris	11.07	1.44	3.2
Fort Bragg	2.47	.27	2.5	Riverside	8.46	.59	.5
Point Arena	....	....	....	San Jacinto	60.26	5.92	5.8
Ukiah	27.05	2.59	1.8				
Willits	34.50	3.18	6.4	**Sacramento Co.**			
				Folsom	43.57	7.75	8.5
Merced Co.				Galt	....	....	....
Atwater	62.83	3.76	9.2	Isleton	124.24	13.13	13.2
Dos Palos	18.07	1.82	1.6	No. Sacramento	32.63	1.93	3.1
Gustine	56.89	3.22	16.8	Sacramento	73.30	3.98	9.9
Livingston	12.73	.88	2.1				
Los Banos	....	....	....	**San Benito Co.**			
Merced	63.41	2.97	2.2	Hollister	42.61	2.58	5.9
				San Juan Bautista	....	....	....
Modoc Co.							
Alturas	35.33	3.25	7.0	**San Bernardino Co.**			
				Barstow	24.56	2.84	4.1
Monterey Co.				Chino	49.22	4.69	9.8
Carmel	4.09	.15	1.4	Colton	100.70	13 69	.9
Del Rey Oaks	....	....	....	Fontana	171.29	17.98	....
Gonzales	123.08	14.83	13.5	Monte Vista	....	....	....
Greenfield	186.91	22.74	13.1	Needles	49.79	6.49	4.7
King City	2.00	.15	4.3	Ontario	34.77	3.38	2.3
Monterey	66.19	4.88	4.2	Redlands	5.74	.47	1.2
Pacific Grove	38.86	3.19	6.0	Rialto	39.26	5.11	7.5
Salinas	105.46	4.83	4.0	San Bernardino	1.03	.09	.6
Seaside	....	....	....	Upland	71.23	5.72	2.9
Soledad	53.13	7.96	13.1				
				San Diego Co.			
Napa Co.				Carlsbad	5.56	.31	1.7
Calistoga	86.88	5.94	15.6	Chula Vista	11.97	1.25	2.5
Napa	208.17	15.39	13.3	Coronado	.80	.05	.2
St. Helena	....	....	....	El Cajon	21.48	2.09	2.8
				Escondido	4.93	.41	1.0
Orange Co.				Imperial Beach	....	....	.3
Anaheim	74.25	6.20	7.4				

Table 7.c

	$ Per Capita	Percentage of Assessed Valuation	Debt Serv. as % of Total Cost of Gov't
San Diego Co. (cont'd)			
La Mesa	24.71	2.24	3.7
National City	3.66	.44	1.6
Oceanside	29.18	2.91	4.3
San Diego	84.02	7.12	8.3
San Joaquin Co.			
Lodi	.65	9.01	....
Manteca	61.08	5.94	11.5
Ripon	23.16	1.69	3.9
Stockton	1.76	1.18	3.6
Tracy	42.23	3.70	4.1
San Luis Obispo Co.			
Arroyo Grande	8.80	.78	1.7
El Paso Robles	51.08	3.33	4.7
Pismo Beach	42.20	6.03	5.6
San Luis Obispo	14.80	1.24	.2
San Mateo Co.			
Atherton	....	....	....
Belmont	10.85	.94	3.2
Burlingame	....	.60	1.4
Colma	....	....	....
Daly City	23.79	2.81	3.1
Hillsborough	49.96	1.32	4.2
Menlo Park	11.40	.94	1.2
Millbrae	80.30	6.21	14.7
Redwood City	67.35	2.58	6.7
San Bruno	9.77	.88	4.6
San Carlos	14.30	.87	3.0
San Mateo	20.09	.81	2.4
So. San Francisco	26.06	1.79	4.3
Woodside	....	....	.3
Santa Barbara Co.			
Guadalupe	17.86	3.06	7.6
Lompoc	15.71	2.11	2.0
Santa Barbara	61.88	3.19	5.5
Santa Maria	....	....	....
Santa Clara Co.			
Alviso	....	....	....
Campbell	....	....	....
Cupertino	....	....	....
Gilroy	2.23	.18	.4
Los Altos	31.82	2.63	....
Los Altos Hills	....	....	....
Los Gatos	18.72	1.03	2.8
Milpitas	....	....	....
Morgan Hill	79.13	7.52	3.1
Mountain View	37.55	3.43	2.7
Palo Alto	138.64	6.58	2.6
San Jose	79.44	4.87	7.0
Santa Clara	77.15	5.95	2.8
Saratoga	....	....	....
Sunnyvale	184.92	15.18	5.0
Santa Cruz Co.			
Capitola	....	....	....
Santa Cruz	34.10	2.05	3.5
Watsonville	108.80	8.79	12.0
Shasta Co.			
Anderson	....	....	....
Redding	22.14	1.28	1.7
Sierra Co.			
Loyalton	10.20	.77	6.81
Siskiyou Co.			
Dorris	43.33	8.20	6.9
Dunsmuir	....	....	....
Etna	38.89	5.83	15.1

	$ Per Capita	Percentage of Assessed Valuation	Debt Serv. as % of Total Cost of Gov't
Siskiyou Co. (Continued)			
Fort Jones	27.50	4.14	4.0
Montague	82.17	4.84	7.4
Mt. Shasta	4.10	.44	1.1
Tulelake	113.33	7.40	21.1
Yreka	.56	4.57	6.5
Solano Co.			
Benicia	.43	.04	1.3
Dixon	45.60	3.80	8.3
Fairfield	85.58	5.68	8.7
Rio Vista	128.00	8.48	7.0
Suisun	1.82	.25	2.4
Vacaville	21.00	2.63	6.9
Vallejo	150.90	16.61	16.7
Sonoma Co.			
Cloverdale	104.00	8.87	4.9
Healdsburg	31.25	2.26	3.5
Petaluma	65.15	4.68	8.4
Santa Rosa	27.98	1.65	2.5
Sebastopol	37.33	2.25	7.1
Sonoma	85.14	3.16	7.1
Stanislaus Co.			
Ceres	16.05	1.64	4.5
Modesto	84.69	6.26	5.4
Newman	....	....	2.6
Oakdale	23.78	2.98	3.9
Patterson	28.57	1.64	10.8
Riverbank	34.65	6.17	5.5
Turlock	89.10	7.76	9.0
Sutter Co.			
Live Oak	142.65	.60	13.9
Yuba City	34.23	3.13	6.0
Tehama Co.			
Corning	71.29	6.54	12.4
Red Bluff	31.20	3.51	3.3
Tehama	....	....	....
Tulare Co.			
Dinuba	....	....	1.6
Exeter	....	....	....
Lindsay	4.74	.33	1.3
Porterville	37.75	2.01	4.0
Tulare	19.23	1.33	3.0
Visalia	.33	.02	.2
Woodlake	45.43	5.95	8.7
Tuolumne Co.			
Sonora	1.25	.13	2.7
Ventura Co.			
Fillmore	50.31	6.04	9.2
Ojai	2.42	.21	1.7
Oxnard	68.71	6.31	8.4
Port Hueneme	14.74	3.42	6.3
San Buenaventura	47.62	4.11	6.2
Santa Paula	28.31	2.28	8.2
Yolo Co.			
Davis	158.68	8.24	11.7
Winters	....	....	....
Woodland	17.31	.98	2.4
Yuba Co.			
Marysville	15.05	.59	1.8
Wheatland	18.33	2.01	3.7

INDEX

Designation: Unless otherwise indicated, all items refer to California; "state," for example, means state of California. Government bureaus and agencies are catalogued by operational title; thus the State Board of Equalization appears as "Board of Equalization."

Cross filing: A few of the more important concepts are cross-catalogued; thus "current operations: city" appears also under "city: current operations." But in the interests of economy and compactness, most items are listed only once; "School district: taxes," for instance, is not cross filed as "Taxes: school district."

Footnote citation: Authors cited in footnotes are indexed to the page where the number of the footnote appears, although the footnote itself is found at the end of the chapter; for example, "Davisson, Malcolm M.; 199n(26)" refers to footnote 26 entered at page 199. Bibliographical footnotes are numbered consecutively within each chapter and printed at the end of that chapter except for the references of Chapters 8 and 9, collected and numbered in alphabetical order at the end of Chapter 9 and employed mainly to show the sources of the tables. Substantive notes, printed at the bottom of the page, are indexed by the symbol n — for instance," 'creeping socialism': 69n."

Appendix, Preface, Tables: The appendix and preface are not indexed; text tables are indexed.